USAF WARRIOR STUDIES

Richard H. Kohn and Joseph P. Harahan
General Editors

Reprinted in 1983 by the Office of Air Force History.

Library of Congress Cataloging in Publication Data

Douhet, Giulio, 1869–1930.
    The command of the air.

    Translation of Il dominio dell'aria.
    Reprint. Originally published: New York: Coward-McCann, 1942.
    1. Air Power. I. Title.
UG630.D62   1983   358.4   83–19318
ISBN 0–912799–10–2

Project Warrior Studies are published by the Office of Air Force History. The views expressed in this publication are those of the author and should not be construed to represent the policies of the United States Air Force or the Department of Defense.

The Command of The Air

BY

GIULIO DOUHET

TRANSLATED BY

DINO FERRARI

New Imprint by the
Office of Air Force History
Washington, D.C., 1983

United States Air Force
Historical Advisory Committee

(As of September 1, 1983)

Lt. Gen. Charles G. Cleveland,
USAF
Commander, Air University

Mr. DeWitt S. Copp
The National Volunteer Agency

Dr. Philip A. Crowl
Annapolis, Maryland

Dr. Warren W. Hassler, Jr.
Pennsylvania State University

Brig. Gen. Harris B. Hull, USAF,
Retired
National Aeronautics and Space
Administration

Dr. Alfred F. Hurley
Brig. Gen., USAF, Retired
North Texas State University

Mr. David E. Place
The General Counsel, USAF

Gen. Bryce Poe II, USAF, Retired
Alexandria, Virginia

Lt. Gen. Winfield W. Scott, Jr.
Superintendent, USAF Academy

Dr. David A. Shannon (Chairman)
University of Virginia

Foreword

This reprinting of *The Command of the Air* is part of a continuing series of historical studies from the Office of Air Force History in support of Project Warrior.

Project Warrior seeks to create and maintain within the Air Force an environment where Air Force people at all levels can learn from the past and apply the warfighting experiences of past generations to the present. When Gen. Lew Allen, Jr., initiated the project in 1982, he called for the "continuing study of military history, combat leadership, the principles of war and, particularly, the applications of air power." All of us in the Air Force community can benefit from such study and reflection. The challenges of today and the future demand no less.

CHARLES A. GABRIEL, General USAF
Chief of Staff

Editors' Introduction

Long before the age of powered flight, men dreamed of employing aerial craft as weapons of war. When in the late eighteenth century the Montgolfier brothers demonstrated free flight by means of a balloon near Paris, others almost immediately speculated about its application to battle. In 1794 the French government established an army balloon unit for the purposes of reconnaissance. Through the nineteenth century, other military establishments experimented with lighter-than-air ships, not only for observation but for attack, including one effort by an Austrian lieutenant to bomb the city of Venice. By the time of the Wright brothers' successful flight in 1903, the world was anticipating military aviation. Within a decade, in a war between Italy and Turkey, powered flight for the first time became integral to the conduct of military operations. As instruments of war able to leap over armies and ignore many of the physical barriers of terrain and water, airplanes and dirigibles stirred public imagination and sufficient controversy to force soldiers to ponder the role the airplane would play in future conflict.[1]

Few thinkers of that era, or any other, were more prominent in airpower thinking than the Italian soldier and writer, Giulio Douhet. Born in Caserta in 1869 and commissioned into the Italian Army in Artillery in 1882, Douhet in 1909 began thinking seriously about the impact of aircraft. He commanded one of the first army air units and directed the army's Aviation Section; by 1915, the year Italy entered World War I, he had already formulated a substantial portion of his theories, in particular the idea of forcing an enemy nation to capitulate by means of a bombing campaign directed against the morale of its population. When the Italian army became locked in a bloody stalemate with Austria, Douhet proposed just such an attack against Austrian cities by an independent bomber force of 500 aircraft. His ideas were rejected, and for criticizing Italian military leaders in memoranda to the cabinet, he was court-

---

[1] Lee Kennett, *A History of Strategic Bombing* (New York, 1982) 1–9.

martialed and imprisoned for a year. In 1918 he was recalled to service to head the Italian Central Aeronautical Bureau. Exonerated finally in 1920, and promoted to general officer in 1921, the same year he published *Command of the Air,* Douhet soon retired from the service. Except for a brief few months as the head of aviation in Mussolini's government in 1922, he spent much of the rest of his life writing and publicizing his ideas on airpower.

Much of what Douhet propounded was not original with him, but his were perhaps the most coherent, the most systematic, and the most prophetic airpower writings of the era. More than any other thinker, Douhet addressed the basic issues that military theorists have grappled with since the beginning of organized combat. In Douhet's thinking, aircraft altered the fundamental character of warfare, and he argued the case at a level of abstraction and generalization that elevated argument to principle and the body of thought as a whole to theory. In that theory, airpower became the use of space off the surface of the earth to decide war on the surface of the earth. He discussed the organization and employment of aircraft in generalities independent of time, place, technology, and even independent of the nature of warfare itself. (Douhet virtually assumed the prevalence of total war.) He believed that the first effort of air forces was "to conquer the command of the air—that is, to put the enemy in a position where he is unable to fly, while preserving for one's self the ability to do so. . . ." His method of gaining superiority was to attack the enemy air force on the ground. For Douhet, aircraft were only useful as instruments of the offense. By bombing cities and factories instead of military forces (except air forces), the enemy could be defeated through shattering the civilian will to continue resistance. He argued that the character of airplanes—their speed and mobility—and the vastness of the ether would prevent the defense from ever stopping a determined bomber offensive. But in order to mount such an effort, and because air forces had little significance as "auxiliaries" to armies and navies, air forces had to be independent of ground and naval forces, and armed, structured, and deployed for the decisive strategic role.[2]

After his death in 1930, Douhet's writings were translated into French, German, Russian, and English and widely disseminated in western military establishments. According to some military leaders at the time, his

---

[2] For studies of Douhet's life and thinking, consult Edward Warner, "Douhet, Mitchell, Seversky: Theories of Air Warfare," in *Makers of Modern Strategy: Military Thought from Machiavelli to Hitler,* ed. Edward Mead Earle (Princeton, N.J., 1943), 485–497; Bernard Brodie, "The Heritage of Douhet," *Air University Quarterly Review,* VI (1953), 64–69, 120–126. Kennett, *A History of Strategic Bombing,* 54–57.

thinking had great impact on air doctrine and organization. Certainly the leadership of the U.S. Army Air Corps considered him important. A translation of *Command of the Air* was available at the Air Service Tactical School as early as 1923, and extracts of his works were circulated at the School in the early 1930s. In 1933, the Chief of the Air Corps, Major General Benjamin Foulois, sent 30 mimeographed copies of an article on Douhet's theories to the chairman of the House Committee on Military Affairs, calling the study "an excellent exposition of certain principles of air war." [3]

Today the extent of his influence and the originality of his thinking remain in much dispute among scholars and airmen. But virtually all of them agree that he "synthesized and articulated a body of thought that had occurred in whole or in part to many others," that "his theories had a sweeping boldness and grandeur that his critics could not match," and that airmen "found him useful in arguing for an independent air force and supplying a conceptual framework for the next year. . . ." [4] "Douhet stated the case for airpower as no one else did—with all the stops out," wrote another historian recently. "Those who read *Command of the Air*, early or late, often found bold confirmation of ideas stirring in their own minds." [5]

Much that he predicted, of course, turned out to be incorrect. Tactical aviation altered the nature of land and naval warfare and so contributed to the outcome of World War II that a few historians have suggested that its influence outweighed that of the strategic bombing campaigns against Germany and Japan. Douhet neglected almost entirely the issue of target selection. He vastly overestimated the physical destructiveness of a ton of bombs and equally underestimated the ability of the defense to defeat attacking air forces. Writing in 1953, the late Bernard Brodie, the greatest

---

[3] Quoted in Robert Frank Futrell, *Ideas, Concepts, Doctrine: A History of Basic Thinking in the United States Air Force, 1907–1964* (Maxwell Air Force Base, Ala., 1971) 35; General Giulio Douhet, "Air Warfare," trans. Mrs. Dorothy Benedict, December 1933, mimeographed typescript at the Office of Air Force History; Giulio Douhet, *Aerial Warfare*, trans. into French by Jan Romeyer, trans. into English by Louis R. Bellanger (Maxwell Field, Ala., 1933) typescript in the Army Library, the Pentagon. See also *The Development of Air Doctrine in the Army Air Arm, 1917–1941* (USAF Historical Division, Maxwell Air Force Base, Ala., 1955), 48–52; Raymond R. Flugel, United States Air Power Doctrine: A Study of the Influence of William Mitchell and Giulio Douhet at the Air Corps Tactical School, 1921–1935 (Ph.D. Dissertation, University of Oklahoma, 1965), 185.

[4] Edward Homze, "The Continental Experience," in *Air Power and Warfare: The Proceedings of the Eighth Military History Symposium, United States Air Force Academy, 18–20 October 1978,* eds. Alfred F. Hurley and Robert C. Ehrhart (Washington, 1979), 42.

[5] Kennett, *History of Strategic Bombing,* 57.

of the American military strategists of the post-war era, said that the "Battle of Britain resulted in an outright victory for the defense—and the attacking Germans were at that time quite literally following Douhet's precepts." Brodie called Douhet's "demonstrable errors . . . considerable and sometimes very crude." Yet at the same time "his insights are more impressive than his failures," and his "thoughts are actually more valid today than they were during his lifetime." Comparing him to Billy Mitchell, Brodie concluded that Mitchell's "thinking was tactical rather than strategic, and events have so fully confirmed and vindicated him that his writing is today completely dated in a way that Douhet's is not." [6]

This reprint of the 1942 English translation of Douhet's works, while titled *Command of the Air,* actually consists of five separate works: the original 1921 edition of *Command of the Air,* a second edition of 1927, a 1928 monograph titled "Probable Aspects of Future War," a polemical article of 1929 called "Recapitulation," and the 1930 study "The War of 19—." The volume is reprinted by the Office of Air Force History as part of Project Warrior. By transporting ourselves back to the 1920s, past not only the Vietnam and Korean Wars, but nearly two decades before World War II, we become silent observers of the unfolding drama of airpower's history. Knowing what transpired after Douhet wrote, we can test our understanding, find the assumptions and conclusions of Douhet that proved false, and read with wonder those that proved true. Some of what he wrote today seems almost timeless, "principles" perhaps of the employment of aircraft in war. Giulio Douhet was a prophet. From the perspective of today, he still bears pondering. Serious thinking about the nature of war and the role of aerospace power will not in our lifetime cease to be of value.

R.H.K.
J.P.H.

[6] Brodie, "Heritage of Douhet," 64, 126.

Preface

THE FIRST EDITION of *The Command of The Air* was published in 1921 under the auspices of the Ministry of War. In the years since then many of the ideas incorporated in the present edition have been put into effect. In fact, the cardinal points of the program for national defense which I proposed have been accepted and incorporated into the organization of the armed forces of the nation; namely:

1. Co-ordination of army, navy, and air force under a unified command, a concept I propounded in the 1922 issue of *National Defense*.

2. The constitution of a Council, then of a Ministry, of Aeronautics.

3. A distinction between an Independent Air force and auxiliary aviation, thereby putting into effect a concept which I held to be of vital importance to national defense and in correspondence with the facts of the present situation.

It may seem that if my ideas have been accepted and put into practice, there is no need for a second edition of my book. But I think there is a need for it, and here are my reasons for reprinting what I wrote then and adding to it a second part:

When I wrote the first version in 1921, more than ten years had passed since I first voiced the ideas expressed there. During all those years I had been trying with all my might to drive home the realization of the importance of air power, but all my efforts met defeat at the hands of military authorities and government bureaucracies. Finally, in 1921, owing to a change in circumstances which need not be mentioned here, I succeeded in getting it published by the Ministry of War and distributed among the personnel of the army and navy. This was the first success won by my long and arduous labors. But at that time, in order to accomplish anything practical and useful for my country, I had to be careful not to oppose too strongly certain notions firmly held in high places. Therefore, I was forced to emasculate my thought, confining myself to indispensable fundamentals, and wait for more favorable circumstances before presenting my ideas in full. Fortunately, conditions are different today. Willing or unwilling, military authorities have had to modify their views on the air arm. The first step has been taken; and now it is fitting that I should round out my thoughts on the subject of air power. Part II of Book One should therefore be considered complementary to Part I.

The ideas expressed in this second part will seem daring, perhaps strange, but I am certain that they too will make their way and finally be accepted like the others. It is only a question of time.

GIULIO DOUHET
[*Second Edition, 1927*]

Contents

Book One

The Command of The Air

Originally published in book form in 1921.

PART I

CHAPTER I

The New Form of War

THE TECHNICAL MEANS OF WARFARE

AERONAUTICS OPENED up to men a new field of action, the field of the air. In so doing it of necessity created a new battlefield; for wherever two men meet, conflict is inevitable. In actual fact, aeronautics was widely employed in warfare long before any civilian use was made of it.[1] Still in its infancy at the outbreak of the World War, this new science received then a powerful impetus to military development.

The practical use of the air arm was at first only vaguely understood. This new arm had sprung suddenly into the field of war; and its characteristics, radically different from those of any other arm employed up to that time, were still undefined. Very few possibilities of this new instrument of war were recognized when it first appeared. Many people took the extreme position that it was impossible to fight in the air; others admitted only that it might prove a useful auxiliary to already existing means of war.

At first the speed and freedom of action of the airplane—the air arm chiefly used in the beginning—caused it to be considered primarily an instrument of exploration and reconnaissance. Then gradually the idea of using it as a range-finder for the artillery grew up. Next, its obvious advantages over surface means led to its being used to attack the enemy on and behind his own lines, but no great importance was attached to this function because it was thought that the airplane was incapable of transporting any heavy load of offensive matériel. Then, as the need of counteracting enemy aerial operations was felt, antiaircraft guns and the so-called pursuit planes came into being.

[1] It was first employed by Italy in Libya during the Italo-Turkish War of 1911-12 for reconnaissance and liaison purposes.—Tr.

3

Thus, in order to meet the demands of aerial warfare, it became necessary step by step to increase aerial power. But because the needs which had to be met manifested themselves during a war of large scope, the resulting increase was rapid and hectic, not sound and orderly. And so the illogical concept of utilizing the new aerial weapon solely as an auxiliary to the army and navy prevailed for almost the entire period of the World War. It was only toward the end of the war that the idea emerged, in some of the belligerent nations, that it might be not only feasible but wise to entrust the air force with independent offensive missions. None of the belligerents fully worked out this idea, however—perhaps because the war ended before the right means for actuating the idea became available.

Now,[2] however, this idea has emerged again and seems to be impressing itself strongly on the national authorities most concerned with these matters. It is, in fact, the only logical answer to the imperative need of defense against these new weapons of warfare. Essentially man lives close to the earth's surface, and no doubt he began his battling there. We do not know whether, when he first began to navigate the seas, he regarded naval warfare as a mere auxiliary to land operations; but we do know that from time immemorial we have been fighting on the sea independently of, though in co-operation with, land forces. Today, however, the sky is of far greater interest to man, living on the surface of the earth, than is the sea; and nothing, therefore, can *a priori* prevent him from reaching the conclusion that the air constitutes a battlefield of equal importance.

Though an army is primarily a land force, it possesses navigable means of warfare which it can use to help integrate its land operations; and that fact does not preclude the navy's accomplishing, solely with its own naval means, war missions from which the army is completely excluded. Similarly, while a navy is primarily a sea force, it possesses land means of warfare which it may use to assist and integrate its naval operations; and that fact does not preclude the army's carrying out war missions solely with its own land means, entirely independent of any naval means. In like

<hr />

[2] 1921, three years after the end of the World War.—Tr.

manner, both the army and navy may well possess aerial means to aid and integrate their respective military and naval operations; but that does not preclude the possibility, the practicability, even the necessity, of having an air force capable of accomplishing war missions solely with its own means, to the complete exclusion of both army and navy.

In such a case, an air force should logically be accorded equal importance with the army and navy and bear the same relation to them as they now bear to each other. Obviously, both the army and the navy, each in its own field, must operate toward the same objective—i.e., to win the war. They must act accordingly, but independently of each other. To make one dependent on the other would restrict the freedom of action of the one or the other, and thus diminish their total effectiveness. Similarly, an air force should at all times co-operate with the army and the navy; but it must be independent of them both.

At this point I should like to outline the general aspects of the problem which faces us today and to emphasize the great importance of it. Now that we are released from the pressure of the World War, with its trial-and-error methods, it behooves us to work toward the solution of this problem by an entirely different method, one calculated to obtain for us the maximum return with the minimum of effort.

The state must make such disposition of its defenses as will put it in the best possible condition to sustain any future war. But in order to be effective, these dispositions for defense must provide means of warfare suited to the character and form future wars may assume. In other words, the character and form assumed by the war of the future is the fundamental basis upon which depends what dispositions of the means of war will provide a really effective defense of the state.

The prevailing forms of social organization have given war a character of national totality—that is, the entire population and all the resources of a nation are sucked into the maw of war. And, since society is now definitely evolving along this line, it is within the power of human foresight to see now that future wars will be total in character and scope. Still confining ourselves to the narrow limits of human foresight, we can nevertheless state, with complete certainty, that probable future wars will be radically different in character from those of the past.

The form of any war—and it is the form which is of primary interest to men of war—depends upon the technical means of war available. It is well known, for instance, that the introduction of firearms was a powerful influence in changing the forms of war in the past. Yet firearms were only a gradual development, an improvement upon ancient engines of war—such as the bow and arrow, the ballista, the catapult, et cetera—utilizing the elasticity of solid materials. In our own lifetime we have seen how great an influence the introduction of small-caliber, rapid-fire guns—together with barbed wire—has had on land warfare, and how the submarine changed the nature of sea warfare.[3] We have also assisted in the introduction of two new weapons, the air arm and poison gas. But they are still in their infancy, and are entirely different from all others in character; and we cannot yet estimate exactly their potential influence on the form of future wars. No doubt that influence will be great, and I have no hesitation in asserting that it will completely upset all forms of war so far known.

These two weapons complement each other. Chemistry, which has already provided us with the most powerful of explosives, will now furnish us with poison gases even more potent, and bacteriology may give us even more formidable ones. To get an idea of the nature of future wars, one need only imagine what power of destruction that nation would possess whose bacteriologists should discover the means of spreading epidemics in the enemy's country and at the same time immunize its own people. Air power makes it possible not only to make high-explosive bombing raids over

---

[3] From *Le Matin*, September 8, 1917, issue: "The newly organized history section of the Naval General Staff has recently brought forth evidence of the greatest interest, from which it is as plain as daylight that, had the Germans shown a little more *cran* [guts] during their unrestricted submarine warfare, and had the extraordinary valor of their submarine commanders not been nullified by the hesitations and vacillations of the Kaiser and his Chancellor, we would have lost the war. It was the Germans themselves who, after the spring of 1917, curtailed, step by step, both the number and the action of their submarines."

any sector of the enemy's territory, but also to ravage his whole country by chemical and bacteriological warfare.

If, then, we pause to take stock of the potentialities of these new weapons—which will no doubt be improved and developed in the future—we must be convinced that the experience of the World War can serve only as a point of departure—a point already left far behind us. It cannot serve as a basis for the preparation of national defense, a preparation which must be undertaken with an eye to the necessities of the future.

We must also bear in mind this fact: we are faced today with conditions which favor intensive study and wide application of these new weapons, the potentialities of which are unknown; and these conditions are the very ones to which Germany has been relegated. The Allies compelled Germany to disarm and to scrap her standing army. Will she accept patiently this inferior status? Or will she, forced by necessity, look for new weapons to replace the old ones now forbidden to her, and with them wreak her revenge? The fact that Germany leads the world in both fields, chemico-bacteriological and mechanical, must not be lost sight of. Already we can see signs that she is thinking along those lines, that she will apply the intensity, the unswerving purpose which have always distinguished her people, to the development of those new weapons of war. She can do so in the secrecy of her laboratories, where all foreign disarmament control—if any such control was ever effective—is bound to be futile.

Quite apart from what Germany may or may not do, however, it is impossible to ignore the value of these new weapons or to deny their vital role in any preparation for national defense. But in order to make an accurate estimate of the importance of these weapons, we must know exactly what their value is, both in themselves and in relation to the army and navy. Such an estimate is the primary object of this study.

THE NEW POSSIBILITIES

As long as man remained tied to the surface of the earth, his activities had to be adapted to the conditions imposed by that surface. War being an activity which necessitates wide movements of forces, the terrain upon which it was fought determined its essential features. The uneven configuration of the land surface presents all kinds of obstacles which hinder movements of solid bodies over it. Hence man has had either to move along the lines of least resistance, or by long and arduous labor surmount the obstacles encountered in the more difficult zones. Thus the surface of the earth gradually became covered with lines of easy transit intersecting at various points, at others separated by zones less easy of access, sometimes impassable.

The sea, on the contrary, being everywhere uniform in character, is equally navigable over all parts of its surface. But because the sea is bound by coast lines, freedom of navigation is often precluded except between points of contact situated on the same coastline or along arbitrary routes under foreign control, to avoid which long journeys around the coasts themselves must be undertaken.

War is a conflict between two wills basically opposed one to the other. On one side is the party who wants to occupy a certain portion of the earth; over against him stands his adversary, the party who intends to oppose that occupation, if necessary by force of arms. The result is war.

The attacking force tries to advance along the lines of least resistance, or easiest accessibility, toward the region he intends to occupy. The defender naturally deploys his forces along the line of the enemy's advance in an effort to bar his way. The better to oppose the advance of the enemy, he tries to deploy his forces where the terrain is in his favor or along lines of obstacles most difficult to pass. Because these natural obstacles are permanent and unchanging, just as are the rich and fertile—hence most coveted—regions of the earth, certain portions of the earth's surface seem singled out by destiny to be humanity's battle grounds for all time.

Since war had to be fought on the surface of the earth, it could be waged only in movements and clashes of forces along lines drawn on its surface. Hence, to win, to gain control of the coveted area, one side had to break through the fortified defensive lines of the other and occupy the area. As making war increasingly required the entire resources of nations, in order to protect themselves from enemy invasion warring nations have been forced to spread out their forces along battle lines constantly extended as the fighting went on, to a point where, as in the last war, the lines extended over practically the whole battlefield, thus barring all troop passage either way.

Behind those lines, or beyond certain distances determined by the maximum range of surface weapons, the civilian populations of the warring nations did not directly feel the war. No enemy offensive could menace them beyond that predetermined distance, so civilian life could be carried on in safety and comparative tranquillity. The battlefield was strictly defined; the armed forces were in a category distinct from civilians, who in their turn were more or less organized to fill the needs of a nation at war. There was even a legal distinction made between combatants and noncombatants. And so, though the World War sharply affected whole nations, it is nonetheless true that only a minority of the peoples involved actually fought and died. The majority went on working in safety and comparative peace to furnish the minority with the sinews of war. This state of affairs arose from the fact that *it was impossible* to invade the enemy's territory without first breaking through his defensive lines.

But that situation is a thing of the past; for now *it is possible* to go far behind the fortified lines of defense without first breaking through them. It is air power which makes this possible.

The airplane has complete freedom of action and direction; it can fly to and from any point of the compass in the shortest time —in a straight line—by any route deemed expedient. Nothing man can do on the surface of the earth can interfere with a plane in flight, moving freely in the third dimension. All the influences which have conditioned and characterized warfare from the beginning are powerless to affect aerial action.

By virtue of this new weapon, the repercussions of war are no longer limited by the farthest artillery range of surface guns, but can be directly felt for hundreds and hundreds of miles over all the lands and seas of nations at war. No longer can areas exist in which life can be lived in safety and tranquillity, nor can the battlefield any longer be limited to actual combatants. On the contrary, the battlefield will be limited only by the boundaries of the nations at war, and all of their citizens will become combatants, since all of them will be exposed to the aerial offensives of the enemy. There will be no distinction any longer between soldiers and civilians. The defenses on land and sea will no longer serve to protect the country behind them; nor can victory on land or sea protect the people from enemy aerial attacks unless that victory insures the destruction, by actual occupation of the enemy's territory, of all that gives life to his aerial forces.

All of this must inevitably effect a profound change in the form of future wars, because the essential characteristics of those wars will be radically different from those of any previous ones. We may thus be able to understand intuitively how the continuing development of air power, whether in its technical or in its practical aspects, will conversely make for a relative decrease in the effectiveness of surface weapons, in the extent to which these weapons can defend one's country from the enemy.

The brutal but inescapable conclusion we must draw is this: in face of the technical development of aviation today, in case of war the strongest army we can deploy in the Alps and the strongest navy we can dispose on our seas will prove no effective defense against determined efforts of the enemy to bomb our cities.

THE UPHEAVAL

The World War was a long-drawn-out war which almost completely exhausted both victor and vanquished. This was owing to the technical aspects of the conflict more than to anything else— that is, to new developments in firearms which strongly favored the defensive over the offensive; and, to a lesser degree, to a psychology which could not grasp immediately the advantage conferred on the defensive by the improvement in firearms. Advocates of the offensive were in the saddle everywhere extolling the advantages of the offensive war, but at the same time forgetting that one must have the means to back it up in order to take the offensive successfully. Of the defensive attitude, on the other hand, there was hardly any talk at all, only occasional casual mentions, as though it were a painful subject not to be discussed. This attitude encouraged the belief, held quite generally by military men, that the increased power of firearms favored the offensive rather than the defensive. This belief proved to be an error; the truth was the exact opposite, and clear thinking could have foreseen it, as subsequent war experiences plainly showed.

The truth is that *every development or improvement in firearms favors the defensive.* Defensive action not only permits the conservation of one's weapons for a longer time, but also puts them in the best position to increase their efficacy. It is therefore understandable that, in the absolute sense, the more powerful the weapon, the more valuable will be those dispositions which contribute to its preservation and the increase of its efficacy. This is clearly demonstrated by the fact that never before had there been such a widespread and thorough use of systems of defense as in the World War, in which they assumed formidable proportions. And to prove the fact, we have only to consider what those formidable systems of defense, which for a long period during the war formed the main bulwark of the battle line, would have been worth if the infantry and artillery manning them had been armed like those in the time of Gustavus Adolphus. They would have been worth next to nothing.

But with the increased efficacy of firearms, the defensive had both absolute and relative advantages over the offensive. Let us imagine a soldier posted in a trench protected by barbed-wire entanglements and the attacking enemy exposed on open ground for one minute; and let us also suppose that both sides are armed with muzzle-loading muskets capable of firing one shot a minute. Then we have the mathematical certainty that for the attacker to reach the trench defended by the single soldier, only two men are necessary, because in the minute of time allowed, only one of the two can be hit and put out of action by the defender. But if both sides are armed with rifles which can fire thirty rounds a minute, to have the same mathematical certainty the trench must be stormed by thirty-one men. All the rounds these men might have fired before attacking would have no bear-ing on the case if the lone defender is effectively covered by his own barbed-wire trench.

In the first instance one man on the offensive is effectively checkmated by one man on the defensive; in the second instance thirty men are effectively checkmated by one man because the rifle used was thirty times more effective. With this increased power of firearms, the offensive must, in order to win, upset this equilibrium by a preponderance of forces.

In actual fact, during the World War the enormous increase in the power of small-caliber arms made it possible for the de-fensive to let waves of attacking infantry come close to its own prepared positions and then stop them dead in their tracks; or the defensive could force the offensive, if desperately bent on reaching its objective, to shift its infantry attacks on men in pre-pared positions and lay down costly artillery barrages of all cali-bers which literally churned up the very ground, burying its defenders along with it. So that never before were offensive opera-tions so difficult and so costly as during the World War.

But to say that the increased power of new weapons favors the defensive is not to question the indisputable principle that wars can be won only by offensive action. It means simply that, by virtue of increased fire power, offensive operations demand a much larger force proportionately than defensive ones.

Unfortunately, this fact was not realized until late in the war. So during that long conflict attacks were launched without ade-quate means, attacks which completely failed or only partly suc-ceeded at a great waste of time, money, and men. Because of the inevitable slowness entailed in the process of getting together the enormous quantity of men and matériel to carry them through, these ill-prepared attempts at offensive action succeeded only in wearing down the forces engaged and prolonging the war. And it is certain that if the armies engaged in that struggle had been armed only with muzzle-loading muskets, we should have seen neither reinforced concrete trenches nor barbed-wire entangle-ments; and the war would have been decided in a few months. Instead, what we saw was a prolonged duel of powerful weapons against even more powerful defense fortresses until, by dint of sheer repeated battering, the fortified defenses were finally crumbled and the heart of the enemy bared. This prolonging of the war saved the day for the Allies simply because it gave them time to procure new allies and fresh troops; but on the other hand it almost completely exhausted both victor and vanquished.

In their war preparations the Germans took into account the value the increased power of firearms might give the defensive. They conceived of war in its most offensive aspect, and so provided themselves with the most adequate means—the 305 and 420 mm. guns—with which to wage war and to clear the road of permanent fortifications as quickly as possible. Thus they began the struggle with decisive offensive action; but when circumstances on the French front forced them to adopt the defensive, they covered their position with a system of defense so thorough and so adequate that it surprised the Allies. It could not possibly have been improvised; it must have been thoroughly worked out and planned long in advance to meet just such eventualities.

Germany had also to consider in her preparations for war the possibility of being compelled to fight on more than one front, and to consider the advantage of a defensive under such circumstances—of holding one front with a minimum of effectives while she struck at the other with her maximum forces. No doubt, therefore, she thoroughly systematized some such plan, and no sooner had circumstances shown the necessity of it than she put it into action. This shows clearly how well aware Germany was of the value of the defensive both in itself and relative to the offensive, even though she held firmly to the principle that victory can be won only by offensive action.

Although the preponderance of forces necessary for the offensive to tip the scale made offensive operations more difficult than defensive ones, yet indirectly the situation worked to the advantage of the offensive by making it possible for the offensive to thin out its own defensive lines and mass the greatest possible force in the sector chosen for attack. All the strategic moves of the Germans can be reduced to this formula: to hold a part of the enemy's forces with a small force of her own along a well-systematized line of defense, at the same time attacking another part of the enemy's forces with the largest force she could thus make available. This strategy was often successful over a long period of time.

Caught by surprise, the Allies no sooner saw the German march into the heart of France halted, than they deluded themselves into believing—their lack of defensive preparations notwithstanding—that they could win the war with comparative ease; so, having failed to do at once what should have been done at the beginning of hostilities to insure victory, they were forced to do it in successive stages. In the purely military sense, the war was prolonged by failure to understand the exact nature and demands of modern war. This lack of comprehension produced a series of inconclusive offensives which used up matériel as fast as it was gathered to launch them, thus time and again frittering away that preponderance of forces necessary to upset the equilibrium between the opposing forces which alone could have ended the war sooner.

Though the destruction wrought by the World War was enormous, the nations were able to keep up the struggle for the very reason that the fighting was sporadic and drawn out over a long period of time, so that they could replace their successive material and moral losses and go on throwing all their resources into the struggle until they were exhausted. Never, at any time during the war, was a death-blow struck—a blow which leaves a deep gaping wound and the feeling of imminent death. Instead both sides struck innumerable blows and inflicted many wounds; but the wounds were light ones and always had time to heal. Such wounds, while leaving the body weaker and weaker, still left the patient with the hope of living and recovering strength enough to deal to an equally weakened enemy that last pinprick capable of drawing the last drop of blood. As a matter of fact, the final decision was reached through battles less bloody than earlier ones which had brought only relative results. There is no doubt now that half of the destruction wrought by the war would have been enough if it had been accomplished in three months instead of four years. A quarter of it would have been sufficient if it had been wrought in eight days.

The special character of the World War, then, was shaped by the development of firearms during the last few decades. Now, since the nature of development is dynamic, not static, if there were no new facts to be taken into consideration, the war of the future would have the same general characteristics as the last one, only those characteristics would be accentuated. In other words, in future wars it would be logical to rely upon the continually increasing advantages of the defensive over the offensive, and concomitantly on the still greater difficulty in tipping the scale between the two sides, a necessity if a war is to be won.

If this were the case, protected as we are by a solid frontier of mountains and having no lust for conquest, we should be in an excellent position to face any enemy. With a small force and limited means we could easily provide for the defense of our territory even against attack by greatly superior forces, and rely upon gaining enough time to meet any eventuality of the conflict. But this is not the case; for the new weapons—as we shall see later in this study—reverse this situation by magnifying the advantages of the offensive and at the same time minimizing, if not nullifying, the advantages of the defensive; and, moreover, depriving those who are not fully prepared and ready for instant action of time in which to prepare for defense. No fortifications can possibly offset these new weapons, which can strike mortal blows into the heart of the enemy with lightning speed.

Confronted as we are by this upheaval in the character of war, which encourages nations who lust for conquest and feel neither hesitation nor remorse, it is imperative that we stop and examine calmly, coolly, but searchingly into the question of what is the right path for us to follow in providing for an effective national defense.

THE OFFENSIVE ARM

Because of its independence of surface limitations and its superior speed—superior to any other known means of transportation—the airplane is the offensive weapon par excellence.

The greatest advantage of the offensive is having the initiative in planning operations—that is, being free to choose the point of attack and able to shift its maximum striking forces; whereas the enemy, on the defensive and not knowing the direction of the attack, is compelled to spread his forces thinly to cover all possible points of attack along his line of defense, relying upon being able to shift them in time to the sector actually attacked as soon as the intentions of the offensive are known. In that fact lies essentially the whole game of war tactics and strategy.

From this it is obvious that those nations which have the means to mass their forces rapidly and strike at whatever point they choose of the enemy's forces and supply lines are the nations which have the greatest potential offensive power. In the days when war was fought with small, light, fast-moving bodies of forces, it offered a wide field for tactical and strategic moves; but as the masses engaged grew larger, the playground diminished in size and the game became more restricted. During the World War the masses involved were enormous, and extremely slow and heavy; as a consequence their movements were reduced to a minimum and the war as a whole became a direct, brutal clash between opposite forces.

The airplane, in contrast, can fly in any direction with equal facility and faster than any other means of conveyance. A plane based at point A, for example, is a potential threat to all surface points within a circle having A for its center and a radius of hundreds of miles for its field of action. Planes based anywhere on the surface of this same circle can simultaneously converge in mass on point A. Therefore, an aerial force is a threat to all points within its radius of action, its units operating from their separate bases and converging in mass for the attack on the designated target faster than with any other means so far known. For this reason air power is a weapon superlatively adapted to offensive operations, because it strikes suddenly and gives the enemy no time to parry the blow by calling up reinforcements.

The striking power of the airplane is, in fact, so great that it results in a paradox: for its own protection it needs a greater striking force for defense than for attack. For example, let us suppose that the enemy has an air force with the offensive capacity of X. Even if its bases are scattered, such a force can easily concentrate its action, gradually or however it sees fit, on any number of objectives within its radius of action. To be exact, let us say that there are twenty of these objectives. In this case, in order to defend ourselves from *what force X can do,* we are obliged to station near each of these twenty objectives a defensive force corresponding to force X, in all twenty times as many planes as the enemy has. So that to defend ourselves we would need a minimum aerial force twenty times as large as the attacking force of the enemy—a solution of the problem which partakes of the absurd because the airplane is not adaptable to defense, being pre-eminently an offensive weapon.

The suddenness with which this weapon appeared during the last war made it impossible to study thoroughly the problems posed by its use as a combat weapon. Aerial offensives were instinctively and empirically met by anti-aerial defense alone, whether operating in the air or from the ground. Thus were born antiaircraft guns, and reconnaissance and pursuit planes. But subsequent experience demonstrated that all these means of defense were inadequate, despite the fact that aerial offensives in the last war were of minor importance, haphazardly planned and executed. Every time an aerial offensive was carried out resolutely, it accomplished its purpose. Venice was bombed repeatedly from beginning to end of the war; Treviso was almost razed under our very eyes; and Padua had to be abandoned by the Supreme Command. In other countries, both Allied and enemy, the same thing happened.

In spite of the most elaborate system of signals, if our pursuit squadrons were not already in the air when the enemy reached its objective—and obviously they could not remain in the air continuously—they could seldom take off in time to prevent the enemy from dropping his load of bombs on his chosen targets. There was artillery fire, but it seldom hit the mark; when it did, it scored by chance, as a sparrow might be hit by chance with a rifle bullet. Antiaircraft guns, too, went into action, giving chase through the streets of towns and cities and through the open country in their effort to hit planes diving here, there, and everywhere at will. They behaved much like a man trying to catch a homing pigeon by following him on a bicycle! In the descending curve of its trajectory, artillery fire was metamorphosed into projectiles falling from above. And all of this defensive fire amounted to nothing but a useless dispersion of enormous quantities of our national resources, sometimes wasted on the notion of preventing, not an actual attack, but a possible one! How many guns lay waiting month after month, even years, mouths gaping to the sky, on the watch for an attack which never came! How many pursuit planes immobilized men and materials without ever getting a chance to defend anything! How many people, after staring long and vainly at the sky for the enemy to appear, went soundly and happily to sleep!

I do not know whether an account has ever been drawn up of the weapons and resources scattered over the countryside for aerial defense; but there is no doubt that the total must have been very large. And all that effort, all those resources, so prodigally wasted, could have been profitably used for other purposes.

This dispersion of means, contrary to the fundamental principles of war and to a sound economy of warfare, was caused, as I have already said, by the disorientation produced by the suddenness with which air power came into being, which made for a fallacious concept of defense against it. When a mad dog runs amok in a village, the villagers do not post themselves separately on their own doorsteps, each man armed with a club, waiting on the pleasure of the dog to make an appearance and be killed. That kind of behavior would interrupt their work, but would not prevent the animal from biting someone. No villagers would behave that way. They would gather in groups of three, four, or more of the bolder spirits and go after the dog, track it to its lair, and there kill it.

Similarly, there is no practical way to prevent the enemy from attacking us with his air force except to destroy his air power before he has a chance to strike at us. It is now axiomatic—and has long been so—that coastlines are defended from naval attacks, not by dispersing ships and guns along their whole extent, but by conquering the command of the seas; that is, by preventing the enemy from navigating. The surface of the earth is the coastline of the air. The conditions pertaining to both elements, the air and the sea, are analogous; so that the surface of the earth, both solid and liquid, should be defended from aerial attack, not by scattering guns and planes over its whole extent, but by preventing the enemy from flying. In other words, by "conquering the command of the air."

This is the logical and rational concept which should be recognized, even for simple defense—namely, to prevent the enemy from flying or from carrying out any aerial action at all.

Conquering the command of the air implies positive action—that is, offensive and not defensive action, the very action best suited to air power.

THE MAGNITUDE OF AERIAL OFFENSIVES

Some conception of the magnitude aerial offensives may reach in the future is essential to an evaluation of the command of the air, a conception which the World War can clarify for us in part.

Aerial bombs have only to fall on their target to accomplish their purpose; hence their construction does not require as much metal as is needed in artillery shells. If bombs containing high explosives require a large amount of metal in proportion to their internal charge in order to ensure an effective explosion, the proportion of metal in bombs containing incendiaries or poison gases may be reduced to a minimum. We may be not far off if we figure roughly the proportion of metal in them at 50 per cent of their total weight. The construction of aerial bombs does not call for high-grade steel, other special metals, nor for precision work. What it does demand is that the active ingredients of the bombs—the explosives, incendiaries, and poison gases—have the maximum efficacy, and that research be directed to this end.

Aerial bombardment can certainly never hope to attain the accuracy of artillery fire; but this is an unimportant point because such accuracy is unnecessary. Except in unusual cases, the targets of artillery fire are designed to withstand just such fire; but the targets of aerial bombardment are ill-prepared to endure such onslaught. Bombing objectives should always be large; small targets are unimportant and do not merit our attention here.

The guiding principle of bombing actions should be this: *the objective must be destroyed completely in one attack, making further attack on the same target unnecessary.* Reaching an objective is an aerial operation which always involves a certain amount of risk and should be undertaken once only. The complete destruction of the objective has moral and material effects, the repercussions of which may be tremendous. To give us some idea of the extent of these repercussions, we need only envision what would go on among the civilian population of congested cities once the enemy announced that he would bomb such centers relentlessly, making no distinction between military and non-military objectives.

In general, aerial offensives will be directed against such targets as peacetime industrial and commercial establishments; important buildings, private and public; transportation arteries and centers; and certain designated areas of civilian population as well. To destroy these targets three kinds of bombs are needed—explosive, incendiary, and poison gas—apportioned as the situation may require. The explosives will demolish the target, the incendiaries set fire to it, and the poison-gas bombs prevent fire fighters from extinguishing the fires.

Gas attacks must be so planned as to leave the target permeated with gas which will last over a period of time, whole days, indeed, a result which can be attained either by the quality of the gases used or by using bombs with varying delayed-action fuses. It is easy to see how the use of this method, even with limited supplies of explosive and incendiary bombs, could completely wreck large areas of population and their transit lines during crucial periods of time when such action might prove strategically invaluable.

As an illustration of the magnitude of aerial power, let us assume that 100 kilograms of active material is capable of destroying the area of a circle 25 meters in radius. This supposition is consistent with present practice. Then, in order to extend the destructive action of this active material over a surface 500 meters in diameter, 100 times 100 kilograms, or 10 tons, will be required. Now, 10 tons of active material requires 10 tons of metal casing or shell. Today there are airplanes which can easily carry 2 tons of bombs in addition to their crews; so 10 such planes could carry all the bombs necessary to destroy everything within this circle of 500 meters diameter. To obtain this result it is necessary only to train the crews of ten airplanes to drop their bombs as uniformly as possible over that area.

This gives us the concept of the basic unit of power needed for effective bombing operations; namely, *the unit of bombardment must have the potentiality to destroy any target on a given surface.* In my opinion, the extent of this surface should be exactly the area of a circle 500 meters in diameter. Then, if the above assumptions are correct, this unit should be 10 planes, each capable of carrying 2 tons of bombs. The exact ratio, however, can well be left to experience.

As I said, bombing pilots should be trained to spread their loads over such surfaces as uniformly as possible, releasing their bombs from a medium altitude of, say, 3,000 meters. This dissemination can be accomplished by artificially extending—by variations of sighting data—the natural rose-shaped aim of the squadron formation. If a specified surface contains very vulnerable targets, the area can be extended beyond the 500-meter diameter simply by increasing the number of planes taking part. Conversely, surfaces containing targets more difficult to destroy can be contracted by reducing the number of planes.

But these details are of secondary importance. Of prime importance is the fact that the adoption of such tactics makes the bomber a definite and precise offensive power, no longer a vague, indeterminate one.

When, on the other hand, the surface of a specified objective is smaller, but nevertheless important for military reasons, it should be so designated on the map. It makes no difference if a few bombs go wide of the mark during the attack. But if an objective with a surface larger than 500 meters in diameter is marked for attack, the entire area should be so designated. If the aim is to destroy everything on a surface of, say, 1,000 meters, it is sufficient to divide the target into separate zones and attack with 4 separate but co-ordinated squadrons of planes, with 9 squadrons if the area is 1,500 meters, with 16 squadrons if 2,000 meters, and so forth. Such bombing expeditions, however, cannot be undertaken successfully unless they are directed against very large centers of civilian population. In fact, we have no difficulty in imagining what would happen when areas of 500 to 2,000 meters in diameter in the center of large cities such as London, Paris, or Rome were being unmercifully bombed.[4] With 1,000 bombers of the type described—an actual type in use today, not a hypothetical type in some blueprint of the future—with their necessary maintenance and replacements for daily losses, 100 such operating squadrons can be constituted. Operating 50 of these daily, such an aerial force in the hands of those who know how to use it could destroy 50 such centers every day. This is an offensive power so far superior to any other offensive means known that the power of the latter is negligible in comparison.

As a matter of fact, this same offensive power, the possibility of which was not even dreamed of fifteen years ago,[5] is increasing daily, precisely because the building and development of large, heavy planes goes on all the time. The same thing is true of new explosives, incendiaries, and especially poison gases. What could an army do faced with an offensive power like that, its lines of communication cut, its supply depots burned or blown up, its arsenals and auxiliaries destroyed? What could a navy do when it could no longer take refuge in its own ports, when its bases were burned or blown up, its arsenals and auxiliaries destroyed? How could a country go on living and working under this constant threat, oppressed by the nightmare of imminent destruction and death? How indeed! We should always keep in mind that aerial offensives can be directed not only against objectives of least physical resistance, but against those of least moral resistance as well. For instance, an infantry regiment in a shattered

4 Witness the terrible destruction of Coventry on the night of November 15-16, 1940, a destruction wrought by perhaps no more than 250 bombers in a single night attack.—Tr.

5 1905-6.—Tr.

trench may still be capable of some resistance even after losing two-thirds of its effectives; but when the working personnel of a factory sees one of its machine shops destroyed, even with a minimum loss of life, it quickly breaks up and the plant ceases to function.

All this should be kept in mind when we wish to estimate the potential power of aerial offensives possible even today. To have command of the air means to be in a position to wield offensive power so great it defies human imagination. It means to be able to cut an enemy's army and navy off from their bases of operation and nullify their chances of winning the war. It means complete protection of one's own country, the efficient operation of one's army and navy, and peace of mind to live and work in safety. In short, it means to be in a position *to win*. *To be defeated* in the air, on the other hand, is finally to be defeated and to be at the mercy of the enemy, with no chance at all of defending oneself, compelled to accept whatever terms he sees fit to dictate.

This is the meaning of the "command of the air."

NOTE I: The municipality of Treviso has published a pamphlet entitled "The Martyrdom of Treviso," which may serve as an illustration of what I have said above. In 32 attacks by Austro-Hungarian fliers from April 1916 to the end of October 1918, approximately 1,500 bombs were dropped in an area about 1 kilometer square. Calculating the average weight of each bomb at 50 kilograms—very likely it was less—a total of 75 tons of bombs was dropped on Treviso in 2½ years of war.

On the basis of the approximate calculation I personally made, the diameter of Treviso at its widest periphery being about 1 kilometer, it would take 4 squadrons of 10 planes each, or 40 planes in all, each carrying 2 tons of bombs, or 80 tons in all, to wreak that much destruction.

If we look at the map in "The Martyrdom of Treviso" which shows the distribution of bomb hits and the photographic reproductions of the damage done, we can readily see that if those 75 or 80 tons of bombs, correctly apportioned among explosive, incendiary, and poison-gas types, had been dropped in one day, Treviso would have been completely destroyed and very few of her inhabitants saved. What made it possible for Treviso to escape total destruction and remain on the map in spite of the grave danger to which it was exposed, and to evacuate the population with the loss of only 30 civilian dead and 50 wounded in the very first bombings, is this: during each attack an average of only 50 bombs were dropped, thus allowing time between attacks to smother the fires started during the attacks.

But during all that time nothing effective was done by our aerial defense forces to prevent the bombings except to take note of the places bombed; so the attacks went on until the very end of October 1918, or until the Armistice of November 3, in spite of our claim, especially toward the end of the war, to the command of the air.

NOTE II: The English fleet, the most powerful in the world today, consists of 30 battleships totaling 792,496 tons, exclusive of her smaller units. The weight of their broadsides, every gun firing one round, is 194,931 kilograms, or about 195 tons, each broadside averaging 6.5 tons per battleship.

In contrast, a squadron of 10 planes carrying 2 tons of bombs each, can in a single flight drop 20 tons of bombs, or *something more* than the broadsides of 3 English battleships. Similarly, an aerial fleet of 1,000 planes carrying 2 tons each can drop 2,000 tons of bombs, or *something more* than the whole English fleet of 30 battleships firing 10 rounds with all guns blazing. A thousand such planes, estimating the cost of each at a million lire, would be a round billion lire, or about the cost of a single dreadnought.

Besides the cost, there is another great difference between sea power and air power. The English fleet can fire its broadsides only against another fleet willing to engage in battle, or against stationary targets along seacoasts. An aerial fleet, on the other hand, can carry out bombing attacks against targets which *have no way of retaliating or of putting up any self-defense at all,* and which may be located anywhere on the surface of sea or land.

Moreover, we may soon see the construction of bombers with a capacity of more than 10 tons of effective load, or of a bomb load equal to or even surpassing the broadside of a battleship. And it is also probable that in the event of a duel between a battleship and airplanes, the battleship, with her heavy guns unable to fire at a vertical angle, would get the worst of it. And even if her guns could fire at such an angle, it would be almost impossible to hit a fast-moving plane diving almost vertically—a plane can do just that—at the ship. Recent experiments conducted in the United States and in France seem to furnish conclusive proof of this.

But apart from that, the figures presented in this note should at least give us a more concrete idea of the magnitude of air power and the simplicity of the means needed to effectuate it.

THE COMMAND OF THE AIR

To have command of the air means to be in a position to prevent the enemy from flying while retaining the ability to fly oneself. Planes capable of carrying moderately heavy loads of bombs already exist, and the construction of enough of them for national defense would not require exceptional resources. The active ingredients of bombs or projectiles, the explosives, the incendiaries, the poison gases, are already being produced. An aerial fleet capable of dumping hundreds of tons of such bombs can easily be organized; therefore, the striking force and magnitude of aerial offensives, considered from the standpoint of either material or moral significance, is far more effective than those of any other offensive yet known. A nation which has command of the air is in a position to protect its own territory from enemy aerial attack and even to put a halt to the enemy's auxiliary actions in support of his land and sea operations, leaving him powerless to do much of anything. Such offensive actions can not only cut off an opponent's army and navy from their bases of operations, but can also bomb the interior of the enemy's country so devastatingly that the physical and moral resistance of the people would also collapse.

All this is a present possibility, not one in the distant future. And the fact that this possibility exists, proclaims aloud for anyone to understand that to have command of the air is to have *victory*. Without this command, one's portion is defeat and the acceptance of whatever terms the victor is pleased to impose. Reasoning from the facts along the lines of logic, this is the conclusion we have reached. But since this conclusion applies to matters of very great practical importance, and since it is sharply at variance with the accepted way of looking at things, it behooves us to stop and amplify our statement before going on.

When conclusions are reached by reasoning with strict adherence to logic from actual verifiable facts, those conclusions ought to be accepted as valid even if they seem strange and radical, in direct contradiction to conventional thought patterns or fixed habits of mind based upon other facts, equally positive and verifiable to be sure, but entirely different in nature. To come to any other conclusion would be to deny reason itself. It would be like the reasoning of a peasant who insists upon cultivating his land exactly as his father and grandfather did before him, despite the fact that by using chemical fertilizers and modern machinery he could double or treble his harvest. Such old-fashioned, die-hard perverseness gets him nothing except a handicap in the market place.

Twelve years ago,[6] when the very first airplanes began to hedge-hop between field and air, hardly what we would call flying at all today, I began to preach the value of command of the air. From that day to this I have done my level best to call attention to

[6] 1909.—Tr.

this new weapon of warfare. I argued that the airplane should be the third brother of the army and navy. I argued that the day would come when thousands of military planes would ply the air under an independent Ministry of the Air. I argued that the dirigible and other lighter-than-air ships would give way before the superiority of the plane. And everything I argued for then has come true just as I predicted it in 1909.

I did not prophesy then, and I do not prophesy now. All I did then was to examine the new problem posed by the existence of the new arm and reason from verifiable data; but I did not hesitate to follow up the implications of the conclusions I reached, in spite of the fact that then, as now, they may have sounded paradoxical. I was convinced with mathematical certainty that the facts would prove me right.

When, by the exercise of cold logic and mathematical calculation, someone was able to find out the existence of an unknown planet and furnish an astronomer with all the data necessary for its discovery; when by mathematical reasoning the electro-magnetic waves were discovered, thus furnishing Hertz the means with which to carry on his experiments—then we too should have faith in the validity of human reasoning, at least to the extent that the astronomer and Hertz had faith in it. And how much more abstruse their reasonings were than the reasoning I am attempting here!

At this point I ask my readers to stop with me and consider what I have been saying—the arguments are worth while—so that each may come to his own conclusion about it. The problem does not admit of partial solution. It is right or it is not right.

What I have to say is this: In the preparations for national defense we have to follow an entirely new course because the character of future wars is going to be entirely different from the character of past wars.

I say: The World War was only a point on the graph curve showing the evolution of the character of war; at that point the graph curve makes a sharp swerve showing the influence of entirely new factors. For this reason clinging to the past will teach us nothing useful for the future, for that future will be radically different from anything that has gone before. The future must be approached from a new angle.

I say: If these facts are not given careful consideration, the country will have to make great sacrifices in an effort to bring its defense up to date; but even these sacrifices will be of little use, for the defenses could not possibly meet the demands of modern military requirements. This can be denied only by refuting my argument.

I ask again: Is it true or is it not true that the strongest army and navy we could muster would be powerless to prevent a determined, well-prepared enemy from cutting them off from their bases of operation and from spreading terror and havoc over the whole country?

We can answer, "No, it is not true," to this question only if we have no intention of providing ourselves with suitable means, in addition to those of the army and navy, with which to meet any such eventuality. But I, for one, have long been answering this question with a categorical "Yes, it is true"; and it is because I am convinced of the imminence of such an eventuality that I have deeply pondered the problem posed by the new forms and weapons of war.

NOTE: In 1909 I wrote: "To us who until now have been inexorably bound to the surface of the earth; to us who have smiled superciliously, almost with compassion, at the efforts of a few intrepid pioneers whom we thought deluded with visions of the impossible, but who proved to be the real seers; to us who have only armies and navies, it must seem strange that the sky, too, is about to become another battlefield no less important than the battlefields on land and sea. But from now on we had better get accustomed to this idea and prepare ourselves for the new conflicts to come. If there are nations which can exist untouched by the sea, there are certainly none which exist without the breath of air. In the future, then, we shall have three instead of two separate and well-defined fields of battle; and, though in each of them the conflict will be carried on with different weapons, they will still have to be co-ordinated toward a common goal, which will always remain the same—namely, to win.

"We are fully conscious today of the importance of having command of the seas, but soon the command of the air will be no less important because only by having such a command—and only then—can we make use of the advantages made possible by aerial observation and the ability to see targets clearly—advantages which we shall not be able fully to enjoy until we have the aerial power to keep the enemy grounded. The struggle for the command of the air will be bitter; and the so-called civilized nations will strive to forge the most telling means to wage the conflict. But any conflict, other things being equal, is ultimately decided by weight of numbers; so the race for supremacy will go on without cease, only checked now and then by economic contingencies. By virtue of this race for air supremacy, air fleets will grow in importance as they get larger.

"The army and navy should not then see in the airplane merely an auxiliary arm of limited usefulness. They should rather see in the plane a third brother, younger of course, of the powerful family of War." ["*I problemi dell' aeronavigazione*," by Major G. Douhet; from the newspaper *La preparazione*, Rome, 1910.]

Now, after the experiences of the World War, I find no need to modify by a single word what I wrote eleven years ago. Time has confirmed my deductions, even though the concept of the command of the air has not yet been realized in practice. For that I am not to blame. But anyhow today—it could not possibly be otherwise—those ideas are rapidly gaining ground—especially outside of Italy.

THE EXTREME CONSEQUENCES

To conquer the command of the air means victory; to be beaten in the air means defeat and acceptance of whatever terms the enemy may be pleased to impose. The truth of this affirmation, which for me is an axiom in itself, will become increasingly apparent to readers who will take the trouble to follow this study, wherein I hope to make it completely clear.

From this axiom we come immediately to this first corollary: *In order to assure an adequate national defense, it is necessary— and sufficient—to be in a position in case of war to conquer the command of the air.* And from that we arrive at this second corollary: *All that a nation does to assure her own defense should have as its aim procuring for herself those means which, in case of war, are most effective for the conquest of the command of the air.*

Any effort, any action, or any resources diverted from this essential aim makes conquering the command of the air that much less probable; and it makes defeat in case of war that much more probable. Any diversion from this primary purpose is an error. In order to conquer the air, it is necessary to deprive the enemy of all means of flying, by striking at him in the air, at his bases of operation, or at his production centers—in short, wherever those means are to be found. This kind of destruction can be accomplished only in the air or in the interior of the enemy's country. It can therefore be accomplished only by aerial means, to the exclusion of army and navy weapons. Therefore, *the command of the air cannot be conquered except by an adequate aerial force.* From this affirmation and the above-mentioned first corollary, we may draw an inference of practical value; namely: *An adequate national defense cannot be assured except by an aerial force capable in case of war of conquering the command of the air.* To be sure, this statement is directly opposed to the prevailing conception of national defense, and it puts the air arm first in order of importance. Nevertheless, to deny this affirmation, we must also deny the value of command of the air. To break away from the past is disturbing; but so is man's conquest of space disturbing.

As I have pointed out, this conclusion means the superseding of traditional values by new ones not yet fully realized. Up to this time the army and navy have been the predominant forces, and no one questioned that supremacy. Space was closed to man. But there is no *a priori* reason why the air arm cannot become the predominant power in its relations with surface forces. In examining these relations, we come to the conclusion that the air force is destined to predominate over both land and sea forces; this because their radius of offensive action is limited in comparison to the vastly greater radius of the air force.

As I said, we find ourselves now at a particular point in the curve of the evolution of war. After this point the curve drops off abruptly in a new direction, breaking off all continuity with the past. Therefore, if we have a tendency to deviate as little as possible from the beaten path, we will find ourselves diverging from reality, and we will wind up far removed from the realities of our time. To catch up with things as they are, we must change our course sharply and follow reality itself. If reason, common sense, and the facts themselves tell us that the army and navy are declining in importance as compared with air power, we are doing a disservice to our own defense preparations when we insist upon crediting the army and navy with fictitious values which have no basis in actual fact.

Nature does not progress by leaps and bounds—still less does man. I do not imagine that between today and tomorrow the army and navy will be abolished and only the air force increased.

For the present I ask only that we give the air arm the importance it deserves—in Italy we are far from doing that—and that during the transition period we adopt the following modest program: *A progressive decrease of land and sea forces, accompanied by a corresponding increase of aerial forces until they are strong enough to conquer the command of the air.* This is a program which will approach nearer and nearer reality as we grow firmer in promoting it.

Victory smiles upon those who anticipate the changes in the character of war, not upon those who wait to adapt themselves after the changes occur. In this period of rapid transition from one form to another, those who daringly take to the new road first will enjoy the incalculable advantages of the new means of war over the old. This new character of war, emphasizing the advantages of the offensive, will surely make for swift, crushing decisions on the battlefield. Those nations who are caught unprepared for the coming war will find, when war breaks out, not only that it is too late for them to get ready for it, but that they cannot even get the drift of it. Those who are ready first not only will win quickly, but will win with the fewest sacrifices and the minimum expenditure of means. So that, when this change is completed, though decisions in the field will be swift, the actual war will be fought with increasingly formidable air forces. But during the period of transition a limited force will be adequate to checkmate any opponent's army and navy.

If we must wait to be convinced of this until someone else sets us an example, we will be left behind; and to be left behind during this period means to be defeated in case of war.[7] And, as I have already pointed out, that, ironically enough, is just what is happening now. In an effort to safeguard themselves against Germany's possible thirst for revenge, the Allies forced her along the surest road toward accomplishing it. It is a fact that Germany, forced to disarm on land and sea, will be driven to arm in the air. As we shall see, an air force capable of conquering the command

[7] This is exactly what happened to Poland, France, Norway, Belgium, Holland, and in a measure to England and America when they were caught unprepared by the war machines of Germany and Japan in the present war.—Tr.

of the air, especially during this transition period, requires comparatively limited means, a small personnel, and modest resources; and all of this can be quietly disposed without awakening the attention of potential enemies. At the slightest chafing of the yoke imposed upon her by the Allies, the inner drive to be free will surely push Germany along the new road.[8]

This new road is an economic road which makes it feasible for us to provide for national defense with a limited expenditure of energy and resources once the respective weapons of air, land, and sea are properly evaluated. We remember that in England there have been Admirals of the Fleet who questioned the value of battleships versus airplanes; and we remember, too, that in America tests have been made which demonstrated that under certain conditions planes can sink armored ships.

Now we have reached the hour when we can no longer ignore this problem, which, in the interest of national defense, we should face squarely.

INDEPENDENT AIR FORCE AND AUXILIARY AVIATION

Surveying the problem of national defense in outline, with particular reference to the aerial phase, we have emphasized aerial independence of surface forces and rapidity of movement; and we reached this conclusion: *An adequate national defense cannot be assured except by an aerial force capable in case of war of conquering the command of the air.* We have seen also that, in order to conquer the command of the air, all aerial means of the enemy must be destroyed whether in air combat, at their bases and airports, or in their production centers; in short, wherever they may be found or produced. And we have noted that neither the army nor the navy can help in any way in this work of destruction. The natural consequence of this situation is that an aerial force capable of conquering the command of the air is,

---

[8] It is only five years since I wrote these words, and already Germany, in addition to her first place in chemistry, is incontestably leading the field in aeronautical construction as well as in civilian aviation. And these are the basic—the sufficient—elements necessary to create rapidly and secretly a formidable air force.

by the very nature of things, organically self-sufficient and independent of land and sea forces in its operations. For the sake of simplicity, I shall hereafter refer to all those aerial means which, taken together, constitute an aerial force capable of conquering the command of the air, by the term, Independent Air Force. The foregoing conclusion may thus be stated: *National defense can be assured only by an Independent Air Force of adequate power.*

At present the only military use made of airplanes is to assist the operations of land and sea forces; and for this reason they are under the commands of the army and the navy. So far, an aerial force able to command the air does not exist anywhere in the world. If there were one, granting the uniformity of the air extending over land and sea alike, it could not depend for its being or for its operation on either the army or the navy, because such dependency would be an arbitrary one which, by forcing the Independent Air Force to divide its forces, would fail to fill the true needs of the situation. There are planes at present under the direct command of land and sea forces. An example is the observation plane, whose function is to direct artillery fire—a function, by the way, which is not essentially aerial; it would be performed by other means if aviation were not yet invented. Other examples are the bombing and pursuit specialties, which, while not operating directly under military and naval command, are nonetheless dependent upon them. The primary function of planes under direct army command is, naturally, the furthering of specifically army aims; of those under navy command, furthering specifically navy aims. In like manner, pursuit squadrons under army command have the specific duty of policing the sky above the land surface; those under navy command, of policing the sky over the sea surface.

In this situation we feel something which offends our sense of fitness. In face of this state of things, we can see clearly how easy a time a well-organized enemy bent on conquering the command of the air would have, and how helpless these auxiliary aerial means employed by the army and navy would be, confronted by an enemy Independent Air Force bent on conquest, inasmuch as no organized opposition would stand in his way. It is only natural that the army and navy should wish to be provided with aerial auxiliaries to assist their operations. But such aerial means, which integrate the separate operations of those two branches of the service, are nothing more than an extension of the army and navy. They cannot possibly be considered to constitute a real air force. Observation planes directing artillery fire are useful observers in aerial form, no more.

That fact is so self-evident that in our discussion of aerial warfare we have come to the inescapable conclusion that an Independent Air Force functioning completely independent of the army and the navy is of paramount importance.

When, a few years ago, we first encountered the term "flying service," it seemed a real triumph for the new instrument of war. But it only seemed so; for the term "flying service" expresses only a bond, inasmuch as a "service" is a mere part of a whole, which is the only entity which can be considered really independent. It is only when we arrive at the term "Independent Air Force" that we perceive an entity capable of fighting on the new battlefield, where neither army nor navy can take any part. Planes operating under command of the army or navy can be considered as no more than auxiliary weapons; so, for the sake of simplicity, I shall refer to them from now on as "auxiliary aviation of the army and navy."

Up to this point I have spoken of aerial means of warfare in general terms only, because I thought best to introduce the problem along general lines at the beginning of the book. But in fact aviation falls into two major categories, lighter-than-air and heavier-than-air ships, or dirigibles and airplanes. I should explain, for the sake of clarity, that from now on I shall confine myself to the heavier-than-air category, airplanes, as the only kind suitable for warfare.

CHAPTER II

The Independent Air Force

STRUCTURE

WE HAVE defined an Independent Air Force as that complex total of aerial means which, taken as a whole, makes up an air force capable of conquering the command of the air; we have seen also that, in order to conquer the command of the air, it is necessary to destroy all the enemy's means of flying. Therefore, an Independent Air Force must be organized and employed with this destruction as the end in view.

But, if I may use a figure of speech, it is not enough to shoot down all birds in flight if you want to wipe out the species; there remain the eggs and the nests. The most effective method would be to destroy the eggs and the nests systematically, because, strictly speaking, no species of bird can remain continuously in flight without alighting. Similarly, destroying an enemy's airplanes by seeking them out in the air is, while not entirely useless, the least effective method. A much better way is to destroy his airports, supply bases, and centers of production. In the air his planes may escape; but, like the birds whose nests and eggs have been destroyed, those planes which were still out would have no bases at which to alight when they returned. Therefore, the best means of destroying such objectives is by aerial bombardment carried out by "units of bombardment."

Bombers, however, are by their very nature not intended for combat; so pursuit planes must clear the sky of enemy interference before the bombers can accomplish their mission. These pursuit squadrons I shall call "units of combat."

An Independent Air Force should be organically composed of bombing units and combat units, the first to direct offensive action against surface targets, the second to protect the bombers against possible enemy opposition. It follows, therefore, that the stronger the bombing units of an Independent Air Force, the greater its destructive capacity. The total strength of the combat units, on the other hand, should be only proportionately greater than the combat strength of the enemy; that is, they need be only strong enough to gain superiority over the enemy's combat forces. Once the Independent Air Force has conquered the command of the air, there will be no need of the combat units. The bombing units, on the contrary, once the Independent Air Force has won command of the air, now freed of aerial opposition, will be able to unleash without risk all their offensive power to cut off the enemy's army and navy from their bases of operation, spread terror and havoc in the interior of his country, and break down the moral and physical resistance of his people.

The following simple outline shows the skeleton upon which an Independent Air Force should be constituted:

1. Maximum bombing power
2. Combat power proportionate to the enemy's possible strength

UNIT OF BOMBARDMENT

The unit of bombardment must possess sufficient striking power to ensure really important results. I have already pointed out the fundamental principle which should govern offensive action from the air; namely, that a bombing attack must completely destroy the target at which it is directed, thus obviating the necessity of returning to make a second attack on the same target.

In my opinion the unit of bombardment should be capable of destroying everything on a specified surface of 500 meters in diameter. The area of that surface, then, should be the basis upon which to compute and establish the degree of power necessary to the bombing unit. Once the area of such a surface is determined by empirical criteria, or the number of targets on it, the next step is to determine the quantity of active material—explosives, incendiaries, and poison gases—necessary to demolish everything exposed on that surface. This quantity will be larger or smaller according to the efficacy of the active materials used in the actual bombs. If we stop to think that upon this necessary quantity of active material depends the number of bombers to a unit, other things being equal, we can easily see how great an advantage it would be to make use of the most efficient active materials.

Once the basic quantity of active materials is established and the ratio between it and the weight of the shell determined, it is a simple matter to calculate the total weight of the bomb load needed to destroy the surface under consideration. Once this weight is computed, we know the number of planes needed in a bombing unit. On the assumption that a quintal of active material is enough to destroy everything within a radius of 25 meters, and that on an average the active material in a bomb accounts for half its weight, we arrive at the conclusion that 20 tons of bombs are necessary to destroy a surface 500 meters in diameter. And further, allowing a carrying capacity of 2 tons of bombs to a plane, I conclude that the bombing unit should be a force of 10 planes. The assumptions upon which this computation is based are not pure speculation; they are derived from existing conditions. So that even if they are not absolutely exact, they furnish us with a reasonably accurate estimate which cannot be far from the truth. Only experience, of course, can establish the exact figures; and only experience can accurately determine the specific details of the organization of the bombing unit. But that is not of vital importance to us here. What interests us now is the principle of the matter and some realization of what should be the strength of a bombing unit capable of destroying a surface of, say, 500 meters diameter.

We may think from all this that a unit of bombardment established according to this principle represents a somewhat indefinite offensive power which might be capable of inflicting a certain amount of damage upon an opponent. That is not the case. Such a unit represents an exactly determined offensive power which possesses a definite known capacity for destruction over a given surface. When such a unit strikes against an enemy target within the specified surface, we have mathematical certainty that that target will be destroyed. The offensive power of an Independent Air Force as a whole, then, is computed from the number of bombing units composing it; and the number of these, in turn, from the number of given surfaces to be destroyed. This offensive—or better still, destructive—power can be launched against an enemy at whatever point it will prove most effective and most painful. Take, for example, an Independent Air Force of 500 planes, each carrying 2 tons of bombs, and capable of destroying 50 surfaces, each 500 meters in diameter. Such an air force could destroy every day 50 enemy aviation nests—i.e. airports, supply depots, production plants, et cetera. At that rate, how long do you think it would take to ground the present air force of any of the great powers of Europe? What opposition, aerial or ground, could any of them offer against such attacks?

In discussing the unit of combat, let us first look into the possibility of aerial opposition, because it is the combat unit which will overcome the opposition. As for any opposition from ground forces, there can be none except antiaircraft guns; and I shall try to show how combat planes can counteract even the action of antiaircraft guns. But quite apart from this point, in actual fact the efficacy of antiaircraft guns can never be anything but very limited, both because of their inaccurate fire and because of the dispersion of means inherent in that kind of defense. Antiaircraft fire can certainly put out of action some planes in a bombing unit —a limited loss; but no one can hope to fight a war without taking some risks, especially when those risks can be reduced to a minimum. And that loss can easily be compensated for by simply keeping up the strength of the bombing units by a constant flow of replacement planes.

As to this question of replacement planes, an adequate supply of such planes should be kept on hand ready for instant action, and the quota of these planes should never be allowed to go below a certain limit. For example, taking the potentiality of the bombing unit as 20 tons of bombs, this amount of power can be developed by 10 machines, each carrying 2 tons; by 5 machines, each carrying 4 tons; or by a single machine—if such a machine existed —carrying the whole 20-ton load. From one point of view, it is better to have as few planes as possible to simplify the organization of the unit. But from another point of view, it is very unwise to make the number of planes in a unit too small, because the loss of even one plane would too greatly reduce the potentiality of the unit. For this reason I consider that the minimum number of planes per unit should never be less than 4; which, in the case under consideration, would mean planes carrying 5 tons each.

Now let us try to determine the general characteristics of planes suitable for bombing units. An airplane must have the characteristics of air-worthiness and usefulness. These are demanded of any flying machine in peace or war. It is the functional characteristics —the performance—of a plane we must determine here; and these include speed, radius of action, ceiling, armament, and useful-load capacity.

Speed: We have already noted that bombing units, which should carry out their mission in spite of enemy opposition, are supported by combat units. This means that they need not have the speed to outdistance enemy pursuit planes; a fact of utmost importance because it makes it unnecessary for bombing planes to enter a speed race, the outcome of which is bound to be uncertain. The nation which stakes its safety or its power simply on speed in the air, gambles on a very doubtful card—especially in view of the ever-increasing speed of airplanes. On the other hand, victory is never won by fleeing. Great speed in an airplane is always obtained at the expense of carrying capacity. So in planes of great carrying capacity we must be content with a moderate speed, which may actually prove to be best for practical purposes. The bombing plane, then, should be a plane of moderate speed, since, protected by combat planes, it need not flee or dodge the attacks of the enemy and thus sacrifice load to speed.

Radius of Action: The radius of action of a warplane is the greatest distance it can travel from its own airfield and return under its own power. A bombing plane's radius of action should therefore be the greatest possible; for the longer its radius of action, the deeper its penetration into enemy territory. The extent of the radius of action depends exclusively upon the fuel consumption of its motors and its carrying capacity. Therefore, the greater the carrying capacity, the longer its radius of action.

A bombing plane's carrying capacity, exclusive of the crew, should be proportionately divided between fuel load and bomb load. It is understood, of course, that, given the maximum total load of the plane—a predetermined fixed quantity—the radius of action can be increased simply by increasing the load of fuel and decreasing the bomb load, and vice versa. What we are concerned with here is determining the normal or average radius of action of the bombing plane; and that depends upon two factors: the disposition of enemy targets intended for attack during normal operations, and the choice of plane capable, within that normal radius of action, of carrying a load of bombs sufficient to destroy the target.

In my opinion, the normal radius of action of a bombing plane today should be between 200 and 300 kilometers. I said "normal radius of action"; in exceptional instances it can easily be modified. If the normal radius is 300 kilometers and an action is planned within 100 kilometers, it would be wasteful to carry a load of fuel sufficient for 300 kilometers instead of reducing the fuel load and using the weight thus saved to carry more bombs. Conversely, if the normal radius is 300 kilometers and an action at 400 kilometers is planned, the bomb load can be lightened by enough to correspond with the increase in fuel load. This elasticity in the radius of action of a plane can be secured by a few extra details of construction to allow for adjustment of the total load between fuel weight and bomb weight.

Ceiling: The higher the altitude, the less a warplane's vulnerability to antiaircraft fire. Since by their very nature bombing operations are characterized by dispersion rather than concentration of fire, bombing raids can be carried out effectively even at very high altitudes. The normal ceiling, therefore, should be between 3,000 and 4,000 meters. Considering the nature of our boundaries, made up for the most part of high mountain peaks, we need warplanes with ceilings high enough to surmount the entire Alpine range at any point without difficulty; which means ceilings between 6,000 and 7,000 meters.

Degree of Armament: Obviously, the first requisite, the chief purpose, of a bombing plane is to carry bombs and to be equipped with the proper mechanism for releasing them. But that is not all; something more is needed. For the sake of the crew's morale, some defensive armament is indispensable. Though a bombing plane cannot possibly be the ideal weapon for aerial combat, it would be poor judgment to leave its crew with a feeling of utter helplessness against possible attack by enemy pursuit planes. It is imperative, therefore, that the plane be supplied with small-caliber rapid-fire guns for its own defense, even though conscious of the fact that aerial combat should be left to combat units.

Useful Load: The maximum useful load of any type of plane is a predetermined fixed quantity equal to the sum of the weights of these three elements: crew, fuel, and armament. The crew, naturally, should be kept to an indispensable minimum, allowing for possible losses in personnel. The relationship between weight of fuel and weight of armament we have already discussed. Given, then, the amount of fuel and armament needed for normal operations, the total useful load of a bombing plane should be such as to allow a bomb weight substantial enough to avoid cumbersome bombing units of too many planes. In my opinion, the number of planes in a bombing unit should be between 4 and 12.

Such are the functional characteristics of a bomber—characteristics which, translated into specifications, should be required to be put into effect by plane designers and builders.

I have already called attention to the great importance of the efficacy of the active materials used in bombs. Doubling the efficacy of the active materials, in fact, automatically doubles the power of an Independent Air Force. It would be foolish indeed to be too economical in these matters or in any way stint appropriations for research into the nature and use of these materials.

Active materials fall into three major categories: explosives, incendiaries, and poison gases. Besides study and research into the efficacy of each of these, we should also investigate the potentialities of possible combinations of them in bombing operations. Even if we still have little knowledge of them, we can at least sense, and experience may confirm the impression, that high explosives will play a minor role in potential combinations, given a more extensive use of incendiaries and poison gases. This will be particularly true as regards civilian objectives such as warehouses, factories, stores, food supplies, and population centers, the destruction of which may be more easily accomplished by setting fires with incendiary bombs and paralyzing all human activity for a time with gas bombs. Only in exceptional cases will high-explosive bombs be useful, as in smashing runways and plowing up airfields with bomb bursts. But this matter of bombs is a particular detail to which I allude only in order to give you an idea of the scope of the whole problem of the formation of a bombing unit.

UNIT OF COMBAT

The essential function of the combat unit is to clear any possible aerial opposition out of the path of bombers while they carry out their mission. They should therefore be designed and equipped primarily for aerial combat.

In the days before the World War the opinion was current in military circles that combat in the air was an impossibility, and, except in rare instances, the first planes used in the war were provided with no armament suitable for combat. But aerial combat is a reality and is here to stay.

Any aerial action on the part of the foe is bound to be to his advantage, and our disadvantage, and we must contest it. During the World War it was considered poor policy to admit that our reconnaissance planes could do practically nothing to prevent enemy planes from carrying out their observations over our lines, and vice versa. But aerial combat developed spontaneously, in the natural course of events. Planes began to carry some armament, and pilots began to learn to attack and to defend themselves—the beginning of aerial maneuvers. And from these dog fights the fact emerged clearly that the faster planes had the advantage over slower ones; they could hit and run at will. Soon after, out of that experience came the pursuit plane, so named precisely because its purpose was to interfere with other planes and prevent them from fulfilling their missions. Speed and armament were the characteristics most stressed in the design of this type of plane; and as a consequence the pursuit plane immediately became master of the air and dominated all other types of plane in combat. Out of the necessity of protecting other types of plane from the pursuit plane, arose the need of another plane as fast or faster, a plane able, as it were, to give chase to the chaser.

Then the race was on to develop more and more speed in airplanes. More speed and greater maneuverability than the enemy, was the cry—for planes capable of performing aerial "acrobatics," by which, in case a pilot found his speed inferior, he could dodge the fight and flee to safety. Everything else was sacrificed to speed and maneuverability, the first requisite for gaining even temporary superiority over the enemy in the air. The crew was reduced to the minimum—a single pilot who also handled the machine gun. The radius of action was reduced to a minimum—an hour or a little more of flying time was all.

The function of pursuit planes, then, was to seek out other types of enemy plane and to protect their own planes from enemy pursuers. Since they were the fastest planes and designed for aerial acrobatics, hence the most difficult to handle, they were assigned to the most daring of the pilots. For two understandable reasons pilots preferred them to other types of plane.

In the first place, other types—reconnaissance, observation, and bomber planes—were sent out on definite missions, which put them at a disadvantage in encounters with enemy chasers. Pursuit planes, on the other hand, were given less definite missions and consequently had more freedom of action. They attacked enemy planes of other types, over which they had obvious advantages when it came to an encounter. Or, encountering enemy pursuit planes, they could engage them in dog fights, evade the encounter entirely, or, once engaged, cut the fight short in the middle and head for home. Their performance was thus more colorful, less restricted, less monotonous, and even, in a certain sense, less dangerous than the operations of other types of plane.

In the second place, pursuit planes usually operated near the headquarters of the High Commands, to whose protection, I may add, they directly contributed. In the war both sides kept trying to bomb Headquarters, and it was soon apparent that pursuit planes were the best defense against these attempts. With their quick take-off and fast climbing speed, these machines were more likely to succeed in intercepting the attacker before he could strike and, more often than not, in bringing down the slower enemy bombers. Policing the sky became the particular province of the pursuit planes, and they enjoyed the favor of the High Commands, whose safety and peace of mind they could safeguard, at least during the day.

This favoritism produced a rapid growth of this flying specialty; but at the same time it obscured the problem of national defense and prevented a correct understanding of what the command of the air consists in. When the pursuit squadrons of one side in the war succeeded in bringing down more enemy ships than they lost of their own, that side would immediately claim command of the air. In reality all that had been gained was a temporary superiority which may have made aerial operations more difficult for the opponent for the time being. But it did not, and could not, preclude his engaging in aerial operations. Up to the very last days of the war, in fact, all belligerents carried out aerial operations against each other.

The fact of the matter is that, in spite of its claim to offensive characteristics, the pursuit plane was used almost entirely as a defensive means. It could not have been otherwise. With its very limited radius of action, the pursuit plane was forced to play a passive role instead of seeking out the enemy on his own grounds. The pursuit planes of those days could not have been differently employed. They were used primarily to shoot down enemy machines on observation patrol or directing artillery fire, and to defend important centers from bombardment. For the rest, their usefulness was as limited as their operations were scattered; and aerial combat became merely a series of duels in which the skill and courage of the individual aces were displayed in all their brilliance. Pursuit squadrons were a loose agglomeration of knights-errant of the air, rather than an effectively organized cavalry of the air.

We can see now that such a situation has something false in it, something that does not ring true; for war is no longer fought in a series of scattered individual encounters, no matter how brave or skillful the individuals may be. War today is fought by masses of men and machines. So this aerial knight-errantry ought to be supplanted by a real cavalry of the air—the Independent Air Force.

Earlier in these pages I remarked that to rely on speed alone in aerial combat is to stake one's all on a doubtful card. For instance, let a pursuit plane be chased by a faster one, and it ceases to be a pursuit plane. By its very nature the pursuit plane must be an exceptional machine, embodying at any given moment all the most recent technical developments, and manipulated by exceptional pilots. But war is fought with men and machines of average abilities and standards; and we must therefore change our present conception of aerial warfare—or go under.

What determines victory in aerial warfare is fire power. Speed serves only to come to grips with the foe or to flee from him, no more. A slower, heavily armed plane, able to clear its way with its own armament, can always get the best of the faster pursuit plane. A unit of combat composed of slower, heavily armed planes is in a position to stand up to the fire of enemy pursuit planes and carry out its mission successfully. As a matter of fact, it is not the business of a combat unit either to seek out an aerial foe or to flee from him. I have said, and I repeat it, that the primary function of a combat unit is to clear enemy aerial opposition out of the way of bombing units intent upon carrying out definite missions.

Let me use this simple example to illustrate what I mean: A bombing unit leaves point A to bomb point B. Combat units have no other purpose in this operation than to clear out of their path any enemy aerial obstacles attempting to bar the way of the bombing unit on the road from A to B. It is up to the enemy to prevent the bombardment of B if he can. He is the one who seeks battle, who makes the attack. If he does not, so much the better—the bombing of B can be performed with more safety. If he does attack, there are the combat units to fight off the attack. Therefore, combat units have no need of great speed in order to seek out the enemy and force him to give battle; all they need is enough to escort the bombing units and put up an adequate fight if the enemy attempts to interfere with their operations.

It is obvious, then, that the speed of combat units ought to be somewhat greater than that of bombing units. And, as a matter of fact, it goes without saying that the radius of action and ceiling of combat planes should be greater than those of bombing units, which they must escort and protect. In general the chief characteristics of combat planes should be speed, radius of action, and ceiling superior to those of bombing planes.

From this the conclusion may be drawn that there should, on the whole, be very little difference between one type of plane and the other, which implies that combat planes, like bombers, ought to be capable of carrying a substantial load in addition to an adequate supply of fuel. This increase in the carrying capacity of the combat unit should be made use of for increasing fire power and, if possible, armor protection. This is merely a matter of increasing the amount of the plane's armament and its ability to concentrate fire in any given direction. A certain amount of protection may be afforded by armor-plating the vital parts of the plane with light metal alloys. Certainly it would be absurd to expect complete armor protection against all possible hits; but it is not too much to expect that a very light armor-plating would deflect a great many bullets.

A plane designed and constructed along these lines would on the face of it be so superior in intensity of fire power as to outmatch any pursuit ship now existing. If a bombing plane capable of carrying two tons of bombs can be made, certainly it should be possible to construct one with slightly superior speed, radius of action, and ceiling, capable of carrying a one-ton load of bombs. Then if the carrying capacity thus saved were used for armament instead of bombs, we would have a plane equipped for combat with a much greater fire power than any pursuit plane now existing.

The organization of a combat unit must be such as to include a number of planes which can fight in formation; and the formation must be of a nature to concentrate maximum intensity of fire in any direction in order to ward off enemy aerial attack, or at least make it hazardous for the enemy to approach. Compared with such units—the purpose of which, I repeat, is not to attack, but to defend themselves against attack—pursuit planes, with all their superior speed and maneuverability, would have no advantage, but rather the disadvantage of light armament. Such a unit could be attacked with success only by a similar unit made up of a still larger number of planes, stronger, better armed, and better armored.

Only practical experience can furnish us with enough data to determine the proper organization of the combat unit in specific detail—i.e. number of planes, formation, and tactics. My purpose here is to present a schematic, but nonetheless concrete, idea of what the combat unit should be like.

STABILIZATION OF ARMAMENT

We have seen how an Independent Air Force should be organized, that it must include both bombing and combat units in order to be fully effective. It may include other types of plane in addition—fast planes for observation, dispatch bearing, and liaison duty between the various commands, for example. But its backbone must always be bombing and combat planes. In that lies stabilization of its armament.

One of the gravest problems confronting an air force is this question of stabilizing its armament. It is often said that military planes should be changed in design and construction every three months because of the constant and rapid technical progress being made in aviation. This is true in view of the concepts which today govern the organization of such forces. For instance, we have noted the importance accorded to pursuit planes at present. Since this branch of aviation derives its potential power from speed, and since new speed records are made and broken every day, pursuit aviation is clearly unstable; the plane which today is the last word in technical developments may be obsolete tomorrow.

This is true not only of pursuit planes. There are machines called "daylight bombers," in which a combination of great speed and bomb-carrying capacity is sought. In the prevailing concept of their purpose, these planes are called daylight bombers because they can carry out limited bombing operations—during daylight only—at the same time taking advantage of their greater speed to escape from enemy pursuit planes. These daylight bombers are considered to be the counterpart of the medium-speed bombers called "night bombers" because they are supposed to carry out their operations under cover of night. In both cases the same concept governs; namely, trying to carry out an operation *by fleeing!* This is a concept that cries aloud for revision. The idea is absurd inasmuch as war demands the power to carry out operations, whether on land, on the sea, or in the air, *in spite of* enemy opposition. But apart from that, these so-called daylight bombers must evidently remain unstabilized inasmuch as they rely upon speed alone for their effectiveness, a factor forever changing.

Very different indeed is my conception of the planes which should form the main body of an Independent Air Force. Whether bombers or combat planes, they need no more than a medium speed. No emphasis need be placed upon speed; it is of little importance that technical advances may soon produce bombing or combat planes which, while retaining other basic characteristics unaltered, will have a speed of 10 to 20 more miles per hour. To keep abreast of technical developments in armament, it will be enough to take into account the gradual improvement in armament itself. Theoretical perfection always demands the extreme; but our interest is in the middle road of practicality.

Therefore, it is the actual armament of an Independent Air Force which governs the stabilization of whatever armament is considered necessary for a really efficient air force. But there is more to it than that. If we examine carefully the functional characteristics of bombing and combat planes as I have tried to define them, we can readily see that they are in general almost identical with the functional characteristics of civil aviation. When all is said and done, the bombing plane is essentially a transport plane of medium speed and sufficient radius of action, especially equipped to carry bombs. In fact, to change its equipment is all that is necessary to transform it into a plane for civilian use. The same thing can be said of a combat plane of normal radius of action and medium speed (even if this is somewhat greater than the speed of a regular bomber), and of sufficient carrying capacity to carry out bombing operations (even if this is slightly less than the carrying capacity of the regular bomber). This also means—since the law of reciprocity works both ways—that, by mutual understanding between military and civil aviation, civilian planes could be turned into military planes in case of need. This in turn implies that, with the strides being made in civil aviation, an Independent Air Force can rely for many of its needs and much of its equipment upon civilian progress in addition to military progress. Based as it is upon planes of extreme characteristics, military aviation in its present state cannot boast of this advantage. As a result, military aviation today not only has failed to stabilize design and construction, but is also almost entirely dependent upon its own resources. I shall return to this argument, which is of the utmost importance, in my discussion of the relationship between military and civil aviation in later chapters.

Aerial Warfare

GENERAL PRINCIPLES

BEFORE WE CAN draw up an accurate estimate of the scope of an Independent Air Force, we must first consider the following point: An Independent Air Force is an offensive force which can strike with terrific speed against enemy targets on land or sea in any direction, and can force its way through any aerial opposition from the enemy. From this fact emerges this first principle governing its operation: *An Independent Air Force should always operate in mass.*

This is the same principle which governs warfare on land and sea; and therefore the material and moral effects of aerial offensives—as of any other kind of offensive—are greatest when the offensives are concentrated in time and space. In addition, keeping together in mass in its operations makes it possible for the Air Force to force its way through aerial opposition successfully.

The radius of action of an Independent Air Force obviously must depend upon the radius of action of the planes comprising its units. But because all its units cannot be located at a single base, the disposition of the various units in relation to one another and to the general theater of war have some influence upon the radius of action. Once the disposition of its units has been decided, the Air Force's field of mass operation against enemy targets can be shown on a military map simply by tracing the periphery which can be reached by *all* units. It is self-evident that any enemy target, on land or sea, within this line can be reached with equal facility by the entire Air Force in a few hours, at most in the time needed to cover the maximum distance between its bases of operation and any given point on that periphery. The attack may therefore be prepared in complete secrecy and launched without forewarning the enemy, with the offensive retaining the advantages of operational initiative. And, considering the suddenness of the attack, it is unlikely that the enemy would have time enough to parry the blow effectively either in the air or from the ground. Whatever he might be able to do, in general he could oppose the attack with no more than a fraction of his air forces.

Whatever the total strength of an Independent Air Force, provided it has at its disposal an adequate number of bombing units, the attack can be successfully directed not only against a single target, but against a number of them within the same zone. Since a bombing unit is potentially able to destroy any target on a specified surface, a fully activated Air Force is potentially capable of demolishing as many such targets, or surfaces, as there are bombing units. An Air Force of 50 bombing units, each capable of destroying a surface 500 meters in diameter, could in a single flight completely destroy 50 enemy objectives, such as supply depots, industrial plants, warehouses, railroad centers, population centers, et cetera.

In considering the objectives situated within striking distance of the Air Force, it would be advisable to subdivide the area into zones of 50 targets each. If we get 10 zones when the subdivision is mapped out, it means that the Air Force has the potential capacity to destroy all enemy objectives in that area of land or sea in ten days of operation, after which its striking power can be transferred to other zones designated for destruction.

All this sounds very simple; but as a matter of fact the selection of objectives, the grouping of zones, and determining the order in which they are to be destroyed is the most difficult and delicate task in aerial warfare, constituting what may be defined as aerial strategy. Objectives vary considerably in war, and the choice of them depends chiefly upon the aim sought, whether the command of the air, paralyzing the enemy's army and navy, or shattering the morale of civilians behind the lines. This choice may therefore be guided by a great many considerations—military, political, social, and psychological, depending upon the conditions of the moment. For example, I have always maintained that the essential purpose of an Air Force is to conquer the command of the air by first wiping out the enemy's air forces. This, then, would seem to be always the first objective of an Independent Air Force. But this is not always the case. Take, for instance, a case when the enemy's aerial forces are so weak it would be a waste of time to devote men and materials to so unimportant an objective. It may be more profitable to subject the enemy to various other offensive actions instead, thereby doing him far more damage. Let us suppose—hypothetically, of course—that Germany had an Air Force of the strength described above, and decided to attack France, who was armed only with the aerial means now at her disposal. How long do you think it would take Germany to knock out not only the French flying forces, but the very heart of France?

The same thing is true of the grouping of enemy objectives into zones and in the disposition of the zones themselves, dependent as they are on diverse factors of vital consequence to the conduct of aerial operations as a whole. On this aspect of aerial warfare I do not believe it possible to lay down any specific rules. It will be enough to keep in mind the following basic principle, which is the same one which governs warfare on land and sea: *Inflict the greatest damage in the shortest possible time.*

In the light of this principle the value of the surprise attack is obvious. A really strong Independent Air Force such as the one described above could inflict upon an unprepared enemy such grave damage as to bring about a complete collapse of his forces in a very few days. To confirm the truth of this statement, I suggest that the reader solve for himself the following military problems:

Given a possible enemy armed with an Independent Air Force of enough bombing units, each capable of demolishing a surface 500 meters in diameter, and with an adequate radius of action—

1. How many bombing units would be needed to cut all rail communications between Piedmont and Liguria, and the rest of Italy, in a single day?

2. How many bombing units would be needed to cut Rome off from all rail, telegraph, telephone, and radio communication, and to plunge the city itself into terror and confusion by the destruction of governing bodies, banks, and other public services in a single day?

If the reader remembers that by a 500-meter surface we mean an area of that dimension upon which a variety of explosive, incendiary, and poison-gas bombs will be dropped, he needs must answer the questions with very small numbers indeed; and his conception of the power of this new weapon of warfare will be that much clearer and nearer the truth.

THE DEFENSE

The very magnitude of possible aerial offensives cries for an answer to the question, "How can we defend ourselves against them?" To this I have always answered, "By attacking."

More than once I have stressed the pre-eminently offensive character of the air arm. Like a cavalry corps (unless it is dismounted), whose best defense is always to attack, the air arm depends upon attack for its own best defense, to an even greater degree, in fact. But before we go on with the air arm, we should thoroughly understand what we mean by the term "to attack."

Let us suppose that Nation A is armed only with combat units and depends upon them in case of war to repel the attack of Nation B's Independent Air Force. What do you think would be their respective situations at the outbreak of hostilities? The probability is that the air force of Nation A would have to seek for B's Independent Air Force, find it, compel it to fight, and defeat it.

To find it is the crux of the matter. One may look—but where? The air is a uniform element everywhere; there are no signposts to show the road Independent Air Force B will follow in attacking Nation A. The word "seek" becomes an abstraction; and "to find" is a possibility, not a probability. For A's air force to compel B's Independent Air Force to engage in battle, A must have greater speed than B; to win, A must be stronger than B and have good luck besides. But while air force A's search for Independent Air Force B is going on unsuccessfully, B can strike at A's territory and do enormous damage, with A helpless to inflict any damage at all on Nation B. If, however, Nation B considers A's air force dangerous, her Independent Air Force will doubtless concentrate her attacks upon demolishing everything essential to the functioning of A's air force. A's wasted time looking for Independent Air Force B will then result not only in a futile joyride, but in a real if indirect defeat, since her air potential will have been wasted without her having had a chance to engage Independent Air Force B in combat.

If we also consider that the air force of Nation A must operate in mass in order to be in the best position to win, the question comes up of where and when to concentrate those forces, operating as they are from scattered airfields.

This kind of action is essentially defensive in spite of its offensive appearance, and it has all the disadvantages of the defensive. To attack on land means to attack, without the need of scouting for them, fixed targets immovable upon the surface, targets which are the very lifeblood of an opponent's air force. On the sea, conditions are different. Naval bases are as a rule so strongly fortified that it is practically impossible for hostile naval forces to destroy them. This fact increases the importance of naval battles fought to prevent or carry out subsequent possible action against land targets by one belligerent or the other. Things would be radically different, however, if naval bases could no longer be protected, and instead were subject to destruction in a few hours by naval forces. In such a case the destruction of naval bases would set the value of battle fleets at naught, because it would prove of incalculable help in crippling the operating efficiency of such fleets without wasting time and matériel trying to catch and sink them on the open seas.

For a nation to be equipped with an air force intended for aerial combat alone is not only to jeopardize the home front, but also to preclude any possibility of offensive action against enemy objectives—a condition of profound aerial inferiority.

The only really effective aerial defense cannot but be indirect; for it consists in reducing the offensive potentiality of the opponent's air forces by destroying the source of aerial power at its point of origin. The surest and most effective way of achieving this end is to destroy the enemy air force at its bases, which are found on the surface. This is the principle which governs the situation: it is easier and more effective to destroy the enemy's aerial power by destroying his nests and eggs on the ground than to hunt his flying birds in the air. And every time we ignore this principle we commit an error. Therefore, even if a nation has no other end in view than self-defense, it should be armed with an Independent Air Force capable of launching powerful offensives on land and sea.

It remains for us to take up the question of what I shall call local defense, meaning defense of singularly important points on one's land and sea territory. Theoretically there are two ways of making this defense effective: by preventing enemy bombardment of them and by immediate repair of the damage inflicted by bombardment. This last appears at once impossible to effect, since it would be impossible to bomb-shelter entire cities with their rail centers, port facilities, supply bases, factories, and so on. In a measure aerial enemies could be kept at a distance and prevented from bombing certain objectives either by antiaircraft fire or by defensive aerial operations. Since antiaircraft guns are limited in range and not effective enough, practically speaking, to be of any great value, large numbers of them would have to be used; and since any country has a great many vital centers to be defended, even partial protection of them would require an enormous number of antiaircraft guns.[1]

Moreover, the fact must be taken into consideration that antiaircraft guns may be neutralized by the escorting combat units' drawing on themselves the fire of the guns. These operations are even safer at a low altitude than at a higher one, for the simple reason that the angular variation of the gunfire would have to be greater to keep the diving planes in sight. A plane flying at 100 meters is far more difficult to hit than one flying at 2,000 meters because the angular variation is about twenty times greater. If, therefore, the escorting combat planes should dive with machine guns wide open straight at the gun emplacements, it would be very unlikely that the gunners could stay at their posts and keep firing at the high-flying bombing units. In all probability, if they were not quite forced to drop the guns and take up the rifle, they

[1] It has recently been estimated by Fletcher Pratt in *America and Total War*, that to defend our northeastern cities and vital centers alone, we would need about 120,-000 antiaircraft guns.—Tr.

would naturally shift their fire, trying to hit the immediate menace, hard as it might be to keep them in sight. For my part, I maintain—and war experience has already confirmed me in my opinion—that the use of antiaircraft guns is a mere waste of energy and resources.[2]

As for the utilization of aerial units for purely defensive purposes, we have only to recall that if an enemy's Independent Air Force operates efficiently, as presumably it will, it will function in mass, so the defensive units must at least be equal to the combat units of the hostile Independent Air Force. To defend effectively all areas threatened by such an Air Force would require a defensive force equal to the total combat strength of the attacking Air Force, multiplied by as many times as there are defensive positions to be protected. To obtain even this negative result it would be necessary to spend an enormously greater amount of resources than the enemy had to spend to obtain a positive result. This clearly demonstrates that it is both cheaper and wiser to put these resources to work where they will do the most good, for offensive purposes.

In conclusion, no local defense can be very effective when confronted by an aerial offensive of this magnitude; therefore, the expenditure of men and resources for such a purpose goes against the principles of sound war economy.

Viewed in its true light, aerial warfare admits of no defense, only offense. *We must therefore resign ourselves to the offensives the enemy inflicts upon us, while striving to put all our resources to work to inflict even heavier ones upon him.* This is the basic principle which must govern the development of aerial warfare.

THE DEVELOPMENT OF AERIAL WARFARE

As long as aerial forces remain mere auxiliaries of the army and navy, there will be no real aerial warfare in case of conflict. True, there will be air battles of major and minor proportions,

[2] Since this was written, in 1921, antiaircraft has been greatly improved in both range and accuracy and has become immeasurably more effective. Still, this does not alter the essential validity of the author's premise and argument.—Tr.

but always subject to land or sea operations. Before any real aerial warfare can take place, its basic elements, such as planes, personnel, and their organization into an autonomous fighting body, must first be created and forged into an efficient fighting organization.

Under the circumstances, the first nation to arm herself with a real Independent Air Force will be in a superior military position, at least until other nations follow her example; for she will be in possession of an offensive weapon of formidable power, while the others will be dependent upon mere aerial auxiliaries. No doubt the necessity of establishing military equilibrium among the nations will induce others to follow her lead.

To study the development of aerial warfare, let us consider two cases: (1) a war between Nation A, armed with an Independent Air Force, and Nation B, without one; and (2) a war between two nations, both armed with an Independent Air Force.

An Independent Air Force must be always ready for action; otherwise 90 per cent of its effectiveness is lost. Given the speed of its units, no matter how widely dispersed their bases of operation may be in time of peace, it should be able to concentrate its forces along its line of battle and be ready for action in a few hours. If civil aviation units, scattered over the country, are a part of the Air Force's organization, they must be located where their integration into the Air Force can be accomplished as quickly as possible. In short, the Independent Air Force must be organically and logistically organized so that it can go into action immediately upon the outbreak of hostilities.

Now let us examine the first case. Independent Air Force A begins its action to catch Nation B in the midst of mobilization. But let us assume that Nation B is found to have immediately mobilized all her military aviation. Only her pursuit and bombing specialties, however, could take part in the battle, because her other specialties are suitable only for integrating the action of her naval and land forces. It is clear, then, that Independent Air Force A will have freedom of action, for B's pursuit aviation certainly could not hinder it. On the contrary, assuming that Air Force A has an adequate number of combat units, it will be able to inflict losses on B's pursuit aviation. Thus Air Force A will rapidly gain command of the air by destroying the mobilization, maintenance, and production centers of Nation B's aviation.

Once the command of the air has been won, the combat units of A's Independent Air Force will naturally cease functioning solely to protect bombing units and will be used to neutralize the fire of antiaircraft batteries during bombing operations by the entire Air Force, and to bomb and machine-gun troop concentrations, supply trains, transport or marching columns, et cetera. Furthermore, if constructed to undergo the necessary conversion in equipment, these combat units can quickly be transformed into first-rate bombing planes. Therefore, with the command of the air an accomplished fact, Independent Air Force A will have won complete liberty of action to strike at will, with no risk to itself, over all the enemy's territory, and quickly bring him to his knees.

By bombing railroad junctions and depots, population centers at road junctions, military depots, and other vital objectives, Air Force A could handicap the mobilization of B's army. By bombing naval bases, arsenals, oil stores, battleships at anchor, and mercantile ports, it could prevent the efficient operation of B's navy. By bombing the most vital civilian centers it could spread terror through the nation and quickly break down B's material and moral resistance.

The reader who thinks this picture overdrawn has only to look at a map of Italy, and imagine himself the commander of an Independent Air Force belonging to any of the nations on our frontiers. Let him remember that his Air Force is capable of destroying 50 surfaces 500 meters in diameter every day; and then ask himself how many days of operation it would take to achieve the aim described above. He must also take into consideration the fact that, even in the present stage of aeronautical development, the daily operational strength of such an Independent Air Force would be, even if only half of it were used on alternate days, about a thousand machines, requiring only a few thousand men to man it. Then he may draw his own conclusions.

At this point I want to stress one aspect of the problem—namely, that the effect of such aerial offensives upon morale may well have more influence upon the conduct of the war than their material effects. For example, take the center of a large city and imagine what would happen among the civilian population during a single attack by a single bombing unit. For my part, I have no doubt that its impact upon the people would be terrible. Here is what would be likely to happen to the center of the city within a radius of about 250 meters: Within a few minutes some 20 tons of high-explosive, incendiary, and gas bombs would rain down. First would come explosions, then fires, then deadly gases floating on the surface and preventing any approach to the stricken area. As the hours passed and night advanced, the fires would spread while the poison gas paralyzed all life. By the following day the life of the city would be suspended; and if it happened to be a junction on some important artery of communication traffic would be suspended.

What could happen to a single city in a single day could also happen to ten, twenty, fifty cities. And, since news travels fast, even without telegraph, telephone, or radio, what, I ask you, would be the effect upon civilians of other cities, not yet stricken but equally subject to bombing attacks? What civil or military authority could keep order, public services functioning, and production going under such a threat? And even if a semblance of order was maintained and some work done, would not the sight of a single enemy plane be enough to stampede the population into panic? In short, normal life would be impossible in this constant nightmare of imminent death and destruction. And if on the second day another ten, twenty, or fifty cities were bombed, who could keep all those lost, panic-stricken people from fleeing to the open countryside to escape this terror from the air?

A complete breakdown of the social structure cannot but take place in a country subjected to this kind of merciless pounding from the air. The time would soon come when, to put an end to horror and suffering, the people themselves, driven by the instinct of self-preservation, would rise up and demand an end to the war —this before their army and navy had time to mobilize at all! The reader who thinks I have overcolored the picture has only to recall the panic created at Brescia when, during funeral services for the victims of an earlier bombing—a negligible one compared with the one I have pictured here—one of the mourners mistook a bird for an enemy plane.

Now to the second case, of two nations each armed with an Independent Air Force. It is easy to see that in this case, even more than in the first one, the nation who struck first would have the edge on the enemy; or, conversely, how imperative it would be to parry as well as possible the enemy's blow before it struck home. To simplify the situation, then, let us admit that both Independent Air Forces could begin operations simultaneously. We have already seen that the fundamental concept governing aerial warfare is *to be resigned to the damage the enemy may inflict upon us, while utilizing every means at our disposal to inflict even heavier damage upon him.* An Independent Air Force must therefore be completely free of any preoccupation with the actions of the enemy force. Its sole concern should be to do the enemy the greatest possible amount of surface damage in the shortest possible time, which depends upon the available air forces and the choice of enemy targets. Whatever resources, of men, money, and equipment, are diverted from the strength and essential purpose of an Independent Air Force will result in slowing down the conduct of the war and delaying its final outcome.

The choice of enemy targets, as I have already pointed out, is the most delicate operation of aerial warfare, especially when both sides are armed with Independent Air Forces. In such a case the final decision depends upon the disequilibrium between the damage suffered by the enemy and his powers of recuperating from a blow which must be struck as quickly as possible, lest the enemy strike at us first. Of course, it may still be possible for one side to use its Independent Air Force to conquer the command of the air, which would ultimately win the war. But there may not be time enough for this if the other side succeeds in striking first and throwing the country into complete confusion.

The truth of the matter is that no hard and fast rules can be laid down on this aspect of aerial warfare. It is impossible even to outline general standards, because the choice of enemy targets will depend upon a number of circumstances, material, moral, and psychological, the importance of which, though real, is not easily estimated. It is just here, in grasping these imponderables, in choosing enemy targets, that future commanders of Independent Air Forces will show their ability.

Once the choice of enemy objectives and the order of their destruction have been determined, the task of the Air Force becomes very simple—to get on with their destruction in the briefest possible time, with no other preoccupation. In the case we are considering, therefore, both Air Forces will, at least in theory, proceed simultaneously in mass from their points of concentration toward their chosen objectives, without seeking each other out on the way. Should they happen to meet in flight, an air battle is inevitable; but I repeat that their purpose is not to seek each other out and fight in the air.

I consider this phase of aerial warfare very important, and I should like to pause here to clarify it further. Let us suppose that one of the Air Forces does seek out the other; but meanwhile the latter, avoiding an encounter, goes straight to its chosen objectives. He who seeks may find; but he may also return empty-handed. If one Independent Air Force deviates from its essential purpose, wastes time and fritters away its own freedom of action by seeking out the enemy in the air, the chances are not only that it will fail to find the enemy Air Force in the air, but also that the latter is at that very moment carrying out unchallenged its operations against the home territory. The one will have accomplished its task successfully; the other will have missed its opportunity and failed. In this kind of war, in which time is a vital factor, such a failure may have grave consequences in the outcome of the war, and should at all costs be avoided.

Speaking of aerial actions, I have already mentioned the possibility of having units of an Independent Air Force operate on alternate days; but I meant it merely as an illustration of how an Air Force might achieve results of major importance even with only half her strength, or with a relatively small number of planes. But during actual operations it would be an error to employ the strength of the Air Force piecemeal; for the purpose of an Independent Air Force is to inflict upon the enemy the greatest possible damage in the shortest possible time. The potential strength of an Independent Air Force should always be used to its fullest, with no thought of economy, especially when confronted by another equally strong Air Force which could do equally heavy damage. To replace personnel and equipment with fresh reserves may be expedient; but the Air Force itself—that is, its full complement of planes—should always remain in the air battering at enemy targets. It is the total effect of these bombing operations which decides the outcome of the conflict in favor of that Air Force which succeeds in dumping the largest quantity of bombs in the shortest time.

In presenting these ideas of the general character of aerial warfare, I have attempted only to show that if aerial warfare in its broad outline looks like a simple matter, it nevertheless presents staggering problems, the solution of which is very complex. But even in this brief résumé we can catch a glimpse of the heights of atrocity to which aerial warfare may reach.

When we stop to think of the magnitude and power of aerial offensives, and realize that no really effective method of parrying them exists; and since it would be futile to divert aerial forces to defense, the phrase "to submit to whatever damage the enemy may inflict" becomes a phrase expressing actual circumstances of tragedy attending aerial warfare.

Tragic, too, to think that the decision in this kind of war must depend upon smashing the material and moral resources of a people caught up in a frightful cataclysm which haunts them everywhere without cease until the final collapse of all social organization.[3] Mercifully, the decision will be quick in this kind of war, since the decisive blows will be directed at civilians, that element of the countries at war least able to sustain them. These future wars may yet prove to be more humane than wars in the past in spite of all, because they may in the long run shed less blood. But there is no doubt that nations who find themselves unprepared to sustain them will be lost.

[3] Exactly what seems to have happened when the Germans bombed and broke the will to resist of Poland, Holland, Belgium, France, Greece, and Jugoslavia (and Norway to a lesser extent) in the aerial Blitzkrieg of 1940-41.—Tr.

THE FUTURE

The matters I have been discussing up to this point are all actual possibilities which could easily be put into practice with the means existing at the moment. By that I mean that any nation, if convinced of its value and expediency, could make practical application of present-day aerial weapons to the science of making war along the lines I have described.

Having accepted this premise, we can now look toward the future—a near future, be it understood, and no idle exercise of the imagination, but a future which takes into account prevailing tendencies in the technical development of aviation; tendencies which point out the road we must follow if we wish to keep abreast of technical advances for tomorrow's use.

The technico-practical problem faced by aviation is to make aerial navigation safer, more dependable, more economical, and in general better suited to the needs of society. Study of the problem is therefore directed toward realizing these four aims:

1. To increase the safety of flying and of take-off and landing facilities.

2. To exclude materials which warp and deteriorate in use today in the construction of airplanes.

3. To increase the carrying capacity and radius of action of airplanes.

4. To increase the speed and give better performance on less fuel.

Improvement along these lines will give the airplane much greater utility in peacetime and in wartime as well.

I shall now briefly analyze these trends.

1. *To increase the safety of flying and of take-off and landing facilities:* While in the air an airplane is self-stabilizing and tends automatically to maintain equilibrium. If an airplane has enough space beneath it, and if the pilot does not willfully keep it off balance against its natural tendency to right itself, whatever positions the plane may go through, eventually it will end up in its natural flying position. This phenomenon is the basis of aerial

acrobatics—nose dives, spirals, spins, loops, and so on. To execute any of these acrobatic stunts, the pilot has only to throw the plane off balance in a certain way; to straighten out, he has only to stop interfering, and the plane will automatically regain its equilibrium. The equilibrium of a plane may also be disturbed by abnormal air conditions—air pockets, storms, cross-currents, et cetera; but in this case too, once the disturbing action of the air has ceased, the plane will automatically regain equilibrium. In short, a plane may lose its natural equilibrium in the air for a number of reasons owing to abnormal air conditions or to actions of the pilot.

These disturbing air conditions usually prevail at low altitude, near the surface of the earth where atmospheric pressure is greatest. Just as sea waves are more irregular near the shoreline, air currents, even if generated by entirely different influences, are more pronounced near the surface, which is in effect the shoreline of the air.

As I explained above, a pilot may willfully throw his plane off balance, in which case the assumption is that he has it under control and can regain equilibrium; or he may make an error in maneuvering and lose control of the plane. Losing control may, of course, happen at any altitude. If the pilot keeps his head he may easily straighten the plane out in time, if he has enough space beneath him. But if he loses his head and the plane continues out of control, he may crash no matter what the altitude.

All in all, we can see that the higher the altitude, the safer flying is. But if some mechanical device could be built into the plane to prevent the pilot from throwing it off balance whether from voluntary or involuntary action, more than half of the accidents in flying would be prevented. Hence the tendency toward the invention of a mechanism—which we need not go into here—to keep the plane automatically self-stabilizing while in flight. An automatically equilibrated plane should be as simple to fly as an automobile to run. That is, an accelerator to increase the power of the motor in climbing or diminish it in descending, and a steering wheel to turn right and left. We shall certainly soon reach this goal.

As early as 1913, in the arsenal at Vizzola, a plane was constructed which took off, flew, and landed, simply with an accelerator and a steering wheel.[4] This plane, which would not allow the pilot to lose equilibrium and reacted automatically to disturbing atmospheric conditions, hung up a world endurance record for automatic flights (over an hour). We can easily imagine the practical results of such an improvement, once it is firmly established.

Take-off and landing are two of the most difficult operations in flying, just as entering and leaving port are two of the most difficult operations in navigation. The reason for this lies either in the difference in the physical resistance of a plane passing from a fluid to a solid medium, or in air disturbances near the surface. Of the two, landing is the more difficult; and, as the shock upon touching ground is proportionate to the speed of the plane, the greater the landing speed, the greater the hazard.

Safety in flying therefore requires that a plane be able to land at a very low speed; while on the other hand more and more flying speed is demanded. Three hundred kilometers an hour have already been surpassed, and 300 kilometers an hour are equivalent to about 83 meters per second, or a little more than a quarter of the velocity of sound.[5] Aeronautical science is therefore trying to develop planes of greater speed in flight and slower, safer landing and take-off speeds. Surface improvements in the form of better airfields, runways, and signal systems will no doubt contribute to safety in aviation.[6]

2. *To exclude materials which warp and deteriorate in use today in the construction of airplanes:* As a machine the airplane has marvelous accomplishments to its credit; but it is still a long way from what could be considered a hundred-per-cent perfect machine. Except in a few recent rare experiments, such perishable materials as wood and canvas are still used in the construction of planes. It is true that wood and canvas have certain characteristics of elasticity and lightness that we have not been able to

---

[4] Not only was this accomplished, but flying machines were constructed which flew without a pilot by means of commands transmitted from the ground through electro-magnetic waves.

[5] Now 400 kilometers have been surpassed.

[6] Already, blind and night flying by means of radio beams has become a reality.

duplicate even today in metals. On the other hand, their lack of structural homogeneity and their rapid deterioration from a number of causes, such as meteorological conditions, create a doubt of their permanent value. The ideal machine should be entirely of metal, because the characteristics of metal are definite and not easily altered. Hence the trend to construct airplanes entirely of metal, which, besides affording greater stability in construction, will minimize if not eliminate the necessity of housing planes in hangars. From this, especially in wartime, a great saving in time and labor can be effected.[7]

3. *To increase the carrying capacity and radius of action of airplanes:* The trend toward increasing the carrying capacity of airplanes is in line with principles of sound economy and with the desire to increase the radius of action of the planes. Greater carrying capacity in a plane proportionately decreases total costs of construction and operation. A two-passenger plane carrying two passengers instead of one has no need to double its personnel because of the extra passenger. It costs less to transport ten passengers, or ten quintals of cargo, with a single plane than with ten planes. Moreover, by varying within certain limits the proportion between useful load and fuel weight, an increase of total carrying capacity of planes would also extend their radius of action. And no regular transoceanic service could be effectuated except with planes of greater carrying capacity than those in use today.

A plane is kept aloft by its wings, the stress of its total weight being distributed over its wing surface. But since the weight per square meter of its wing surface cannot be increased beyond a certain predetermined limit, its carrying capacity will depend upon its wing surface. Therefore, the greater the carrying capacity desired, the greater will have to be the wing surface. At one time triplanes seemed to offer the best possibility for maximum wing surface, but even this maximum could not be forced beyond certain limits. Recently, however, a new type of plane made its appearance in Italy—a tailless plane based on a series of triplane

[7] As a matter of fact, canvas and wood already seem an aeronautical anachronism.

cellules and operated by a new system of controls. It was tested in the air, and the experiment proved practical.

Since planes of such weight [8] probably could not land or take off except on liquid surfaces, we may have to build artificial lakes for their landing. That would be of some military advantage, because in case of war enemy bombardment could not put liquid fields out of service as easily as ground fields.

4. *To increase the speed and give better performance on less fuel:* The increased speed of planes is mainly due to increased power of their motors. It follows that the greater the power of the motor, the greater its power to conquer air resistance, and the greater the resulting speed. But we can see that such a system cannot possibly be economical. The need is to increase the speed not by increasing motor power, but by diminishing air resistance. But that is not in our power. Air resistance is what it is. But it is a fact that air resistance grows less as a plane gains altitude. Therefore, the higher we go, if we could continue to develop the same horsepower, the greater would be the speed and the economy in performance.

But the matter is not so simple as it would seem at first sight, and the difficulty lies in keeping motor power. One of the factors in determining the power of a motor is the intake volume of its cylinders; that is, the amount of air and gasoline mixture used by a cylinder at each intake stroke. If the cubic displacement of a cylinder is one liter, it means that with each explosion in the cylinder a liter of carbureted mixture is used up.

The density of air varies with the level under consideration. If this density is 1 at sea level, at 5,000 meters it would be about $\frac{1}{2}$, and at 18,000 meters it would be about $\frac{1}{4}$. That means that at 5,000 meters a motor, while keeping unaltered the *volume* of its cylinders, would absorb only half the quantity (weight) of the carbureted mixture it would absorb at sea level; and at 18,000 meters it would absorb only one-tenth as much. Therefore, if the power of the motor is 1 at sea level, it decreases as it climbs, to $\frac{1}{2}$ at 5,000 meters and to 1/10 at 18,000 meters.

---

[8] Already there are planes in service of 2,000 h.p., and others under construction of 6,000 h.p., with 6 to 12 motors.

This phenomenon is actually more complex than that, but what I have said here should be enough to show how, owing to rarefaction of the air, the power of a motor decreases as the altitude increases. This explains why every type of airplane has, as we say, a "ceiling," a limit to the altitude it can reach. At that altitude the power of a plane's motor is almost exhausted, and it cannot climb beyond that.

Theoretically, to develop the same power at various levels, a motor would have to absorb at any altitude air of the same density as at sea level. To obtain such a result, still theoretically, it would be enough to compress the air intake of the motor to the density of 1, the density of sea level, as the air becomes gradually lighter on climbing. Studies to find a practical solution to this problem are being conducted by technicians all over the world; and there is nothing to keep us from thinking that some day or other it will be solved for all practical, if not for theoretical, purposes.

But, since air resistance is proportionate to its density, if the resistance is 1 at sea level, it becomes roughly ½ at 5,000 meters and 1/10 at 18,000 meters. Therefore, if we could succeed in keeping the same motor power irrespective of altitude, an airplane capable of 150 kilometers per hour at sea level could theoretically do 300 kilometers an hour at 5,000 meters and 1,500 kilometers at 18,000; and there would no longer be any limit to its ceiling, for the higher it climbed, the more easily it could climb.

Naturally, these are all theoretical goals which practice will never be able to reach, but toward which aeronautical progress is tending; and in fact technicians do not despair of making it possible in the near future to travel regularly and economically at the 10,000-meter level, and at 500 kilometers an hour.[9] When flying at such an altitude becomes the normal thing, passenger cabins should of course be hermetically sealed with constant air pressure at sea-level density, as in the case of the motors. This possibility of heavy air traffic at great speed and economy will permit the extension of the plane's radius of action and greater comfort aboard.

From what we can see of present tendencies in technical de-

[9] The transoceanic clippers and stratospheres of our days.—Tr.

velopments, we can be assured that aerial navigation will make a great spurt of progress, especially in long-distance travel. The day will come when no one will think of crossing the ocean by steamer, just as no one today thinks of doing it by sailboat. And since the offensive power of planes, considered as war machines, will be constantly increasing, there is nothing to prevent us from thinking that in the not too distant future Japan may be able to attack the United States of America by air, or vice versa.

I have dwelt upon the future only to emphasize the necessities of the present; and to the present I shall immediately return.

CHAPTER IV

The Organization of Aerial Warfare

GENERAL OUTLINE

IN 1910 I wrote: "Besides the technical question of weapons involved, aerial warfare also demands solution of the problems of preparation, organization, and utilization of aerial forces; that is, it calls for the creation, *ex novo,* of a third part of the art of war, the art of aerial warfare." [1]

I believe that this statement today may meet with agreement by a consensus of opinion; and in compiling this study of the art of aerial warfare, I have been led to make it simply to point out the heights which aerial warfare may reach, and thus be given the importance it deserves, so that students of war would try to create the third branch of the art of war—aerial warfare.

The problems involved are many and difficult; but they must be solved, for before forging an arm we must first know *what* we intend to do with it and *how* to use it. So far in this study I have merely tried to indicate, without making any pretense of solving the many problems involved, the character and scope of aerial warfare in general and to define the means necessary to actuate the Independent Air Force, formulating as I went a few basic principles which I do not despair of having accepted.

But even from the little I have said, it is evident that the establishment of an Independent Air Force requires an organization founded not on empiricism, but upon a comprehensive study of all those logistical dispositions necessary to operate it. While the strategic utilization of an Independent Air Force may result from wise application of a few basic principles, its tactical use requires an accurate theoretical and practical study of its armament and formation of its units. A study of aerial logistics or tactics would

[1] *I problemi dell aeronavigazione,* Rome, 1910.

be out of place in this book. Instead I believe it timely to go a little deeper into its organization here, since it is with its organization that we must begin. And since the organizing of an Independent Air Force does not admit any flights of the imagination, I shall try to correlate to the best of my ability present and future needs.

CO-ORDINATION

The use of military, naval, and aerial forces in war should be directed toward a single end, to win. To attain maximum effectiveness these forces must be thoroughly co-ordinated and in harmony with one another. The three forces should function as ingredients—or factors—of a single product in which the best results can be obtained only by a proper apportioning of the ingredients used.

The resources which even the richest nation can put at the disposal of national defenses are not limitless. With a given quantity of resources it is possible to secure a national defense just as efficient as the correct proportioning of the three factors. The more nearly just the proportions of these factors, the smaller will be the nation's expenditure for its national defense. But even when the three factors are so justly proportioned, the maximum results cannot be obtained unless they are perfectly co-ordinated. Allowing the greatest freedom of action to the respective commanders of the army, navy, and air forces, it would be in the interest of national defense to have the three branches of the service co-ordinated under a supreme authority. But even this is not enough. What is needed further is the proper subdivision and allocation of the resources destined for national defense where they can be most effective in war or any other eventuality.

These considerations are so self-evident in nature that it would be superfluous to explain them further. It logically follows, then, that the following is what is needed to carry out the program:

1. An authoritative body to study the needs of national defense and to determine and allocate the proper proportions of national resources to the three branches of the service—land, sea, and air forces; and

2. An authoritative body prepared to assume the Supreme Command of the three armed forces and co-ordinate their action.

There are no such authoritative bodies in existence now. Instead the resources of the country allotted to national defense are now allocated by loose empirical methods, so that the proportion granted to each armed force is more a matter of happy combination of circumstances than of real planning. It cannot be otherwise when each branch of the service is directed by separate bodies, each jealous of its prerogatives. In case of war whatever co-ordination there is among them cannot be other than contingent, especially since there is no precedent for it.[2] Lack of co-ordination among the various branches of the service has always been the cause of serious drawbacks; and it will cause even worse ones in the future because war is tending more and more to absorb all the activities of a nation making war, and because of the new factor of air power, which is constantly increasing in importance.

More than ever in the past, we need today to keep within the logic of strict necessity and create a national body which would be neither army nor navy; a body that would have the clear vision to perceive the totality of war and to weigh the value of the three basic arms without preconceptions, in order to obtain the maximum result from their co-ordination.

But since this is not the case, and since we must begin with the present, we must take the situation as we find it and begin there. Aeronautics today is something which is neither army nor navy, even though it participates with both no less than with civilian life. Stating the case exactly as it is, is all that is needed to make it clear why the present forms of organization of the air forces fall far short of their potential scope. In my opinion we need to establish the following fundamental principles:

1. Aerial means used by the army and navy to facilitate and integrate their own actions in their respective fields, no matter what those actions may be, are an integral part of the army and navy and must be considered as such.

2. Aerial means destined to carry out war missions in which

2 With the establishment of a High Command under a Chief of the General Staff, by order of Mussolini in 1927, this fundamental necessity has been provided for.

neither army nor navy can take part and beyond their radius of action, must be made independent of both of them and constitute what we may call an Independent Air Force, an entity that, while paralleling and co-ordinating its action with the army and navy, must act independently of them.

3. Civil aeronautics, like any other national activity, should be supported and encouraged by the state quite independently of its bearing on national defense, in all those phases which have no direct bearing on national defense. I say *direct,* because *indirectly* all national activities have a bearing on national defense.

4. But in all activities bearing *directly* on national defense, civil aeronautics must be supported by the organs of national defense.

As we shall see later, application of these four axiomatic principles could bring about logical and effective organization.

AUXILIARY AVIATION

By the phrase "army and navy auxiliary aviation" I mean all aerial means utilized by the army and navy to facilitate and integrate operations in their respective fields of action. If these auxiliary aerial means form an integral part of the army and navy, they must be: (1) included in the budgets of the army and navy respectively; and (2) placed absolutely under the direct command of the army or the navy, beginning with their organization and ending with their employment.

There is no valid reason why the auxiliary aviation of the army and navy should be financed under a separate budget. On the contrary; for the auxiliary aviation of these two branches of the armed forces should be proportionate to their total strength and organization, and this would be impossible if these auxiliaries were provided for under a separate budget. The only body competent to decide upon the proper organization of this aerial auxiliary is the army or navy, as the case may be; for they are in possession of the data necessary for determining the aerial weapons most suitable for furthering their respective actions. There is, in fact, no good reason why the army, in determining the formation of an artillery unit, for example—number and kinds of guns, gun carriages, ammunition, et cetera—should not also determine the number and type of planes needed to direct its artillery fire.

For instance, if it seems advisable to put reconnaissance or observation planes under the command of large ground units, these commands should obviously have complete control of them, all the way from their organization in peacetime to their use in wartime, in order to get the best results. In planning their operations these commands can then take into account the exact aerial strength at their disposal. This in turn permits the aerial units to familiarize themselves with the tactics of the ground forces. This system not only conforms to logical concepts of the organization and use of such units, but also avoids the dangers of dual control, which may easily happen when auxiliary aviation becomes almost independent of the army.

Military aviation, then, being an integral part of the army, should be placed under its direct control for provisioning, discipline, utilization, and training. But before this first principle of organization can be adopted by the armed forces, a preconceived notion which has so far prevented reciprocal relations between aviation and the army must be dispelled—that is, the notion that aviation is too technical a field for it to deal with and should be left exclusively to technical specialists—a notion originated by the novelty of aviation, with the essence of which only a few specialists concerned themselves.

Dispelling this notion is an easy matter once we state the exact terms of the problem. It is true that military aviation, like any other kind of aviation, is highly technical and depends upon personnel trained in the techniques of aviation. But considered as a weapon of war, aviation must also meet the requisites of usefulness as a weapon. In directing artillery fire, for instance, there is need of planes and personnel trained to fly them, both of them utilized to control artillery fire. Therefore, both must answer to this need in flight. If they fail in this, the artillery is utterly useless. As a matter of fact, it is the artillery which, knowing its own needs, must determine the prerequisites of its planes and give the special training needed by the personnel which mans them.

Once the problem has been thoroughly examined, the artillery can say: "We need so many observation planes, of such and such models, equipped with such and such instruments, and capable of landing in such and such restricted fields," et cetera. Once the artillery had made their choice, the responsibility would be theirs. It is not the function of aviation technicians to decide which types of plane should or should not be used by this or that branch of the armed forces. Their responsibility is to produce air-worthy planes according to the specifications furnished them by the armed forces, not to pass judgment upon the military usefulness of their planes. This they are not qualified to do. If the army or navy required a new type of plane not yet in existence, it would of course be up to the technicians to study the requirements and produce the desired plane, at the same time suggesting the right direction for aeronautical science to follow in the production of useful planes. Such requirements must, of course, be reasonable and feasible. We might otherwise have some such absurd requirement as a plane capable of remaining immovable in midair. To avoid such absurdities it is enough to be aware of those general ideas which are the common heritage of our culture; and it is certain that, once those who employ aviation felt the responsibility of their choice, that aeronautical culture too would not be long in becoming part of the common heritage of mankind.

In conclusion, what aviation technicians should be concerned with is the production of air-worthy planes according to specifications; and the military should furnish the aviation instructors to fly and take care of them. In this way the military and the aviation technician would each be fulfilling his proper function and would assume full responsibility for his acts, avoiding interference with the other's sphere of activity.

I have declared that the responsibility for the organization of the army auxiliary aviation rests with the army. I shall not enter into a discussion of its merits here; I shall only say, to forestall objections, that assigning an auxiliary aviation to the army does not imply a duplication of military organization. This I shall be able to demonstrate later on.

INDEPENDENT AVIATION

To avoid words which at the beginning may sound extreme, I shall make a distinction between "auxiliary aviation" and "independent aviation," the term I shall use instead of Independent Air Force to refer to all those aviation means destined to accomplish war missions to which neither the army nor the navy can in any way contribute. These means exist today in embryo in the so-called bombing and pursuit specialties.

Aerial offensives, which can be carried behind the enemy's lines where neither land nor sea weapons can reach, may prove helpful to either the army or the navy. But just because such aerial co-operation may prove helpful to them does not necessarily mean that such aerial weapons should be placed under the direct control of either of them—if for no other reason, to avoid dividing them. Nor does it follow that in bombing operations the army should use only land-based planes and the navy only ship-based planes. An enemy port or inland city can be bombed by either type of bomber, operating from either land or sea bases, as experience taught us during the last war. Even in the present limited conception of the command of the air, the function of pursuit aviation should be, if not exactly to wage aerial warfare by itself, at least to fight in the air. Therefore, for the very reasons discussed above, it should not be under the control of the army or the navy. If either branch wishes to make use of pursuit units to police the sky above its field of operation, that is the concern of the organization of its auxiliary aviation.

I have dwelt at great length on the reasons why I consider an independent aviation having the mission, in case of war, of conquering the command of the air, to be indispensable. I have also said that, in my opinion, the prevailing concepts governing bombing and pursuit aviation do not answer this purpose; and I have pointed out how they could be made to do so. Whatever the dissent on this phase of aerial organization, I believe that this at least must be admitted: *To be unprepared for the coming struggle for command of the air would be foolhardy indeed.*

The first step toward preparedness would be to separate bombing and pursuit aviation from the army and navy, thus setting up the first independent nucleus, the seed, which, whatever the form it may take, will in a not too distant future become an Independent Air Force. This independent aviation will be strong or weak according to the means placed at its disposal. But because it must be independent to enjoy the widest latitude within its limits, its means must be provided for under a separate budget. There is no doubt in my mind that this budget will be increased as the public gradually comes to realize the importance of the command of the air. Likewise, the organization and functioning of this independent aviation must be free of outside control. Although it stemmed from the army and navy, aviation has reached maturity and should be emancipated—hence the need of creating a competent body to supervise its growth, a body made up of men familiar with the art of war in general and open to new ideas. These men need not be technical experts; they need only be aware of the great possibilities of this new aerial weapon. That will be enough to begin with; for it is not a question of deciding the best profile of a wing, but of determining the best technical means available for creating a combat force and the best method of utilizing it in war.

This body must examine and solve the problems involved. Though those problems are complex and far-reaching, the fact that we must start from the very beginning will make their solution easier, since errors committed along the way can be righted as they occur. And it must be this body which creates this third branch of the art of war, that relative to aerial warfare. I say "creates" because nothing exists today. But the present bombing and pursuit aviation, made independent, could serve as a means of experience for it.

In fine, this proposed body should, within limits, bear the same relation to the air force as the Supreme Army Council bears to the army; and it should function accordingly.

By this time my readers should be convinced that, despite the majestic scale of the canvases I have painted, what I have proposed is nevertheless practicable within modest limits.

CIVIL AVIATION

As to the future of aerial navigation as a means of civil progress, there may be differences of opinion; but one thing is certain: this new means of transportation is here to stay.[3] This machine which man has forged out of his genius and daring after millenniums of trial and failure, is the swiftest and most marvelous invention in the history of transportation. Its eventual development cannot be predicted now, but all the signs point to a long life for it.

Two basic characteristics distinguish this new aerial means of transportation from all others, namely:

1. It is the fastest known, whether one considers its actual speed in itself or the fact that it connects the point of departure and the point of arrival by a straight line.

2. It requires no roads, in the commonly accepted meaning of the word.

Heretofore all means of transportation were made up of two elements, one of which is the roadway. The locomotive does not in itself serve as a means of communication, nor does the automobile negotiate two points connected only by a mule path. In ocean travel the road element is not so vital, but nevertheless laborious tasks like building the Suez and Panama canals have sometimes been necessary to shorten distances by water. Only the airplane can travel without restriction over the whole surface of the globe, needing only a point of departure and one of arrival.

By virtue of these two essential characteristics, the airplane has speeded up existing communications and made possible even more rapid and economical ones between points on the surface of the earth no matter how separate and distant. The establishment of more and better means of communication is a vital factor in our social structure, a fact which encourages the development of aerial navigation. Because of these two special characteristics, this development will take the form of long-distance air lines which will save much time, and others across barren country without the usual roads and railroads, which will solve the problem of communication in such regions. It is impossible to conceive that man would neglect to develop a means of transportation capable of reducing the distance between Rome and London to a few hours' travel; and it seems inevitable that Alexandria, Egypt, will be linked to Capetown, South Africa, by air sooner than by rail.[4]

Local air lines between shorter distances and trunk lines between longer ones will develop as travel by air becomes little by little more popular and practical. But even now it is easy to foresee the rapid

[3] This statement shows that Douhet was looking into the future as far as is humanly possible.—Tr.

[4] It was so linked by Imperial Airways in 1931.—Tr.

expansion of the plane used in air sports and private travel. The airplane has already withstood the most trying tests, fulfilled the most daring hopes; and the war has shown incontrovertibly the shortsightedness of skepticism about it. What should interest Italy about all this is that great air lines will surely be established, and soon; the greater part of which will necessarily span the Mediterranean basin. The axis of the three great European powers lies NW-SE, and if it is extended across the Mediterranean, it falls on Suez, where Asia and Africa meet. Thus the majority of these air lines will follow the direction of this axis, and will constitute a vast aerial network gathered together by England, spanning France and Italy, and fanning out from here to Asia, Africa, and the Balkan peninsula.

Because of the geographical and political position accorded Italy after the war, she must necessarily become the crossroads of the aerial communications of the Old World. This undeniable fact puts her in a privileged position in regard to aerial communication, but it also imposes on her the duty of being as quickly as possible in a position to meet the exigencies which will arise, lest she lose the immense advantages within her grasp and become a field of exploitation for foreign aerial navigation.

If we exploit our geographical and political position in the Mediterranean in the maritime field, there is even more reason why we should take advantage of it in the air, a field even larger and one in which we are the first arrivals. Everything remains to be done in that field, and we are on our home ground. For political, moral, and economic reasons, as well as for national security, aerial navigation over our own territory and over the Mediterranean should fly the Italian flag. That should be the guiding principle of our aeronautical policy. Italy should not be content to be merely the pier at which foreign lines tie up. To take full advantage of her privileged position, she must be ready to meet the demands of aerial navigation in the Mediterranean, and to foresee the needs which will stimulate such navigation herself.

Obviously, the establishment of an air line from Turin to Rome to Alexandria would promote one from London to Paris to Turin, and further lines from Alexandria to the Sudan and Palestine. We must, therefore, provide not only for the establishment of the main internal and colonial arteries, but for all those which will link our coasts to Africa, Asia, and the Balkan peninsula. That is, we must be the clearing center for the air lines of the Old World. Since the Balkan peninsula is nearer to us than to the other great powers, and since the aeronautical industry lags there, it is also up to us to take care of the internal aerial navigation there, a task which will be made easy for us by the fact that our ports on the eastern coasts of the Adriatic constitute the natural bases from which to push on to southern Russia and Asia Minor—precisely across the Balkan region.

From these considerations it is evident that Italy is, perhaps more than any other nation, vitally concerned in the development of aerial navigation. Apart from the general advantages described above, adequate development of aerial navigation would bring others which should be justly valued, as follows:

1. Economic and industrial advantages. The development of a flourishing aerial navigation would in turn stimulate the development of the aeronautical industry as a whole. This industry is best suited to the genius and to the resources of our country. It requires only a limited quantity of raw materials, and it needs skillful workmanship; and though we are poor in the first, we are rich in the second. The aeronautical industry is an industry in which Italy can excel if she seriously applies herself to it.

2. Advantages of national security. It is to be hoped the World War was the last war; but it would be folly to rest on this hope. That war revealed the air arm, even though there was not time enough to show all of its importance. There is no doubt that the perfecting of civil aerial means will enhance the military value of the air arm, and that in an eventual conflict the possession of the command of the air will be a greater advantage than command of the sea. To have at one's disposal a large fleet of air transports is equivalent, in terms of military power, to having a large Independent Air Force always ready to defend one's rights.

In conclusion, for Italy the intensive development of aerial navigation in the Mediterranean is a chance to avail herself of the magnificent geographical position in which destiny placed her, and of the political prestige bought with the blood of her sons. It gives her an opportunity to excel in a great industry, and it constitutes a means of political power, national wealth, and military security.

In planning for the establishment of internal, colonial, and Mediterranean air lines, we must start with comprehensive ideas, taking into account the advantages enumerated above, and not be halted by miserly considerations of immediate expense. Certainly the first air lines will not pay for at least the first few years, because of the high cost and the fact that flying goes against the atavistic habits of man and will encounter difficulties and some hostility. But all these drawbacks will be conquered in a short time, competition will develop, and the cost of air lines will rapidly diminish.

The flying machine is marvelous in every sense of the word, far exceeding the boldest imaginings. The man who said before the World War that airplanes would be numbered in thousands was considered a visionary; but aerial navigation will go on developing in the same strain. In a few years express trains will become mere third-class locals, the Compagnie des Wagons-Lits will have changed its name, and international mail will be carried exclusively by air transport.

To put ourselves definitely in the stream of this development would in our situation be wise and far-seeing. The initial expense of establishing such air lines would not be money thrown away, but a solid insurance for the future.

The development of aerial navigation is a matter of national concern, and it should have the close attention of the government. The establishment of air lines presents a number of problems from divers fields—political, economic, social, military, et cetera; and these problems must be solved by a competent national body with the authority of a cabinet minister. During the World War a General Commissariat of Aeronautics, more or less dependent upon the Ministry of War or of Arms and Munitions, was considered sufficient inasmuch as its activities were limited to procuring certain arms specialties. But during the subsequent period of peace this proposed body dedicated to furthering aerial navigation should be invested with greater authority and more freedom of action, at the same time co-operating closely with the various ministries of transport, industry, mail, war, and so on.

A Ministry of Aeronautics should have the authority and the competence to pass upon all questions, of whatsoever nature, dealing with aeronautics. Gradually such questions will increase in number and importance; and, considering the newness of the field and the scarcity of men educated in it, the fact that this increase will be gradual rather than rapid will have the advantage of familiarizing the people with the importance of the Ministry and preparing more men to deal effectively with the ever-vaster problems implicit in the future development of aeronautics.

Relative to air lines, the function of the Ministry of Aeronautics may be either activating or co-ordinating. That is, the main air lines may be run directly by the state, or by concessions granted to private corporations under the supervision of the state. But the state should in no case turn over control of aerial navigation to private interests, whose chief concern is bound to be personal gain, to the neglect of the broader, less direct interests of the state, which are far more vital to the nation. Since peacetime civil aviation can and should be quickly converted into military aviation when the occasion arises, the Ministry of Aeronautics should keep a vigilant eye upon the organization and armament of the proposed fleets of air transports, so that both organization and armament can be quickly and easily converted into means of war. In addition, the Ministry should encourage and integrate secondary aerial activities such as local air lines, sport and recreational interests, as well as aerial navigation in the Balkan peninsula and South America, and the aeronautical industry as a whole so as to give Italy a position of first importance in the aerial world of the future.

From this exposition of a subject of far-reaching importance and recent development—a subject which calls for daring and imaginative ideas to deal with it—we can see how necessary it is for this national body to rise to the occasion and carry through the project. In a very short time both the plane itself and the useful application of it have developed and improved with a truly fantastic speed. Delay in this matter may be fatal. In order not to be left behind, we must work fast—clay feet are irreconcilable with the lightness of wings. In this relatively unexplored field the war has set free an enormous quantity of new energies and new resources, all of which are ready to combine enthusiastically in the work of peace which must follow the Allied victory. Everywhere in the civilian world, large numbers of technical experts, skilled workmen, and industries have been converted to production in this new field. Large interests have banded together in the new industry, and a long roster of courageous youth has learned the art of flying.

All these new energies will surge forward over a new road—none other than the road of the air; and fierce competition among the nations will follow to get possession of the principal air routes, the ones which will give the best returns in various ways. Since Italy is at the center of clearance for the most important international lines, Italy and the Mediterranean will certainly become the field for the peaceful competition of international aerial navigation in the Old World. The only way to come out ahead in the competition is to be prepared to meet the requirements of this new means of transportation. Hence the necessity not only of undertaking the task, but of doing it quickly and well. Timidity and hesitation now will be bitterly regretted later.

In conclusion I must add that, in my opinion, the nation should promptly undertake to further a sagacious aeronautical policy based on the following points:

1. Favoring the development of internal, colonial, and Mediterranean aerial navigation by exercising a co-ordinating state supervision on the principle that internal, colonial, and Mediterranean aerial navigation from Africa, Asia, the Balkan peninsula, and in South America must fly the Italian flag.

2. Favoring the development of the aviation industry by giving it protection, publicizing it, and giving it funds for research and experiment.

3. Favoring the development of aerial navigation and a national aviation industry by provisions for transforming them quickly into instruments of war; whereby a large part of the money assigned by the state for national defense could profitably be employed to further the development of peacetime civil aviation.

A detailed examination of the questions here briefly sketched would require a thorough exposition. It is enough for us here to call attention to the aeronautical problems which, in the press of national affairs, might easily be overlooked entirely or considered as of secondary importance; whereas in reality they are of capital importance for the future of aviation.

Let us take a map of the Roman Empire and see how power radiated from Rome across the sea basin which bathes the great mole of Europe. In those days the radiating power was one of conquest and civilization. Today the new position of Italy and the new means which makes man master of space can form a similar radiation, this time peaceful. Rome, which was the center of the greatest empire of early civilization, for the last conquest of civilization must become the center of the fastest means of communication—the most important airport of the world. And over this center of civilization must fly the tricolor, still warm from glorious battles.

So I wrote soon after the end of the World War in an article on "Mediterranean Air Policy" in the *Nuova Antologia* of January 16, 1919. What I wrote then is still valid today; nothing has happened to invalidate the concepts I expressed in those lines. But unfortunately Italy has not been able to find her way in the air, and much has already been accomplished abroad in these two years. If we look on the map of Europe at the air lines in existence or projected, we can see how they circle about Italy, making her almost an obstacle to the aerial communications of the Old World. This situation cannot last, either from the point of view of our own interests or from that of national duty. It is plain that if we fail to develop the aeronautical value of our own country, we will have to give foreigners a right-of-way in Italy for their air lines.[5]

All that I have said about civil aviation I said to show that the state should promote its development in the interests of national security. Some of the activities of civil aviation have a direct bearing on national defense, others do not. The organs of national defense should have no concern with the ones that do not, for these activities lie outside their province. They should be the concern of the state in general. The activities which do have a direct bearing should be the concern of the organs entrusted with national defense.

ACTIVITIES OF CIVIL AVIATION WITH A DIRECT BEARING ON NATIONAL DEFENSE

These activities are those which prepare means directly utilizable by national defense—that is, by independent aviation and

[5] These words were written in 1921. This year (1926) I have had the satisfaction of seeing a promising beginning toward putting into effect the ideas expressed in them.

auxiliary aviation. They are the bombing and combat specialties constituting the nucleus of what may become an Independent Air Force.

Civil aviation employs planes, trains pilots and maintains them in active service, and makes use of various aviation accessories—all means directly utilizable by the organs of national defense, provided they meet certain conditions—such as, for instance, that the planes be easily and rapidly convertible into warplanes. Hence the interest of the organs of national defense in the development of civil aviation insofar as its means also meet the needs of national defense. In the matter of training of personnel, the only conditions imposed upon civil aviation are that it must be ready for instant mobilization in case of war, and in time of peace must undergo a minimum of training to fit it for war service at the instant of mobilization. The fulfillment of these conditions should be directed and supervised by the aerial branch of national defense; and to this end subsidies should be granted to civil initiatives. And in this sense the subsidy may be considerable: If we actually calculate the cost to the military administration of training and maintaining a pilot, this cost is the maximum limit of the subsidy which the military administration may grant to civil initiatives for each pilot trained and maintained in operation. But this maximum limit is so high that the subsidies may be brought down to a much lower sum, thus effecting a great economy.

As for the planes themselves, even in military aviation circles the misconception is held that civilian planes cannot be used for war purposes because the two types of plane must have different characteristics. I call this opinion a misconception because, apart from any other consideration, the fact is that no nation on earth is rich enough to keep up an adequate military air force ready for instant action. All nations, rich and poor alike, will be forced by necessity to put the resources of their civil aviation facilities to military use.

No one will dispute the fact that, in the absolute sense, a plane which must meet both civil and military requirements cannot be the perfect machine for either purpose. But the absolute does not exist. In practice we must always strive to compromise between extremes. Such compromise would be of advantage to military aviation for this reason: by basing itself upon civil aviation, which is constantly active, it would always have at its disposal the latest types of plane; whereas, if it relied entirely upon its own means, it would often find itself armed with antiquated models.

This misconception also results from the fact that military aviation today uses almost entirely planes of extreme characteristics; whereas civil aviation uses planes of moderate characteristics. And, I repeat, aerial war is not fought with planes of extreme characteristics, in spite of occasional air battles.[6] War is fought by masses of men and machines; and masses, whether of men or machines, are composed of the average and not of the extreme. In discussing the Independent Air Force, I pointed out that it requires planes of moderate characteristics, more or less similar to the characteristics of commercial planes. Military aviation can, therefore, utilize civilian planes fitted with special, though not exceptional, equipment; and civilian aviation would have no difficulty in fulfilling these conditions in view of the advantages ensuing from such a relationship to the military. If we stop to think what the per diem operating cost of a military plane would be, we immediately have an idea of the amount of the maximum subsidy which the military administration should grant to a civilian plane for each day of operation. These considerations are sufficient to show how much assistance military aviation could give to civil aviation.

The financial assistance should logically be included in the appropriations for military aviation. As civil aviation developed, as it expanded and became self-sustaining, the amount of this financial assistance would be gradually reduced, so that military aviation of a permanent character, so to speak, would be brought down to a minimum while still having the power to absorb these civilian complements, in case of war, into an effective striking force. This financial aid, being in the interest of military aviation, must be left entirely in the hands of the military authorities, because they are the only body competent to determine the condi-

---

[6] The superb account the United States Flying Fortresses have given of themselves in the present war is ample proof of Douhet's point, inasmuch as they are evolved from commercial transport designs.—Tr.

tions to which the resources and activities of civil aviation must conform in order to be directly useful to them.

This is not enough. Military aviation can co-operate still more in developing civil aviation by entrusting to the latter all activities not strictly military. The training of pilots, mechanics, maintenance and repair men—in short, all special technical instruction not strictly military—can be left to civil aviation. After all, pilots, whether civilian or military, must be masters of their ships; and mechanics, in or out of uniform, must know their motors and how to keep them running. All technical aviation instruction can therefore be left to private initiative, thus lightening the burdens of the military authorities, reducing costs, and stimulating private responsibility.

Military aviation can do much for civil aviation while still acting in its own interest and avoiding interference, provided that the diverse interests of the two branches are clearly defined, and that we act with magnanimity, without misconceptions, cutting away the traditions which have already grown up about aviation in spite of its youth.

ACTIVITIES OF CIVIL AVIATION WITH NO DIRECT BEARING ON NATIONAL DEFENSE

Like all other activities, these have an indirect bearing on national defense, but they should not burden the military administration with problems beyond their scope. Activities of this kind should be supported by the state to the extent that they represent the collective interest of the nation; but this support should come through a separate budget apportioned according to their usefulness. These activities include everything relating to the scientific and industrial progress of aviation, everything which is found to improve the position of our aviation industry, commercial or otherwise, in the field of international competition, a field in which national defense can never take a direct part for obvious military reasons.

All organs of national defense profit indirectly from all scientific and industrial progress in aviation, but they are not competent to promote such progress. All military establishments for aero-nautical research and experiment should be in the hands of trained civilians under the supervision, in my opinion, of the Ministry of Public Instruction; for scientific study and experimental research in the techniques of aviation do not have a special military character. All such establishments should be within reach of all students of aviation, whether or not they wear a uniform, thus avoiding a monopoly which, like all monopolies, is bound to bring about scarcity. In this situation, if the military authorities should need, for example, a special type of plane or a plane with special equipment, they would need only to make their requirements known to these civil aeronautical establishments and request that they study the problem and produce the plane; and I am certain that the military authorities would get a quicker and more satisfactory response than is possible otherwise.

The military authorities should not be burdened with the responsibility of supervising the air-worthiness of civilian machines and training of pilots, any more than with the construction and regulation of automobiles. If the state considers it its duty to take a hand in such matters, it should do so through some organ of civil administration, as it does in supervision of public utilities and driving licenses. For the military to intervene in such matters, besides burdening itself with extraneous functions, would create dissension between civil and military aviation, which should be avoided in the interests of both.

To increase appreciation of such a national industry, it should be publicized by air races, air shows, competitions, exhibitions, et cetera. These activities also should be left in civilian hands, or to private initiative. The military should stay clear of them except in such special cases as military horse shows. Very likely more sport and competitive air activities of a similar kind will be developed, as well as new ones of quite different character. But the military authorities, I repeat, should stay clear of them and get rid of the hybrid harness which lies a dead weight on their shoulders and cramps their movements. They have enough to carry as things are.

As I said, the state should establish a special budget to take care of activities of civil aviation not bearing directly on national defense.

But the military administration is not competent to apportion this budget among the various activities. What is needed is the creation of a Civilian Consultive Commission to study the matter and recommend the appropriations.

CENTRAL ORGANIZATION

From the investigation conducted in the preceding chapters we reach the conclusion that the central organization for both a national military air force and civilian aviation should be based upon the following principles:

1. Integration of auxiliary aviation with army and navy, and provision for it under their respective budgets.

2. A separate budget for independent aviation, to serve as a nucleus for the Independent Air Force of the future.

3. A separate budget for civil aviation.

The adoption of these three principles in no way implies a larger expenditure for the development of aviation. On the contrary, it means merely the logical apportionment of funds which now are arbitrarily allocated.

4. Transfer of all nonmilitary aerial functions from military to civil aviation, thus lightening the burdens of military aviation.

5. Exact definition and control, as to both quantity and quality, of all aerial means allocated to army and navy auxiliary aviation and to independent aviation by their respective organizations; and with it absolute control over the organization and employment of these means by these same organs.

Adoption of this point is in line with the criterion of differentiation of function, which is the index of progress.

The central organization based on the foregoing major principles could be realized along the following lines:

1. (a) Army and navy auxiliary aviation would have no technical aeronautical function in respect to their materials, because special technical materials would be supplied to them in the amount and quality requested, by a technical body which I shall discuss later. (b) No technical aeronautical instruction should be given its personnel by the army and navy auxiliary aviation, be-

cause this kind of instruction would be given by a technical aviation body which I shall discuss later.

2. A body should be created, as I have already indicated, constituted to superintend the organization of the proposed independent aviation within the limits allowed by the budget appropriation granted to it. At the beginning this body would use its time experimenting with existing bombing and pursuit planes placed at its disposal, in order to determine the organization, command, instruction, and utilization of the independent aviation. As in 1 (a) and (b) above, no technical aeronautical function would devolve upon this body.

3. A body (Direction of Construction) should be created to provide in quantity and quality the special materials requested by the various aerial organizations, with the understanding that such materials must come solely from private industry.

4. A body (Direction of Personnel) should be created to provide in quantity and quality the special instruction for the personnel of the army and navy auxiliary aviation and independent aviation, with the provision that such instruction come solely from civilian sources.

Both the Direction of Construction and the Direction of Personnel should function without the encumbrance of operating establishments or schools—they should be, as it were, light organs, almost simple clearing houses for directing civilian activities and for passing on materials and personnel. Both of them would be responsible for the technical aviation standards of the men and materials passing through their hands. To obviate dissipation of energies if these departments were left to themselves, they should be under the direct supervision of a body which would superintend independent aviation, as being the most air-minded.

5. A Consultive Commission should be created to study and propose the best uses for the appropriations for civil aviation, and also the transfer to civil aviation of all aeronautical activities now under military jurisdiction which are not essentially military.

That is enough; and we must not be dismayed by the word "create" in paragraphs 2, 3, 4, and 5. I have used "create" because I prefer it to "transform." However briefly we consider the ideas promulgated above, it is a fact that the organization outlined in them demands the creation of a new body as compensation for abolishing a number of organs now in existence, the functions of which are confused, overlapping, or belong elsewhere entirely.

I said, "That is enough"; but on second thought it is not. There must be some agency to co-ordinate all these aviation organs and their functions into a responsible, smoothly functioning whole; a bond which would unite them under a single comprehensive direction. This unity can only be effected through a Ministry of Aeronautics. Someone must be invested with authority to assume full responsibility, and he must be free to devote all his time and energy to it.

If our national aviation today is on a very small scale, it does not matter. Aviation, military and civil, is expanding rapidly, and we do not know what proportions it may reach tomorrow. If our present aviation is of modest proportions, a modest Ministry of Aeronautics will be sufficient if it is alert and capable of preparing for the future. If we have the will, we can begin with little and end up with much; when we are unprepared for the new, we have to begin with little.

I maintain, then, that our aviation body needs its own directing head; the creation of a Ministry of Aeronautics. To go into the details of a central aviation organization would serve no practical purpose here. Details will follow when the central organization has been realized. We must plan and work for this first of all. The rest will follow of its own accord.

THE AIR ROUTES

Before concluding this study I must pause a moment over the subject of air routes, which I consider of paramount importance. The airplane has no need of roads in the accepted meaning of the word; all space is an unlimited roadway for planes. The sea is also an unlimited roadway for ships; nevertheless the best results in navigation of the sea depend upon the preparations made on land. The same thing is true of aerial navigation. In theory a plane needs only a point of departure and a point of arrival;

but in practice thorough preparations on the ground are necessary before a plane can fly over it. Facility and safety in flying depend to a large extent upon the preparations made on the surface, particularly when a country is rugged, broken, intensively cultivated, like ours.

So we can hardly hope to develop an aerial navigation until we have prepared for air routes. We managed somehow without much preparation in the last war; the answer is that the risks of war itself were so great as to make other risks seem negligible. But in peacetime all risks must be reducd to a minimum.

Air routes demand very little: good take-off and landing fields, some emergency landing fields, an effective signal system, efficient maintenance and repair service in the main centers. But that indispensable "little" must be done. A network of air lines is made up of large links connecting great arteries; and to be of the greatest benefit to the nation, it must be of a kind to facilitate the development of civil aviation and the utilization of military aviation. To open new air routes is to further the national interest.

Provision for establishing air lines is to the interest of the state as a whole, and therefore is a duty of the state. The shape of our country clearly shows the routes that our major air lines should take: two along the coast and in the Po Valley, to which all air lines converging in the Mediterranean can be connected. This triangular network will rapidly assume international importance and change our country from an obstacle to a junction which will facilitate aerial communications between Spain and southern France and the Balkan States, and between Central Europe, Africa, and Asia. At the same time this triangular network will lend itself to eventual strategic aerial movements, for instance, if rapid concentration of aerial forces is required in the Po Valley or along the littoral fronts.

This is the *absolute minimum* without which it is futile to hope for progress in aeronavigation in our country; and it is therefore one of the first provisions the state should make.

This does not, of course, mean that the state should be the entrepreneur of the undertaking, be the active manager of the air lines. On the contrary, the state should merely encourage, see to it that the air lines are created and efficiently run. In view of the doubtful results so far shown by state-controlled undertakings, the management of air lines should indubitably be entrusted to private enterprise. With the right kind of airfields and other ground works accomplished, with well-disposed civilian enterprise encouraged and amply subsidized, with each function of the military air forces differentiated and co-ordinated under competent authorities, with new enthusiasm for adventure and aspiration toward a future that cannot fail, aviation will finally be ready to rise to the freedom of the skies. That much aviation offers to us, who have men of genius and courage, an unclouded sky, and a land embraced by the seas, where civilization was born.

CONCLUSION

Readers who have kept pace with me so far must now be convinced that I have dared to look into the future, but that in so doing I have based my views, not on idle imaginings, but upon the reality of today, out of which grows the reality of tomorrow. Not only that; they must also have noticed that, though I see in the reality of tomorrow something which cannot but disturb the coolest minds, when I have dealt with practical problems in order to stress what should be done today I presented no revolutionary proposals. Instead I limited myself to simple proposals for co-ordinating and integrating what already exists.

This necessity stares us in the face: to plan to increase the present output; and to create the possibilities of tomorrow instead of resting inert in the present moment, which even as we speak has already fled. If I may be so bold, I have mathematical certainty that the future will confirm my assertion that aerial warfare will be the most important element in future wars, and that in consequence not only will the importance of the Independent Air Force rapidly increase, but the importance of the army and navy will decrease in proportion. Nevertheless, coming down to present realities, I have not proposed the constitution of an Independent Air Force; I have simply proposed that a competent body be created to study the problem and to furnish experimental means. This is the minimum proposal that, in the present state of the question—a question discussed everywhere—could be made; and we cannot ignore it unless we deliberately choose to bury our heads in the sand.

No matter how minimum my proposal **is**, it is enough for me because I have the mathematical certainty that to propose the problem is to solve it, if not in the letter, certainly in the spirit, of the deductions I have made. If my long study of and deep concern with the subject have enabled me to induce those in authority to sow the good seed, I shall consider myself amply rewarded. The plant will flourish and grow to be a giant.

Rome, 1921

PART II

(Added in 1926)

1

WHEN THE first edition of *The Command of The Air* was published,[1] I thought it wiser not to express all my thoughts on the problems of aeronautics because I did not want to upset too violently the prevailing ideas on the subject. My purpose then was simply to break ground for the acceptance and execution of a minimum program which would have constituted a point of departure for further progress.

In 1921 we had only an auxiliary air force—it could hardly be called even that—that is to say, some aerial means intended to facilitate and integrate land and sea operations. Notwithstanding the services rendered by the air arm during the war, it was really considered superfluous, especially in military circles. At that time if few paid attention to the needs of the army and navy, no one gave any attention to the needs of the air force. This being the case, it was a question at that time of bringing to notice the concept of the "command of the air," of giving a preliminary notion of its importance, of pleading for consideration of means better adapted to conquering the command of the air, of gaining acceptance or the idea of an air force independent of the army and navy. All this had to be done shortly after a major war during which the air force operated only as an auxiliary, and against the cherished convictions of all those—they were and are legion—who make ready for the future by looking at the past.

This was dangerous territory; and, notwithstanding the semi-official status given to *The Command of The Air* by its publication under the auspices of the Ministry of War, none of the high army

---

[1] The first edition contained only Part I. Part II appeared for the first time in the second edition, published in 1927.

93

and navy authorities deigned to concern themselves with the question, about which complete silence was preserved until the march on Rome. Then came a revolution which really provoked thought. Apparently the ideas expressed in Part I must have seemed doubtful, if not altogether insane, unless the indifference sprang from general congenital mental laziness. But had I not sacrificed much in permitting the retention of the auxiliary air force in order to propitiate the goddess of incomprehension? I had. In Part I I tried to make clear the essential importance of an independent aviation; but I made the admission that for the time being the auxiliary air force should be retained, though I was, and still am, convinced that one is incompatible with the other. This was a weakness on my part, I admit. But the things one must go through to make common sense prevail! For the rest, anyone who read Part I with attention must have understood perfectly that I considered auxiliary aviation *worthless, superfluous, harmful.*

In the section on "Independent Air Force and Auxiliary Aviation," after stating the conclusion: "An adequate national defense cannot be assured except by an aerial force capable, in case of war, of conquering the command of the air," I added: "We can see clearly how easy a time a well-organized enemy bent on conquering the command of the air would have, and how helpless these auxiliary aerial means employed by the army and navy would be, confronted by an enemy Independent Air Force bent on conquest." This means that an auxiliary air force is worth nothing if it does not succeed in conquering the command of the air. Now, in wartime an auxiliary air force is worthless; not only that, but harmful because its means could have been usefully employed in another way. In short, as I said in Chapter I, "Any effort, any action, any resources diverted from this essential aim (the command of the air) makes conquering the command of the air that much less probable; and it makes defeat in case of war that much more probable." Any diversion from this essential aim is an error.

I considered it an "error" to keep an auxiliary air force which was incapable of conquering the command of the air, but I admitted its right to existence so as not to upset too violently those whose minds found it too great a leap to abolish the auxiliary air force, the only air force allowed then, and create an independent aviation, an innovation which did not grow out of the war.

Even though I conceded it, I did not want to discuss it then, and in the section on "Auxiliary Aviation" I wrote: ". . . the responsibility for the organization of the army and navy auxiliary aviation rests with the army and navy. I shall not enter into a discussion of its merits here." Earlier in the same section I said that auxiliary aviation must be: " (1) included in the budgets of the army and navy respectively; and (2) placed absolutely under the direct command of the army or the navy, beginning with their organization and ending with their employment."

As long as I conceded the auxiliary aviation, that stand was perfectly logical; but in making the concession I had in mind a further aim. I thought that when a really worth-while auxiliary aviation had been organized and the army and navy compelled to pay for it out of their own budgets, and their authorities had been obliged seriously to study the organization and employment of it, they would automatically come to the conclusion that such auxiliary aviation was useless—and therefore not only superfluous, but contrary to the public interest.

These are the essential reasons why I did not then, as I do now, state that the only aerial organization whose existence is fully justified is the Independent Air Force.

2

By the term Independent Air Force—it seems to me I have made it clear since 1921—I do not mean any air force capable of carrying out any military action whatever, but *an air force fit to strive for conquest of the command of the air*. By the expression "command of the air" I do not mean supremacy in the air nor a preponderance of aerial means, but *that state of affairs in which we find ourselves able to fly in the face of an enemy who is unable to do likewise*. Given these definitions, the following affirmation is axiomatic: *The command of the air provides whoever possesses it with the advantages of protecting all his own land and sea ter-*

ritory from enemy aerial offensives and at the same time of sub-jecting the enemy's territory to his own offensives.

In view of the carrying capacity and range of modern airplanes and the efficacy of present destructive materials, these advantages are such that a country *in possession of adequate air forces* can crush the material and moral resistance of the enemy; that is to say, that country can win *regardless of any other circumstances whatsoever.* This cannot be denied; for the material and moral resistance of the enemy is destroyed by means of the offensive, and offensives can be carried out by means of airplanes. The question will be one of delimiting *the quantity and quality* of the air offensive necessary to destroy the moral and material resistance of the enemy, but this need not concern us for the moment. With the proviso, "if adequate air forces are possessed," I intend merely to state that the air force must accord with the objective; that is, it must have the power to bring against the enemy that quantity and quality of offensives which will suffice to crush the enemy's material and moral resistance. Now, if the command of the air, controlled with an adequate air force, assures victory regardless of any other circumstances whatsoever, it logically follows as an immediate consequence that the air force adapted for the struggle for command of the air—*namely, an Independent Air Force*— *is the means suitable to assure victory regardless of other circum-stances when it is capable of winning the command of the air with adequate forces.*

To deny this axiomatic truth, considering that it cannot be denied that airplanes fly and explosives destroy, it is to deny the possibility of the struggle for command of the air, or to deny the possibility of commanding the air in the sense in which I use the expression.

In order to conquer the command of the air—that is, to prevent the enemy from flying while keeping the power to fly oneself— the enemy must be deprived of the use of all his planes. For the present we need not investigate how this end may be achieved. It is enough to show the actual possibility of achieving it. This possibility does exist, because the enemy's planes can be destroyed, either in the air with airplanes or on the ground with air attacks directed against the places of maintenance, concentration, and production. These actions aimed at the destruction of the enemy's planes will, on the other hand, provoke retaliatory counteraction from the enemy to prevent the launching of such actions. Action and counteraction; hence, battle.

When I say that the Independent Air Force must be an air force capable of fighting for the command of the air, I mean that it must be *so fashioned* as to be able to crush the enemy's counteraction and destroy his airplanes. To prevent the enemy from flying does not, of course, mean to prevent even his flies from flying. In the absolute sense, it will certainly be hardly possible to destroy *all* the enemy's means of flying. The command of the air will be gained when the enemy's planes are reduced to a negligible number incapable of developing any aerial action of real importance in the war as a whole. A fleet can be said to have conquered the command of the sea even if the enemy still has a few boats; an Independent Air Force can be said to have conquered the command of the air even if the enemy still has a few flying machines. To say that having command of the air means to fly in the face of an enemy who has been prevented from doing likewise means *to have the ability to fly against an enemy so as to injure him, while he has been deprived of the power to do likewise.*

I must beg indulgence for dwelling so long on my definition of "the command of the air." I have done this because in general the expression is used ambiguously. "Command" of the air is often confused with "preponderance" or "supremacy" in the air. But these are two very different things. Whoever possesses preponderance or supremacy in the air will be able to conquer the command of the air more easily; but until he has conquered it he does not possess it and he cannot make use of it.

During the last phase of the war it was often said that we possessed the command of the air, when all we had was aerial preponderance and we even neglected to use this preponderance to conquer the command of the air—so much so that notwithstanding our preponderance in the air we did not have command of the air, and the enemy continued to make attacks up to the day of the Armistice. Some people, especially of late, have discovered the *relative command of the air,* namely, command of the air restricted to a particular zone of the sky, again, naturally, confusing preponderance with command. Considering the speed and range of action of the air arm, characteristics which prevent the cutting up of the sky into small slices, such a conception is faulty indeed. To be stronger in the air does not mean to command it, because to command means to be master of and excludes any suggestion of the comparative; and if we are content to be stronger, we are content with a potential condition which will not prevent a weaker opponent from injuring us.

Thus the Independent Air Force is shown to be the *best way to assure victory, regardless of any other circumstances whatever, when it has been organized in a way suitable to winning the struggle for the command of the air and to exploiting the command with adequate forces.*

To become the essential factor in victory, the Independent Air Force must therefore meet two conditions:

1. It must be capable of winning the struggle for the command of the air.

2. It must be capable of exploiting the command of the air, once it has been conquered, with forces capable of crushing the material and moral resistance of the enemy.

The first of these conditions is essential, the second is integral. An Air Force which meets the first condition only—that is, one which is capable of winning the struggle for the command of the air but is not able to exploit it with forces sufficient to crush the resistance of the enemy, will be in a position to: (1) prevent its own territory from being subjected to aerial offensives of the enemy; and (2) subject all the enemy's land and sea territory to aerial offensives—without, however, having enough offensive power to crush the material and moral resistance of the enemy. In other words, an Independent Air Force which meets only the first condition cannot decide the issue of the war, which will then depend upon other circumstances besides the aerial warfare. But an Independent Air Force which meets both conditions, essential and integral, decides the issue of the war without regard to any other circumstances whatever.

When an Independent Air Force meets only the first condition, the issue of the war will be decided by the struggle on land and sea. In what situation will this struggle put the one who conquers the command of the air? Plainly, a very advantageous situation if the Air Force retains the greater power after having conquered the command of the air, because (1) it will have blinded the army and navy of the enemy, while providing far-seeing eyes for its own army and navy; and (2) it will have retained the possibility of carrying out air offensives against the enemy—offensives which, if not completely successful in crushing his material and moral resistance, will seriously damage and weaken that resistance. Thus, an Independent Air Force which meets only the first condition will nonetheless be able to develop effective action for victory.

3

Auxiliary aviation is defined as that mass of air power which facilitates or integrates land and sea actions, or a mass of air power delegated to render designated services to the army or navy and strictly confined to that purpose; therefore not designed for the conquest of the command of the air. Consequently, *auxiliary aviation can in no way influence the issue of the struggle for command.* On the other hand, since to gain the command means to put the enemy in a position where he is no longer able to fly, the one defeated *will have been deprived even of the use of auxiliary aviation.* In other words, *the possibility of using auxiliary aviation is dependent upon the issue of the struggle for command of the air, an issue on which auxiliary aviation can have no influence at all.*

Consequently, *aerial means set aside for auxiliary aviation are means diverted from their essential purpose, and worthless if that purpose is not pursued.* Since diverting force from its essential purpose can bring about failure of that purpose, diversion of aerial means to auxiliary aviation can bring about defeat in the struggle to conquer the command of the air; consequently, auxiliary aviation is made useless.

Considering, then, that, if it seems worth while, there will be nothing to prevent detaching some of the planes from the Independent Air Force to use as auxiliaries after the command of the air has been conquered, we must logically conclude that auxiliary aviation is worthless, superfluous, harmful. *Worthless* because incapable of taking action if it does not have command of the air. *Superfluous* because a part of the Independent Air Force can be used as an auxiliary if the command of the air has been conquered. *Harmful* because it diverts power from its essential purpose, thus making it more difficult to achieve that purpose.

To make this assertion while auxiliary aviation is a dominant idea may seem bold; but it was even bolder to say in 1909:

> ...not less important than the command of the sea will be the command of the air.... Civilized nations will arm and prepare for the latest war; and, as has been the case for the army and navy, and still is, a headlong race checked only by economic limitations will begin in the field of air power.... Automatically, inevitably, air forces will make a dizzy ascent.... The conquest of the air will be bitterly contested.... Aeronautics will inevitably give rise to aerial warfare in its widest possible significance.... Henceforth we must accustom ourselves to the idea of aerial warfare.... From now on aerial means must be governed by a concept similar to that governing war means on land and sea, with aerial warfare in view.... Warplanes must essentially be capable of fighting in the air against other aerial weapons, and not merely of carrying out such special missions as observation, liaison duty, and so forth.... Besides the solution of the technical problem of aerial means, aerial warfare also involves the solution of a great many problems of preparation, organization, employment, et cetera, of aerial forces; and that calls for the creation, *ex novo*, of a third branch of the art of war, which branch may be accurately defined as the art of aerial warfare.... The army and navy must look upon airplanes not as auxiliaries to be put to use in certain circumstances only, but rather as a third brother, younger but no less important, in the great warrior family.... We shall have assisted and contributed toward the beginning of aerial warfare... and it would indeed be strange if we had never been aware of it! [2]

Yet these bold assertions, offspring of iron-clad logic, an iron-clad logic based on facts, have now become mere common sense, even thought their true inwardness has not yet been understood.

[2] See *La preparazione*, 1909.

So I may be permitted to hope that the things I say today may some day become common sense, since they rest on the same foundations.

Let us check this reasoning by the following: A and B are two nations which have the same amount of resources and the same standards of technical proficiency in their respective air forces. But, while Nation A uses all its resources to build an Independent Air Force capable of striving for conquest of the command of the air, Nation B divides its resources into two parts, one to create an Independent Air Force, the other to create an auxiliary aviation. Plainly, the Air Force of Nation A will be stronger than that of Nation B. Therefore, in case of war, all other things being equal, Nation A will win the command of the air, and Nation B will be unable to use its auxiliary aviation. In other words, Nation B will be defeated in aerial warfare simply because she diverted part of her resources from an Independent Air Force to establish auxiliary aviation, which became the cause of her defeat and from then on was worthless. However we look at it, the conclusion is the same: *auxiliary aviation is worthless, superfluous, harmful.*

In the World War airplanes were employed exclusively as auxiliaries, it is true. But what does this show? Simply that the value of the command of the air was not appreciated, hence was not sought, and no means designed to conquer it were prepared. The war broke out when aviation was still in its infancy. Few believed in it, and they were not in power. Indeed, they were regarded as enthusiasts, fanatics. The military authorities of the nations engaged in the war did not believe in aviation. Worse, the greater part of them knew nothing about it. Only in Germany was there some conception of aerial warfare; but fortunately Germany was led down the blind alley of the Zeppelin and put her faith in dirigibles instead of airplanes.

Aviation entered the war more from tolerance than from conviction, more in deference to public opinion—which was more clear-sighted than the military-technical authorities—than in the belief that it might be valuable. It was left to itself and treated as a secondary service—in Italy it was placed for a short time under the General Intendency! [3] No one took any notice of it until bombs rained down on General Headquarters.

What use could this newest arm be put to under such conditions? Plainly, to an empirical use, for partial and particular objectives. In other words, it served as an auxiliary.

The credit for everything accomplished by aviation in the war belongs to the personnel, who displayed valor and initiative and accomplished things in spite of, sometimes in contradiction to, the actions of the army authorities. But the aviation personnel could not embrace the whole field of war in its entirety; it had to limit its vision to the narrow fields open to it. When someone like me—in 1915 I proposed the institution of a national Independent Air Force and in 1917, an Allied Independent Air Force—tried to bring to the attention of the high military authorities the importance of aerial means as a separate arm to be used in pursuing the general objectives of the war, the military authorities did not deign to take the matter under consideration.

Under such conditions a consistent, authentic aerial warfare could not, and did not, develop. Instead there could, and did, develop local aerial actions, chaotic and unorganized because directed by instinct rather than by reason.

Because it is easy to see well and to drop things from a high altitude, reconnaissance and bombardment are accepted; because defense against the damage inflicted by them is necessary, pursuit is accepted. Upon this simple fact rests all the action of aviation in warfare; it goes no further. Opposing air forces reconnoiter, bombard, and pursue throughout the war. The one which gains preponderance in the air reconnoiters, bombards, and pursues more than the inferior one; and aviation, securely chained to the surface forces, does not leave them, but limits its action to the direct service of those forces in their own fields. It is not understood that this tie hampers the air arm, whose field of action is essentially different from the field of the surface arm; and the idea has not yet been born which can make aviation do all it can do once that chain is broken. Despite all this, circumstances forced the recognition of the great value of the air arm. What could this newest arm not

---

[3] A service analogous to our Quartermaster Corps.—Tr.

have accomplished in the hands of someone who really understood it!

In view of this situation, what can the experience of the last war teach us? Nothing; in fact, less than nothing; for aviation was used with poor judgment, and it is easy to see that good sound judgment cannot grow out of the use of an arm which is not understood and is abandoned to its own devices. Just because in the last war aviation was used empirically, with no guiding principle, must we do likewise in a future war? In my judgment, to say this would be even bolder than not to say that auxiliary aviation is worthless, superfluous, harmful.

4

I have said that an Independent Air Force must meet two conditions: (1) the essential condition—namely, *to possess strength enough to conquer the command of the air;* (2) the integral condition—namely, *to keep up that strength after command of the air has been won and exploit it in such a way as to crush the material and moral resistance of the enemy.*

Also I have shown that if the command of the air means, as I define it, being in a position to fly in the face of an enemy who has been prevented from doing likewise, then (1) *an Independent Air Force which succeeds in conquering the command of the air, but does not keep up its strength and use it to crush the resistance of the enemy, will nevertheless be able to carry out actions very effective in the achievement of victory;* and (2) *an Independent Air Force which conquers the command of the air and keeps up enough strength to crush the resistance of the enemy will be able to achieve victory regardless of what happens on the surface.*

These two propositions are axiomatic. They cannot be refuted without altering the meaning of the expressions given here.

Now, to conquer the command of the air—that is, to put the enemy in a position where he is unable to fly, while preserving for oneself the ability to do so—it is necessary to deprive the enemy of all his means of flying; and this can only be done by destroying his means and still keeping at least a part of one's own means intact.

To exploit the command of the air in a manner calculated to crush the material and moral resistance of the enemy, it is necessary to have at one's disposal after command of the air has been won a sufficient number of aerial means to carry out offensives against the enemy strong enough to crush him.

These two propositions also are axiomatic and cannot be equivocated.

The enemy's flying forces can be found in the air or on the surface, in centers of maintenance, concentration, production, and so on; in either case they can only be destroyed by aerial offensives; and neither land nor sea forces can co-operate or collaborate in any way in such destruction. Air attacks which can be launched over the enemy's land and sea territory after command of the air has been won, obviously can be carried out only by air forces; and neither army nor navy can co-operate in any way in this purpose. Therefore, when considering the matter of the struggle for the command of the air and the launching of air offensives, one sees that the air forces assigned to accomplishing this—namely, the Independent Air Force—should not and cannot depend in any way upon the army and navy.

This is not in any sense to say that the Independent Air Force should not co-ordinate its actions with the actions of the army and navy in order to attain a common final objective. It is merely to say that such co-ordination should be planned by the authority which directs the use of all the armed forces of the nation. Neither does it mean that the Independent Air Force should never in any instance co-operate directly with the army and navy to give them assistance in special operations, just as the army and navy co-operate with each other. Plainly, there will be instances when the authority in charge of all the armed forces of the nation will consider it necessary—once the command of the air has been won—to put the Independent Air Force, or a designated part of it, temporarily in the service of a land or sea commander, thus depriving it of its independence.

To succeed in destroying enemy aerial means, one must be able to overcome the obstacles the enemy will put in his way to prevent that destruction. In this struggle we have authentic aerial warfare carried to its logical conclusion. In fact, whoever conquers the command of the air will find himself opposing an enemy who is unable to fly; and there can be no aerial warfare against an enemy deprived of his aerial means. All the actions an Independent Air Force can perform after conquering the command of the air must necessarily be directed against the surface. These actions will play a large, perhaps a decisive, part in deciding the issue of the war, but they can never be accurately classified as actions of aerial warfare. Therefore, the struggle for and conquest of the command of the air constitute the unique object of aerial warfare which the Independent Air Force should set up for itself.

To deprive the enemy of his means of flying, they must be destroyed wherever they are found, in the air or on the surface. Therefore, if an Independent Air Force is to be equal to the task of conquering the command of the air, it must be capable of carrying out destructive actions either in the air or on the surface. One air force cannot destroy another in the air except by aerial combat—that is, by subjecting the enemy to a more effective fire power than he can employ. In other words, destructive action in the air can be carried out only by means adapted to aerial combat, which for simplicity I have called "combat means." To destroy an air force on the surface, that surface must be attacked with destructive power, which, generally speaking, can be effected only by bombardment. It follows that the enemy's forces found on the surface can be destroyed only by means of *bombardments. Thus the Independent Air Force must possess both combat planes and bombers.* Thus, by a different route, I reach the same conclusions as I expressed in Part I.

Can either of these two kinds of forces be spared in an Independent Air Force? My answer is, absolutely not, for these reasons:

1. An Independent Air Force made up of combat planes alone —that is, forces capable only of carrying out destructive actions against enemy aircraft in the air—might be put in the position of failing in its action whenever the enemy avoided an encounter—

something he can do simply by descending to the surface, scarcely observed by the opposing Air Force. An Independent Air Force made up of combat planes alone, even if it had superiority in these means, would end by exhausting itself in futile actions directed at empty space. Whenever it was opposed to an Air Force inferior in combat planes but provided with bombers, it would have great difficulty in achieving even the negative objective of safeguarding its own territory from enemy air attacks, because the enemy, taking advantage of the rapidity with which air attacks can be carried out, might evade combat and try a surprise attack. Thus, an Independent Air Force made up of combat planes alone is not a true Independent Air Force, because it is unfit to strive for command of the air, and it is also unfit for the simple protection of its own territory from enemy attacks.

2. An Independent Air Force provided only with bombers could not operate except by evading air encounters and making surprise attacks, and it could offer no resistance to the will of the enemy.

The Independent Air Force in possession of both combat planes and bombers could travel with impunity to the enemy's sky and there launch offensives against the ground.

Lack of combat planes is therefore the lesser of the two evils; even though an air force provided only with bombers is not an Independent Air Force at all, merely the beginnings of one.

Consequently, there must be both combat planes and bombers in an Independent Air Force. In what proportion? For an Independent Air Force to maneuver freely and to be in a position to impose its will on the enemy, it must be able to travel to the designated points in the enemy's sky *in spite of the enemy's opposition.* That is, it should put itself in a position to overcome the enemy's opposition, an opposition manifested in the action of the adversary's combat means. To be in a position to win, all other things being equal, one must be stronger in the field of battle. Therefore, combat means should tend to be stronger than those of the enemy. As for bombers, it is obviously desirable to have the greatest possible number, because, whatever the circumstances, it is always opportune to launch major offensives. Therefore, there can be no set proportion of combat planes and bombers since both depend upon diverse independent circumstances.

For these reasons it can be said of the composition of an Independent Air Force only that (1) combat forces should aim to be stronger than like forces of the enemy; and (2) bombing means should strive to reach a maximum of power to produce the greatest effects, always remembering that an Independent Air Force cannot dispense with either type of plane and must at all costs prevent being left without one or the other.

In relation to what has been said, let us suppose that we have an Independent Air Force which disposes (1) a combat power superior to the enemy's and (2) a power of bombardment of limited capacity for the offensive. With such an Air Force we can fly anywhere in the enemy's sky, over any objective of our choice, traveling swiftly by the route most favorable for us, because (1) the enemy's Independent Air Force will not try to oppose us, so we have a free path, or (2) the enemy will try to offer resistance but will fail to contact us, so we have a free path, or (3) the enemy will offer resistance with an inferior combat force, thus putting us in a position to overcome it, so we have a free path.

Consequently, in the first and second cases we will be in a position to operate against the surface with impunity, inflicting damage upon the enemy in proportion to our bombing power. In the third case we will make the enemy suffer an aerial defeat, after which we will be in a position to inflict damage upon the surface in proportion to our bombing power.

If we have chosen as our objective the enemy's means of flying —centers of maintenance, concentration, production, and so forth —in any of the three cases we will have inflicted damage which will result in a diminution of his air potentiality. Therefore, *every time our Independent Air Force attacks the enemy's surface objectives directly, whatever else it may do, it will diminish his air potentiality.* The reduction of the enemy's air potentiality to zero, or conquering the command of the air, will be effected as rapidly as our Air Force can operate intensively, can possess the greater means of surface destruction, and can pick its objectives with care.

What action could the enemy's Independent Air Force bring against this action of ours? Will he try to oppose it directly? Obviously not, because he will either not succeed in contacting us and thus operate in empty space or succeed in contacting us and be defeated. Will he try to avoid combat and strike in turn against our territory? Plainly, that is what he must do, for only when he succeeds in avoiding combat can he strike against us in a way which can force a diminution of our air potentiality.

The battle for the command of the air between two Independent Air Forces of different combat powers will show these features:

1. The Air Force having the greater combat power, not being fettered by enemy action, hence in a position to impose its will, will operate with full freedom of maneuver, choosing those objectives it considers most useful to its purpose.

2. The Air Force weaker in combat power will try to avoid combat and destroy those objectives it considers most useful to its purpose.

That is, the actions of the two Air Forces will be similar, but the struggle will be characterized by the preoccupation of the weaker Air Force with maintaining itself in action. Let us say that during such a struggle the weaker Air Force does succeed in keeping in action—that is, in avoiding battle. In this case every action of either Air Force will diminish the enemy's air potentiality, and that Air Force which first inflicts cumulative damage sufficient to wipe out the other's air potentiality will conquer the command of the air. Therefore, if the stronger Air Force must operate as intensively as possible, must employ the greatest possible destructive power against the surface, and must choose the objectives which will have the greatest effect in diminishing the enemy's air potentiality, all the more reason why the weaker should do likewise.

From this we can draw these conclusions of practical interest:

1. Immediately upon the opening of hostilities, aerial warfare should be conducted with the greatest possible intensity. The Independent Air Force should always be ready for action, and once the action is begun, it should be ready to carry on without

let-up until the command of the air is conquered. Considering the magnitude of the offensives which the Independent Air Force can develop and the intensity with which they will be carried out, it is not possible to hope that new planes not yet ready at the opening of hostilities can carry any weight in aerial warfare—that is, in the conquest of the command of the air. In other words, the war will be decided by the air means ready to go into action at the opening of hostilities. Those prepared later will at best be used to exploit the command of the air after it has been conquered.

2. If the choice of objectives is of great importance for one side, the way those objectives are disposed in one's territory and how they present themselves to the enemy is of equal importance. That is to say, the location of a nation's potentiality should be so disposed as to make it difficult for the enemy to destroy them. It can readily be seen that if the planes, the life-blood of the Independent Air Force, are concentrated in a few centers along the frontier, the enemy will have an easy time of destroying them.

3. The issue of aerial warfare will of course depend upon the forces opposing each other, but in particular it will depend upon how the forces are employed—that is, upon the genius of the commanders, their prompt decisions and swift action, their exact knowledge of the air resources of the enemy.

In preceding paragraphs we concluded definitely that aerial warfare must be between two Independent Air Forces solely concerned with inflicting the greatest possible damage upon the enemy without giving heed to damage the enemy may inflict in turn. This conception of warfare, which has been explained in Part I, consists *in resigning oneself to submit to enemy attacks in order to use all possible means for launching the greatest offensives against the enemy.* It is difficult for this idea to penetrate the minds of people, because it departs from the conception of general warfare prevalent in the past. We are used to seeing the offensive and the defensive aspect in every battle, and we cannot grasp the idea of a battle which is all offensive, with no defensive aspect. Yet aerial warfare must be exactly this and nothing else, because the characteristics of the air arm are eminently offensive and completely unsuited for the defensive. The fact is this: with the air arm it is easy to strike but not to parry.

Let us take now the most favorable case, that of a nation whose Independent Air Force is much stronger in combat planes than the enemy's. Can this Air Force defend the nation from the enemy's Air Force? Two methods of defense offer themselves. One is to go in search of the enemy; the other is to wait and strike at him when he appears. Can an Independent Air Force go in search of the enemy's? Of course it can; but it may not find it, or if it does, may not be able to give battle and so will find no opportunity to attack it, especially if it is deliberately avoiding battle. Now, whenever an Air Force goes in search of an enemy force and finds no opportunity to attack it, that Air Force is thrusting at empty space, is exhausting itself to no end, and inflicts no damage on the enemy; but the enemy's Air Force, which has succeeded in evading the attack, can inflict indirect damage. So this first method of defense is illusory; it is nothing but sport for the enemy.

It can be said that nothing prevents the Air Force which sets out in search of the enemy's from inflicting some damage with its bombers. That is true. But in this case the Air Force does not have free choice of objectives, for these are secondary to its main purpose and contingent upon being located in the particular spot happened upon in the search for the enemy Air Force.

Can an Air Force lie in wait for the enemy and strike at him as he comes along? Certainly it can. But what are the chances of its gaining its objective? If the enemy Air Force comes in mass, as it must to have any chance of winning, the first Air Force must necessarily first concentrate in mass. Can any Independent Air Force, particularly if it thinks it is the stronger, passively await the enemy's convenience, submit to his initiative, with no assurance of ever contacting him and with the probability of being forced to endure his attack without being able to retaliate? Certainly not. So this second method of defense is illusory, is nothing but sport for the enemy.

Hence we must conclude that there is only one attitude to adopt in aerial warfare—namely, an intense and violent offensive, even at the risk of enduring the same thing from the enemy. The one effective method of defending one's own territory from an offensive by air is to destroy the enemy's air power with the greatest possible speed.

Any means of defense against an enemy aerial action will fail, and therefore benefits the enemy. This statement applies generally as well as to the specific Air Force action already examined. The intention is to oppose aerial offensives with aerial defenses made up of groups of airplanes, and with antiaircraft defenses employing surface arms. To be effective, the aerial defense of a center must crush the enemy's action, since its purpose is to hinder an offensive against that center. That means the aerial defense of a center must confront the enemy with a combat force at least equal to his own. Now, if the enemy operates by the sound rules of warfare, he will operate in mass. To be effective, the aerial defense of a center must have at its disposal a number of combat planes equal to the number of the enemy's combat planes in mass. Otherwise the aerial defense will be overcome and the center destroyed.

But since the air arm has a long range of action, potentially an Independent Air Force can threaten other centers. And since air offensives are carried out very rapidly, in order successfully to defend all centers potentially threatened, it would be necessary to station air forces in various parts of the territory attacked, and each of these forces would have to be equal in combat power to the mass combat power of the enemy. Besides that, it would be necessary to set up a complicated network of communications and keep all the air forces in constant readiness for action.

I repeat, the air arm is so essentially offensive in character that to use it defensively dooms it to the absurdity of being stronger than the attacker and yet being obliged to keep this preponderant air force completely inactive, because unable to pursue any positive objective, and thus at the mercy of the enemy's initiative.

Even admitting that defensive air forces could always arrive in time to be of some use, would it be wise to use air forces in this manner? Plainly not, because this would mean an extremely dangerous dispersion of forces. Undoubtedly, one should instead use all possible resources to strengthen to the utmost one's own Independent Air Force, because the stronger the Air Force, the more easily and rapidly it will be in a position to conquer the command of the air, the only effective way of protecting one's own territory from enemy air offensives.

To be effective, an antiaircraft defense of a center must be able to prevent the execution of an air offensive against the center. The range of action of the antiaircraft arm is very limited, hence there would have to be an adequate supply of antiaircraft guns for the protection of each center. Hence, to be of any use, antiaircraft defense would require an enormous quantity of equipment spread over the entire surface.

On the other hand, antiaircraft guns can easily be neutralized by air action, by attacks at low altitudes or wrapping in clouds of smoke, and so forth, so that effective retort could not be made. Certainly if the resources used for antiaircraft defense were employed to strengthen the Independent Air Force to the same extent, the rewards would be much greater, for the only valid method of defending one's territory is by conquering the command of the air. Therefore, there should be no air defense and no antiaircraft defense. The surface is defended from the air just as coasts are defended from the sea—by gaining command. No one would think of scattering ships and cannon along the coast in order to defend it from bombardment. The coast cities are left open and their defense entrusted indirectly to the fleet.

Therefore, all possible resources must be used to strengthen the Independent Air Force so that it can operate and defend itself in the air solely by means of intensive and violent offensives. I urge my readers to think about this statement, which is fundamental and admits no exceptions, implications, or reservations, because it must be made the basis for the formation and use of our aerial power.

To reach this conclusion it has been sufficient to consider aerial warfare in its general characteristics, or in the essential characteristics of the airplane itself—wide radius of action, great speed, ability to fight in the air, power to carry out an offensive against the surface—without going into technical details. Therefore, the conclusion itself is general in nature and does not depend upon technical details which can alter the essential characteristics of the planes at one's disposal, the future perfecting of which cannot but add weight to the conclusion drawn here. Proof of this conclusion can easily be obtained—simply contrast any other conception of air power with an Independent Air Force conceived and operating according to my ideas.

Let us imagine an encounter between such an Independent Air Force and an air force organized according to prevalent ideas, the resources for constructing them being equal in both cases.

It is clear that the Independent Air Force, having utilized all the resources at its disposal for building combat and bombing planes, will be able to employ a combat force superior to that of the other air force, because the latter will have subdivided its resources to provide a variety of planes designed for special uses, generally excluding combat. For the same reason the Independent Air Force will be superior in bombers.

In these circumstances the Independent Air Force will immediately take the initiative and pursue its aim intensely and without interruption, by means of a succession of offensives against the surface executed with the mass of its forces, paying no heed to contacting the enemy and so neither searching for nor evading him. Against this action the other air force could not retaliate directly except by confronting the Independent Air Force with its pursuit planes which, if they come to grips, will be beaten; and indirectly by using its bombers which, inferior to those of the Independent Air Force in offensive power, will conduct their operations in a way calculated to avoid combat. Not being adapted for combat and bombing operations, all this mass of auxiliaries cannot effectively influence the issue of the struggle for command of the air. They will have to remain almost entirely inactive, seeking to avoid destruction, especially on the surface.

Therefore, other things being equal, command of the air will certainly be conquered by the Independent Air Force. Nothing could oppose an Independent Air Force constituted according to my ideas except just such another Independent Air Force. Any other form of air force, any other standard of action, will result in an improper use of the air arm. I challenge anyone to prove the contrary.

5

All the conclusions I have stated have been made simply to establish that (1) combat forces must be suited to combat in the air and (2) bombers must be suited for offensives against the surface. Now we can go on to more concrete ideas of what should be the characteristics for combat or bombardment which the aerial means of an Independent Air Force must possess.

MEANS OF COMBAT

An aerial battle is fought by fire action between warplanes. The fitness of a plane for aerial battle is determined by its power of attack and defense. In aerial battle a warplane may be attacked by enemy fire from any direction. It must therefore be capable of returning this fire; and, all things being equal, the advantage lies with the plane which is more heavily armed and has greater fire power than its adversary. To best withstand enemy fire, the greatest measure of self-protection is needed. Therefore, other things being equal, the advantage lies with the plane which is more heavily armored.

Obviously, in an air battle it is an advantage to have greater speed and maneuverability than the adversary, which permits one to engage or refuse battle at one's discretion; or, once engaged, to cut the battle short. Again, other things being equal, the advantage lies with the faster and more maneuverable plane.

In fine, other things being equal, the plane with the greater radius of action will have the advantage because it can carry the action deeper into the enemy's territory.

Therefore, a warplane should possess to the maximum degree compatible with technical exigencies, the following four characteristics: *armament, armor protection, speed,* and *radius of action.*

These characteristics are reducible to terms of physical weight, the sum total being determined by the aerodynamic structure of the plane, subdivided to harmonize with these four characteristics.

The problem here is analogous to the problem presented by warships. Nor could it be otherwise, considering the similarity of purpose. There are, however, other considerations to be taken into account in this case.

Armament: The combat planes of an Independent Air Force are not designed to fight alone, but in formation. They must therefore be grouped in units of combat capable of fighting together; and in this lies the basis of their tactics. Hence the maximum intensity of fire is wanted, not so much in the single plane, but essentially in the combat unit as a whole, the formation of which may be modified according to the direction of the attack by the enemy or the direction of the intended attack against the enemy. Hence the armament problem concerns both the individual plane and the formation of the unit, whether emphasis on the plane or emphasis on the formation as a whole is the deciding factor.

In fire power, likewise, it is not the individual plane that matters so much, but the unit of combat, a unit which must be considered indivisible. Here, too, the emphasis must lie on the formation, rather than on the individual plane, which must integrate in the best possible way the fire power of the individual planes. But in any case we can see that, though it is desirable for each plane to have a potential fire power above the bare minimum, we must not exaggerate the importance of such fire power, because it would seem that, as between two combat units of equal fire power, the unit which gets its power by the possession of more planes is in a better condition to effect a more enveloping action. Only experience can decide this for practical purposes, however.

Armor Protection: The purpose of armor protection is to conserve the power of the weapon by reducing its vulnerability. Obviously, as between two planes with equal armament, the one with the best armor protection has twice the offensive capacity of the other, because it can keep up its offensive power twice as long in the same action, or double its power for the same period of action. This characteristic of protection has not only a material but a moral value, and therefore it is erroneous to think that the weight used for armor protection is always a waste of power and material, even though it may exist at the expense of armament itself. The problem of armor protection has to do with the individual plane, not with the formation as a whole. Nevertheless, it is obvious that the total physical weight of armor protection grows relatively less as the number of planes is reduced, even though the formation as a whole keeps its total offensive capacity unaltered.

Speed: Though superior speed is indisputably an advantage in battle, the fact remains, as I have fully demonstrated, that an Independent Air Force should neither seek an encounter nor force a battle. Superior speed has therefore only a relative importance for a weaker Independent Air Force in avoiding an aerial battle. So it is not advisable to exalt speed at the expense of the other three characteristics.

Radius of Action: Possible offensive actions against enemy territory more or less depend upon the radius of action of the planes. Therefore, there is a radius of action, depending upon the operational distance necessary to reach enemy objectives, below which an Independent Air Force loses its value. Naturally, the radius of action should be the maximum whenever possible.

MEANS OF BOMBARDMENT

The function of bombing planes is integral with the action of combat planes, which are entrusted with clearing the air of enemy obstacles. Therefore, their characteristics should meet the following conditions:

Radius of Action: Equal to that of combat planes.

Speed: Equal to that of combat planes.

Armor Protection: If armor protection is considered necessary for a combat plane, there is no reason why it should not be equally necessary for bombers. Therefore, armor protection equal to that of combat planes.

Armament: Essentially the armament of a bomber should consist of bombs with which to attack the surface. But for the sake of the crew's morale, no warplane, which may be attacked in the air, should be completely unarmed. All characteristics except armament shall be the same for both combat and bombing planes. The difference between the two types of plane lies in the difference in distribution of weight for armament in the combat plane and for bomb-load in the bomber.

BATTLEPLANE

From this fact emerges the conception of a plane suitable for both combat and bombing, which for simplicity I shall call "battleplane." This type of plane should have the radius of action, speed, and armor protection as described; but should have armament sufficient both for aerial combat and for offensives against the surface. If, after satisfying the other three characteristics, we denote by the letter W the rest of the weight at our disposal for armament—consisting of firearms, munitions, and crew—and if an Independent Air Force consists of combat planes, C, and bombing planes, B, its combat strength will be CW and its bombing strength B(W-w), w being the weight taken up by defensive armament in the bombing planes. But if the Independent Air Force consists entirely of battleplanes, the number of planes will be C+B, and the weight allowed for combat armament will be W (C+B), or CW+BW. Now, if the two types of arms—for aerial combat and for surface attack—are proportionately distributed in each plane, the total value of the armament which can be used against the surface is BW. In other words, this Independent Air Force would be identical with the other in combat power; but in offensive action against the surface it would be slightly superior owing to lack of defensive armament.

In this respect we should make another observation. If the total number of planes in an Independent Air Force is divided between combat and bombing planes, in case of an encounter with an enemy the action will be not simultaneous, but at different times. First will come an aerial battle to overcome the enemy opposition, then afterward the bombing action against surface objectives. Thus, only combat planes can take part in the first phase of the action and only bombers in the second. Similarly, only machine-gunners will be able to operate in the first phase, and only bombardiers in the second.

But if, instead, the Independent Air Force consists entirely of battleplanes, the same personnel could employ all the armament of the planes in aerial battle in the first phase of action, then strike against surface targets in the second phase. This means that the same crew can function both as machine-gunners and bombardiers, thus utilizing the weight saved in personnel to increase the fire power of the Independent Air Force as a whole.

Moreover, an Independent Air Force made up of bombing and combat planes will have to fight, in case of an encounter with the enemy, with only an aliquot part of its planes and without freedom of action, because this number will have to devote itself to protecting the bombing planes during the engagement. If the Air Force were made up entirely of battleplanes, all the planes could take part in the engagement, with full freedom of action. Therefore, from all points of view it is best that the bulk of an Independent Air Force be made up entirely of battleplanes designed for aerial combat and for bombing offensives against the surface.[4]

We can go even further in this respect. As a matter of fact, it would be better if these characteristics, or at least some of them, were *elastic*. For instance, since radius of action, armor protection, and armament can be translated into carrying capacity, and since the sum total of the weight of these in a given plane is constant, the weight of any of them may be increased at the expense of any or all of the others. Now, it may be expedient to do so because of the intended use. Consequently, it would be very useful to have these details in the construction of battleplanes allow of easy alteration of these characteristics.

If an Independent Air Force undertook an operation within a short radius of action, obviously it would be more useful to decrease the weight of the fuel load and increase the armament a corresponding amount. Conversely, if the action is far from the bases, it would be more useful to decrease the armor protection and

---

[4] If this interpretation of Douhet's thought is correct, the plane he is describing resembles our modern Flying Fortresses but is much more powerful.—Tr.

perhaps even the armament. Once the command of the air had been conquered, there would of course no longer be any need for an Independent Air Force to engage in aerial battle—so there would no longer be any need of heavy armor protection and defensive aerial armament. The construction of a battleplane should therefore be such as to allow the ready adjustment or substitution of these two weight characteristics to increase the plane's radius of action or its striking power against surface targets. Everything being equal, it is better for a battleplane to be elastic in its characteristics.

We have determined all the basic characteristics of the battleplane which should make up the mass of our Independent Air Force. The problem left for technicians and builders is to produce the plane which will best meet the conditions desired within the limits of practicability. Such a plane must certainly be a heavy type, multimotored, and of medium speed if it is to fill all the requirements. Since the Independent Air Force will have to operate in mass over land and sea, the battleplane ought to be an amphibian. If it is impossible to realize this kind of plane at present, the Independent Air Force will have to be made up partly of hydroplanes and partly of land planes, both to have identical characteristics. The present state of technical development permits the realization of a plane which will meet these requirements to a certain degree, and surely further progress will tend to make the battleplane ever more efficient.

We have been able to determine through deduction the characteristics a battleplane should have—the *only* type of plane which should make up the operating mass of an Independent Air Force— the *only* organism necessary, because sufficient in itself, to wage aerial warfare.

But an Independent Air Force must maintain an efficient information service to keep from being surprised by the enemy, so it must be provided with reconnaissance means. Before we go on any further we must define "reconnaissance," a term which lends itself easily to ambiguity. Reconnaissance is obviously a war operation undertaken for one's own advantage and against the enemy's interests; and therefore, like all war operations, is subject to enemy counteraction. To accomplish this kind of operation successfully, it is first necessary to be in a position to defeat or circumvent the enemy's counteraction. That holds true on land or sea or in the air. For instance, cavalry may reconnoiter against the enemy either by employing large masses of cavalry troops capable of breaking through the enemy's lines to see what goes on behind them, or by using small, well-mounted patrols who can avoid contact with the enemy and slip behind his rear, then return with the needed information. In the air the situation is the same. If a reconnaissance in force to overcome enemy resistance is wanted, it is up to the Independent Air Force, or at least a part of it, to perform the task. If a small scouting operation is planned to report enemy moves in order to use the information to avoid contact with the enemy in subsequent operations, a type of plane entirely different from the combat plane is needed. We shall call this type of plane a *reconnaissance plane.*

To get behind the enemy aerial defense and at the same time avoid aerial combat, *superior speed* and more skillful flying than the enemy can oppose to it are necessary. To carry out successful reconnaissance, an active Independent Air Force needs special observation planes with a greater radius of action than that of the mass of the Air Force if it is to be of any use during the time the Air Force is operating in the air. In short, the essence of successful reconnaissance is to *see, understand,* and *report.* Therefore, a reconnaissance plane needs two eyes, an alert brain, and suitable means of communicating with the Independent Air Force.

RECONNAISSANCE PLANES

The characteristics of this plane should be as follows:

Speed: The maximum possible compatible with the actual state of technical aeronautical developments.

Radius of Action: At least equal to that of the Independent Air Force. If the Air Force has a range of six hours of flight, for example, the reconnaissance plane should have at least an equal range.

Armament and Armor Protection: It is useless to arm a plane intended to *avoid combat*. It is better to use the weight thus saved to increase speed and radius of action.

Means of Communication: The most perfect.

Crew: The absolutely indispensable minimum, possibly one person only.

To avoid combat, reconnaissance should be undertaken by individual planes operating singly, or by small groups, to allow for any possible loss during operations. An Independent Air Force operating in mass, preceded and surrounded at a convenient distance by a covey of such reconnaissance planes, will be protected from any surprise attack. At the same time it can use these reconnaissance planes to discover ground targets for eventual attack.

6

The characteristics of battle and reconnaissance planes defined so far are valid for any Independent Air Force. But we are essentially interested here in *our own* Independent Air Force, so we must take into account two other conditions particularly applicable to us. Our eventual enemies will be found either beyond the Alps or beyond the narrow sea surrounding us. Therefore, if we want to be in a position to strike at them, we must have an Independent Air Force capable of crossing the Alps and the narrow seas surrounding us. The first of these conditions determines the minimum ceiling the planes of our Air Force must have; the second the minimum radius of action of the whole Air Force. If we do not meet these two conditions, the value of the whole Independent Air Force will be nullified.

In this connection we should be careful not to confuse the radius of action of the individual plane with that of the Independent Air Force itself. The latter may be much less than the former. An Independent Air Force intending to act in mass must first of all assemble its forces, then operate, and finally disperse, each unit re-entering its proper base. The radius of action of an Independent Air Force is equal to the radius of action of the planes constituting it, minus twice the distance from the point of concentration to the base farthest from it.

From this consideration derives the importance of the disposition of air bases, or the home bases of the various units composing the Independent Air Force. The closer these bases are to the point of concentration, the more efficient the Air Force will be. But the points of concentration may vary with the enemy in question, and sometimes also with the operation intended against the chosen enemy. From this springs the necessity for numerous air bases more or less grouped to make the best use of the radius of action of each individual plane, so as to effect the maximum radius of action for the entire Independent Air Force.

That is part of aerial logistics, which must determine the best conditions for utilizing the greatest operating efficiency an Air Force is capable of. But I do not intend to speak of that now. For the present I merely want to point out the necessity of these numerous air bases to be used simply as landing fields. Wartime bases cannot be provided with hangars, because it would be practically impossible to dispose such a large number of them, and because the bases would be too easily identified by the enemy. The planes should therefore be made of metal resistant to all kinds of weather. Large peacetime air bases, at least those of no practical value, should be abandoned immediately upon declaration of war and the planes dispersed to substitute airfields.

An Independent Air Force should disappear from the surface immediately upon landing, and should never be left exposed to enemy attack on the open field. An able and daring enemy force, even if inferior, can make good use of this critical moment. When an Air Force is on the ground, it should be widely dispersed and camouflaged as much as possible. And, as we have seen, an Independent Air Force should dispose different groups of bases so as to have freedom of maneuver and to facilitate its dispersal. Aerial forces should be able to function at will, independent of the ground.

It is necessary, therefore, to create a logistical aerial unit, which will have to be provided with all the needs of life, movement, and combat, which must in turn be supplied by its own aerial organization. To fulfill its purpose, an Independent Air Force must be a completely self-sufficient organization able to move in the air and to change its location on the surface autonomously. That proves that an Independent Air Force worthy of the name is something very different from what is generally thought.

7

The type of battleplane suitable for our Independent Air Force —that is, a plane with a wide radius of action, a high enough ceiling to navigate the Alps, sufficient speed, and a carrying capacity large enough to allow a safe margin of armament and armor protection—is similar to a commercial transport plane utilized by civil aviation, once an equal weight of armament and armor were substituted for passengers, cargo, and mail. This shows the possibility of converting a civil machine into a battleplane by means of appropriate technical arrangements. I believe we should hasten and bend all our energies to this end: *to organize a civil aviation capable of being converted into a powerful military air force in case of national need.*[5] During times of peace, which is to say normally, a military plane has only a potential function in what it may be able to do when war breaks out. All kinds of resources needed to maintain such a military plane in power during all the time when the life of the nation flows normally are consumed in view of that potential action. On the other hand, a civilian plane capable of conversion immediately on the opening of hostilities has a potential value identical with that of the military plane. But it also represents a real value in peacetime in that it can perform useful civilian services.

It is understandable, therefore, how in choosing between two masses, one made up of military planes and the other of civilian ones capable of immediate conversion to military ones, there are moral and material advantages in choosing the second. No matter how limited the returns of a civil air service, materially speaking, the returns will always be a plus value. Therefore, a mass of civilian planes capable of being converted into military ones will

[5] An ideal magnificently followed in Germany.

always cost less than an equal number of military ones. By using convertible civilian planes we obtain from the same expenditure greater military power and at the same time the possibility of actively maintaining a very comprehensive civilian air service. This is so great an advantage that I have no hesitation in saying that the end we must work for is *to organize a powerful civil aviation capable of immediate conversion, in case of need, into a powerful military aviation, reducing the latter during peacetime to a skeleton force for instruction and command.*

I have already shown that the possibility for this unit exists as far as the mass of planes constituting an Independent Air Force according to the idea expressed here is concerned. The aeronautical world in general denies such a possibility. Considering the prevalent conception of air power—a conception which demands a great variety of specialized types of planes and sometimes even of extreme characteristics—is this denial altogether wrong? It may not be possible now to make civilian planes capable of immediate conversion into battleplanes, since these require, besides suitable armament for aerial combat and for surface offensives, installations for suitable armor protection. But it is certainly possible even now to make civilian planes capable of immediate conversion into bombing planes, because to do this we need only substitute bombs for the weight of passengers, cargo, and mail.

So from now on it will be possible to increase the bombing power of an Independent Air Force by using civil aviation to complement it. Depending upon circumstances, such complements could be used to increase the bombing power of an Independent Air Force during the struggle for command of the air or after the command has been conquered. Therefore, there is nothing to stop us from aiming at this goal.

I have said, and proved, that only those who have learned how to conquer the command of the air will be in a position to employ aerial means as auxiliary services with the army and navy, and that the only aerial force a nation must create for itself is the Independent Air Force. Conversely, an Independent Air Force which has conquered the command of the air can lend part of its complements to the army and navy for auxiliary services.

But are such complements adapted to such services? Most certainly they are. First of all we must note that when an independent Air Force confronts an enemy made incapable of flying, any aerial action, auxiliary or not, undertaken against him is accomplished with great ease and important results because the enemy is powerless to retaliate.

Once it has conquered the command of the air, an Independent Air Force may lend the army and navy, for auxiliary service, battle units (or units of combat and units of bombardment) and also observation units. These units can carry out with great facility, because in complete safety, all the auxiliary tasks of exploration, reconnaissance, and observation which the army and navy may require of them. The combat units, powerfully armed and capable of maximum intensity of fire in all directions, can serve best to attack marching troops, supply trains, rail movements, and so forth; while the bombing units can serve to destroy objectives bearing directly on surface operations. Therefore, there will be no need of pursuit planes once the command of the air has been conquered. And therefore the constitution of an Independent Air Force according to my ideas will make it able to render all imaginable auxiliary aerial services after it has conquered the command of the air.

8

In all the foregoing my purpose has been to demonstrate that an Independent Air Force, once it has conquered the command of the air, can also meet the needs of all auxiliary services required by the exigencies of war. I have made my demonstrations in abundance because I am convinced that, even after conquering the command of the air, an Independent Air Force should operate independently and not waste its time and disperse its means in actions of secondary importance. Once the command of the air is conquered, the Air Force should attempt to carry out offensives of such magnitude as to crush the material and moral resistance of the enemy. Even if this aim cannot be achieved in entirety, it is still necessary to weaken the enemy's resistance as much as possible, because that, better than any other means, facilitates the operations of the army and navy. But to achieve such an end, we must avoid dispersing our means and make the most possible use of them.

The maximum returns from aerial offensives must be sought beyond the field of battle. They must be sought in places where effective counteraction is negligible and where the most vital and vulnerable targets are to be found—targets which are, even though indirectly, much more relevant to the action and outcome on the field of battle. In terms of military results, it is much more important to destroy a railroad station, a bakery, a war plant, or to machine-gun a supply column, moving trains, or any other behind-the-lines objective, than to strafe or bomb a trench. The results are immeasurably greater in breaking morale, in disorganizing badly disciplined organizations, in spreading terror and panic, than in dashing against more solid resistance. There is no end to what a powerful Independent Air Force in command of the air could do to the enemy!

It seems paradoxical to some people that the final decision in future wars may be brought about by blows to the morale of the civilian population. But that is what the last war proved, and it will be verified in future wars with even more evidence. The outcome of the last war was only apparently brought about by military operations. In actual fact, it was decided by the breakdown of morale among the defeated peoples—a moral collapse caused by the long attrition of the people involved in the struggle. The air arm makes it possible to reach the civilian population behind the line of battle, and thus to attack their moral resistance directly. And there is nothing to prevent our thinking that some day this direct action may be on a scale to break the moral resistance of the people even while leaving intact their respective armies and navies. Was not the German Army still able to go on fighting at the time when it laid down its arms? Was not the German fleet turned over intact to the enemy when the German people felt their power of resistance weakening?

We must keep in mind, not what aviation *is* today, but what it *could be* today. Certainly if we said that the actual air powers of the various nations could decide the outcome of a war, we would be uttering not only paradox, but downright absurdity. But that means nothing, because we do not say that the actual aviations of today are what they should be in effectiveness. We should think, for example, what would happen if an enemy were to conquer the command of our sky with his Independent Air Force, enabling him to rove at will over Piedmont, Lombardy, and Liguria, dumping great quantities of explosive, incendiary, and poison-gas bombs on the most vital centers of these three northern provinces. If we think of that, we must conclude that the resistance of our surface forces would soon be broken by the disruption of every-day life in those three provinces—a disruption directly brought about by air power.

Even assuming—although I by no means concede it—that today it would be impossible to launch aerial offensives of the necessary magnitude, still the constant improvement of aerial weapons and increase in the efficiency of destructive materials show that the necessary magnitude will be possible in the not too distant future.

In any case, by common consent the fact remains that aerial offensives have already attained such material and moral efficacy as to compel surface armies to undertake arduous, time-consuming defensive measures—secret night movements of troops and sup-plies, et cetera—which tie up the movement of surface aerial defenses and antiaircraft guns which might be more useful else-where, thus causing a serious dispersion of means. This is true whenever we give credit to aviation for what it is, and for what it may and should be.

We must not rely on the fact that other nations organize and employ their air forces much as we do. One fine day one of our eventual enemies may decide to organize and employ his air forces as I would do myself, for example. And in that case, I ask anyone disposed to give me an honest answer, whether, taking into account the concepts of aerial organization and employment which prevail in our country and the location of our aerial re-sources on the surface, this potential enemy would not be in a position rapidly to conquer the command of the air over our sky; and whether, having conquered it, he could not perhaps inflict irreparable damage upon us. If anyone can conscientiously give me an unequivocal "no," I will lay down my arms and admit that I am wrong. But until I hear this unequivocal "no," for which someone is ready to assume full responsibility, I shall not cease to point out this grave danger and fight with everything in my power, thus fulfilling my solemn duty.

Following is a recapitulation of my ideas on the constitution of our air power:

1. The purpose of aerial warfare is the conquest of the command of the air. Having the command of the air, aerial forces should direct their offensives against surface objectives with the intention of crushing the material and moral resistance of the enemy.

2. We should seek no other purposes except the two described above if we want to avoid playing the enemy's game.

3. The only effective instrument for carrying out these purposes is an Independent Air Force made up of a mass of battle units and an aliquot part of reconnaissance units.

4. The Independent Air Force should embody the greatest power compatible with the resources at our disposal; therefore no aerial resources should under any circumstances be diverted to secondary purposes, such as auxiliary aviation, local air defense, and antiaircraft defenses.

5. The efficacy of destructive materials should be increased as much as possible, because, other things being equal, the offensive power of an Independent Air Force is in direct proportion to the efficacy of the destructive materials at its disposal.

6. Civil aviation should be so organized as to be utilized as a complement to military aviation in case of war. That organization should be in the direction of a powerful fleet of transports capable of immediate conversion into a powerful military air force. The latter should be reduced, in time of peace, to a simple organization for instruction and command.

7. Aerial warfare admits of no defensive attitude, only the offensive. Of two Independent Air Forces, the one stronger in combat units should neither seek nor avoid aerial combat; the weaker should try to avoid it. But both stronger and weaker

should always be in readiness to act even before hostilities break out; and once action has begun, both should keep in action incessantly and with the utmost violence, trying to hit the enemy's most vital targets—that is, targets more likely to cause repercussions on his air power and moral resistance.

8. Once an Independent Air Force has conquered the command of the air, it should keep up violent, uninterrupted action against surface objectives, to the end that it may crush the material and moral resistance of the enemy.

9. An Independent Air Force should be so organized as to move as quickly as possible over its own territory with its own means, in order to be of the greatest use against any potential enemy.

10. Aerial warfare will be fought and decided solely by aerial forces which are ready to act at the instant hostilities break out, because, owing to the great violence with which it will be fought, if the adversaries are fairly well matched in strength, it will be conducted and decided very rapidly.

11. An Independent Air Force formed with all the resources a nation has at its disposal for its aerial forces, made up of a mass of battleplanes and an aliquot part of reconnaissance planes, acting decisively and exclusively on the offensive, will soon wrest command of the air from an enemy air force constituted, organized, and performing in a different way.

In spite of the close reasoning by which I have arrived at these affirmations, I am sure they will seem extravagant to many. That does not affect me in the least. I am used to hearing my ideas, which often contrast with those of many people, who have clung fanatically to the same old ideas, called extravagant and worse. On the other hand, this will not prevent my ideas, even the most radical ones, from little by little being accepted by general opinion. Such stubbornness leaves me absolutely unaffected, because I have the mathematical certainty that the time will come when air forces of nations everywhere will conform exactly to the concepts described above.

Naturally, I wish we might be the first to conform to them, because I am convinced that the first nation to create an air force along rational, logical lines will have an inestimable advantage over other nations. But even if my wish is not to be fulfilled, I have done all that is humanly possible to bring it about, and my conscience will have nothing to reproach me for.

General Bonzani said in *L' Epoca:*

Italy needs an air force capable of defending her own sky during the necessary time after the beginning of hostilities for her industry to turn out the latest types of plane.

This statement carries over into the field of the air a concept applied to the shield and the lance on the ground. According to this concept, an aerial shield would be sufficient protection against an aerial lance, or for all aerial purposes. That is to say, it admits the possibility of an air force able to protect our centers of production of means and personnel-training from aerial offensives during all the time necessary to set up an air power able to take the offensive; and at the same time holds out the hope of having means incorporating the latest improvements of science and industry for the decisive encounter.

The shield-and-lance concept is justified on the ground because of the enormous disproportion of forces needed by the offensive in order to break through a well-organized defense. But there is no justification for applying it to the field of the air, where the means employed have no defensive value, but present the most outstanding offensive characteristics in the highest degree. Unfortunately, we cannot dig trenches in the air, nor throw up barbed-wire entanglements, nor prevent infiltration. Also unfortunately, our essential aeronautical industries are well within the range of aerial offensives from our eventual worst enemies. I do not say what security, nor what probability, I say what possibility is there of our preventing, by aerial defense, an enemy from destroying our most essential aeronautical industries during all that time we are turning to mass production? Even if there were such a possibility, are we to suppose that the enemy would be sitting with his hands behind his back during all that time, instead of starting his own mass production too?

That kind of thing is fantasy. Aerial warfare will be waged and

decided by the available means in hand. He who is caught unprepared will be irrevocably defeated in the air. The stronger one
will try for a quick decision; he will not wait upon the pleasure of
his weaker adversary, nor permit him to go on producing under
his very nose. In the name of charity, let us forget the last war!
Then it was possible to create an air force from the very beginning, by establishing industrial plants and creating the various
types of plane. But at that time aviation itself was just being
born, and every nation was in the same situation. But in future
wars aviation will have grown to adulthood and will know its
own value. And that will be a very different matter.

We must not waste time talking about it. We should get to
work and do it, always keeping abreast of the latest developments
in armament. And for that reason our industry must always be in
a position to produce the best materials, and to produce them in
greater quantity than normal needs require. It is of supreme importance to national defense that our aeronautical industry should
develop a large export trade, because in that way it will produce
better materials in greater quantities, thus meeting the demands
of abnormal times. As far as national defense is concerned, it is
infinitely better to have an aeronautical industry with an export
trade and fewer squadrons of up-to-the-minute planes than a hit-
or-miss industry compelled to depend sometimes on imported materials and a larger number of makeshift armed squadrons. Therefore, it is to the interest of national defense that aeronautics also
should make some sacrifice so that our industry can compete with
foreign industries.

But economic sacrifices are not enough. What is needed to
stimulate the expansion of our aeronautical industry is a definite
direction and a measure of security—objectives which for obvious
reasons cannot be reached unless we formulate a definite aeronautical policy.

If we analyze the air forces of the principal nations, we can see
that they are all constituted according to the same concepts which
governed during the last war. Today we often speak of aerial
warfare. War is a struggle fought out with deadly weapons. And
yet, though all the air forces have innumerable types of plane for

many different purposes, not one of them has a *combat* type of plane. It seems as though they are prepared to do anything that can be done in the air except fight. There are pursuit planes, I know. But pursuit planes are not combat planes; they are for the purpose of pursuit. In spite of their apparently offensive character, pursuit planes are essentially suited for defensive purposes only. That is owing to their very origin and to their limited radius of action, which precludes their carrying out effective operations inside enemy territory.

The true combat plane, able to impose its will upon the enemy, has not yet been invented; nor does it seem likely it will be soon, because we have stopped with the World War—in the infancy of aerial action—and have not yet learned that in war the most necessary thing is to be fit for combat. On the contrary, generally speaking we are convinced that many things are possible in aerial warfare without being forced to fight, so much so that the great majority of warplanes are unfit for aerial combat.

It is on this very concept—that action of an offensive nature can be developed without combat—that the bombardment aviation of the nations is founded. Generally speaking, bombardment aviation is divided into two specialties, daylight bombing and night bombing. The first *flees* combat by virtue of having greater speed than the enemy; the second *flees* combat by grace of darkness! Now, one who intends to *flee* is at the mercy of enemy action or special circumstances, and therefore he is not master of his own actions and his initiative is limited. On the other hand, what else can he do if he lacks the concept and the means for *conquering* enemy opposition, as is the constant rule of war on land and sea?

During the last war the purpose of a bombing action was limited to merely annoying the enemy, and it was admissible that bombing operations were possible by *fleeing* enemy counteraction. Now this is no longer admissible, because today the tendency is to get positive and very great results from aerial bombardment. During the World War there were some night bombings carried out by a limited number of planes scattering a few bombs on enemy objectives. We made some on the northernmost section of the Isonozo front and across the Piave. But to carry out bombing raids under present conditions, whoever our eventual enemy may be, we would have *to take off with a considerable number of planes from the lowlands, cross the Alps, reach the enemy objectives, and return across the Alps.* Is it possible to do all that at night? And if it is possible, is it worth while? If we admit the possibility of bombing by daylight, what is the necessity of keeping nighttime aviation? In either case, why divide our strength in two instead of collecting it into a single striking force, which would also facilitate training of personnel and replacement of materials?

Lack of a clear conception of an Independent Air Force gives rise to a curious notion of its formation. According to this notion, it is generally understood to consist of daylight-bombing units, night-bombing units, and pursuit units. The very term, Independent Air Force, implies something unified. As a matter of fact, an Independent Air Force as generally conceived would consist of three specialties, because their essential characteristics would prohibit their working together even in pairs, inasmuch as daylight bombing requires great speed and a wide radius of action; night bombing, low speed and a wide radius of action; and pursuit planes, great speed and a short radius of action.

The bulk of existing air forces consists of reconnaissance units. But even as concerns this specialty, we note the predominating influence of the past and the idea that it is possible to accomplish war operations without being forced to fight. Because of such notions the reconnaissance plane is held up as the ideal, possessing all the essential characteristics best fitted for facilitating reconnaissance operations, intended not as war operations, but as operations sufficient in themselves and apart from the struggle as a whole. So we look for ideal visibility, medium speed, good photographic equipment, good radio, a hook to fish up orders, and so on. In fact, we expect of a reconnaissance plane everything we have found suitable and convenient in peacetime, without stopping to think that, in order to observe the enemy in war, it is necessary first to spot him; and without taking into account the fact that, if it is important for us to observe him, it is equally important for him not to be observed.

Let us consider this hypothetical case: Two enemy lines, A and B, are facing each other. Line A has 500 reconnaissance planes and line B has 500 pursuit planes. Obviously, Line A will not succeed in accomplishing its mission because its reconnaissance planes cannot fly over Line B without being shot down by B's pursuit planes; but Line B, however unsuitable its pursuit planes for observation, will be able to observe something of the enemy because its planes will be able to reach Line A. This demonstrates that in war, where the essential is to fight, machine guns are more effective than photographic equipment for carrying out a reconnaissance operation.

Reconnoitering is a war operation which, like all war operations, is accomplished at the expense of the enemy; and therefore the enemy will try his best to prevent it. Therefore, in order to perform aerial reconnaissance successfully, it is necessary to be able either to checkmate the enemy's counteraction by force, or to escape by speed and stratagem. Consequently, reconnaissance units should be either combat units or pursuit units capable of avoiding combat.

For lack of the realization that in war the primary need is the capacity to fight, we neglect the fighting capacity in our so-called warplanes in order to concentrate on essentially secondary auxiliary capacities. The result is a great deal of specialization which breaks up our air power into fragments and diverts it from its essential purpose.

In peacetime maneuvers this may be all very well, because then we have two identical parties, each provided with the same means. Since neither the "reds" nor the "blues" have combat units, obviously no combat can take place, and each party can employ its aerial means as though there were no such thing as combat. But in war things may be different. If one of two confronting sides excludes aerial combat, and the other considers it the essential function of air power and is armed accordingly, the situation is completely different, because the one who is not in a position to fight could not fight, nor observe, nor bomb, nor make use of all the other aerial specializations which detract from the essential purpose of an air force.

In preparing for war, we must always begin with the assumption that the enemy is not only as brave and as able as we are, but also that he will always try to act in ways least advantageous for us. As far as aerial warfare is concerned, it is always an advantage to have the enemy armed chiefly with hybrid aerial auxiliary weapons, for defense, observation, pursuit, et cetera; because then he has at his disposal less combat and bombardment means capable of hindering our own aerial actions and inflicting damage on our territory.

Since that would be advantageous to us, we must assume that the very opposite will be the case, that the enemy will use all his resources to provide himself with combat and bombardment means. Then we should arm ourselves in accordance with this, the worst, hypothesis, because if we are armed to face the worst, surely we can, with better reason, face any other hypothesis.

Whoever our enemy may be, we will encounter him in the high mountains near the frontier; and in the mountains our army will have to wage a long and bitter fight. Therefore, our auxiliary aviation will have to operate above the Alps and be able to act above the highest peaks in case these areas are occupied by the enemy. So we can say that such aviation must be able to operate at 3,000 meters above the ground, or at a minimum ceiling of 5,000 to 6,000 meters. As for our Independent Air Force, it too will have to cross the Alps, presumably guarded by the enemy, with a full load if it wants to launch offensives against important enemy objectives.

These are particular and essential conditions which impose themselves upon our aviation, and they demand special characteristics in its armament. If our aviation does not meet these requirements satisfactorily, its value will be nullified. But there is more to it than that. Since we must depend on the hope that our army will be able to drive back the enemy, and since it is not easy to find places in the high mountains adapted for airfields, our aviation will have to operate from its airfields in our lowlands until the army reaches the enemy's lowlands on the other side of the mountains. Therefore, *all* of our aviation must be able to operate from our rear bases, across the Alps, and over enemy territory.

Everyone agrees that the characteristics of the air arm make it the one weapon which will go into action first—immediately, in fact, perhaps even before war is formally declared. For this reason the air arm should always be ready to *mobilize* and to *deploy*. To mobilize means to move—specifically, to be able to pick up and leave peacetime locations, and with only the means at one's disposal, live and act autonomously. To deploy means to make the most opportune disposition of one's forces for action against the enemy. For an Independent Air Force, deployment is that disposition which proves most opportune in developing those aerial actions intended to be carried out unswervingly. For an auxiliary air force, it is that disposition most opportune to further auxiliary actions in relation to the deployment of the army or the disposition of the fleet.

Deployment naturally varies according to the hypothesis of war under consideration, but in each case it must be exactly determined so that each unit or command may know where to go as circumstances may require. Consequently, all units of a military aviation should always be ready for *immediate* mobilization and *immediate* transfer to the localities assigned them by the deployment, to be put into effect in accordance with a predetermined plan of war.

To be ready for immediate mobilization, an aerial unit must have in permanent possession all means necessary for autonomous living and acting during the whole period of time needed, once the disposition has been made, to establish a regular, uninterrupted flow of supplies between the air unit and the supply service in the rear. All these means may be lumped together under the term "mobilization supplies." They should include replacement parts, planes and motors, small repair units, fuel deposits, depots for materials and personnel, arms and ammunition, maps, and various other necessary equipment. There must be a constant flow of these supplies, far in excess of the amount needed for ordinary peacetime requirements. Since it is evidently necessary to be in the best condition for instant action—and therefore ready to move armed with the most efficient machines—the aerial unit should possess more planes and motors and other equipment in peacetime than are mobilized, because they must be constantly kept at top operating efficiency.

To effectuate proper disposition and to make possible other variations in the order of deployment, all the equipment of mobilization supplies not possible to transfer by air, must have some other means of transfer. In general the only possible way will be by motor transport. Therefore, an aerial unit must have not only mobilization supplies beyond peacetime needs, but also "automotive means" for transporting all of them which cannot be transferred by air. Only on these conditions can an aerial unit be speedily and effectively mobilized, deployed, and utilized in case of war.

Of necessity, the dispersion of aerial units will have to be on improvised airfields during the war, thus avoiding disaster by camouflaging them as much as possible and by being ready to change location as fast as the bases are identified by the enemy. This means the aerial units must be highly mobile and autonomous. Large permanent airfields near the front should be moved back to prevent the destruction of the materials in them.

We must realize that the problem of air power is very complex. It is not limited to production of a certain number of planes and training a certain number of operating personnel. A great many requirements must be met to make this arm, the efficacy of which may reach formidable proportions, function properly. They are all linked one with the other; and if one of them fails to be met, the air arm, if not made completely useless, would certainly lose most of its efficiency.

I have mentioned deployment according to various hypotheses of war. To say that aerial units should deploy is to state a fundamental necessity of war. But in order to satisfy this necessity in the case of a powerful aerial mass which must be put into action immediately, it is necessary above everything else to study the best disposition of all aerial units in relation to the objectives of aerial action and the deployment of land and sea forces under the circumstances of the particular war. This means determining for each aerial unit the locality to which it should be transferred, and, in view of the intensively cultivated nature of our land, predisposing the chosen terrain which can immediately be adapted as take-off and landing fields.

I have already spoken of the supply problem. To maintain air forces in efficient operation, it is necessary for supplies of all kinds to reach them during the conflict. To get an idea of the enormous amount of work entailed, we have only to remember what the last war showed; namely, that to maintain 100 first-line planes in efficient operation, it was necessary to keep 300 in reserve, and for industry to produce about 100 every month for replacement. Since in future wars aerial forces will be used much more intensively and in much greater numbers than in the last war, the supply problem will demand even more work.

The real power of an aerial force depends, then, on such a large number of coefficients that none of them can be reduced to zero; and when we wish to judge the real value of an aerial force we must take into account all the coefficients which go to make it up.

The number of planes a military aviation can put in the air means little in itself as regards the power of that aviation, because in the true military sense, flying is not an end in itself, but a means for accomplishing actions of war. Now, in order to accomplish war actions, aerial means must be: gathered into organic units; armed accordingly; trained in aerial combat; easily employed; ready for instant mobilization; and so forth—all of them harmoniously co-ordinated to meet the reality of aerial warfare.

CONCLUSION

I feel sure there cannot be anyone today who can honestly maintain that the problem of air power is of only secondary importance. More and more every day the air arm is being consolidated, its radius of action widened, and its carrying capacity increased; and the efficacy of destructive materials is constantly being raised. With our geographical and political situation, all of our land and sea territory is exposed to eventual enemy offensives of imposing dimensions operating from land bases. The Alpine arc embraces our richest and most industrious provinces, *all* of which can be reached by enemy aerial offensives operating from the opposite slopes; and the narrow seas surrounding us offer little protection from aerial attacks launched from enemy shores.

Our extremely concentrated industries, with large centers of population exposed, the ease with which our main communication lines can be broken, and the degree to which we employ hydraulic resources, all put us in a position to fear aerial offensives more than any other nation. If on the one hand the Alpine barrier gives us the power to bar the door of our house, on the other hand, because of the difficult terrain and scarce roadways, it favors an enemy effectively armed in the air and bent upon cutting off from their bases our land forces operating in the mountains.

If we consider all this seriously, we cannot but agree that the command of its own sky is an indispensable condition of Italy's safety. Nevertheless, even today anyone who tries to point out the importance of air power in future wars is called a visionary. It is admitted that the enemy can compel us to evacuate entire cities by using aerial offensives; but it is denied that this can weigh heavily in the outcome of the war—as though an army deployed in the Alps would not be affected by the evacuation of Milan, Turin, and Genoa; or as though the evacuation of a city could be compared to moving out of an apartment house. Even though it is admitted that aerial offensives can stop industrial production, it is maintained that this small inconvenience can be obviated by transferring the factories farther inland, as though all industrial plants were not compelled to intensify their production during wartime. The idea that a war could be decided by the collapse of the nation's morale is considered paradoxical, and this in spite of the fact that the World War was decided by the collapse of the moral resistance of the defeated peoples.

The armies involved in that war were only the means by which the nations of each side tried to undermine the resistance of the other; so much so that, though the defeated side was the one whose armies won the most and greatest battles, when the morale of the civilian population began to weaken, these very armies either disbanded or surrendered, and an entire fleet was turned over intact to the enemy. This disintegration of nations in the last war was indirectly brought about by the actions of the armies in the field. In the future it will be accomplished directly by the actions of aerial forces. In that lies the difference between past and future wars.

An aerial bombardment which compels the evacuation of a city of some hundreds of thousands of inhabitants will certainly have more influence on the realization of victory than a battle of the kind often fought during the last war without appreciable results. A nation which once loses the command of the air and finds itself subjected to incessant aerial attacks aimed directly at its most vital centers and without the possibility of effective retaliation, this nation, whatever its surface forces may be able to do, must arrive at the conviction that all is useless, that all hope is dead. This conviction spells defeat.

Even admitting—I by no means concede it—that the command of the air exercised with adequate forces could not defeat the enemy without regard to other circumstances, it is nevertheless indisputable that the command of the air can bring serious material and moral damage to the enemy, thereby contributing effectively to his defeat. Therefore, apart from the value that may be attributed to the command of the air, it is of paramount importance that we should dominate our sky. The primary concern of the army and navy should be to see that their own aviation conquers the command of the air; otherwise all their actions will be put in jeopardy by an enemy in command of the air.

Though military and naval forces are not yet fully aware of the value of the air arm, they do feel the necessity of protecting themselves against aerial operations. The mere fact that it is possible to fly, and by flying to accomplish war operations, must be the determining factor in modifying the methods of combat on land and sea. A single example will suffice: It is no longer possible to imagine fuel deposits in the open sky. We must therefore consider seriously the new aerial factor in itself and its influence upon military and naval forces no less than upon the total civilian resources of the country. But if we are in a position to dominate our own sky, we will automatically be in a position to dominate the Mediterranean sky as well—that is, to control the sea which must be ours if we wish to create for ourselves an imperial destiny. The Independent Air Force must become Italy's impregnable shield and the sharp sword with which to carve out her future.

At present such ideas are in the embryonic stage, but it is certain that the nation which first learns to use them in the right way will have an advantage over all others. With time and experience, the Independent Air Forces of all nations will take on a similar form, as long ago their armies and navies did. Today ingenuity may still be useful; tomorrow quality alone will count. Thanks to the native aptitude of her people, though poorer than other nations, Italy may still forge for herself an Independent Air Force capable of commanding respect from others.

I have been harping on this theme for years, and I intend to keep on harping on it, confident of doing my duty as a citizen and a soldier, and at the same time of doing a work of sound collaboration in a period when the national government intends to lead Italy toward its bright future. We possess all the necessary elements for creating a superb air power: daring pilots, resourceful technicians, large guilds of skilled artisans and craftsmen, a unique geographical situation, and a strong government which knows what it wants and how to get it done. All we need do is unite in silent, intense labor, with the firm determination to get to the top and stay there.

Aviation has already shed its primitive, or I should say sporting, character, and has now entered upon a period of serious industrial production. At the beginning its aim was simply to fly; now its purpose is to accomplish something worth while through flying—to shorten great distances in peacetime, to fight in wartime. We must enter this second period with the determination to try to do something in the air, something better than the rest of the world.

NOTE: For various reasons, nearly a year went by between the time the manuscript of this book went to the printers and its publication date. During this interval 2,000-horsepower planes were put in service by various nations, and construction of 6,000-horsepower planes was undertaken. These are the very means from which to realize the battleplane, an equal of the battleship in striking power, and the true Independent Air Force according to the concepts I have expounded in this book.

Faced by these formidable machines, powerfully armed, strongly armored, with a radius of action wide enough to cross the ocean, and each capable of destroying the nerve center of a city, is it still possible to cling to the concepts of the use of the airplane which prevailed during the World War? One hundred planes of 6,000 horsepower may cost as much as a dreadnought; but the nation which, once it has conquered the air, can maintain in operation, not 100, but 50 or even 20 such planes, will have won decisively, because it will be in a position to break up the whole social structure of the enemy in less than a week, *no matter what his army and navy may do*. In face of this state of affairs, is it possible to deny that a revolution has taken place? Is it possible to refuse to admit the truth of the affirmation which forms the basis of this book—namely, that *the command of the air is a necessary and sufficient condition of victory?*

Book Two

The Probable Aspects of The War
of The Future

Originally published as a monograph in April 1928.

Introduction

THE STUDY OF WAR, particularly the war of the future, presents some very interesting features. First is the vastness of the phenomenon which makes whole peoples hurl themselves against one another, forgetting for a time that they all wear the aspect of human beings, that they belong to the same family of humanity striving toward the same goal of ideal perfection, to become wolves and throw themselves into torment and a bloody work of destruction, as though possessed by blind folly. Next comes the impressive scale of war, which demands the assembling, ordering, and directing toward the single goal, victory, all the formidable material and moral forces of whole nations—the destructive forces to hurl against the enemy, the productive forces to turn out more destructive ones. This is an immense and varied undertaking which must still be done with foresight before the crisis, and must be integrated with fervor during the crisis, but always scientifically, so that it may yield the maximum results from the national resources poured into it. And, finally, there is what might be called the mysterious aspect of war, which, no matter how hard an individual may try to think of it as something improbable and far away, presses upon everyone, and is shrouded by a heavy veil of mystery in that it bears within it, vaguely descried, an eventuality of the future.

To prepare for war is to prepare to face this vaguely felt eventuality of the future. The preparation for war demands, then, exercise of the imagination; we are compelled to make a mental excursion into the future. A man who wants to make a good instrument must first have a precise understanding of what the instrument is to be used for; and he who intends to build a good instrument of war must first ask himself what the next war will be like. And he must try to find an answer which approximates most closely the reality of the future war, for the closer that approximation, the more suitable for dealing with the future reality will be his instrument. Research into the war of the future is not, therefore, an idle pastime. It is, rather, an ever-present practical necessity. And when we consider that such research proposes to discover the nature of the cataclysm which may come upon humanity, and that analysis of it cannot be accomplished except by exercise of the imagination within the confines of rigid logic, it becomes a fascinating study.

Defining with a larger measure of probability what the forms and characteristics of future wars will be like is not, as some lazy minds affirm, the province of the fortuneteller or the idle speculator. It is, rather, a serious problem, the solution to which must be worked out by logical progression from cause to effect.

There is a simple method of foretelling the future, simply asking of the present what it is preparing for the future, asking of the cause what its effect will be. Tomorrow is only the outgrowth of today; and the man who foretells it is like the farmer who knows what he will reap from what he sows, or the astronomer who can tell the precise instant at which the conjunction of Venus and Mars will occur.

In the period of history through which we are passing, war is undergoing a profound and radical change in character and forms, as I shall show; so that the war of the future will be very different from all wars of the past. That makes the problem even more interesting, because the war of the future will be a new and different thing. I shall try to accompany you on this excursion into the future. Our itinerary will be simple: we shall start from the past, look over the present, and from there jump into the future. We shall glance at the war of the past long enough to retrace its essential features; we shall ask of the present what it is preparing for the future; and, finally, we shall try to decide what modifications will be made in the character of war by the causes at work today in order to point out their inevitable consequences.

You will find the road easy and even. I shall not try to tell you, for I do not know how, about matters abstruse or transcendental. War is simple, like good sense. Perhaps I shall tell you things quite different from what is commonly said, but even these things will be the modest offspring of common sense.

CHAPTER I

IN THIS FIRST chapter we shall glance briefly at the World War and trace its essential features. This is an event in which we have taken part, a war which we have won—won as allies, and thrice won as Italians: the first time by breaking our bonds to the Triple Alliance and permitting France to win the Battle of the Marne; the second time by entering the war at a critical moment for the Allies; and the third time by leading the Allies on the road to triumph. This is, then, an event we should recall with pride, a memory which should make our hearts beat faster. Nevertheless, if we want to build a solid base of departure for our journey into the future, we must for the moment ignore its spiritual beauty and moral grandeur and examine it dispassionately, as a surgeon dispassionately dissects a nameless corpse to question it about the mysteries of life without letting himself be moved by thoughts of the life that once pulsed in it.

The World War was a colossal tragedy, with the whole world for its theater and humanity for its protagonist. To retrace the course of its action, we must betake ourselves to a high point of observation and look at it through the reverse end of binoculars, counting off time with the small hand of our watch, ticking off months instead of hours. If we do this, we see immediately that the World War displayed a character different from any preceding war, a character which I shall call social. Past wars were larger or smaller conflicts between more or less imposing armed forces. In those days, as an *ultimo ratio,* nations delegated, by tacit conventional accord, the solution of their conflicts to special groups organized and destined for that end.[1] The outcome of clashes be-

[1] The professional armies of the past, often mercenaries.—Tr.

tween such groups on land and sea was accepted by the nations concerned, and they resigned themselves to bear the consequences. A single battle between a few thousand men was often enough to decide the destiny of entire peoples for long periods of time.

The heads of nations used to draw from the people the material for their armed forces, and with these they would play their big game of war, the stake of which was often the destiny of the people themselves. The game of arms won or lost, the matter was settled until it was renewed by fresh troops. Only these troops, a small part of the whole strength of the peoples involved, sometimes a very small part indeed, counted in the decision of those conflicts. The majority of the people remained aloof, almost oblivious, if not completely indifferent to the whole thing. In short, these heads of nations were playing for their own fortunes and the fortunes of their peoples with special pawns, called armies and navies, moving them over special gambling tables called theaters of war. The outcome of those conflicts were therefore dependent upon the number and quality of the pawns and the ability of the players. Hence the "art of war," which consisted in a set of rules and standards for playing the game, a codification of the best methods for: arranging the pawns—organization; moving them —strategy and logistics; striking with them—tactics; rules and standards, the more or less brilliant application of which made the fame of great captains.

The principal rules of this game—those fundamental, intuitive, so-called basic principles—remained unchanged, because the players were always alike and the game always the same, even though the forms of the pawns changed. But even if the main principles did not change, their application in specific cases depended on the player; and great captains were only clever and lucky players who found themselves confronted by inferior players, and therefore won the stakes even when they held less in their hands than the enemy did. And they were essentially players who could cut free of tradition and revitalize old and obsolete methods of playing the game. In fact, the great captains were men with the psychology of great gamblers. They had confidence in their own luck, audacity at the right moment, intuitive understanding of the enemy's play, ability to bluff, the art of trickery and surprise, and absolute faith in their last card.

This explains events in history which otherwise seem absurd. It explains, for example, the phenomenon of Napoleon carrying his eagles through Europe with only a handful of men. But the people, especially in the period just prior to the World War, began to realize their power and almost unconsciously came to feel that it was absurd to let their fate hang upon the outcome of a conflict fought by only a part of their total strength. When two men or two animals fight to the death, they throw all their strength into the struggle. They have a single aim, to win. Once the peoples of nations became aware of their individualities, the same thing was bound to happen in a struggle between nations. All their strength and resources were bound to be entered in the game. All saving is vain for him who is about to die.

Universal conscription had increased the bulk of the armed forces, but that was not enough; there were other formidable resources at the disposal of the people, and all these, too, had to be entered in the game. Thus the World War had to, as it did, assume the character of a titanic struggle for life and death between two coalitions of peoples armed with all their energies, all their resources, all their faith.

In the World War, then, the pawns in the game were the people themselves, with all their spiritual and material wealth. The armed forces were only one of the manifestations of the power of the peoples involved in the struggle. In preceding wars the armed forces had been the sole agents in the conflict; in the World War the agents were the people themselves, and the armed forces were merely the means they used and remained firmly in their hands as long as they themselves remained firm. But when, as in the case of Germany, the people began to give, an army still strong and disciplined gave up and an entire fleet was surrendered intact to the enemy.

The decision of such a war could not be based on the outcome of a game of pawns moved over a board by more or less clever captains; it could not be decided by a purely military fact or series of facts. Groups of highly civilized people, millions and millions of conscientious men, could not possibly delegate the decision as to their own future, nor allow their destiny to hang upon the more or less dashing move of a *condottiere* or to the heroism of an armed mass. Inevitably the two groups of nations had to enter the conflict directly, throwing themselves into the vortex with reckless abandon; and neither group could have resigned themselves to acknowledge defeat except as a consequence of complete general collapse. And this collapse could not have happened except by a long and onerous process of disintegration, moral and material, of an essential nature—a process which came about almost independently of the purely military conduct of the war.

This explains why the side which won the most military victories was the side which was defeated. This explains the length of the war, because it was necessary to beat a group of nations, not merely a group of armies. In short, this explains the conditions in which both victor and vanquished found themselves after the war.

When wars were decided by armed forces alone—that is, by only a small part of the resources of nations—all those resources which were not put into the game remained untouched in the case of both victor and vanquished. The effects of the war were relative, hardly felt by the people, simply the exaction of tribute from the vanquished with which to begin the game all over again. But the World War exhausted the resources of all the people involved in it; as a consequence of its having been decided by the complete disintegration of all the forces of one side under the pressure of all the forces of the other side, the victors were left prostrate and the vanquished stripped of everything. The conquered nations were wrecked, as though struck by a hurricane. The victorious ones were exhausted by the supreme effort they had put forth and found it impossible to recoup their losses from their fallen enemies.

Looking through our reversed telescope, we today can perceive this social character of that war and recognize its consequences. It would have been useful to have seen it first, as the inevitable effect of existing causes. Nor would it have been difficult to see it first. As proof of that I take the liberty of including a few excerpts from an article which appeared in the *Gazzetta del Popolo* of Turin in the issue of August 11, 1914, entitled, "Who Will Win?"

To say today what will be the outcome of this gigantic war seems a daring thing to do, but it is not. The elements of this formidable struggle are well known in their larger outlines, because they are made up of all the material and moral powers of the nations involved. Nations today no longer entrust their destiny to an army which, once beaten, leaves the nation beaten. Today the struggle is larger in scope and more complex—a struggle between nations rather than armies. In such a struggle, a victory or a series of victories in the field is not enough to decide the outcome; more important is the strength of the nations concerned to resist.

If we were to make any prognostications, on the basis of the strength and disposition of armies, on their probable actions, on the major or minor preparations of the General Staffs, we would be committing a gross error because we would be ignoring the real clashing agents, the nations themselves, whose armies are but exponents in the struggle. It is not a case of the Franco-Russian armies arrayed against the Austro-German armies; rather, it is France, Russia, and England arrayed against Austria and Germany. The difference is enormous.

In so gigantic a struggle the idea of gaining advantage by action through interior lines by the Austro-German armies is a dream destined to come to nothing. Sooner or later, inevitably, the Central Powers will find they have on their hands all of France, all of Russia, all of England; and the victory will go to the side which knows how to bring to the fight the greater resistance of means, of energy, of faith. With their seaports closed to them, with their land borders surrounded by enemies fighting for their very existence, Germany and Austria are locked in as though by an iron ring. They are like a couple of wild boars cornered in their den by a pack of baying hounds, who make wild rushes now to one side, now to the other, widening the ring around them on one side while it tightens on the other; and the threat of the hounds grows more fiercely insistent until the boars fall exhausted and are mangled while the forest rings with triumphal howls as the bleeding hounds prepare for their banquet.

In this article, written during the first week of the World War, is a forecast of that war which shows it would not have been difficult to foresee its essential character. That did not happen; the governments involved were unable to see what was bound to be the character of the war about to begin.

Today it seems impossible to believe that the idea of *Deutsch-*

land über alles could have taken root in the minds of a group of cultivated, intelligent men, such as the German General Staff no doubt was, simply from the execution of a mere military maneuver, no matter how clever; and it seems even more incredible that the men governing Germany, outside of the military element, could have taken in such an idea and made it theirs. And yet so it was.

This absurdity was given strength because other absurdities had been at work for a long time. As a matter of fact, though the tendency was increasingly toward total war—that is, in interesting an evergrowing number of citizens—an increasingly sharper distinction between political power and military power was drawn. When the heads of the government ruled their people, the two powers overlapped; but with the transformation of governments into agents representing the will of the people, a kind of incompatibility between political power and military power grew up. The more war came to interest civilians through a process of natural evolution, the more the civilians left all matters pertaining to war in the hands of a special category of people, to whom military matters were entrusted with absolute unquestioning faith. A wall was erected between the civil and the military, a wall which cut off all relations between them and shut them away from each other's view. And because the people on the inside of the wall were engaged in something which seemed mysterious to profane eyes, those on the outside considered that something beyond their comprehension and bowed to it with a respect almost religious.

Any judgment pronounced from within that enclosure came to be accepted as indisputable; and at the outbreak of the crisis the fate of the nation was put completely in the hands of men competent only by definition, who had remained out of touch with the living, acting, operating nation. Political power ceased to function upon the declaration of war, delegating to the military power the task of waging the war while the political sat by the window looking on. The military power on its own part tended to limit the activities of the political and enlarge the field of its own activities. The government, by definition incompetent in military matters, had the power to appoint and dismiss Supreme

Commanders. Now, appointment and dismissal implies a judgment; and such judgment was the judgment of an incompetent upon whom rested the responsibility of the war. Obviously, the nations had to pay the price for this strange dance of competence and incompetence by definition.

This state of affairs still exists in many states. In Italy the wisdom of the Chief of State put an end to it. The chief of the government is also the chief of the armed forces, having supreme control over preparations for war and, if need be, supreme direction of its conduct.

The most important effect of this incomprehension of the character of the conflict was the war itself. Having taken into consideration only the military angle and being confident of the excellence of its plans and the preparation of the forces at its disposal, the German General Staff had concluded that a decisive victory could be gained quickly and at relatively low cost. But this conviction was based upon a wrong evaluation of the situation; yet it was accepted in political circles without careful examination because it had come from the organ competent by definition, the General Staff. Had the shrewd men who governed Germany not been dazzled by the high reputation the General Staff enjoyed, had they examined the reality of the problems involved, very likely they would have gained clearer insight into the situation, the unlikelihood of victory, and the prodigious cost of the game. And perhaps they would have refrained from throwing the dice.

The war on land can be divided into two periods: the first from the beginning to the Battle of the Marne; the second from the subsequent establishment of the continuous front to the end of the war. The first period, very short compared to the second, was a period of adjustment, and on the face of it presented an aspect almost similar to that of preceding wars. I say "almost similar" because it was a war of movement, and I say "on the face of it" because the clashes which characterized it were not decisive and led only to the formation of the continuous front, which was destined to become the essential form of the World War for the duration.

The German war plans were strategically unassailable, above all from a classical point of view. They were reminiscent of Napoleon and were based on the famous maneuver over interior lines. One who finds himself in a central position, by utilizing its advantages can strike at one or more of his adversaries in succession on the periphery. Of course, in order to succeed he must decisively defeat one of them before the others pounce upon him, or he will find himself encircled. In the case of the Germans, they had to defeat the French Army before the Russians could throw their whole weight into the action. Therefore, with their powerful, well-organized army, they launched a speedy, resolute offensive against the French. To get through quickly, they avoided a frontal attack by turning the French left wing. That made it necessary to pass through Belgium, but they did not hesitate, as strategy made it imperative. They knew that violation of Belgium would draw England into the war, but they relied on the unpreparedness of the English Army. The strategical advantage gained by turning the French left wing to reach Paris quickly was considered to overbalance the entry of Belgium and England into the war. Once the French Army had been beaten, they would have had plenty of time to beat the Russians and whatever forces the English could raise in the meantime. Thus the German General Staff, not fully realizing the situation and regarding the war as the traditional chess game on the battlefield, put its classical plans into effect and did not hesitate to draw England, with all her might, into the war against Germany. The German Government followed the lead of the General Staff and declared that treaties were scraps of paper.

The war plans of the French General Staff, based on the same theories, were simple and aggressive, independent of the plans of the enemy and the size of his forces. It would be difficult to imagine a simpler strategy than that which France followed, for it can be condensed into these few words: "Forward, and trust in victory!" No one in the nineteenth century, the century of positivism, would have thought of trusting the safety of the nation to such a naïve theory. But the French General Staff, certainly with a high sense of patriotism, but closed within itself, living

apart from present reality and influenced by an almost mystic
ideology, conceived and attempted to execute just such a naïve
plan until it gave way before the brutal impact of events.

In fact, the French Army was deployed all the way from the
Belgian to the Swiss frontiers, with a reserve army behind its center; and it was instructed to pounce on the enemy and overwhelm
him before he could execute any maneuver at all. As soon as it
was deployed, the French Army was supposed to attack with all
its forces on both wings simultaneously. Undoubtedly the French
General Staff knew of Germany's intention of turning its left
wing, but it gave little thought to this possible danger. In case
the Germans passed through Belgium, the French left wing was
supposed merely to extend itself still more toward the northwest.
That was all.

But the war began, the French attack petered out after a few
inconclusive initial successes, the German right wing overwhelmed
the scant French forces which opposed it, and on September 2 the
French General Staff ordered a 100-kilometer retreat, while
Millerand asked the Council of Ministers to declare Paris an open
city. But God had not chosen to punish France so severely. The
Battle of the Marne came and the subsequent rush by both sides
to the Channel ports, which led to the establishment of the continuous front.

From that moment on the war assumed its predominantly static
character, which lasted until the end; and it is from that moment
that the true conflict among the nations dates. Everything which
could have made this war like preceding ones, every traditional
war move of the past, disappeared.

On the contact lines, anchored to insurmountable natural or
political obstacles, trenches were dug, parapets raised, barbed-
wire entanglements constructed; men, rifles, cannon, and machine
guns were distributed along their length; and the game of trying
to push back the enemy began, now on one side, now on the
other; now here, now there. It was no longer war in the traditional
meaning of the word. Rather, it was a single endless battle extending along hundreds and hundreds of kilometers. Its intensity
alternately flared and died down along various sectors of its long

front; it lasted for years, during which its continuous front lines were never really broken, because as soon as a break occurred anywhere, the severed ends promptly united again along a different line ahead or behind.

It was a static war, not a war of armies which fight each other. It was a war of nations besieging each other. It was like two wrestlers who, instead of getting holds and trying to pin each other down, stand shoulder to shoulder and strain at each other, each patiently waiting for the other to collapse from nervous prostration induced by the constant muscular and nervous strain. It was a struggle without precedents, with an entirely new aspect, a struggle which puts to shame all the traditional classical rules of war.

Maneuvering was out of the question; you cannot maneuver against the Wall of China. Strategy was useless; for strategy is the art of deploying masses of men on the battlefield, but in this war the masses of men were already there facing each other and rigidly deployed. Tactics, the art of choosing one's own ground of attack or defense, was useless too, because in this war there was no choosing of ground; there was only one field, and no one could change it. There was no more use for the art of war because potential forces could not be brought into play; all the material forces were already on the spot. It was a war in which the most brutal carnage went on unendingly; it was simply a war of killing and destroying as much as possible.

The establishment of the continuous front was a surprise to everyone. It was in direct opposition to all current theories and the habits of thought of all the General Staffs. There had been previous instances in history of defensive actions attempted by establishing a solid line of defense, but always the attacker had massed his forces and broken through it easily. The idea was considered heresy—and so it would have been called by the very wooden benches in all the war colleges in the world—that an attacker had to deploy his mass of men along a solid line opposite the solid defensive line of the enemy. But now the past had been left behind. The two lines sat opposite each other and did nothing but hammer at each other.

Something even stranger happened. Other nations entered the war, and immediately their armies took places along similiar continuous lines, always along the longest line possible. We ourselves on May 25, 1915, deployed our army along an uninterrupted line from the Stelvio to the sea, and we found the Austrians facing us along an uninterrupted line from the sea to the Stelvio. Not one of the General Staffs had foreseen such a form of war, and so they were all surprised by it and tried to react, but uselessly; for the continuous front was the brutal, threatening, unalterable reality.

What were the causes of this strange, widespread phenomenon? This phenomenon, which had appeared in spite of the men who directed the war, naturally must have been caused by something of a general character, present everywhere, and not to be removed by the will of men alone.

That cause was purely and simply *the formidable efficacy of firearms, especially small-caliber ones.* And the reason is that *any increase in the efficacy of firearms, especially small-caliber ones, increases the value of the defensive.* If I am in a trench and I have a gun which fires one shot a minute, at the most I can stop only one attacker coming at me from one minute's distance. If two enemies attack me at the same time, I can stop one of them but not the other. But if my gun fires 100 shots a minute, I can stop 100 attackers coming at me from one minute's distance; therefore, my attackers must number 101 so that at least one of them can reach me. In the first case, I, on the defensive, can checkmate one attacker; but in the second case I can checkmate 100. And nothing in the situation has changed except the efficacy of my gun.

If in both cases I put up on the field enough barbed-wire entanglement to slow the attacker down so it takes him 5 minutes to cross the field, in the first case I can stop 5 attackers, and in the second case 500. Nothing has changed but the efficacy of the gun; but indirectly this efficacy is changed in value by the barbed-wire entanglement, as in the first case it allows me to checkmate 4 more attackers than I could without it, and in the second case 400 more.

These considerations give great importance to defensive systems; that is, the means suitable for protecting one's own arms—

the trenches—and the means suitable for slowing down the enemy's advance in the immediate vicinities of the trenches—barbed-wire entanglements and other such devices—because they make it possible for small forces to checkmate forces far larger. Therefore, all improvements in firearms favor the defensive and make the offensive pay a heavier price, for the offensive must be carried out with a preponderance of strength.

In actual practice the increase in value of the defensive became immediately and impressively clear. The most violent attacks were easily stopped by smaller entrenched forces, even if the trenches and entanglements were improvised. That led to the crystallization of the lines, because both sides were unable to break through once they came in contact and had to stop and dig in. After the Battle of the Marne and the rush to the Channel ports, the two lines underwent the crystallizing process by sectors all the way to the North Sea. The value acquired by the defensive allowed the lines to be thinned till they stretched unbroken from Switzerland to the sea, because even when they were thinned out they were still impregnable, thanks to the superior strength of the defensive.

Nothing of the kind could have happened if guns had still been the old muzzle-loading kind. But everybody on both sides had rapid-fire arms, and no human will could have made them go back to the traditional methods of waging war, based on muzzle-loading guns of the past.

No one, with the possible exception of the Germans, had foreseen any such phenomenon. On the contrary, the opposite belief was prevalent everywhere—that is, the belief that the improvements in firearms would favor the offensive. This concept was openly expressed in official documents and instruction manuals of the time. Why was this technical error made, an error bound to have such serious consequences? It is hard to say why, but certainly it can be said that it must have come from some kind of collective suggestion. The War of 1870 had been thoroughly studied for the lessons to be learned from it—it is traditional to draw instruction from preceding wars. In 1870 the Germans had been constantly on the offensive, and they had always won. Therefore, it was deduced that they had always won because they had been always on the offensive, and the fact was ignored that they could keep on the offensive because they were stronger. Going a step further, it was declared that the offensive was the right recipe for victory. Therefore, the military mind turned whole-heartedly to the offensive, always the offensive at any cost. In France a trend of thought which gained a good deal of ground at the time went so far as to advocate that a commander should concentrate everything on the offensive to such an extent that he should not even bother to try to get information about the enemy.

In peacetime maneuvers the offensive was always successful, because no umpire would have dreamed of daring to give any credit to the defensive. The idea that the defensive, though never decisive, might be of help in gaining time and mustering strength, was completely disregarded, and the thing was carried so far that some armies did not even mention the word defense in their manuals of tactical instruction. It is no wonder that such a habit of mind made it impossible to realize that the increase in the efficacy of firearms increased the value of the defensive more than the offensive. Instead, the increased efficacy of firearms was seen as an increase in offensive potentiality, perhaps owing to the idea that a gun which fires 100 shots a minute offends more than one which fires only one shot.

The spontaneous and unexpected rise of the continuous front, the surprising revelation of the efficacy of the defensive, and the failure of the prevailing rules of war, caused a serious disorientation. The boldest, best trained, most enthusiastic troops were stopped on the barbed wire by the rapid fire of rifles and machine guns. Attacks were repeated, always with the same results. It ended with the attackers exhausting themselves while the defenders remained in position or retreated, and the struggle would die down and wait for a renewal. Abel Ferry, deputy from the Vosges, took part in the war as an infantry lieutenant, as Under-Secretary of State, and as a member of the Army Commission, and died on the battlefield on September 25, 1918. Twenty-two months after the beginning of the war, he wrote:

Only one who has taken part in this war can realize how deeply ignorant was the French General Staff of the character of the war, of machine-gun fire power, of the value of barbed wire, and of the necessity for heavy artillery. Our General Staff, having a high sense of moral duty and great personal virtues, worked very hard to prepare for the war—but unfortunately in the wrong direction. Our General Staff officers had made themselves experts in the Napoleonic war, but ignored the function of economic, industrial, and political forces; they were not experts in the modern war between nations. The trench war, made up chiefly of small details, had not been foreseen nor studied. The great General Staffs know nothing about it yet; they have not lived it, and they have not led it. The experience has not yet permeated from the lower ranks to the top.

When all plans of strategy had failed, when one wall had been erected facing another wall, the struggle became diffused and unco-ordinated. Since no strategical results could be gained even at the cost of heavy sacrifices, the contending armies had to resign themselves to tactical results. And because these tactical results were also very costly, they came to have a great importance. Since by paying the price one could gain tactical results anywhere, tactical actions were the rule all along the line. During the favorable season, after a good stock of men and munitions had been laid in, actions on a large scale were periodically attempted, actions which would turn out to be very expensive in men and matériel, and the results at best would be measured only by an indentation in the enemy's lines. After a long series of this kind of action, the battle line grew fantastically twisted and bizarre, not because of any strategical or tactical requirement, but according to the points where the various ineffectual offensives of both sides happened to stop. Only very occasionally was a deep break made through the front, and even then the front lines were somehow always re-established. In reality, though very costly actions—perhaps more costly than in any other war in the past—often took place, each of them was only an episode in the single battle which continued without any let-up from the Battle of the Marne to final victory.

The offensive action is always more expensive than the defensive, until it succeeds in overwhelming the defense. After conquering, the offensive reaps the fruits of its labor in large measure. But the offensive is a net loss when it is stopped before it reaches its objective, because then it costs the attacker more than the defender. This fact was not unobserved. But as the idea of the offensive for the offensive's sake, it brought into being the French theory of the *grignotage*.[2]

This theory was based on the premise that the Allies had a great numerical preponderance over the Central Powers, and the reasoning went: It is true that every offensive costs us more than it does the enemy; but since the enemy has less man power than we have, in the end we will exhaust him even if in the meantime we have to suffer more serious losses than he does. This theory bankrupted the art of war and seriously jeopardized the final victory, because after the Russians collapsed, the Allies no longer had numerical preponderance, and the great losses they had suffered had already had a demoralizing effect on the Allied armies on the Western Front.

In July 1916 Abel Ferry sent to the members of the Viviani Cabinet a memorandum on the Woëvre operation, in which he said:

The war of attrition, besides being a patent acknowledgment of strategical impotence, besides leading to a devastated France in the future, is a journalistic formula, not a military one; and after all, that kind of war is a war against ourselves. When I rejoined my regiment on March 18, it was animated by heroic folly. Of my company 250 men went to the attack; only 29 returned. The same thing happened to the 8th Company. In the German trench, first taken, then lost, they found only one German killed. On the twenty-seventh we attacked again, and again we were checkmated. On the fifth, the sixth, the twelfth of April we attacked again. Captain X, glorious defender of Fort Tryon, went so far as to go out of the trenches alone to get killed. This brave regiment has now lost all its offensive strength, and at best is fit only to stay in the trenches. I could say the same of twenty other regiments I know.

They claim that to fire human grapeshot at the enemy, without preparation, gives us a moral ascendancy. But the thousands of dead Frenchmen lying in front of the German trenches are instead those who are giving moral ascendancy to our enemy. If this waste of human material keeps on, the day is not far off when the offensive capacity of our army, already seriously weakened, will be completely destroyed.

2 Gnawing or nibbling away, as a rat gnaws or nibbles.

Outside of the great offensives, for which all sacrifices are justified, these small local attacks, good only for the sake of the daily communiqué, have meant from 300,000 to 400,000 men uselessly lost. During last December the attacks against the Hartmann Willerkopf alone cost us 15,000 men without gaining one meter of trenches.

And in May 1917, after the famous Nivelle offensive, which cost France so much blood without result, Ferry, as relator of the Army Commission, ended his report as follows:

The tragic hour has struck. The morale of France has been seriously injured. Some soldiers on vacation have been heard shouting: "Long live peace!" These are the fruits which we are reaping from the systems of war followed during these last three years. The French Government has not defended the lives of French soldiers from the thoughtless policies of the High Command.

The hour was indeed tragic, not only for France but for all the Allies. Pétain, who came after Nivelle, sensing a collapse of Russia in the near future, inaugurated a new policy of avoiding useless offensive actions in order to save lives and improve the morale of the army and the nation itself. But during all the summer and fall of 1917, the English launched a series of offensives at a cost of more than 400,000 men, losses which they could not replace. And therefore, during the second half of 1917, when the Russian Armistice was signed, the Allies were short of men and low in morale. A balance was re-established only when American troops began to march along the roads of France.

The closing period of the war was characterized by a radical change in methods and policies. The Allies realized they had to husband their forces and gain time until American reinforcements could be made available and fully trained. The Germans realized that the issue must be decided as soon as possible, before American help, with all the strength back of it, should weigh in the balance. Besides, reversing their previous attrition theory, the Allies realized it would be better to leave the offensive to the enemy until he exhausted himself, then go on to counteroffensive. From that point on the conduct of the war led to victory.

Retaining the initiative does not necessarily mean having the freedom to attack at will; it may also mean having the freedom to let the enemy attack when it seems more profitable. This was the rational, economical method the Allies should have adopted at the outbreak of the war; and they would have done it if their minds had not been dazzled by the myth of the offensive. The Allies had been caught unprepared, not only for war, but also for full comprehension of its realities. They should have played for time to increase and bring into play their latent strength, to make up the preponderance in men and materials necessitated by the increased value of defensive action. They should have avoided any useless effort, for time was their best ally and their enemy's worst foe. One should always do the opposite of what suits the enemy, so they should have tried to put off the decision until they had ready all the means needed to make it in their favor. This is what they should have done at the beginning, instead of plunging in like a bull after a red cloth waved by the enemy.

If the Central Powers had taken the offensive during this period of waiting, so much the better; they would have exhausted themselves more quickly. Instead of hurling men and munitions against the enemy at periodic intervals as they became available, without appreciable results, it would have been better for them to make their lines impregnable, then mass behind them formidable forces which would have had potential weight until the day when they could be effectively utilized in action.

The great waste of man power, not always justified, besides being an error in itself, also proved to be a serious political disadvantage for the Allies, because they were compelled to acknowledge that it was American help which turned the scale in their favor. This led to the dominant place of the United States in the peace treaty and afterward.

This fleeting glance at land operations during the World War has enabled us to note the essential characteristics of them. It was a struggle of nations, who plunged into the war with all their strength, trying to shatter each other by attrition, pitting one army against the other in positions they could not move from because of the greatly increased value of the defensive, a new value given by the efficacy of small-caliber firearms. We have also seen how the wrong evaluation of a technical factor—the improved small-caliber firearms—made the armies take the field morally and materially unprepared for the kind of war they would have to wage. In fact, everything had to be changed and much had to be made over during the course of the crisis. Civilian mobilization took place slowly. In England military conscription was debated bitterly and at length; and the program for rapid-fire heavy artillery was adopted by the French General Staff only on May 30, 1916, after twenty-two months of war. The inability during the period just before the war to answer the question of what the war would be like in the near future, jeopardized the successful outcome of it, lengthened the war, and made victory more costly.

It was the fault of systems, not of men. Considering the conditions under which they had to act, men did everything humanly possible, spurred on by ardent patriotism and burning faith. We should salute them reverently.

But even war has economic needs which cannot be disregarded. Even victory is a purpose, a maximum result which must be attained with a minimum of means. In this case the means is the blood of citizens and the purpose the saving of the country. War is all-inclusive, and no one can be allowed to dissociate himself from it and take no part in it. During the era of her greatest splendor, Rome drew her best soldiers from her prominent citizens, all of whom were passionately interested in the art of war. After being initiated into politics, law, public administration, philosophy, oratory—in short, after having known and lived Roman public life, young Romans tried to get military commissions to earn fame and renown, after which they resumed their political and administrative careers. Caesar did not have to go through a military career to become a great captain; he used the natural abilities which had brought him success in politics. His genius, lively intelligence, sure intuition, adaptability, firm will—all contributed to the military fame he earned.

It was true then, and it will be true tomorrow, that the leader of a nation at war must not limit himself to military matters, but interest himself in the manifold life of his nation and others. In other words, he must really be a leader.

If in looking at the past we can see what errors we have committed, errors for which we must share the guilt, we can feel more pride in the victory we won, because then we had to conquer ourselves as well as the enemy. This is the reason why I, who bear the undeserved reputation of being hypercritical, conceived the idea of glorifying the Unknown Soldier as the sacred symbol of our magnificent people, who were victorious over all.

CHAPTER II

IN THE LAST chapter we briefly examined the land aspect of the World War, its outstanding characteristics and the consequences of an error in evaluating a technical factor. In this chapter we shall consider the sea aspect of the war, and there we shall find that another technical factor, this one peculiar to the sea, was wrongly evaluated, a mistake which entailed almost exactly similar consequences.

Admiral Lord St. Vincent once attacked Prime Minister Pitt in the House of Lords because he seemed in favor of encouraging experiments with the torpedo and submarine. He told the Prime Minister: "I think you are the biggest fool that ever lived if you are in favor of an instrument of war which we who dominate the sea do not need at all, and which if successful will take that domination from us."

Well, the great English Prime Minister was certainly not a fool; but neither was Lord St. Vincent a false prophet. That instrument was perfected, and after almost a century took away the dominion of the seas from the English. In spite of the improvements of the submarine arm during the 110 years which had passed since Fulton with his *Nautilus* and his torpedo for the first time in history blew up a ship, the brig *Dorothea,* the technicians of the English Navy did not realize the truth of Lord St. Vincent's words. Therefore, the German submarine war caught them by surprise and found the English Navy totally unprepared.

During that long span of time some people with imagination had foreseen and tried to call attention to the possibilities of the submarine arm for war; but it did no good. Wells, the English novelist, foresaw the submarine war completely; but because he was a novelist, and a writer of fantasy besides, serious people could not take him seriously. Shortly before the war, the English Admiral Sir Percy Scott, famous innovator in firing tactics for naval artillery and an expert on guns and armor, wrote:

Given the actual power of the submarine, battleships have become useless for offense as well as defense; and therefore to keep on building them would be a waste of the money citizens contribute to the defense of the Empire.

But even Sir Percy Scott's opinion was sunk by a barrage of criticism from the upholders of the ultra-superdreadnought. During the English naval maneuvers of 1913 a submarine attacked the Admiral's ship six times in a row, and six times the imprudent submarine commander received the following acknowledgment from the Admiral: "Go to hell!"

Admiral Sims of the American Navy wrote:

Until the great war, the opinion held about submarines by most admirals and naval captains was that they were wonderful toys, good for spectacular feats, but only in carefully selected localities and under good weather and sea conditions.

Competent naval circles declared that the submarine could operate only by daylight and with favorable weather, that it was useless in fog, that it had to rise to the surface to fire torpedoes, that its interior was unfit for human life, so that crews had to be changed every week or so, that it had no probability of success on the high seas, that it needed mother-ships in order to operate, and several other such objections. All this despite the fact that the submarine was already a tangible reality!

These strange prejudices were not dispelled even by the sinking of the *Hague, Cressy,* and *Aboukir,* because, it was claimed, these three cruisers had been sunk under circumstances exceptionally favorable to submarines, while navigating inside a narrow stretch of sea. Only after the sinking of the *Audacious* on the northwest coast of Ireland, several hundred miles from the nearest German base, did the possibilities of the new arm begin to be realized.

The German submarines [wrote Admiral Sir Percy Scott] deprived the English ships of their freedom of movement, as on account of them no big ships dared to go out of a naval base without being protected by an escort of torpedo boats and destroyers; they prevented the Great Fleet from bombarding the German ports; they sank 100,000 tons of our warships; compelled us to keep as far away as we could from enemy shores; compelled the Fleet to go to Bermuda in order to carry on fire drills, and to hide ships which were sent against the Dardanelles inside the Bay of Mudros, except those that were sunk during that expedition. In other words, they greatly impaired the fighting potentiality of the greatest war fleet in the world, which for the first time in its long history felt itself incapable of safeguarding England.

The toy had turned out to be a formidable weapon after all. Lord St. Vincent's prophecy had come true, and England had lost the undisputed command of the sea. In fact, during the spring of 1917, when the submarine warfare was at its height, English naval circles and the English Government began to feel that the war might be lost because of the submarine action. About the beginning of April in the same year, a meeting between Admiral Sims of the American Navy and Admiral Jellicoe, First Lord of the Admiralty, concluded with this exchange of opinions:

"It seems to me the Germans are winning the war," said Admiral Sims.

"They certainly will if we don't succeed in stopping these losses, and at once," answered Admiral Jellicoe.

"Isn't there any solution to the problem?" asked Sims.

"None that I know of, for the present at least," answered Jellicoe.

This exchange gives an idea of the seriousness of the submarine warfare, the more so as the United States entered the war at just about that time. The great English Navy, undisputed mistress of the seas, in spite of having the French and Italian navies at her side and also being able to rely on help from America, was already sensing defeat by submarine action. That moment marks the loss of England's naval supremacy, the victory she gained afterward notwithstanding.

The German submarine warfare did not win its objectives, for these reasons:

1. The Allies were able to oppose to the destructive action of

the submarines the shipbuilding production of the rest of the world in addition to their own.

2. The Germans themselves did not realize fully and at the right time the value of the submarine arm. If they had had a true idea of the value of the submarine, they would have allocated to this arm part of the money they spent to create the great surface fleet which proved almost useless; and they would have begun the submarine warfare right away at the beginning of the war, and with a number of submarines which would have enabled them to prosecute it successfully. When we stop to think that by the middle of 1917, when the submarine warfare was at its height, the number of German submarines in English waters was never more than 35, we can get some idea of the importance of this arm.

3. The Germans hesitated to launch their all-out submarine campaign until January 1917; they lost time in vain discussions between military and political authorities, military and naval staffs, and kept on hesitating even after they did begin it. In other words, they were half-hearted about it, which is always the worst way of all, especially in war.

These delays gave the Allies time to devise more or less suitable defensive means, but did not allow Germany enough time to get ready and build enough new submarines. When at last the partisans of the all-out submarine warfare had their way in Germany, it was already too late. Building of new submarines was begun, but the needed raw materials and skilled labor had grown scarce. Toward the end of 1917—this will prove that there was little or no co-operation between the German General Staff and the navy—the General Staff refused to release to the navy 2,000 skilled workmen then serving in the army. Even crews were hard to find because of the demoralization engendered by the long enforced inactivity of the German Fleet. In spite of this the History Section of the French Navy General Staff stated:

We would have lost the war if the Germans had not delayed in launching their all-out submarine warfare, and if the extraordinary courage of their commanders and crews had not been offset by the doubts and scruples entertained by the Kaiser and his Chancellor.

It can therefore be concluded that the Allies won the war partly on their own merit and partly because of the Germans; that failure of both sides to realize the realities of naval warfare lost the war for the Germans and endangered it for the Allies.

America's entry into the war—April 7, 1917—was probably owing to the fact that prospects for a German victory were brightest just at that time, a victory which would have meant not only the doom of the Allies, but also great danger to America. Thus the United States came to have a predominant position even in naval affairs, since they could claim with some truth that their entry into the war tipped the scale, even in the naval field, in favor of the Allies. It was therefore impossible for the United States to acquiesce in her naval inferiority to England. It can be said that a naval race between the United States and England began as soon as the American Fleet was put side by side with the English Fleet.

Admiral Sheer has written:

Until now few nations have been able to afford the luxury of having big ships which would have enabled them to rule the seas; but now the submarine has upset this situation and *the dread of the English Navy* as a compelling political argument has disappeared.

That is the reason why the richest nations, those who can afford big ships to be used as compelling political arguments, have a decided dislike for submarines and declare, shuddering with self-righteous horror the while, that they are inhuman.

The naval aspect of the World War took on a special characteristic which at times has been wrongly interpreted. To a superficial observer it may seem that the navy's functions had been limited to attacking enemy traffic and defending its own. A few naval clashes took place, it is true; but they were limited in scope and therefore indecisive. This leads some people, perhaps too many of them, to say that the navy's essential purpose in the future will be simply defense of its own traffic and attack on the enemy's. Magazines and newspapers carry more or less serious articles along these lines.

But this impression is completely false and may lead to serious errors. The naval struggle during the World War was carried on under exceptional conditions. The preponderance of the Allied fleets over the enemy's and their excellent geographical and strategical positions constituted such great advantages that the navies of the Central Powers thought themselves defeated before the fight began. Unwilling to commit suicide, they shut themselves inside their fortified bases, made impregnable by their own submarines, and lay there in ambush waiting for an opportunity, which could only come to them as a result of some mistake on the part of the Allies. The Central Powers gave up their sea traffic of their own accord and laid up their cargo ships in their own ports or had them interned in neutral harbors. In actual fact, the Allied navies were not confronted by enemy navies; yet they had to keep constantly on the alert and keep a strict watch on fleets which were out of their reach, bottled up of their own accord; and they had to do this for the whole time of the war, always hoping to catch them if they came out. For them it was not a question of attacking enemy traffic, for enemy traffic did not exist. The enemy had willingly given it up. Their task was to defend their own traffic from ambush by submarines.

Therefore, there was no naval warfare in the true sense of the term. The English Fleet acted *potentially,* inasmuch as her *potential capacity for action* compelled the enemy to shut up its naval forces and give up its sea-borne traffic without even waiting for this *potential* capacity to become *actual.* That would never have happened had not the Germans felt their naval inferiority. For this reason people who look at the matter superficially say lightly that the great surface fleets, especially the big ships, were no great help or no help at all in the World War. Such people make a great mistake, and the deductions they draw from their mistaken premise are wrong.

As a matter of fact, the great surface fleets won the war without firing a single shot, the moment war was declared, by virtue of their *potential capacity;* and the immediate consequences of their naval victory was the cessation of all enemy traffic and the disappearance of the enemy naval forces. The enemy had to rely upon submarine ambush. Submarine action might have reversed the situation, it is true; but this fact does not detract from the value of an initial naval victory on the surface. This proves also that, though a naval victory on the surface is the surest way to prevent enemy traffic, it is not yet a sure way to safeguard one's own traffic, because it must be defended from submarines even after a surface victory. The side which compels the enemy's naval forces to hole up, or in any other way prevents them from navigating, can attack enemy traffic with surface means. He does not need to have recourse to the submarine arm for the purpose, and it would not pay him to, because surface means have a capacity for destroying traffic far superior to that of submarines.

So, if the submarine has reduced the over-all efficacy of surface fleets by taking away some of their functions, it has not reduced it at all as far as the essential task of the navy is concerned—namely, fighting and defeating the enemy. A naval situation would be normal when there was little disparity in the strength of the contending forces, a disparity so small it would not make one side consider himself beaten before the battle begins. If this were the case, a naval war in the full meaning of the term would have to be fought.

The expression "command of the sea" has lost the meaning it had in the past; that is, the ability to be free to navigate while at the same time making it impossible for the enemy to do likewise, because it would be very difficult to destroy all the naval forces of an enemy who has naval bases. When a naval force comes out of a naval battle with its strength greatly reduced, it will do as the German Fleet did during the last war, and then the victorious fleet will have to keep watch on the remainder of the defeated one. Therefore, it will have no full freedom to navigate, but it will completely prevent enemy traffic, defending itself and its own traffic from the submarine menace.

Nowadays the *command of the sea* is to be understood only as a state in which the side which enjoys it has much more freedom of navigation than the enemy, a state similar to that which prevailed for the Allied navies during the World War. Although they did not have command of the sea in the old meaning, they had it to the extent of preventing enemy traffic and keeping enemy naval forces bottled up until they had to surrender. The essential task of a navy is to conquer that kind of command of the sea; and until such a struggle is decided, neither fleet can risk detaching forces from its mass in order to defend its own traffic or attack the enemy's. Anything like that can be attended to only after the struggle is won. The side which gains such a command of the sea will at once stop all enemy traffic, but it will have to defend its own from danger of submarines.

This is the difference characteristic assumed by the naval struggle in the last war; but it is a difference which did not affect the essential value of the surface naval fleet.

From the foregoing examination of the World War we can draw the following conclusions:

1. It was a war between nations, and it affected the interest and welfare of all citizens.

2. Victory went to the group of nations which succeeded in breaking the material and moral resistance of the enemy group before their own was exhausted.

3. The armies functioned as agents of attrition for the nations involved. From time to time the nations would send their resources, made into war means, to the battle lines, where they would be used up by attrition. After they were used up, they were replaced by others; and this process of attrition and replacement went on until one of the two groups, materially and morally exhausted, was no longer able to replace the means he had used up.

4. The navies functioned as accelerating and retarding organs of attrition—*accelerating* when acting to prevent the inflow of resources to be used for replacement, and *retarding* when used to facilitate such inflow.

5. War on land took on a static form contrary to the intentions of those who directed it, the reason being the great efficacy of small-caliber firearms, an efficacy which increased the difficulties of the offensive to the point where it came to need an enormous preponderance of forces.

6. War on land was decided only when the nations had endured a long, painful process of attrition and were no longer able to support their armies materially or morally.

7. Owing to the great preponderance of Allied forces, the naval war was decided before it began; therefore, it developed for the Allies into a long, wearisome period of keeping watch on the enemy forces, and for the Central Powers into a long, demoralizing wait for a chance to strike at their foes.

8. Though the Allies were in a position to prevent enemy seaborne traffic, which the enemy had given up of their own accord anyway, they were nevertheless compelled to defend their own traffic from the submarine arm, whose action became during one period very dangerous to the Allies' chances of success.

9. Because of wrong evaluations of technical elements, both armies and navies failed fully to understand the realities of the war when they began to fight; and they were therefore compelled to remedy the effects of their lack of adequate preparation, materially and morally, as they went along.

Such are the premises upon which we can base our excursion into the future. At once we can say:

1. The war of the future will once more involve all nations and all their resources, with no exceptions.

2. Victory will go to the side which *first* succeeds in breaking down the material and moral resistance of the other.

3. The armed forces will be better prepared for the war of the future to the extent to which they have correctly answered the question of what that war will be like and how nearly they have been trained to meet its requirements.

I think we can all agree on these three indisputable points.

4. Of the war on land taken by itself, it can be said that it will take on a static character very similar to that of the World War, since the causes of that character still exist and will be more important in the future than they are now.

From the Armistice to the present day, the efficacy of firearms has been increasing, and it will go on increasing even more rapidly in the future. Everything is constantly improving, and in all armies the number of very rapid small-caliber firearms issued has been increasing constantly. Consequently, the value of the defensive has kept on increasing, which means that the offensive must have greater preponderance than before in order to be able to break a stalemate. New arms will not affect the situation, because they will be found on both sides equally, and they will always tend to favor the defensive. Offensive action will be seriously difficult *even against a much weaker enemy*, especially if the enemy has mountainous borders which prevent a large deployment of forces and complicate the supply problem. Since one of the two sides will always find it more profitable to try to delay the decision until a more favorable time, that side will go on the defensive; and thus inevitably the continuous front will spring up even against the will of the war leaders. To break through the enemy's continuous front, prodigious quantities of means will be needed, such as no nation can have ready before the beginning of the war. Therefore, it will be necessary to go on during the war converting national resources into means of war by intensifying industrial production. Since both sides will be doing this, the stalemate will be hard to break unless and until one side suffers complete attrition of national resources. Without doubt the war of the future will be long, slow, and onerous.

On the whole it can be said that long, continuous fronts will be set up in the future war as in the World War, fronts hard to break through and easy to join together again in case of a minor break, fronts which will slowly wear down the resources of the fighting nations until one side collapses from exhaustion. All theories and concepts of a war of movement will fail against these continuous fronts because, no matter what the stronger side would like to do, the weaker one, being less well prepared and less confident, will avail itself of the advantages of a defensive attitude in order to stop the attacker and gain time to grow stronger, better prepared, and more confident. Inevitably, the weaker side, buttressed by the advantages of the defensive, will impose his will on the stronger, who, in spite of being the stronger, will not be strong enough to overwhelm the adversary. Aggressiveness and the will to maneuver cannot overcome the fact. It is true that an army must foster aggressiveness, because a submissive spirit would be absurd in an army; but it is equally true that if I butt my head against a stone wall in order to show my aggressive spirit, I will break my head without even marring the wall. Men with a task to do must be imbued with an aggressive spirit; but the man who makes decisions and gives orders must have clear vision and know how to be guided by it. A war of movements and maneuvers will be possible only after the stalemate of a static war has been broken.

5. Considered by itself, the naval war will take on a character very like that of the last war, allowing for the fact that the naval struggle would first have to be decided, except in cases where one side has a decisive initial preponderance over the other. If no great disparity exists between the forces of the two sides, each of them will try to gain preponderance by inflicting losses on the other. That will mean the naval victory, which will greatly curtail the losing side's freedom of navigation. The victor will be able to prevent the loser's traffic with his surface forces; while the loser will have to limit his action to submarine warfare against the victor's traffic. Nevertheless, the winner will still be compelled to defend his traffic from the submarine threat of the enemy.

It would seem logical to conclude that, since similar causes lead to similar effects, and since all the causes which shaped the forms of the last war are still applicable and have suffered no substantial changes, land and naval warfare of the future, considered by themselves, should show characteristics similar to those of the last war.

CHAPTER III

But that will not be the case, because, even if no new developments have taken place on land, on the sea, or under the sea, there has been a new development in the air—one which, because the air is over land and sea alike, tends to change war as a whole and also those of its aspects peculiar to land and sea warfare. This new development is the existence of the air arm, which, since it was born about the time the World War began, did not greatly influence that war.

To get an immediate realization of the radical change the air arm is making in the characteristics and forms of war, we need only consider that it has suddenly upset the characteristics which were fundamental to war ever since man first began fighting man. As long as man was earth-bound, all human activities, including war, were localized on the surface of the earth. War has always been the result of a clash of two wills—one the will to occupy a certain territory; the other, the will not to let it be occupied. Every war has therefore consisted of movements of and clashes by forces deployed on the surface; one force trying to break through the opposing force to seize the land beyond it, the other trying to repel the attackers in order to protect its own territory. The forces thus aligned on the surface had two purposes: one struggling to break the enemy force to reach its objective, the other struggling to protect the objective sought by the first.

This has been the fundamental character of war from its origin up to the present day; and such were the essential functions of the forces deployed on the surface up to the time of the World War, which presented the most formidable example of this fundamental character and the functions of the opposing lines of forces. The ability to leave the surface and fly in the air, which man now possesses, has changed the character of war and curtailed the functions of surface forces, because the character of the war and the functions of the forces originated in the fact that war was restricted to the surface.

In other words, there is no longer any need to break through the enemy's lines to reach an objective. The lines no longer protect what is behind them. If you stop to consider the new state of things caused by the appearance of the air arm, you will realize that it is bound to produce a radical change in the forms and characteristics of war.

Armies and navies have lost the ability they once had to protect the nation behind them. That nation now lies open to enemy aerial attack regardless of the existence and location of its army and navy. The battlefield can no longer be limited; it now extends to all the lands and seas of all the nations in the war. No longer can a line of demarcation be drawn between belligerents and nonbelligerents, because all citizens wherever they are can be victims of an enemy offensive. There will be no place where life and work can go on in comparative safety and tranquillity; the countinghouse will be just as exposed as the trench—perhaps more; imminent danger will hang over everyone and everything.

Many people think the air arm is only an improved weapon based on a new invention, as firearms were based on the invention of gunpowder, or as steamships took the place of sail after the invention of the steam engine. These people are mistaken. Never before in all the history of humanity has there appeared a war arm which can be compared to the air arm. The difference between the stone thrown by primitive man and the projectile fired by the famous Bertha is simply a difference of performance, not of kind. Between primitive man and Krupp's stretches a series of improvements in giving force to the propulsion of a projectile. But all these improvements have been along the same line of thought; and as long as we move along the same line of thought we have evolution, but never revolution. Between the triremes and the great steamships there is nothing but a series of improvements in methods of propelling a floating ship. Ever since man began to fight, war has been waged with identical means having identical characteristics in differing degrees; therefore, in its general lines war has always been the same. But the aerial machine is not an improvement; it is something new, with characteristics of its own, and it gives man possibilities he has never had before.

It is a new and different factor which brings its own peculiar characteristics and possibilities into the group of age-old factors which shape the forms and characteristics of war. From this point the graph line of the evolution of war loses its continuity from the effects of this new factor and veers sharply in a completely different direction. It is no longer a matter of evolution; it is revolution. Woe to him who keeps on following the old graph line during this period of transition. He will find himself out of touch with the reality of the present. Disrupting violently the age-old form of war, the air arm has by itself broken the evolutionary continuity of the character of war.

The almost simultaneous appearance of the poison-gas arm lends still sharper point to this revolution. The chlorine-gas attack of April 25, 1915, was called the most terrifying episode of the last war. Besides that, it must be considered the beginning of the poison-gas era in war. Until April 25, 1915, it seemed that, as had been the case since ancient time, human life could be attacked only by cutting, piercing, or bruising instruments handled by man, or by other means having a force of impact. From the natural primitive arms we had arrived through numerous improvements to modern arms. From the stone ax and the rough flint stone we arrived at the bayonet; from throwing rocks by hand, to the rifle, cannon, and machine gun, simply by substituting the expanding force of gunpowder for the muscular force used before its invention. But to be hit by a projectile, using the word in its widest meaning, one must at some given time be at a given point along its trajectory. The offensive action of the projectile is therefore *instantaneous* and *linear*. But to be hit by the action of poison gas, one need only be within the space occupied by the volume of gas at any time during the period in which its action is effective. The offensive action of poison gas is therefore exercised in *volume* and *duration*. The projectile is harmless once its propulsive forces is spent; the poison gas, on the contrary, remains active as long as it lasts within a certain space in the atmosphere.

A 305 projectile is more harmless than a child soon after it has exploded; but an Yperite bomb is mortal from the moment of its explosion until whole days later. The gun shell is noisy; the poison gas is silent and often invisible. The trajectory of a projectile can be intercepted by suitable surfaces behind which man can shield himself; but poison gas penetrates, expands, enters any crack or crevice, permeates the element man cannot do without for a moment, and can therefore kill simultaneously masses of men over wide stretches of ground. The offensive power of poison gas is therefore greatly superior to that of the projectile. When we consider that everything in this world undergoes improvement, it is clear that the atrocious gas attack of April 25, 1915, will be child's play to soldiers and civilians of tomorrow.

It is useless to delude ourselves. All the restrictions, all the international agreements made during peacetime are fated to be swept away like dried leaves on the winds of war. A man who is fighting a life-and-death fight—as all wars are nowadays—has the right to use any means to keep his life. War means cannot be classified as human and inhuman. War will always be inhuman, and the means which are used in it cannot be classified as acceptable or not acceptable according to their efficacy, potentiality, or harmfulness to the enemy. The purpose of war is to harm the enemy as much as possible; and all means which contribute to this end will be employed, no matter what they are. He is a fool if not a patricide who would acquiesce in his country's defeat rather than go against those formal agreements which do not limit the right to kill and destroy, but simply the ways of killing and destroying. The limitations applied to the so-called inhuman and atrocious means of war are nothing but international demagogic hypocrisies. As a matter of fact, poison gases are being experimented with and improved everywhere—and certainly not for purely scientific purposes. Just because of its terrible efficacy, poison gas will be largely used in the war of the future. This is the brutal fact; and it is better to look it squarely in the face without false delicacy and sentimentalism.

The airplane affords the means to drop great quantities of poison gases over armies and large extents of territory. The airplane makes it possible for chemical warfare to produce terrifying effects over wide extents of ground.

So wrote Marshal Foch awhile ago. In fact, the aerial arm can take the poison gas to any point in the enemy territory. The two arms thus combined have a much greater offensive capacity than any other arm employed up to now. Everyone knows the terrible effects of poison gas in the World War, and everyone is aware that studies and experiments are going on in the quiet of the chemical laboratories all over the world to increase these effects in intensity and duration. Each nation tries to keep it a secret in order to take its enemy by surprise; but there is no end of published information, especially abroad, about the best ways of poisoning people. There is therefore no reason why we should not talk about some of them.

In the United States, father of the most humanitarian and pacifist proposals, experiments have been made with gases which would make the ground over which they were released barren for years to come. The only protection against these gases for human beings would be a diving suit of some special material with a suitable apparatus for artificial breathing. It is well known that there are slow-evaporating gases whose poisonous action would last for weeks. It is claimed that with 80 or 100 tons of poison gas, it would be possible to envelop a great city like London or Paris, and that with a proportionate number of explosive, incendiary, and poison-gas bombs it would be feasible to destroy completely great centers of population, because the poison gas would make it impossible to put out the fires.

The Germans, always a romantic people, have devised a system which they call the "gas cloak." The idea is to release, over a city for example, an invisible cloud of heavier-than-air poison gases. This cloud would slowly fall to the ground, destroying everything on it. No safety, no way of escape would be left, neither in basements nor skyscraper terraces.

Airplanes and poison gas were used in the last war, but these two terrible arms were in their infancy then, and the proper techniques for their use had not yet been developed. Though little can be said now about the present and future use of poison gas, a great many facts are available about aerial arms. The potentiality of the aerial machine is about ten times more today than it was at the close of the World War. Machines with 2,000-, 3,000-, even 6,000-horsepower motors are in use today or about to be built. In this field, thanks to the ingenuity and initiative of His Excellency the Honorable Balbo, Italy is ahead of all other nations. He has already commissioned Caproni to build the 2,000-, 3,000-, and 6,000-horsepower airplanes. Some of them are ready now, others are in the process of construction. The total weight of the 6,000-horsepower machine is about 40 tons, half of which is useful load.[1] In other words, it is equal to four freight cars supplied with wings. These machines are ideal for safe transportation of passengers at great speed, but also they make very powerful war weapons, veritable air cruisers, when armed with two cannons, one foreward and the other aft, with from sixteen to twenty-four machine guns of larger caliber than usual, and six tons of bombs. Eventually these planes can be protected with light armor over their vital parts. Their large fuselages allow them to alight safely on water. By being multimotored, they largely avoid the danger of forced landings, because they can keep on flying even if half their motors stop, since it is feasible to repair minor motor troubles in flight.

These are the aerial machines of the present and the near future, machines built of metal and independent of hangars. The aerial machines of the last war look like toys in comparison. When thinking of airplanes we can forget the admirable but fragile machines of yore, made out of wood and canvas, and be thankful that progress in the construction of airplanes is being made in geometrical progression. The 300-horsepower Caproni became progressively a 600-, 1,000-, 2,000-, and now 3,000- and 6,000-horsepower plane.

An English officer has figured out that today an Independent

[1] This is one of the developments Douhet foresaw as early as 1909.—Tr.

Air Force can release in *a single flight* a weight of bombs superior to that of *all* the bombs released by *all* the English airplanes during the *whole time* of the last war, a weight which was computed at 800 tons. As a matter of fact, it is computed that today an Independent Air Force of normal size can carry on each flight 1,500 tons of bombs, equal to the carrying capacity of 150 railroad freight cars.

The English Fleet, firing one shot from each of her guns, can throw a total of 200 tons of projectiles. Therefore, an Independent Air Force can drop bombs weighing seven times as much as a broadside from the whole English Fleet. But the English Fleet can fire her broadsides only against another fleet, which can fire back at her, or against coastal objectives, which can also retaliate in some measure; whereas an aerial fleet can hurl its bombs anywhere on the land or sea territory of the enemy, including its most vital points. While the English Fleet must throw much steel and little explosives, an Independent Air Force can drop much explosives, much poison gas, and little steel. An Independent Air Force of this kind would have an offensive power much greater than the English Fleet, even if the latter could be made to fly.

During the World War the city of Treviso had to be evacuated; and the evacuation was accomplished long before it was hit by the 80 tons of bombs which were dropped on it. If those 80 tons had been dropped in one raid, the damage to Treviso would have been much greater, owing both to fires which could not have been put out and to the effect on the morale of the population. A normal Independent Air Force of today can drop 80 tons of bombs on twenty centers like Treviso; and it is logical to think that such an action would have an incalculable effect upon morale in addition to the material damage it would do.

Every day planes fly from London to Paris and back. It is entirely feasible, then, that a thousand airplanes could take off from northern France at any time and fly over London just as easily as a thousand planes could take off from southern England and fly over Paris. No one can deny that today an airplane can carry a ton of bombs from Paris to London. Neither can it be denied that 1,000 tons of explosive, incendiary, and poison-gas bombs dropped on Paris or London could destroy these cities, the heart of France and England.

I wish my readers would think long and deeply about the possibilities and figures I have mentioned. They are the reality of today, not a vision of what might happen tomorrow or ten or twenty years from now. The undeniable fact is this: whatever the situation of the armies and navies on the surface, today the airplane makes it possible to launch over enemy territory offensive actions larger and stronger than any action which could have been imagined. The air arm gives the means of reaching the most vital of the enemy's centers, and poison gas makes such an offensive as terrifying as it could possibly be.

It will be an inhuman, an atrocious, performance; but these are the facts. And no one will shrink from using such terrifying offensives, tomorrow if need be, no matter how inhuman and atrocious they might be considered. Up to the present, enemies could protect themselves with armor and deal each other heavy blows in an attempt to break through the armor. But as long as the armor lasted, the heart beneath it was safe. Now the situation has changed. Armor has lost its protective power. It no longer shields the heart, which can be reached by the air arm and paralyzed by poison gas.

Lord Rothermere wrote:

From now on no nation can boast of naval supremacy; it is for us English a bitter pill to swallow, but we have to swallow it.

Baldwin, then Prime Minister, said on July 24, 1924:

It is easy to say, as many people do, that England should isolate herself from Europe, but we have to remember that the history of our insularity has ended, because with the advent of the airplane we are no longer an island. It does not matter whether we like it or not; we are now indissolubly tied to Europe.

This was the second very bitter pill the English have had to swallow. And in fact, no navy, no matter how powerful, can prevent an adequately prepared enemy, be it Germany or France, from attacking London from the air—London, the great metropolis until now rejoicing in her inviolability. It cannot prevent an attack against her mercantile ports—her stomach; nor against her naval bases—her heart. The English Fleet has lost its ability to protect; the safety of England now lies in an air force able to keep off the aerial menace.

This situation at once gives a picture of the revolutionary changes which have taken place in war, and should be enough to convince anyone that the war of the future will inevitably be completely different from all wars of the past. But it means even more. It means that the influence of such purely technical factors as the submarine and the airplane extend beyond the military sphere into the political. There is no doubt that the submarine and the airplane have altered the very foundation of England's political situation, and certainly not in favor of the Empire on which the sun never sets. It would be interesting to make a study of the political influence exerted by technical means; but I shall be satisfied with showing, as I hope I have, that in an eventual future war, necessarily different from the last one, it would be extremely dangerous not to recognize or properly evaluate the air arm—that is, to repeat the errors of evaluation made in the period just before the last war. It is therefore important and necessary to give passionate attention to the effects of the aerial factor on the forms and characteristics of war.

CHAPTER IV

I COME NOW to the most interesting problem, the problem of the future. This may seem difficult to the reader, but that is appearance rather than reality. We have already well established our starting point—we have seen the events which have been maturing. Now all we have to do is to deduce from them the effects which must follow. Human reasoning has this divining power which brings man closer to God. Using abstract calculus as a basis, Maxwell discovered and defined electromagnetic waves, which we cannot perceive with our senses. On the same basis Hertz built the instrument which revealed them; and Marconi in his turn put them to use and gave them to mankind. In the matter we are examining, we are confronted with facts which our senses can see and perceive, and therefore we should easily be able to define the consequences which must inevitably ensue from them, provided we free our minds from the set traditions of the past.

In a book of mine in 1921 I asked the following question: Is it not true that the strongest army deployed on the Alps and the strongest navy sailing our seas, could do nothing practical against an enemy adequately armed in the air who was determined to invade our territory and destroy from the air our communication, production, and industrial centers, and sow death, destruction, and terror in our population centers in order to break our material and moral resistance? The only possible answer then was: "It is true"; today the answer is the same, and tomorrow it must still be the same, unless one denies that airplanes fly and poison gases kill, which would be absurd. As I have said about the last war, the armies then functioned as organs of *indirect* attrition of national resistance, and the navies as organs to *accelerate or retard* this attrition.

While the armies and navies tend *indirectly* to break the enemy's resistance, the air arm, having the capacity to act upon the very source of resources, tends to break it *directly*—namely, with more speed and efficacy. Once one had to be content with destroying a battery with shells; today it is possible to destroy the factory where the guns for the batteries are being built. During the last war tons of explosives and whole mines of iron were fired at regions covered with barbed-wire entanglements in order to destroy them; the air arm can ignore that kind of objective and use its shells, explosives, and poison gases to much better advantage. An army can reach the enemy's capital only after facing the enemy army, defeating it, and pushing it back by a long, painful, onerous series of operations; the air arm instead may try for the destruction of the enemy's capital even before war is declared.

There is no comparison between the efficacy of direct and indirect destructive action against the vital resistance of a nation. In the days when a nation could shield itself behind the stout armor of an army and navy, blows from the enemy were barely felt by the nation itself, sometimes not at all. The blows were taken by institutions such as the army and navy, well organized and disciplined, materially and morally able to resist, and able to act and counteract. The air arm, on the contrary, will strike against entities less well-organized and disciplined, less able to resist, and helpless to act or counteract. It is fated, therefore, that the moral and material collapse will come about more quickly and easily. A body of troops will stand fast under intensive bombings, even after losing half or two-thirds of its men; but the workers in shop, factory, or harbor will melt away after the first losses.

The direct attack against the moral and material resistance of the enemy will hasten the decision of the conflict, and so will shorten the war. Fokker, the famous airplane builder, who understands the mentalities of all his international clients, said:

Do not believe that tomorrow the enemy will make any distinction between military forces and the civilian population. He will use his most powerful and terrifying means, such as poison gas and other things, against the civilian population, even though in peacetime he may have professed the best intentions and subscribed to the strictest limitation of them. Squadrons of airplanes will be sent to destroy the principal cities. The future war, of which we now have only a vague idea, will be frightful.

Fokker is right. We dare not wait for the enemy to begin using the so-called inhuman weapons banned by treaties before we feel justified in doing the same. This justification, useless anyhow, would be too costly since it would leave the initiative to the enemy. Owing to extreme necessity, all contenders must use all means without hesitation, whether or not they are forbidden by treaties, which after all are nothing but scraps of paper compared to the tragedy which would follow.

This is a dark and bloody picture I am drawing for you; but it is bound to happen and there is no use in burying one's head in the sand. And the picture grows still darker when one realizes that defense against aerial attacks as it is commonly envisaged is *illusory*, owing again to the essential characteristics of the air arm. An airplane taking off from the center of the island of Corsica, with a 500-kilometer radius of action, could attack, besides all of Sardinia, every place else on the peninsula, from Trent and Venice in the east to Termoli and Salerno in the south. To defend all the centers exposed to the potential threat of this one airplane, we would have to distribute defense planes and antiaircraft artillery to each of these centers.

How many defense planes and how many antiaircraft guns would be needed to make sure of repelling that one plane? What look-out service should be organized on the ground so as not to be surprised by it? How long should the look-out service, the defense planes, and the antiaircraft guns be on the alert for it to put in an appearance, and all this without any certainty of being able to prevent its offensive if it should come? Anyhow, how many resources and how much energy would be immobilized for such a defense? And all for one lone airplane, which could accomplish the immobilization of all these resources and energies merely by its potential existence, without needing to take off and fly at all.

If that lone airplane is multiplied by a hundred or by a thousand—in other words, if we consider the size of the air forces we would have to contend with in case of war—we will realize immediately that defensive action would compel us to immobilize for a purely negative purpose a much larger amount of resources than those which would attack us—perhaps so much larger that we could not afford it. Would it not be better to renounce this passive and expensive attitude and send out against that threat, which could become a nightmare, an offensive aerial force of our own which would go in search of the enemy and destroy him in his nest, thus putting an end to the nightmare and the threat? Wouldn't this be the best way out, the way which would accomplish the most with the least?

The air arm is eminently offensive, but completely unsuitable for defensive action. In fact, one who used it defensively would be in the absurd situation of needing a defensive aerial force much larger than the enemy's offensive one. Although there were no exact rules for large-scale aerial offensives in the last war, those which were carried out with determination were successful. We bombed Pola every time it suited us, and the Austrians kept on bombing our Treviso right up to Armistice Day, although our aviation was in preponderance during the last months.

In England a few months ago an experiment was made in the aerial defense of London. The defense had at its disposal as many airplanes as the offensive side, besides the antiaircraft batteries and organization. Furthermore, it knew the days during which the offensive would be attempted. The offensive side, equal in strength to the defensive, had its objective limited in time and space. All the conditions were in favor of the defense; but the experiment proved that London would have been bombed.

Aerial defense should therefore be limited to the organization of all those means which would lessen the effects of aerial offensives, such as decentralization of vital organs, preparation of bomb shelters, protective measures against poison gas, and similar means. Only a center of exceptional importance should be defended by antiaircraft artillery, because it would be physically impossible to have as much as it would take to defend the whole national territory efficaciously. I have heard that 300 antiaircraft batteries would be necessary to defend Milan with some measure of efficacy. How many would be needed to insure the safety of all the important centers of Italy? The situation is the same for aerial offensives as for naval ones. Since it would be impossible to defend the whole coastline, or even the more important coastal points, from a naval offensive, defense is limited to the most important points from a military point of view—fortified naval bases—leaving all other points undefended, even the great maritime cities, their protection being entrusted to the fleet. Similarly, the protection of the national territory from aerial offensives should be entrusted to the aerial arm, which will be capable of repelling, defeating, and destroying the enemy's aerial force.

There is only one valid way to defend oneself from aerial offensives: namely, *to conquer the command of the air,* that is *to prevent the enemy from flying, while assuring this freedom for oneself.* To prevent the enemy from flying, one must destroy his means of flying. His means may be found in the air, on the ground in airfields, in hangars, in factories. To destroy the enemy's means of flying, one must have an aerial force capable of destroying them wherever they may be found or are being manufactured. In line with this concept, I have been preaching for years the necessity of an Independent Air Force, a mass of aerial means adequate to fight an aerial war to conquer the command of the air.

During the last war this concept was unknown. Aviation was used then as auxiliary means intended to facilitate and integrate land and sea actions. There was no true aerial warfare; there were aerial struggles and clashes, but only partial, limited, isolated, often individual ones. Aerial victory was not sought, only aerial preponderance. Until Armistice Day there were auxiliary aerial actions carried on by both sides in proportion to the available forces. Today things are quite different; the magnitude of possible aerial forces leads to real aerial war, the struggle between masses of means.

Without going into details, which would be out of place here, we can easily understand that an Independent Air Force capable of aerial combat and of bombing the surface can aim at the conquest of the command of the air, because it can destroy enemy aerial means in the air or on the ground, wherever they are found or manufactured. Through its aerial offensive, therefore, an Independent Air Force can reduce the enemy's aerial means to a minimum, insignificant in relation to the economy of war in general. When it gets such a result it has won, inasmuch as it has conquered the command of the air.

The command of the air carries with it the following advantages:

1. It shields one's own territory and seas from enemy aerial offensives, because the enemy has been made powerless to carry out offensives. It protects, therefore, the material and moral resistance of the nation from direct and terrifying attacks by the enemy.

2. It exposes the enemy's territory to one's own aerial offensives, which can be carried on with the utmost ease, because the enemy has been made powerless to act in the air. It therefore facilitates a direct and terrifying attack on the enemy's resistance.

3. It completely protects the bases and communication lines of one's own army and navy, and threatens those of the enemy.

4. It prevents the enemy from helping his army and navy from the air, and at the same time insures aerial help for one's own army and navy.

To all these advantages must be added the fact that the one who has command of the air can prevent the enemy from rebuilding his aerial force, because he can destroy the sources of materials and the places of manufacture. This is equivalent to saying that the conquest of the air is final.

In consideration of the advantages which ensue from the command of the air, it must be admitted that the command of the air will have a decisive influence on the outcome of the war.

I have said that the command of the air is final, inasmuch as the one who conquers it can prevent the enemy from rebuilding his aerial forces. But there is more than that—the one who has command of the air can increase his own aerial forces to his liking. The nation dominated in the air must suffer without possibility of effective counteraction the aerial offensives carried by the enemy to its territory—offensives which will increase as the enemy increases his offensive aerial forces. Its army and navy will be powerless against these offensives. Quite apart from material damage, how great must be the moral effects both on the nation enduring this nightmare and on its armed forces, who would be conscious of their impotence to help?

In their turn the army and navy will see their lines of communication cut and their bases destroyed; the forwarding of supplies from the nation to its armed forces would be cut off completely or made irregular and dangerous. By simply destroying facilities in enemy mercantile ports, the dominant Independent Air Force can cut off maritime traffic even if the enemy nation is able to protect its seaways. Then is it not logical to assume that a nation placed in such a position of inferiority would begin to despair of a favorable outcome of the war? And would not that be the beginning of the end?

If you think about it you will realize how true it is. Dominated from the air, England would be lost. Her magnificent fleet, her naval predominance, would be of no avail. Even if her merchant marine could bring supplies to her ports, they could not be unloaded and forwarded. Hunger, desolation, and terror would stalk the country. These are some of the probabilities of the war to come. Do they not revolutionize all past ideas on the subject?

The conquest of the command of the air will be a necessary condition of future wars, even if it will not insure victory by itself. It will always be necessary; it will be sufficient if and when the Independent Air Force is left with enough offensive strength to crush the material and moral resistance of the enemy. If the Air Force is not left with enough strength, the conflict will be decided by the land and sea forces, whose task will be greatly facilitated by having the command of the air on their side.

Considering the decisive importance of the conquest of the command of the air, it is imperative to put oneself in condition to reach toward this aim. It is essential to have an Independent Air Force able to fight an aerial battle, the most powerful possible within one's resources; and to have this it is necessary to make use of *all* the *available resources* of the nation. This is the inflexible principle I advocate, allowing no exceptions; for any resources diverted from that essential end, or only partly used, or not at all, would reduce our chances of conquering the command of the air.

I have shown how aerial defense would demand immobilization of a larger quantity of means than the offense needs, since the defensive value of the aerial arm is much less than the offensive. One hundred airplanes offensively employed by an Independent Air Force would be worth more than 500 or 1,000 used defensively. If the enemy should conquer the command of the air, our army and navy auxiliary aviations would be destroyed without even having a chance to go into action; but if we conquer, our victorious Independent Air Force would be able to give substantial help to the army and navy. Therefore, auxiliary aviation will be useless in the first case, superfluous in the second.

Consequently, I say: No aerial defense, because it is practically useless. No auxiliary aviation, because it is practically useless or superfluous. Instead, a single Independent Air Force, to include all the aerial resources available to the nation, none excepted. This is my thesis. Some people call it extremist; but really it is just a thesis which differs from the average thesis. The latter is always a poor solution, and in wartime the worst of all. Supporting this thesis brings me into conflict with valorous opponents who hold a different opinion; but I am confident that I shall win this battle too.[1]

Since the only way to defend oneself from aerial offensives is to attack and destroy the enemy aerial forces, and since every resource diverted from this fundamental aim might jeopardize one's chances of conquering the command of the air, the fundamental principle of aerial warfare is this: *to resign oneself to endure enemy aerial offensives in order to inflict the greatest possible offensives on the enemy.*

At first this principle seems atrocious, especially when one thinks of the suffering and horror which would be caused by aerial offensives. But that is the principle upon which all war actions are based. An army commander resigns himself to the probable loss of a hundred thousand men if he can inflict a larger loss on

---

[1] The "battles" to which Douhet refers were his battles for a unified command, an Air Ministry, and the creation of an Independent Air Force distinct from the auxiliary air force.—Tr.

the enemy—a loss which, disregarding the number of men involved, might bring victory. A commander of a fleet resigns himself to the loss of some of his units in order to sink more of the enemy's. In like manner a nation must resign itself to endure the enemy's aerial offensives in order to inflict heavier ones on him, because victory comes only through inflicting more damage than one suffers.

When this general principle of war is applied to aerial warfare, it seems inhuman to us because of a traditional notion which must be changed. Everyone says, and is convinced of it, that war is no longer a clash between armies, but is a clash between nations, between whole populations. During the last war this clash took the form of a long process of attrition between armies, and that seemed natural and logical. Because of its direct action, the air arm pits populations directly against populations, nations directly against nations, and does away with the intervening armor which has kept them apart during past wars. Now it is actually populations and nations which come to blows and seize each other's throats.

This fact sharpens that peculiar traditional notion which makes people weep to hear of a few women and children killed in an air raid, and leaves them unmoved to hear of thousands of soldiers killed in action. All human lives are equally valuable; but because tradition holds that the soldier is fated to die in battle, his death does not upset them much, despite the fact that a soldier, a robust young man, should be considered to have the maximum individual value in the general economy of humanity.

In employing submarines the Germans had an end in view which, as we have seen, they came close to reaching. We were justified in stigmatizing the submarine warfare as atrocious in order to play upon the sensibilities of world public opinion. It was to our interest, and we had a right to do it. But the real reason we were worried about it was not that it was inhuman, simply that it was dangerous to us. Compared with the carnage wrought by means recognized as humane and civilized, which amounted to millions of dead and millions of mutilated, the approximately 17,000 victims of the submarine are insignificant. If the last war had been wholly a submarine war, it would have been decided with much less blood. War has to be regarded unemotionally as a science, regardless of how terrible a science.

A great furor was raised about submarines' leaving shipwrecked men to their fate without giving them any help. But the submarines were only doing as the English did when, after one of their ships was torpedoed in the act of picking up the survivors of another ship, the commander gave orders that shipwrecked men must be left to their fate to prevent the torpedoing of rescuers; and in this case the men in question were fellow Englishmen, not enemies. War is war. Either one wages war or one doesn't; but when one does, one must do it without gloves and without frills on either side. The French Jeune École advocated ideas on this subject very like the Germans'. Anyone who likes to pretend that war is something different from what it is, puts himself at a disadvantage because of that thinking.

Any distinction between belligerents and nonbelligerents is no longer admissible today either in fact or theory. Not in theory because when nations are at war, everyone takes a part in it: the soldier carrying his gun, the woman loading shells in a factory, the farmer growing wheat, the scientist experimenting in his laboratory. Not in fact because nowadays the offensive may reach anyone; and it begins to look now as though the safest place may be the trenches.

War is won by crushing the resistance of the enemy; and this can be done more easily, faster, more economically, and with less bloodshed by directly attacking that resistance at its weakest point. The more rapid and terrifying the arms are, the faster they will reach vital centers and the more deeply they will affect moral resistance. Hence the more civilized war will become, because damages will be corresponding to the number of people involved. The better arms are able to attack citizens in general, the more private interests are directly hurt, the fewer wars will be, for people will not be able to say any more: "Let us all arm for war, but you go and do the fighting."

A belief generally held nowadays is that wars will begin in the air, and that large-scale aerial actions will be carried out even before the declaration of war, because everyone will be trying to get the advantage of surprise. Aerial warfare will be intense and violent to a superlative degree; for each side will realize the necessity of inflicting upon the enemy the largest possible losses in the shortest possible time, and of ridding the air of enemy aerial means so as to prevent any possible retaliation from him. Independent Air Forces will hurl themselves against their enemies and try to repeat their offensives as quickly as possible in order to compress the effort into as short a space of time as possible. Therefore, the war in the air will be decided by *those aerial forces which are in being and ready when hostilities break out.* No reliance can be placed on forces to be activated during the war. One who is defeated will not be able to create another aerial force. All available forces must be thrown into the fray at once; every means reserved for some other use will be that much less weight on the scale of destiny. The principle of mass must be implicitly followed.

In land warfare it is possible to rely on the defensive to offset a disparity in strength and gain time to dig trenches, throw up barbed-wire entanglements, and occupy strong positions; but in the air nothing of the kind is possible. The air is uniform everywhere, and there is no chance to stop anywhere and make a stand to gain time. In the air, fighting forces are as naked as swords.

The intense, violent, naked, immediate action, the impossibility of gaining time and creating new forces, the rapidity and efficacy of aerial actions—all lead to the conclusion that the aerial conflict will come to a quick decision. The length of the last war, as I have shown, was caused by the great value acquired by the defensive. In the air the defensive has no value at all. He who is unprepared is lost. The aerial war will be short; one of the two sides will rapidly gain a preponderance which will mean the command of the air, a command which, once gained, will be permanent.

Undoubtedly a decision will come in the air sooner than on land and sea. Consequently, the army and navy will have to be prepared to fight on even if dominated from the air, because such an eventuality, no matter what we may think of it, will have to be taken into consideration, even if only for a short while.

In what situation would an army and navy find themselves if they were dominated from the air? Up to the present, war on land

and sea has been chiefly dependent on the safety of bases and communication lines. Occupying the enemy's bases or cutting off his lines of communication was a brilliant tactical and strategical success, because it put the enemy in difficulty and danger. If an army and navy were dominated from the air, this very fact would expose their bases and communication lines, not only to enemy offensives, but to offensives they could not effectively counteract; which means that an army and navy dominated from the air would be permanently virtually cut off. Therefore—and please note well this inevitable consequence—if an army and navy want to keep their potentiality of action even when dominated from the air, they must arrange their forms and methods of action to make them as independent as possible of their bases and lines of communication.

The problem with which the air arm confronts the army and navy is a formidable one; but it is imperative that it be solved, even if radical and far-reaching changes have to be made. If it is not solved, the efficiency of an army and navy would be nullified almost automatically by the enemy's conquest of the command of the air. Because of their heavy equipment and large consumption, the huge modern armies have to be backed up by a large regular supply service by rail and road. If this service is disrupted, made irregular, or cut off, it means the debilitation of the army which relies upon it and the weakening of its striking power. It might also deprive the army of its strength, perhaps even immobilize it and make it impotent. An army dominated from the air may be the more easily put in a precarious situation, the more intense, regular, and continuous a supply service it needs. To visualize such a situation, we need only imagine our army deployed on the western Alps, and only four of our railroad centers destroyed— Ceva, Nizza Marrittima, Asti, and Chivasso. As a result no supplies could reach the army from the provinces of Lombardy and Liguria—that is, from its own country. Now, these four railroad centers are about a half-hour's flying distance from the border, and no one can doubt the ability of an enemy in command of the air, given the present potentiality of aerial offensives, to destroy them and keep them destroyed. In my opinion, therefore, it **is** imperative for modern armies to be less ponderous, and as much as possible autonomous and independent of their bases.

Similarly, a navy which means to keep on operating even under domination from the air must free itself from the bonds which at present tie navies to their bases. The large military ports, with their arsenals, warehouses, supply depots, and equipment of all kinds, are good targets for aerial offensives, whether they harbor a fleet or not. They may be defended by antiaircraft artillery, but their safety will always be doubtful, and certainly they will never be as invulnerable as they have been heretofore. It is imperative that navies think over the changed situation and do something about it.

Besides, an enemy in command of the air can easily cut off our maritime traffic regardless of his naval strength, simply by putting our commercial ports out of service. A Swiss Independent Air Force could cut off our maritime traffic if it succeeded in commanding the air. It does seem absurd; but it is nevertheless one of the possibilities of modern war.

These short summaries of the influence of the air arm on the forms of war on land and sea, an influence which should lead armies and navies to reorganize on a new basis, should suffice to make people realize the magnitude of the revolution and the seriousness of the problems which face the armies and navies. The necessary changes apply not only to exterior forms; they deeply affect the essence of these two organizations, and the new problems cannot be solved merely by adding an auxiliary aviation of one sort or another.

Another characteristic of the air arm is that it, shall we say, facilitates the waging of war. An Independent Air Force is comparatively much easier to prepare than an army or navy. A thousand 6,000-horsepower planes may cost approximately as much as ten battleships, will need only 20,000 tons of material—about the weight of one average battleship—and will need only 20,000 to 30,-000 men, only 4,000 to 5,000 of them pilots. But an Independent Air Force a thousand planes strong can drop on an enemy nation, and every locality in it, from 4,000 to 6,000 tons of bombs on each flight, besides carrying 16,000 to 24,000 machine guns and 2,000 small-caliber cannon for combat in the air. In other words, an offensive capacity the like of which has never before been imagined, and one which only another similar Independent Air Force would be able to oppose and fight.

A thousand airplanes of this kind can be built very quickly by a nation with an adequate industrial organization, and ammunition for it can easily be supplied by a well-organized chemical organization. Instructing and training pilots is no difficult task in a country in which aerial transportation is well developed. Furthermore, a passenger plane can be converted into a military plane in a few hours' time, and its crew can be militarized in no time by simply changing their uniforms.

Thus the hope of revenge can be more easily nourished; for it would no longer imply the destruction of huge armies and formidable navies. Perhaps it has been a mistake to forbid the losers to recreate their army and navy, because that forced them to look toward the sky.

In order to get a better idea of the importance of the action of an Independent Air Force, we can compare the airplane to a special gun capable of firing shells a distance equal to its flying range, and with a special observer to guide the shells to their targets. Then we can compare the Independent Air Force to a large battery of guns which, though stationed over a wide area, can at will concentrate its fire on various objectives within its flying range.

Let us suppose, for instance, that we have in the Padua Valley an Independent Air Force with a range of 1,000 kilometers. The fire of this gun battery could be concentrated at will upon any objective in France, Germany, Austria, Yugoslavia, even on London. Let us think for the moment, not of our Independent Air Force, but of its equivalent, the large gun battery. Our eventual enemy, no matter who he is, will have a similar large gun battery capable of striking us almost anywhere in our territory. What would be the best way for us to ward off these special enemy shells? Certainly we could not put an armored umbrella over the whole country. Obviously, the easiest and most practical way would be to silence the battery by destroying it. And that would be the struggle for the command of the air.

After we had destroyed the enemy gun battery, we would be free to choose targets at our own convenience, because our country would be safe from enemy attacks. Which targets would we choose? Those which best suited our convenience under the circumstances. They might be targets directly affecting the resistance of the enemy, such as his capital cities, industrial and population centers, and so on, in which case we would be choosing to hammer the nation itself to make it give in. Or we could choose the bases and communication lines of the enemy's army in order to weaken its resistance to our army. Or we could attack the enemy's naval bases if the navy was annoying us too much; or destroy the enemy's mercantile ports if the nation was dependent on sea-borne supplies. The selection of targets for our powerful gun battery should be the province of the Supreme Commander of the war, because he would be the only one in possession of all the facts for intelligent selection. But in any and all cases, the battery would have to function in all its mass to get the maximum results from concentration of effort in time and space.

The advantage of having such a large gun battery with which to face an enemy deprived of a similar battery constitutes the value of the command of the air; but as the conquest of it implies the destruction of a similar battery belonging to the enemy, it is evident that not a single gun should be taken from our battery before it has accomplished its purpose. Therefore, aerial defense and auxiliary aviation should be ruled out, because they would be useless anyway if our own battery is destroyed, and superfluous if our battery succeeds in silencing the enemy's.

One more remark: The offensive strength of an Independent Air Force against the surface is determined by the quantity of destructive materials—explosive, incendiary, and poison-gas bombs —it can carry and drop on the enemy. But these materials may be of different efficacies; and therefore it is clear that the destructive power of the Independent Air Force is in direct proportion to the efficacy of the materials employed. Doubling the efficacy of the materials employed is enough to double the offensive power of the Independent Air Force if nothing else is altered. This gives us an idea of the importance of the task of improving the quality of destructive materials or, in other words, the importance of co-operation with war efforts on the part of the chemical industry. The air arm is built and strengthened not only in the aviation training fields, but in the factories where the wonderful air machines are built and in the laboratories where the chemist leans over his test tubes in quest of ever more powerful compounds.

I think I have made clear the importance of the air arm and victory in the air in a future conflict, and the revolutionary changes being made by the air arm on the forms and characteristics of war in its general aspect, including all forms of land and sea conflicts. Logically and rationally our imagination enables us then to visualize the war of the future.

Whatever its aims, the side which decides to go to war will unleash all its aerial forces in mass against the enemy nation the instant the decision is taken, without waiting to declare war formally, trying in this way to exploit to the utmost the factor of surprise by direct attack and by use of the chemical arm. Balanced against the advantages of surprise and prevention of counteraction, the time-honored diplomatic niceties will be discarded. Some morning at dawn capital cities, large centers, and important aviation fields may be struck and shaken as though by an earthquake. For instance, the Germans might decide to destroy Paris instead of fifty French aviation centers, preferring to destroy the heart of France instead of her aviation. Of course, counteraction from enemy aerial forces would not be long in coming; and then, while the aerial struggle rose to the climax of violence, the armies would mobilize and the navies begin their hostile actions, hampered in greater or less degree by aerial offensives. As the aerial struggle neared a decision, aerial offensives from one side against enemy nation, army, and navy would weaken, while similar offensives from the other side would grow stronger and more intense. Then the side which won the command of the air would insure its own territory from any aerial offensives, and the losing side would be helpless against them.

At that moment the most tragic phase of the war would begin. The side dominated from the air would have to fight an unequal fight and resign itself to endure implacable offensives. Its army and navy would have to function with bases and communication lines insecure, exposed to constant threat, against an army and navy with secure bases and lines of communication. Its sea traffic would be cut off at the ports. All the most vital and vulnerable points in its territory would be subject to cruelly terrifying offensives.

Under these conditions, can a long, slow land war—which needs enormous quantities of supplies, means, labor, and matériel—give the air-dominated side any chance of a favorable decision? That is a question open to grave doubt. In all probability, unless there is a great disproportion of means and resources, a collapse in morale of the air-dominated nation will come before the outcome of war on land and sea could be decided.

Therefore I say, above all else, let us dominate our sky.

CONCLUSION

THE PICTURE I have drawn is naturally an imaginative one. Since it is an attempt to visualize the future, it could not be otherwise. But because I have painted with the colors of present realities and drawn according to logical reasoning, I think the future will be very much like my picture. At any rate, I think we can now answer along general lines the question: "What will a war of the near future be like?" with the following positive assertions:

1. It will be a struggle of nations grappling with each other, which will directly affect the lives and property of all citizens.

2. It will be a struggle in which the one who succeeds in conquering the command of the air will have secured a decisive advantage.

3. It will be a very violent struggle, terrifying in its nature, waged in order to strike at the moral resistance of the foe; a struggle which will be decided quickly, and therefore will not be very expensive economically.

4. It will be a struggle in which the side which finds itself unprepared will have no time to get ready; and therefore it will be decided by the forces ready at hand when hostilities begin.

In consequence of the foregoing, an adequate preparation for war at the present time requires:

1. The constitution of an Independent Air Force capable of conquering the command of the air, and the strongest possible to achieve within the limits of our national aerial resources.

2. The readiness of the Independent Air Force at all times, because it has to go into action instantly, even without a declaration of war, and cannot rely on reinforcements before the decision of the aerial struggle is reached.

3. A change in the organization of the army and navy and their methods of war, so as to make them as much as possible independent of bases and lines of communication in order that they may go on functioning even after the enemy has secured command of the air.

4. A study of the problem of co-operation between the armed forces, beginning with the premise that a new set of facts have given rise to different circumstances, showing the various functions each of the forces can perform.

5. A study of all provisions of various kinds which will put the nation in a position to withstand aerial offensives with the least possible damage. Since the offensives will be aimed mainly at the morale of civilians, national pride and a sense of discipline must be strengthened as much as possible in the masses.

These general characteristics of the war of the future, and the new requirements which ensue from them, show how formidable are the problems concerning national defense which confront us today. I do not intend that my words, meant to show the importance of the air arm's role in future wars, should be construed as minimizing the value of land and sea forces. More than anyone else, I have always asserted that the three armed forces constitute an indivisible whole, a single three-pronged instrument of war. All men and means used to defend their country have the same value— they are all necessary, whether they function on land, on the sea, under the sea, or in the air. In all these fields there are equally important duties to perform, equally important functions to carry on, equal honors to be earned. But that does not mean that, in the interest of the Fatherland, which considers all its sons equals, we should not build a new instrument, more adequate to its defense, by changing when necessary the size, form, and function of any one of its three prongs in order to make it better fitted to bite deeply into the resistance of an eventual enemy.

I think our glance into the future has not been unprofitable, especially if it has been successful in convincing people of two simple truths.

1. All citizens must be interested in the aspects of the war of the future, because all of them will have to fight in it. As I said in the beginning, war is essentially based on common sense, especially in its broad outlines; but because it demands all the material and moral resources of a nation, it cannot be limited to a certain section of the nation, nor to a special class or number of its citizens. All forces and materials, tangible and intangible, have to be marshaled for the prosecution of war; and all citizens must become deeply interested in it, discussing and understanding it, in order to prepare themselves for the ordeal if it should come. If I may be forgiven the heresy, I have often wondered why, in the universities and colleges, where all subjects under the sun are taught, even to Sanskrit, no place has yet been found for the science of war.

2. We must look toward the future with anxious, wide-open eyes to steel ourselves for what may come, so that the reality may not take us by surprise. This is all the more necessary in the revolutionary period we are living through—so much so that he who is not ready will have no time to get ready or to correct the errors of the past. So we must not let ourselves be led astray by the magic of the past. It is always dangerous to keep looking backward when marching forward, and still more so now when the path is full of sharp detours.

Students of war are induced to rely on the experience of the past for their preparation for the future conflict by the fact that theories of war can't be proved except in a real war. This was the reason why the nations who went to war in 1914 entered the conflict with their minds on the War of 1870. But they soon found out their mistake and had to adapt themselves to the exigencies of the 1914 situation. They could do this with comparative ease, in spite of the serious difficulties and tremendous expense they endured in the process, because the intervening time between the two wars was a period of evolution only. But woe to him who tries to fight the war of the future with the theories and systems of 1914!

I do not mean to imply that the experience of past wars should be discarded as useless; I want only to say that it should be taken with a grain of salt—in fact, with a great deal of salt—because the future is closer to the present than to the past. Experience, the teacher of life, can teach a great deal to the man who knows how to interpret experience; but many people misinterpret it. Napoleon was a great captain; but we should not ask Napoleon about what he did, rather about what he would do if he were in our shoes, in our circumstances, in our time. It is likely that Napoleon could give us some valuable advice; but we should not forget that when the Corsican closed his eyes, the world was not yet girdled by ribbons of steel, guns were not yet breech-loading, machine guns were unknown, words were not transmitted over wires or ether waves, the automobile and the airplane were unknown. I think it is a good thing he cannot rise from his splendid tomb. Who knows what words would come from his disdainful lips in scorn of those who too often misuse his name and reputation?

This is the end of my analysis; but before closing it I want to point out an intimate characteristic of the air arm. The colossal armies and navies of today, although they cannot do without the human element, the soul of every machine, cost enormously; and so only the richest nations can afford them and enjoy their advantages. In comparison to these and in proportion to its offensive capacity, the air arm is much less expensive. Moreover, it is still very young and in a state of rapid and constant change. Everything in it, from its organization to its employment, is in the process of creation. The art of aerial warfare is not yet standardized, like the art of land and sea warfare, and there is still room for ingenuity. The war in the air is the true war of movement, in which swift intuition, swifter decision, and still swifter execution are needed. It is the kind of warfare in which the outcome will be largely dependent upon the genius of the commanders. In short, the air arm is the arm of high courage and bold deeds, material and spiritual, physical and intellectual.

The air arm is the arm not of a rich people, but of a young people, ardent, bold, inventive, who love space and height. It is therefore an arm eminently suited to us Italians. The importance it has attained and its influence on the general character of war are favorable to us; it is the arm best suited to the genius of our race; and surely the solid organization and strong discipline which bind the Italian people in unity is the most adequate force to give us courage to face the terrible effects which would come from an aerial war, even if victorious. Our geographical position, which serves us as a bridge across the Mediterranean, makes the air arm still more vital to us. Visualize Rome as the center of a zone with a radius of 1,000 kilometers, normal range for a plane today, and you will find within the circumference the whole of the ancient Roman Empire.

To dominate our own sky will mean to dominate the Mediterranean sky. Let us therefore look to the future with hope and confidence and give thanks to all those whose daring and ingenuity have made this arm powerful.

Book Three

Recapitulation

This polemic was written to clarify the many which ap-peared in Italy on the subject of Military Aviation. It first appeared in Rivista Aeronautica *for November 1929.*

Introduction

THE EDITOR of this review has opportunely intervened to make peace between the contestants. Like war on land, the discussion had become stabilized. The attackers repeated the same attacks, and the defender was forced in retaliation to repeat the same defensive arguments. The result was monotonous repetition which left the spectators cordially bored. But now a recapitulation of this long and bloodless war of words may be of some interest and utility—if for nothing else, to sum up the respective arguments as a basis for the renewal of the controversy at the proper time. Therefore, I have accepted the editor's courteous invitation to present an analysis of the discussion. I must ask indulgence if now and then I have to repeat myself, and not always as briefly as I could wish.

My first affirmation of the importance of the aerial arm goes back to 1909, twenty years ago. Even then I stated definitely, with no reservations, that only the heavier-than air machines would solve the problem of human flight, especially in the military field; that the aerial arm was destined not to perform auxiliary actions to facilitate and integrate actions of land and sea forces, but to constitute an armed force, the third arm, parallel to, and of equal importance with, the land and sea forces; that the military plane should eventually have the capacity for combat in the air; and that the command of the air would soon be at least as valuable as the command of the sea.

Since 1909 I have done nothing but repeat and amplify these fundamental assertions, always elated by the course of events, which indubitably has supported my original deductions. Following this same line of thinking, in the first edition of *The Command of the Air,* which appeared in 1921, I tried to show the necessity of creating an independent aerial force instead of auxiliary ones—that is, forces dependent upon the arm to which they are attached—which I called Independent Air Force, able to perform acts of war with its own means. I tried also to show the necessity of giving this organization a status equal to the army and navy, and of putting its organization under an Air Ministry.

At that time Italy was in a troubled and uncertain state, and my book was not given due consideration. It was, however, destined for the highest honor—namely, being put into execution. The National Government did in fact create first the Aeronautical Ministry and later the Independent Air Force. Thanks to no merit of mine, but to the enlightened thinking of the Head of the Government, the air arm has acquired a status equal to that of its sister arms, the land and sea arms. The Independent Air Force has been placed in a position parallel to the army and navy. The fact that the three military ministries were united under the Head of the Government, and that the rank of Chief of the General Staff was created, defined and perfected the central organization of our armed power. Thus the most important step had been taken in regard to the air arm, and at last the Independent Air Force could show clearly what it was worth.

Though the fundamental concept of an Independent Air Force was clear and definite, there was still a great deal of vagueness and confusion about it in the minds of the people in general. An Independent Air Force? What for? What is it supposed to do, and how will it work? What is it worth? There was nothing for me to do in answer but to amplify in more detail the ideas I had already expressed in *The Command of the Air.* At that time I had explicitly stated that the conquest of the command of the air is absolutely necessary for victory. A logical corollary of that idea is that it is essential to be prepared for the conquest of the air, and that therefore most of our aerial forces ought to be concentrated into the Independent Air Force, the organization designed for the conquest of the air.

To concentrate is the opposite of to disperse. So, taking one more step, in Part II of *The Command of the Air,* added in the edition of 1927, I affirmed the necessity of concentrating all available aerial forces into an Independent Air Force designed to sustain the struggle of which the final objective is the command of the air. In order to accomplish this, I said, it would be advisable to do away with auxiliary aviation and aerial defense forces, both of which I considered a futile dispersion of strength, useless, superfluous, and harmful.

That started the fireworks. Most of the opposition, especially in this review, was directed against that assertion. I tried to parry the attacks. Still better, I used them as a springboard to launch into general argument on the subject of controversy. I not only stood firmly on my position, but added that, by keenly examining the future of war, anyone could see that a radical change was in process, a change brought about by facts and circumstances which would make the air the decisive field in future wars. For this reason, I contended, according to the basic principle of the art of war, it was not enough to concentrate all aerial resources into an Independent Air Force by doing away with auxiliary and defense aviation forces. Still another bolder and more revolutionary step must be taken—namely, to concentrate the bulk of all national resources in the decisive field, the air. Thus I promulgated a new doctrine of war based on the principle of resisting on land in order to mass one's strength in the air. Naturally, this contention of mine stirred up the controversy, and I saw the number of my opponents swell rapidly. It was just what I hoped for.

The best way to assay the worth of a theory is to put it to the test of fire. I was the first to realize the novelty and daring of the ideas I was expressing; and obviously I could not expect them to be embraced like old friends. My ideas were so new, so different from those heard on the street corner, that people were naturally surprised and look at them askance. I found it most interesting indeed to study the reaction they provoked, and for this reason I was grateful for the opponents who honored me with their criticism. Even if my ideas have not yet been fully accepted, I feel well satisfied to see that the long debate they started has not elicited any argument which makes me entertain a doubt of the worth and soundness of my opinions on the serious problem of war in our times. Seeing that so many opponents of recognized ability, hailing from army, navy, aviation, and even civilian circles, have not been able to muster a single new argument against my theories, has been a great source of satisfaction to me; and I have often patted myself on the back and said: "Well, old man, you're not so bad after all!"

Some readers may think this is obstinacy inspired by foolish presumption or lack of conscience. It is true that anything is likely to happen in this world; but it is also true that every opinion deserves respectful consideration. Therefore, I respect the opinion of those readers, but they cannot stop me from reasoning the way I do, and I ask them to be so good as to follow my reasoning with me.

Several articles of great importance have recently been published on the subject under discussion, articles important because written by well-known authorities belonging to land and sea armed forces and civilian circles. To mention a few: "Concerning Aerial Battles and the Ratio between the Whole and Its Component Parts," by General Bastico, in *Rivista Aeronautica* Vol. VI; "Aviation, Tactical Code, and Armed Forces," by General Bollati, in *Rivista Militare Italiana;* "To Resist on Land in Order to Mass One's Strength in the Air," by Captain A. Fioravanzo,[1] in *Rivista Aeronautica,* Vol. VII; and "The Aerial Arm As a Decisive Factor of Victory," by Engineer Salvatore Attal, in *Rivista Aeronautica,* Vol. VII.

On the whole these articles can be said to contain all the criticisms of my theories and to represent the views of my opponents. They will often be referred to in the following synthesis, which will be divided into the following sections: (1) Auxiliary Aviation, (2) Aerial Defense, (3) Aerial Battle, and (4) The Aerial Field As the Decisive Field.

[1] Of the Italian Navy.

CHAPTER I

Auxiliary Aviation

IN OPPOSITION to my assertion that auxiliary aviation is useless, superfluous, and harmful, my opponents have been content to emphasize the importance of these auxiliary forces during land and sea operations, and therefore the paramount necessity of keeping and even increasing them. In a recent article, "For the Naval Aviation," Beta, the pseudonym of a high naval authority, analyzes the importance of ship-based aviation, *outlining in summary the principal needs for auxiliary aerial help for a naval force operating in the Mediterranean from the moment it leaves its base.* These needs, according to the author are: (1) anti-submarine scouting, (2) aerial defense, (3) reconnaissance, and (4) tactical co-operation. Going on with his argument, the author declares a certain number of aircraft-carriers are *indispensable.*

Anyone who reads a succinct article like this must conclude that the author is right. In the same way all the worthy military and civilian authors are right who say that an army or navy without auxiliary aviation would be seriously inferior in face of an army or navy with its own auxiliary aviation. It is all so true that I am proud that I issued, when I was commander of the Aviation Battalion, the *first* "Rules for the Employment of Airplanes in War," in 1913. At that time the airplane was so little understood that I was directed by order of the Ministry of War to delete the word "arm" every time it occurred in these "Rules" in reference to the airplane.

Certainly it is true that when two armies or navies meet, one with and one without auxiliary aviation, the one without will find itself seriously at a disadvantage. This is an argument which needs no discussion. Even stones recognize its soundness. But the trouble with this argument is that it is impossible to visualize two armies or two navies acting in complete isolation, entirely by themselves.

We are not judging here the value of the aerial arm on land or sea. Instead we are judging its value in the whole field of war as a unit. These are two very different points of view. When the aerial arm was considered *solely* suitable for auxiliary service in land and sea operations—in other words, when it was thought that the only actions feasible for aerial means were auxiliary actions—then my opponents were in the right. But now the Independent Air Force exists, it has been legally constituted, and willy-nilly it must be taken into account. The Independent Air Force—that is, an aerial force of impressive size—flies and performs in the air above the armies and navies; these forces fly and perform in the same field in which auxiliary forces are supposed to fly and perform. No argument is possible now on the subject of aviation without taking the Independent Air Force into account; the air above the armies and navies is no longer reserved for auxiliary aviation forces. On the contrary—and most important— it is possible now to argue only about the co-existence of the Independent Air Force and auxiliary aviation forces in the same field.

Auxiliary aviation acquires its greatest value only when acting in concert with surface operations; and this maximum value is nullified if auxiliary aviation cannot co-exist with the Independent Air Force. I maintain that the two cannot co-exist; and therefore auxiliary aviation is useless, superfluous, and harmful.

In a fight between two Independent Air Forces, no matter how the fight takes place, one must necessarily prevail over the other. Assuming that fact, is it possible to imagine a dominating Independent Air Force which would allow the enemy auxiliary aviation to act at will, especially if it would cause serious trouble by doing so? On the face of it, it would not. In fact, either auxiliary aviation cannot influence the outcome of the war—in which case it would be left unmolested, free to go on burning gasoline—or it can influence the outcome to some degree—in which case nothing would stop the dominating Independent Air Force from attacking and destroying it, the more easily as the auxiliary aviation is not equipped for combat. In order to make use of one's auxiliary aviation, one's Independent Air Force must be predominant, for auxiliary aviation can co-exist only with a predominant or victorious Independent Air Force.

In order to enjoy the advantages which obviously can accrue from the use of auxiliary aviation, one must first of all be victorious in the air. Therefore, before anything else, one must put one's Independent Air Force in condition to defeat the enemy Independent Air Force as easily as possible. In other words, one must make it as strong as possible, avoiding any dispersion of forces, and consequently doing away with auxiliary aviation. Discarding auxiliary aviation is the best way to enjoy these advantages, which cannot be gained by keeping it.

This may sound like a play on words, but it is not. If by discarding my auxiliary aviation I can increase the strength of my Independent Air Force so that it can conquer the enemy Independent Air Force, I can also destroy my enemy's auxiliary aviation, and in addition put aerial means at the disposal of my army and navy—means which can then function with no fear of opposition from my enemy. But if to keep auxiliary aviation I am compelled to reduce the strength of my Independent Air Force, and as a result it is defeated by the enemy, I will also see my auxiliary aviation destroyed or prevented from giving any help to my army and navy.

Therefore, although auxiliary aviation seems valuable when land and sea operations are considered by themselves, in the whole picture of the war—the army, navy, and Independent Air Force functioning simultaneously—it seems useless, superfluous, and harmful.

Let us visualize two armies fighting in a theater of war flanked by the sea. Obviously, such armies would be greatly assisted by naval auxiliary means capable of facilitating and integrating the land operations taking place along the shore. But to visualize the existence of such naval auxiliary means, the navy must be supposed not to exist. But as a matter of fact navies do exist and naval auxiliary means do not. And it is entirely feasible for an army operating on the seashore or any short distance from it to be helped by naval means, provided its navy is predominant over the other. The same thing holds when the surface is considered in relation to the air. As soon as the Independent Air Force was created, the usefulness of the auxiliary aviation forces came to an end. The only aerial assistance the army and navy should rely on is help from their own victorious Independent Air Force. In their own interest the army and navy should do away with their own auxiliary aviation forces.

Nowadays anyone considering land and sea operations of any importance must of necessity remember that above the land and sea is the air. Once, when only the swallow and the albatross flew in the air, to think of land and sea operations as isolated events was justified, because, with very few exceptions, operations in the two theaters were independent of each other. But now land operations can be considered independent of aerial operations only up to a point. Furthermore, since aerial operations can be directed against both land and sea objectives, while the reverse is not true, it is logical to agree that aerial operations are the only ones which can be carried on independently of the others. This undeniable fact is not generally taken into consideration, perhaps because it lacks the sanction of historical precedent; and land and sea operations are still visualized as isolated in space and time, as though they took place inside closed theaters. At the most, the only consideration given to aerial means is to those which operate inside these closed theaters.

This is nothing less than a refusal to face realities. In the article entitled "For the Naval Aviation," the author says he intends to draw "the picture of the principal needs for aerial help for a naval force operating in the Mediterranean *from the moment it leaves its base.*" The author starts by implicitly admitting the safety of the base from which the naval force leaves; for naturally an unsafe base is no base at all. Now, this safety cannot be taken for granted until the enemy Independent Air Force has been reduced to inability to carry on significant actions. As long as the enemy's Independent Air Force has threatening power, an aerial force at least equal to the enemy's is necessary to ensure the safety of the naval base. Since there can be more than one naval base, it would be impossible to assign to the defense of each base an aerial force equal to the whole enemy Independent Air Force, unless the enemy were greatly lacking in aerial means. It would be still more impossible to assign to the fleet all the other aerial means which Beta considers essential.

On the other hand, as long as the enemy Air Force is intact, the fleet operating in the Mediterranean could always be attacked by it; and in that case the fleet would need a ship-based aerial force equal or superior to the enemy Independent Air Force, a manifest impossibility.

Everything Beta describes as indispensable aerial help for a naval force operating in the Mediterranean would be sensible only if flying over the Mediterranean could be forbidden to any but naval aviations, ship-based or not. But a situation like that in the Mediterranean cannot be assumed. An Independent Air Force can fly in any direction over this great sea, against naval bases, cruising fleets, commercial ports, and lines of communication. To free a naval force in the Mediterranean from this menace, her own Independent Air Force must be victorious. Only after victory in the air can the navy rely on aerial help—help which would be of great value because the enemy would be without it.

Beta's contention is right only in case of naval forces operating in zones where Independent Air Forces could not fly; and such zones are now found only in the oceans. His ideas would apply to an English, American, or Japanese naval force operating in the Atlantic or Pacific Ocean; but even then it would apply only up to a point—that is, as long as the ships kept far enough away from enemy shores. Once they got within the range of the enemy's Independent Air Force, they would have to fight not only ship-based aerial forces, but also the Air Force itself. That shows that even in the oceans the Independent Air Forces have a not inconsiderable value.

Because I always keep in view our own particular situation, lying athwart the Mediterranean Sea, I affirm that our navy should be deeply interested in an Independent Air Force able to defeat an enemy's, and that it should therefore willingly give up its auxiliary aviation in order to increase the Independent Air Force, which would quickly conquer the command of the air in case of war.

Several times I have addressed to my opponents in the army and navy the following question: "What would happen to an army or navy compelled to operate against an enemy who has conquered the command of the air?" I have never received an explicit answer. I understand that the question is a difficult one, especially for critics who do not like to give due consideration to the Independent Air Force. But it should be answered, because the situation predicated in it may easily come to pass owing to the weakening of the Independent Air Force now going on in order to reinforce auxiliary aviation. Some critics took the position that there can be no victory and no defeat in the air. Others disputed desperately and philologically the meaning of the words, "the command of the air."

I had to explain repeatedly and at length what I meant by those words; I had to swear that, according to me, "command of the air" did not mean we had to succeed to an extent where even the enemy flies were prevented from flying, but simply where we had put the enemy in a position that made it impossible for him to execute aerial actions of any significance. I also said I had no special affection for that particular phrase and no objection to using a better-sounding one, such as "predominance in the air," or "preponderance in the air," or "aerial supremacy," providing the meaning was not changed. But I repudiated the idea that aerial conflict cannot be won or lost. It offended my common sense. Conflict in the air is like conflict on land or on the sea, or any other kind. By its very nature any conflict must end in a victor and a loser; otherwise it would be no conflict. Aerial forces are similar to any other forces, and out of a conflict of opposing forces comes victory and defeat. I leave this matter to the common sense which nature has given mankind.

Many other people held the opinion that the command of the air (or supremacy or predominance) can be won only *locally* and *temporarily*. But if there is any field in which a struggle would be difficult to localize, the air is certainly that field. And why should the command of the air be temporary? If my Independent Air Force puts the enemy in a position where he cannot execute warlike actions in the air of any appreciable significance, its command of the air will be complete and lasting as long as the enemy remains in that position.

But that my opponents understand. In defense of the word "temporary" they claim that one conquered in the air may still build up another air force and reverse the situation. Of course, anything can happen in this world; but when that happens it would mean simply that the command of the air had passed to the other side. That is possible, just as it is possible for one beaten on land to raise a new army able to conquer the victor, just as it is possible for one beaten on the sea to build a new fleet, and so on and on. But it is really very difficult for anything like that to be done, on land, on the sea, or in the air; and here we are not dealing with the exceptional, but with the normal.

In the aerial field, the possibility of the defeated side's rebuilding an Independent Air Force able to get revenge is based on the assumption that the victorious Air Force would be so chivalrous as to allow the enemy to reorganize its forces, or so naïve as not to increase its own forces by as much as the enemy could rebuild. Such an assumption in war is foolish.

Captain Fioravanzo writes:

In the case of such a hypothesis (that the enemy, owing to inferior means, lack of political courage, or fear of risk, would try to avoid a decisive battle), the command of the air in the hands of the stronger side would be unstable, at least potentially, owing to the fact that the enemy's forces would still exist; and if the weaker side refused to risk a decisive battle, it might be difficult to force him to it. This might happen if, for instance, a weak enemy had a well-organized active and passive local defense and underground airports, so that it would be impossible to draw out his aerial forces or attack his industrial or population centers without grave risk.

And as time goes on, the aerial forces which were so strong and numerous at the beginning of the war might even become weaker little by little from the wear and tear of war, until they reached a state of inferiority. Then, if the enemy is alert and wise, and if he has been purposely temporizing, the roles could be interchanged. And then the battle would take place, just as might happen in naval warfare.

There is too much of the "just as" in his assumption. To arrive at his conclusion, the author has had to assume that the conditions of sea warfare and aerial warfare are identical. But that is an unjustifiable assumption. On the sea it is not only possible but easy to draw in one's forces in such a way as to make it difficult if not impossible for the enemy to draw them out or harm them in any way. On the sea it is absolutely impossible to prevent an enemy from supplying his naval forces with everything they need. Unless one is willing to take heavy risks, it is impossible on the sea to act against industrial or population centers if they are protected, and in any case they can only be centers on or near the coast.

But in the air, while the possibility of drawing in one's forces to underground shelters has to be admitted in the absolute sense, in practice it must be recognized as a very difficult feat, especially if the forces are large. But to draw in the forces would not be enough; one would have to draw in also everything which gives life and means to those forces—depots, factories, repair shops, and other necessities—and that would be even more difficult. Aerial means for keeping an offensive away from an industrial or population center are more limited and less effective than the means which can be used to keep naval means at a respectful distance from coastal centers. Furthermore, those aerial defense means must be widely scattered, because all centers can be attacked from the air instead of only the coastal ones, as in naval warfare. The World War demonstrated clearly that naval bases which were safe from the strongest battle fleets proved easy prey to the very primitive aerial means in existence then, and they were attacked with very little risk, too. Therefore, the conditions under which the two conflicts take place are alike only up to a point.

If it were admitted that a *stronger* Independent Air Force could not act at will against the bases and supply and production centers of the *weaker* one; if, furthermore, it were admitted that a *stronger* Independent Air Force could be held in check purely by the active and passive aerial defense of the enemy, we would have to conclude that it is useless, superfluous, and harmful to have an Air Force *stronger* than the enemy's, inasmuch as all it could do would be to "thin out from the wear and tear of war," and thus become weaker.

"And then the battle would take place," writes the author. Why? Why should the *stronger* Air Force, which has now become the *weaker*, accept the battle which, when the initially weaker Air Force *refused* it, had the virtue of making it stronger?

The author continues:

But it seems that the usual resulting situation will be an *unceasing active contest between the contending forces,* and that from the contest will emerge a victor and a loser *within a comparatively short space of time.* That is, the battle (one or many of them) is more likely to happen in an aerial war than a naval one, because the characteristic of the air which prevents standing without movement has to be taken into account.

I admit that I do not understand at all. If the usual resulting situation will be an "unceasing" contest, how can it lead to a decision within a comparatively "brief" space of time? How can the battle be a probable event if the *weaker* Air Force is always in a position to refuse it, and if only by refusing it can he hope to become the *stronger* one?

The author goes on:

Immediately after the decisive combat, the victor will enjoy unopposed freedom of flight—in other words, he will have command of the air; but this does not mean he will enjoy this unbounded freedom of flight without obstacle, because there is no reason to think that the destruction of the enemy main aerial forces would also have nullified his local defenses.

Evidently, there is no reason to think so. But there is every reason to believe that an Independent Air Force able to destroy the *main* enemy aerial forces will also be able to take care of the *secondary* forces, the more so as they are subdivided into *local defense* units and could oppose the offensive action of the Air Force only *separately*.

The author adds:

And if, like Germany, who, thanks to her industrial organization, was able to launch almost as many submarines as the Allies destroyed, the dominator of the air should not have enough remaining forces to make use of his temporary superiority in a way decisive enough to end the war before the other side succeeds in rebuilding an aerial force of appreciable value, the war will drag on and on, just as the World War did.

Quite so. If the victor is left in a condition in which he cannot make use of his victory, it would not be decisive, but only a *temporary* advantage. But that is nothing peculiar to the aerial field; it happens in all of them, land, sea, and air. Nevertheless, the author's comparison is not just. The German industrial organization which made it possible for Germany to replace submarines as fast as she lost them was located out of reach of the offensive action of the Allied naval forces, which had to wait while the submarines were built, equipped, and sent out to sea, because it was only at sea that they could deal with them.

But an organization capable of rebuilding an Independent Air Force would be located in a place easily accessible to the Air Force in command of the air; and the dominator of the air could attack and destroy the enemy aerial means as they were being built, armed, equipped, and launched into the air. Meanwhile, he himself, with the utmost safety, could build, arm, equip, and launch as many aerial means as he was capable of producing. There is no doubt that the command of the air may turn out to be *temporary,* but only if the conquest proves to be a Pyrrhic victory— if the one who conquers the air is satisfied with moral domination of it or sleeps on his victory instead of creating new aerial arms for himself, and lets the enemy go about rebuilding his aerial forces. But if the one who conquers the command of the air also knows how to exploit it, he will not make the mistake of letting the enemy do what he pleases. Because, once the command of the air is conquered, whether or not it becomes "temporary" depends not upon some peculiar characteristic of the air arm, but solely upon the mental caliber of the commander of the victorious Independent Air Force. Let us pray to God for a good commander.

General Bastico, to whom I particularly referred my question, "In what conditions would an army find itself if it were compelled to operate under a sky dominated by the enemy; that is, an army over which enemy aerial forces could operate *freely?"* confined his answer to some witty remarks on the word "freely" and kept silent about the rest. But there is nothing especially humorous about the word "freely." Just as an army which has broken enemy resistance can *freely* invade the enemy's territory, occupy its important centers, and seize its wealth; just as a navy which has sunk the enemy navy can *freely* roam the seas and interfere with the enemy's traffic—so an Independent Air Force which has destroyed the enemy's aerial forces can *freely* rove the air in all directions and *freely* drop whatever it pleases wherever it pleases. As usual, I shall let common sense be the judge.

It is strange how the people who claim that the army and navy absolutely must have auxiliary aviation at their disposal, and take great pains to point out the disadvantages under which they labor without auxiliary aerial forces, show no concern at all about the eventuality that the army or navy, even with an auxiliary force, might be compelled to operate under a sky dominated by the enemy. But such an eventuality may well come to pass and should be taken into consideration, particularly by those people who uphold the theory that national aerial forces should be scattered in a thousand different directions, thus decreasing the potentiality of that force whose essential function is fighting for the command of the air.

No one can deny that a dominating Independent Air Force can operate against the bases, communication lines, and supply centers of the army and navy, causing some damage and some hindrance. No one can deny that a dominating Independent Air Force can at least hamper the task of the auxiliary aerial services. No one can deny that it is a serious disadvantage for an army and navy to operate under the enemy's predominance in the air. No one can deny that the lowered morale of a country subjected to the aerial offensives of an enemy predominant in the air would have a damaging effect on its armed forces.

And yet everyone treats the subject with complete indifference, as though it were no concern of theirs. Why? Because if they once stopped and considered it seriously, they would have to come to the same conclusion I do—namely, that when confronted by an aerial conflict, one must first of all put oneself in a position favorable for victory, which implies concentration of all available aerial forces into a single mass expressly designed to conquer the enemy. But they do not want to reach this conclusion, so, like ostriches, they bury their heads in the sand.

"Nonsense!" some of them say. "Nonsense! The experiences of the World War are all we need to remember. Isn't it true that then the contending aerial forces did nothing but seesaw back and forth without coming to any decision at all? Then . . ."

Yes, it is true; in the World War it was exactly like that. Then only auxiliary aviation shone. But during the Napoleonic wars it was still worse—then not even auxiliary aviation shone. In the World War the conception of real aerial warfare had not been born, and therefore there were no means suitable for fighting one. Similarly, in the Napoleonic wars there was no auxiliary aviation, for the simple reason that the airplane had not yet been born.

I am willing to admit that if in a future war there are two adversaries who both believe that an aerial war can be neither won nor lost, as some of my critics opine, the aerial conflict will seesaw inconclusively, just as it did in the World War. It is hard to prepare for victory and go and win it with a preconceived notion that it is impossible to win. But I am convinced that such a situation is most unlikely to arise, because now Independent Air Forces exist, and many people everywhere are studying how to make themselves predominant in the air.

To begin an aerial war, the real aerial war, meaning the struggle for the command of the air, it is enough if one contestant decides to follow this idea, which can occur spontaneously even to people uninitiated in the art of war: "It would be very profitable for me to make my enemy powerless in the air; therefore, instead of scattering my aerial forces and using them up in sterile seesawings, I should use them to bring down my enemy's aerial forces."

The experience of the past has no bearing on this matter. On the contrary, it has a negative value, as it tends to distort sound reasoning. During the World War aviation was a mere child; and as we know, children play at war, but they cannot wage war. Now aviation has come of age. It knows its strength and its aims; it can accept and perform its mission, which is fighting in the air, just as the missions of its sister arms on the surface are fighting on land and on the sea. Like the army and navy, the Independent Air Force is made to wage war; and in the name of charity, let us never forget it!

In *Le Forze Armate* Colonel Aimone Cat writes as follows:

If the army and navy auxiliary aeronautical forces should be developed to the point which many people advocate, the entire aeronautical budget would not be enough to cover it.

That is true; it could even be said that if all the help the auxiliary aerial means could give the army and navy should be assigned to them, the whole national defense budget would not be enough to pay for it. In fact, owing to its peculiar characteristics, the aerial arm lends itself to anything which may be useful in war. It has speed, and by soaring high it sees everything and sees it well. This makes it useful for all services of exploration, strategical and tactical, far and near; for topographic and photographic reconnaissance; for fire direction and control; for observation and liaison; for the transmission of orders and news; and for all other imaginable services which may be rendered by an instrument which sees well and travels fast.

It is armed, it is fast, and it is powerful; and that is why it is to be found doing all tasks directly and indirectly connected with combat: bombing targets out of reach of artillery fire; extending artillery fire in length and breadth; machine-gunning troops at low altitude in the critical moment of the attack or in retreat; bolstering the morale of wavering troops; hampering enemy troop concentrations at night; bombing staff headquarters and convoys on back roads; and other co-operative tasks which need an instrument which is armed, goes fast, and inspires fear. It is the only arm which can fight in the air. Therefore, it can be used for policing the sky and to prevent the action of enemy auxiliary aviation forces while assisting its own.

Everything the aerial arm can do for the army applies equally well to the navy, and little imagination is needed to visualize new and varied auxiliary services, all of a nature to put the side which doesn't have them at a great disadvantage. Nor is that all. For instance, it is evident that a land or sea unit with Q quantity of aerial means as its disposal would be at a disadvantage faced by a similar enemy with 2Q quantity of aerial means. The result is that auxiliary services would tend constantly to increase. The supporters of auxiliary aviations, realizing that they tend to decrease the strength of the Independent Air Force but not daring to ignore the Independent Air Force, which now has legal status, say: "As far as auxiliary aviation is concerned, we are satisfied with an *indispensable minimum;* give us this minimum and do what you like with the rest." General Bollati writes:

> ...given the importance of the Independent Air Force,...the principal element to be considered is its efficiency in relation to its foreseeable tasks; therefore, we must give to Z (the quantity of aerial means for the Independent Air Force) the *maximum* possible value compatible with the *minimum* exigencies recognized as essential for X and Y (the quantities of aerial means for the army and navy auxiliary aerial forces).

The word "maximum" in connection with the value of Z is pleonastic, as General Bollati himself sets down the following equation, in which T stands for the total of available aerial means and resources: $T = X + Y + Z$. Once the minimum for the essential exigencies of the army and navy is established, it is easy to find the value of Z: $Z = T - (X + Y)$ or $Z = T - X - Y$.

Now, Z cannot be a minimum or a maximum; it is what it is, the *result* of a *subtraction,* that is, a *residue* or, if the word is preferred, a *balance.* This balance can be so small as to reach zero, depending upon the values given to X and Y, as T is a constant. The principal element is the efficiency of the Independent Air Force, but this efficiency is only whatever the *balance* is after all provisions have been made for the auxiliary aviations. The General adds:

> The two older forces—the army and navy—*cannot help* recognizing that their younger sister—the Independent Air Force—already is able to act on her own [in the general picture of war operations] *where they could not act,* or *taking their place in certain circumstances,* or *validly*

co-operating with them in their actions. It would be absurd for them
to deny her the means to accomplish these tasks. But she is now also
in a position to give them the precious means they could not do without. . . . Therefore, even if she can get little or nothing in exchange,
she is in duty bound to be generous within the limits of her possibilities.

General Bollati's idea is that the younger sister should be the
Cinderella of the family. The two older sisters "cannot help"
recognizing her existence and her ability to act on her own—in
favor of the older sisters, of course, going where they cannot go,
substituting for them in certain circumstances, giving them a
lift when they need it; but Cinderella is also in duty bound to
deprive herself in order to give generously to her sisters. But she
should not be afraid; somehow there will always be something
left for her.

No thought is given to the value of the Independent Air Force
in relation to the whole picture of war operations. She has to do
the best she can with what is left over. She cannot do much in any
case! The army and navy must be kept up to a certain standard
of efficiency. Now that aeronautics has arrived and can help the
other arms, her first duty should be to give that help without
stint, all else being secondary. That is what is called co-operation
with the armed forces; but in reality it is the spirit of an armed
force not only unable to rise to being the spirit of the national
armed forces, but degenerating into pure egotism.

If the Independent Air Force has a specific function in the
whole picture of war operations, it must have power enough to
perform it, just as the army and navy have. As long as the Air
Ministry has to provide for the auxiliary aviations out of its own
funds, harmful conflicts of interest will always come up between
them. Each will try to bring grist to its own mill, and neither
will be satisfied.

Do the army and navy believe they cannot get along without
auxiliary aerial means? All right, why do they not provide them
for themselves out of their own funds, as they do everything
else they need? In the same way, the Independent Air Force
should have its own budget which would let it live by itself with-

out interference. Otherwise it would be incorrect to say, as General Bastico does, that a certain nation spends 5 billions for its armed forces, of which 700 millions go for aerial forces, when in effect a large part of the 700 millions goes for auxiliary means to increase the efficiency of the surface forces. I have been saying this since 1921.

Only the army—or the navy—is competent to estimate what auxiliary aerial forces it needs; and this estimate should not be a compromise arrived at by bargaining between the army and the Air Ministry. It is better to face this situation squarely and settle it once and for all in the only sensible way so as to avoid interference and recriminations. In actual practice, when the size of its auxiliary aviation has been settled by compromise agreements, the army will always complain that it did not get enough, and the Air Ministry will feel that it has been much too generous.

The army and navy should not let their efficiency depend upon the *generosity* of the Air Ministry or on *sacrifice* on the part of the Independent Air Force. If the auxiliary aviations are acknowledged to be indispensable to the functioning of the surface armed forces, they should have their own place in the organization of these armed forces, like all their other means and equipment. Fixed proportionate quotas of aerial means should be included in the organization of the great land and sea units, just as fixed quotas of artillery and other war means are; and the determination of these quotas should be the exclusive business of the authorities of the land and sea armed forces. In its turn the Independent Air Force should have its own fixed budget, not its present vague, fluctuating one. Then it could study the best ways to use its available funds without the ever-present worry of having to defend its appropriations from requests from other institutions.

This arrangement would not conflict with the principle of aeronautical unity. Certainly this unity must be kept, for there is only one best way of flying no matter for whom the flying is done, the army, the navy, the Independent Air Force, or civil aviation. The Air Ministry would supply the aviation means and personnel to the army and navy according to request and be reimbursed for the cost of production, thus doing away with tasks and responsibilities not in its province. This system would prove satisfactory to the army and navy, too; for they would get the auxiliary aerial means they consider necessary without outside interference, and could organize, instruct, and employ them as they think best.

Why do the supporters of the auxiliary aviations not propose and support this system? In his interesting article, "Employment, Organization, Mobilization, Training, and . . . Functions of the Auxiliary Aviation for the Royal Army," Colonel Aimone Cat writes:

There is no doubt that the problem of auxiliary aviation is still far from a solution. It is much more complex than Sandalli thinks, if by solution is meant the complete organic suitability of the auxiliary aviation to all foreseeable circumstances of war. It is perfectly true that everything is to be made anew.

Not a very encouraging statement! The author continues:

An agreement between the Royal Army and the Air Ministry would be of no benefit to the auxiliary aviation. The road of agreements is a doubtful one, neither military nor rational because it is paved with personal opinions and influences which are not, and never will be, objective.

All too true. Colonel Cat goes on:

The solution is not to say, "Let us sit down and see what we can do." Rather it should be as follows:
Royal Army: "My aeronautical needs, strategic, tactical, and logistic, are as follows."
Air Ministry: "My resources for filling your needs are as follows."
Royal Army: "The organization of my auxiliary aviation, based on my needs and adjusted to your resources, is as follows."

To my way of thinking, all this would perhaps be a step ahead, but not a decisive one. It is only human nature that if you can get something *free* you try to get *as much as you can;* and if you have to give away something *free,* you try to give *as little as you can.* In practice the system proposed by Colonel Cat would lead to this situation: In order to get as much as possible, the army would exaggerate its needs. In order to concede as little as possible, the Air Ministry would be tempted to minimize its resources. In the end, therefore, the organization of the auxiliary aviation would again be arrived at by compromise, bargaining, that is, agreement.

What is needed is a decisive step. The army and navy should say: "I need this much. Here is the money; give it to me." Then the Air Ministry would fill the request and be paid for it. Then there would be no need of compromise agreements; each would be satisfied and would accept the responsibility which belonged to him.

Colonel Cat writes further:

Nowadays it is out of the question to expect an institution to have complete knowledge of everything pertaining to the land and aerial fields [and the sea fields too, I would add]; and it is necessary that the most important collaboration—in organizing—should be closer and continuous. One way to develop this most important form of collaboration might be to institute a Command of the Auxiliary Aviation of the Royal Army. Such an institution should exist in time of war.

This would be another step ahead, but still not the decisive one. Certainly in time of war there should be commands for the auxiliary aviations of the army and navy; and no doubt it would be advisable to organize them now in time of peace, at least in skeleton. But their function should not be a closer and continuous collaboration; for a collaboration is characteristically vague and indecisive, subject to personal influence, and can function only through concessions and compromises. Instead, their main function should be to develop their own plan of action.

The decision as to the quality and quantity of auxiliary aerial means needed by the army and navy belongs exclusively to the organizing authorities of these two institutions. The one who has charge of the organization of the army is the one to say, for example, that the army needs an aerial service for strategical exploration, and so on. No special knowledge of aviation techniques is required for that; it needs only a knowledge of the general characteristics of aerial means, and nowadays this is part of the general culture. Then the commands of the auxiliary aviation for the army and the navy should use their special technical competence to decide upon the organization of the aerial means needed and their cost. The organizing authorities of the army and navy would thus come into possession of all the data needed for their final decision. As soon as the decision was made, the commands of the auxiliary aviations would send their requests for personnel and means to the Air Ministry, which would furnish them at production cost.

This is the only clear, precise, radical solution of the problem. It would do away with the necessity for compromise agreements and would be a solution materially and morally clear-cut. The following advantages would ensue from such a solution:

1. The auxiliary aerial means would constitute an integral part of the army and navy, on the same footing as all other war means these institutions have at their disposal. The organizing authorities would have as much interest in them as in other means; the employment of them would be synchronized with other means; and the result would be perfect because all would be under the direction of a single mind, and the maximum efficiency would be achieved thereby.

2. Having the task of organizing their own auxiliary aviations and paying for them out of their own budgets, the organizing authorities of the army and navy would correlate their aerial forces with all the others in order to get the most benefit from the money they had. Only then would we know exactly how much importance these authorities really do attach to aerial assistance! Today all they have to do is ask for it, and quite naturally they do not bother about the cost, which will come out of someone else's budget; and so they feel that whatever they ask for is an absolute necessity. If an automobile were given away free to anyone who swore that he absolutely had to have one, would not everybody be riding in an automobile?

3. The Independent Air Force would have its own budget and be free to organize according to its possibilities.

I am convinced that, if such a system should be adopted, not only would the auxiliary aviation really function, but little by little the army and navy would dispense with them. The supporters of the absolute necessity of the auxiliary aviations would no longer ask: "What shall we ask from the generosity of the Air Ministry?" The problem would be quite different. Having to pay the cost out of their own budget, regardless of its size—and even if it should be increased to cover the new expense—they would ask themselves: "Which will better increase the potentiality of the army (or navy), devoting a part of our budget to aerial means or spending it all on land (or sea) means?" The problem would then be more realistic and bring down to earth the soaring imaginations; and probably the answer would be something like this: "What would be the use of aerial means anyway unless our Independent Air Force conquers the command of the air? And if it does, couldn't we then ask for its co-operation against an enemy deprived of aerial strength? Then the best thing to do is to use all of our appropriation to increase our land (or sea) means." Thus the auxiliary aviations would die, killed by their own defenders.

CHAPTER II

Aerial Defense

My worthy opponents have often been pleased to call me a "theorist"—meaning a visionary—when confronting me with their "practical" and "realistic" points of view. Engineer Attal writes in the article cited above:

> I am not an opponent of General Douhet. I discuss his ideas, not to refute but to clarify them. As I am accustomed by my profession to single out the *reality* of any problem I have to consider, I will try here to translate the theory into *practice*. From the general I will come down to the specific.

Engineer Attal—my courteous opponent will bear with me—reminds me a little of one of those ladies who, when gossiping about their friends, say: "Oh, so-and-so? Oh, yes, she is lovely, charming and virtuous, but . . ." and then go on to paint so-and-so blacker than the devil himself.

He begins by complimenting me so much I blush. He repeats several times that he is not one of my opponents, but. . . By the contents of his article he always ends by pointing out that, at least practically and realistically, I am sunk in error up to my neck. In fact, he supports the absolute necessity of auxiliary aviation, attaches great importance to aerial defense, and recognizes only the relative decisiveness of the aerial field. Practically, he is against everything I stand for; and I am inclined to ask myself what he would have written about my theories if he had not declared at the beginning that he was one of my "fervent followers."

But, jesting aside, I must admit that his system of criticism is very convenient, especially when valid arguments are lacking. In effect he says, "Oh, yes, theoretically it cannot be said that you are wrong; but practically you are grossly mistaken." This is convenient, because no one can have practice in this particular question. If I am a theorist—and Engineer Attal will allow me to say it—he is a poet and a dreamer. In regard to aerial defense, the question to which I shall limit myself for the time being, he makes statements of this sort:

> . . . we have to put ourselves in a position to *guarantee at any time and against any enemy the safe development of our national effort!*

This is the statement of an ideal. Now we must see if we could put ourselves in such a position in *practice.*

> . . . our aeronautical budget should answer the following *practical* idea: *"What is the minimum quantity of aerial forces needed to ensure the command of the air in our own sky?"* After this minimum is arrived at, it should be increased by one-third.

This is no *practical* basis for a budget, it is a *poetic* one. At least, that is the way any Finance Minister would look at it.

> . . . our defense should not be limited by the extent of our budget; but the budget should conform to the necessities of defense.

This kind of thing may be practical for the United States of America, but certainly not for us. It is only poets who are not confined by the extent of their budgets.

General Douhet is always worrying about budget limitations. He reasons very well as a military chief used to fighting for large enough appropriations to carry out his plans; but I reason like a businessman. During my professional career I have had the opportunity of carrying out several business deals, and I have found that the only thing that counts is whether the deal is good—that is, worth while. When the deal is worth while, the money is always found.

Although I am not a business expert, I should like to point out that the end sought in business deals is the largest profit from the money and means invested. That is what counts *practically.* *Practically* it is necessary to get the highest return from the money and means invested. The businessman who does not give due attention to the amount of money available when he puts his best ideas in practice, usually succeeds in bankrupting himself. War is a business, like any other; it is the business of distribution. Even in war one must try not to go bankrupt. It is always a question of budget. Italy can afford a Fiat; America can afford a Ford.[1] The fact is as uncomfortable as the mythical shirt of Nessus, but one cannot get away from it.

It is not the province of the war expert to decide what a nation can allocate to its own defense, just as it is not the province of an electrical engineer to decide about the capitalization of an industrial company. Both must be satisfied with utilizing to the best advantage what is made available to them.

The war expert must realize that the economic potentiality of a nation is what it is, no more and no less; and that nation must live first and arm itself afterward. Otherwise it would be like fastening a dead man inside of a strong suit of armor. It would do him little good even if it were made of the toughest steel. If Italy were a rich country like the United States, I might not have bothered myself with my theories. But that is not the case. Nowadays, the less a nation can afford, the more carefully it must utilize what it has. I consider this a very practical principle, even from the business point of view.

I do not say [writes Engineer Attal] that defense needs should come out of military budgets alone; civilian budgets also may be drawn on.

Engineer Attal cartainly has a strange idea of the budgets of a state. He does not realize that all budgets, military and civilian, make up an indivisible whole. Does he think it would be "good business" for the nation to take funds away from agriculture and education, let us say, and devote them to aerial defense?

But let us drop questions like these, which are outside the scope of a technical discussion, which should simply define *the best way to utilize available resources.*

It would certainly be ideal if we could put ourselves in a position to "guarantee at any time and against any enemy the safe development of our national effort"; just as it would be ideal if we could ensure for ourselves the command of our sky. But it is precisely the possibility of reaching these *ideals* that I say is lack-

[1] Douhet intends to compare the *number* of automobiles in the two countries, not the relative costs of the two kinds.

ing. I did hope that Engineer Attal would forget his idealistic assertions for a moment and point out somewhat practically how and where and by what means these ideals could be realized. Instead he gives out more general assertions:

Flying over one's own territory is *infinitely* easier and less expensive than flying over someone else's territory.... When airfields of the future have been *conveniently* distributed over *appropriate* zones, when all supplies and other necessities have been made ready, the command of one's own sky can be ensured with an *adequate* aerial force.... We could always arrange our aerial defenses *within practical limits* so as to reduce to a *minimum* the damage from enemy bombings, even if the chemical arm should be used against us.

Fine words, all of them; but not a word, not a single verb or adjective, to clarify even summarily the quantity of means necessary to attain those aims of his. There has been a lot of talk going on about the "moral factor," and we do agree on that; but when he has to talk about material means, Engineer Attal lightly gets out of it with these words:

What counts is not the number but the organization; in case of war the number is multiplied to the maximum degree within the limits of the organization.

What organization, pray? What number? Besides the moral factor, which is irrelevant to the discussion, preparing an aerial defense demands aerial forces, antiaircraft forces, and matériel to arm them. Naturally, these forces have to be organized. But that is not enough. What is necessary is that they should *exist* already organized and prepared to go into action as soon as hostilities begin. We cannot wait for war to come before we "multiply" them; we cannot expect that the state budget will be transformed in case of war into a single *war budget;* we cannot wait for the enemy to come and bomb us before *spending what will have to be spent for aerial defense*. What counts in aerial defense, no matter what is meant by the term, is not to *organize* it, but to *have it at one's disposal*.

I wrote: "If anyone can prove to me that we could *surely* and *completely* protect our country from eventual aero-chemical offensives by means of a *determined* organized aerial defense, practically possible to bring into existence, I am ready to give up all my theories."

In rebuttal Engineer Attal with much zest makes plays upon the words "surely" and "completely," forgetting it is his fault that I used them, because he had previously affirmed the possibility of *guaranteeing at any time and against any enemy* the safe development of our national effort and of *ensuring the command of our sky.* But I will pass over that and correct myself to read: "I will give up all my theories if someone will prove to me that, by means of a *determined* organized aerial defense, practically possible to bring into existence, we could reduce the force of eventual aerochemical offensives against our country to a point where they would be *unimportant and not dangerous to its safety.*" I will say further: "If, thanks to aerial defense, we had to fear from the enemy aerial offensives only unimportant and not dangerous damage, I would be the first to uphold such a defense *even if it required all our national aerial resources.*"

And I really would! But I am acutely conscious of our unfortunate geographical situation in relation to an aerial conflict; and therefore I know it is much easier for others to attack us than for us to attack them. For this reason a neutralization of aerial offensives would work to our advantage and not to theirs; for then, having done away with the aerial field, we should fight, as in olden times, only on land and sea.

If I am against aerial defense inasmuch as it takes means away from the Independent Air Force, it is not just because I like setting myself against the majority. I am against it because I have a reasonably justified conviction that the aerial defense will be very disappointing in action. I am convinced that it cannot fulfill its aim because much larger forces are needed for defense in the air than for offense. I have demonstrated this hundreds of times; but none of my opponents, Engineer Attal included, have ever discussed or criticized my demonstration. Nonetheless, that is the most important point in the whole question.

To demonstrate that the command of one's own sky is "infinitely" less expensive—or even just "less expensive"—than the command of the air, besides affirming it, Engineer Attal should have demonstrated that *few* aerial forces can keep *many* enemy forces away from our sky. But that is hard to do, because in practice just the opposite happens.

Similarly, Captain Ugo Malusardi's article in *Rivista Marrittima* is valueless. He asserts that "the useful percentage of bombings carried out by the Allies decreased progressively from 73 per cent in 1915 to 27 per cent in 1918." This is merely a statistical item of unknown origin, as no source is given. It is vague, since no explanation of what "useful percentage" means has been made. And anyway, its validity is destroyed, as far as Engineer Attal's point is concerned, by the first words of the paragraph in which it occurs.

The employment of aerial bombings, even toward the end of the World War, was based more on the element of surprise and the special skill of certain aviators than on the matériel itself.

But in future wars aerial bombing operations will be based on something more positive and concrete. We can place no reliance on statistics from a period when there was no true aerial warfare, although some empirical and sporadic bombings were carried out, as well as some absurd ones. I can still remember heroic Captain Salomone, a gold-medal aviator who died in 1918, returning at night to the airfield from which he had taken off with his squadron of Capronis to bomb the terminal of a "Teleferica," when everyone knew that the station was nothing but a make-shift arrangement. I believe that in the future aerial squadrons will not be sent out to bomb make-shift arrangements—something which must have contributed handsomely to decreasing the useful percentage of bombings. Instead, they will be sent against large, vulnerable, easy-to-hit targets, even from altitudes over 1,500 meters. Without worrying about statistics, it is enough to remember that our Treviso was bombed 100 per cent and had to be evacuated in spite of the aerial defense; and at that time, toward the end of the war, our aviation was stronger than the Austrians'.

Engineer Attal sees a marked difference between the command of our own sky and what we might describe as the general sky. It is a distinction which I do not understand. There are no natural borders in the sky, nor artificial barriers. In order to command our sky we should be able to face at any time any enemy aerial force which might try to cross the imaginary line dividing his sky from ours. Therefore, we would need to be everywhere, always ready and able to repel the mass of the enemy aerial forces, because we could not prevent him from trying to come over in mass if he wanted to. But if we were able to repel him, who or what could prevent our aerial forces from crossing the imaginary border between the two skies and flying in the enemy's sky? The only thing which could stop us would be lack of gasoline.

The sky cannot be cut up into sections just to please an aerial defense or an auxiliary aviation. No one can command his own sky if he does not command the adversary's sky. Engineer Attal should realize this: the most practical and realistic way of preventing enemy planes from coming over and bombing us is to destroy them, just as the most practical and realistic way of preventing land and sea offensives against our country is to destroy the enemy's land and sea forces. This is the real solution. All others are palliatives or superfluities, like putting a mustard plaster on a wooden leg. An aerial force in any way subtracted from the offensive force is a force rendered powerless to damage the enemy or offset a corresponding enemy offensive force. This statement is wrong. If two nations, A and B, have equal aerial resources, and A uses *all* of them offensively while B uses *all* of them defensively, B automatically and gratuitously ensures A against any aerial offensive but does not ensure itself against an offensive from A. Consequently, B plays into the hands of A, and does not defend itself either. This is not a theory; it is plain common sense.

Anyway, in war one must know how to *take it*. We agree on that; I myself have said it several times. But one must not exceed certain limits in training oneself to *take it*. Even the strongest boxers are knocked out once in a while. One should not exaggerate the benefits of training, or he may suffer the fate of the horse who was being trained to fast.

The need of *training* oneself to take it comes from the need of *resigning* oneself. Inasmuch as I have stated as a principle that one must *"resign himself* to endure enemy offensives *in order to inflict greater damage on him,"* I have long been one of the most fervent supporters of the need of moral preparation among the population, a necessity which I feel more keenly than anyone else, especially more than those who hope to lower the effectiveness by aerial defense, or those who believe that after all the devil is not as black as he is painted. But the fundamental necessity in preparing the population to face aerial offensives unflinchingly is to make them fully conscious of the gravity of them, not to delude them about the effectiveness of aerial defense; and above all, to make them understand that scattering defensive means here and there would do them no good and divert means from the essential task, hence would be harmful in the final outcome.

Even if I were wrong in my ideas, this is the kind of propaganda I would engage in, for it is useful. A population inured to enduring aerial offensives and convinced that they cannot be adequately protected against them, would certainly be cheered to see that in practice the aerial defense was really capable of keeping away offensives, in spite of what they had been told to the contrary. He who is prepared for the worst is also prepared for the best. But the other way about is very dangerous. A population led to believe in the efficacy of aerial defense would be frightened and their morale lowered if they found out that it did not protect in practice. They could not be made to understand the shortcomings of aerial defense then. They would clamor for more aerial defensive means; and because they could not blame the means, which they believe to be good and sufficient, they would blame the men who man them, accusing them of not knowing how.

We do need a moral preparation, then; but it must be one which will answer the purpose. Besides the moral, material preparation is needed too, which will help to decrease the effects of the offensive. These two preparations together constitute a whole of *passive aerial protection* which does not employ offensive aerial means, and therefore is not contradictory to the principle of resigning oneself to endure the enemy offensives in order to inflict greater ones on him. I consider the organization of this passive protection not only useful but indispensable. I regret to disappoint Engineer Attal, but I stand firmly on my statement: "I acknowledge the value of anything which can be done to lessen the effect of the aerial offensives against us, *provided it would not decrease the strength of the offensive which we might carry to the enemy.*"

I am often accused of being an extremist, but that is wrong. The truth is, two and two will always make four to me, never three or five. Employing an aerial means offensively is *more profitable* than using it defensively. A hundred, a thousand, ten thousand aerial means employed offensively are *more profitable* than fifty, five hundred, five thousand employed defensively and the same number offensively. Two and two make four. I repeat that this is not theoretical or extremist; it is arithmetic, pure and simple.

The Aerial Battle

UNLIKE ENGINEER ATTAL, who at least recognizes that my writing is coherent, General Bastico has filled several pages of this review with an attempt to prove that I am guilty of flagrant contradiction in my evaluation of the aerial battle. Certainly not to prove that I am coherent on this theme, but to clear up misunderstandings and show up the reasoning of my opponents in its true light, I shall say something about the aerial battle, which is of great importance to the thesis I support.

The simplest concept for the guidance of the *stronger* side is this: look for the enemy and defeat him wherever he is encountered. In a land war this is easily done. There are few easy lines of transit on the rugged surface of the earth, and they are well defined. To compel the enemy to fight, all you have to do is march against him and invade his territory. That is the way you meet your enemy on land. In a war on the sea, the concept is less easily carried out. The weaker side can easily avoid combat, even if he has to seek refuge in his own fortified bases. In the last war the weaker side was always being hunted and was never found.

In the aerial war the enemy remains on the surface if he does not want to be found. Just as it is profitable for the *stronger* side to look for the enemy and defeat him wherever he is found, so it is equally profitable for the *weaker* side to avoid defeat by not letting himself be found. Therefore, a stronger Independent Air Force which *looked for* battle—that is, looked for the *weaker* Air Force—would be taking the risk of flying in all directions in vain and exhausting itself without finding its quarry. In other words, it would play into the hands of the *weaker* enemy.

Similarly, if the *weaker* Independent Air Force went looking for battle, it would play into the hands of the *stronger,* very likely committing suicide. In war one must always do his best not to play into the hands of the enemy; therefore, I have always maintained, and I say it again, that an Air Force must never go *looking for* battle, neither the *stronger* nor the *weaker* one. This statement seems to me so clear, so exact, that it should not be misunderstood.

But if the *stronger* Independent Air Force happens to meet the *weaker* by chance, it has everything to gain from a battle because it is the stronger; while the other has everything to lose because it is less strong. Consequently, I have always maintained, and I say it again, that the *stronger* Independent Air Force *must not avoid battle,* but the *weaker must avoid it.* Even this seems to me clear and unequivocal.

Since the *stronger* Independent Air Force *must not look for battle* and the *weaker must avoid it,* and can easily do so, if the aerial war were decided by a battle, it could last for centuries without a conclusive ending, and the two Air Forces would grow old in their own airfields. Therefore, I assert that today, as ever, it is not enough for an Independent Air Force to be able to fight in the air, but it must also have an offensive capacity against the surface.

When I say the *stronger* Independent Air Force, I mean one stronger in its ability to fight in the air, regardless of its bombing capacity. The *stronger* Independent Air Force *must not look for nor avoid the battle.* If it obeys that rule, it can operate with the utmost freedom against the surface; that is, during each flight it can attack the objective which best suits it, and fly straight for it without giving a thought to the enemy Air Force. The latter is either powerless to put up any opposition, in which case the offensive will be accomplished without fighting, or it will decide to show opposition, in which case it will be defeated. In this way the stronger Air Force will damage the enemy in some way or other on each of its flights.

The weaker Independent Air Force *must avoid meeting the stronger.* Therefore, the only thing it can do is attack the enemy's surface, but always trying to *avoid meeting* the stronger Air Force.

Since the *stronger* Air Force must neither look for nor avoid meeting the *weaker,* it has no need of *higher speed;* but for the weaker it might come in handy when *trying to avoid* the stronger. The aerial struggle thus resolves itself into a series of offensive acts against the surface, with the stronger Independent Air Force enjoying the advantage of a larger freedom of maneuver.

The offensive against the surface can seriously affect the potentiality of the two contending Air Forces if it is directed to the destruction of aerial forces on the surface, centers of aeronautical production, and similar objectives. The conquest of the command of the air may result from these indirect attacks on the enemy aerial potential. Only once in a while, for the reasons mentioned above, will it be the result of an aerial battle. A *weaker* Independent Air Force may also happen to gain an initial advantage by an action more intelligent, violent, and intense than the action of the *stronger.*

It may happen that special circumstances and environmental factors lead an Air Force to attack the enemy population and leave objectives of purely aeronautical importance alone. Certainly the outcome of the aerial struggle will depend largely upon the vision of the leaders, the courage of the pilots, and the morale of the people.

That is a clear statement of my opinions. They may be criticized, but they should not be casually dismissed. Let us look at General Bastico's ideas now. He will remember that he wrote as follows:

The peculiar conditions of the aerial field will *always, or nearly always,* allow the weaker adversary to avoid at will a battle which might turn out unfavorably for him.

So far we agree. But in the same article he wrote:

It is true that if the latter [the stronger Independent Air Force] prefers to acquire freedom of movement, it must leave equal freedom to the enemy; that it must let the enemy carry on offensive actions, and it cannot be said that the stronger will not feel them. They may turn out to be weak offensives, pinpricks instead of spear-thrusts; but even pinpricks can be irritating. Then the stronger may *very probably* lose his patience and *try* to engage *that same battle he had wanted to avoid.*

To be accurate, General Bastico should have written, "that he had not wanted to look for," because I never said that the stronger Air Force had to *avoid* battle.

And, I add [it is still General Bastico who writes] that in doing that *he would not be wrong;* on the contrary, he had been wrong heretofore because *he had waited so long before using the necessary and most efficacious way to put the enemy Independent Air Force out of action.*

I must wonder at my colleague's strange reasoning. Why should the stronger Air Force give up its *spear-thrusts* simply to avoid *pinpricks,* and start looking for an enemy who can *always,* or *nearly always,* avoid the battle? Why should looking for a battle with the enemy be the necessary and most efficacious way to put out of action the enemy Air Force, which can *always,* or *nearly always,* avoid it at will? In my opinion, if the commander of the stronger Independent Air Force lost *his patience* under mere pinpricks, he would be showing such nervous instability that he had better go home and grow cabbages.

Farther along in the same article General Bastico feels that it is useless to look for something which cannot be found, and writes:

I have said that *the battle has to be looked for,* but did I say that the Air Force which desires it must find it by searching through the immensity of the sky for something which very probably cannot be found? Is it possible to attribute to me such naïveté?

Really, no one wants to think of General Bastico as naïve. But still, it leaves one a bit puzzled to think of a battle *which has to be looked for without the more or less deliberate intent to look for it.* What does it all mean? Perhaps that the battle has to be looked for without looking for it? And one is still more puzzled to find in the same article:

...I repeat that the battle *must be considered the apogee of the conception of the aerial struggle;* and I make bold to affirm that the Independent Air Force which does not so consider it will lower its fighting capacity, and still more its spirit of aggressiveness.

The apogee of the conception of aerial warfare, then, should be *the battle;* that is, *that action which results from a clash which the weaker Independent Air Force can avoid at will, and the stronger cannot look for deliberately without betraying colossal naïveté.*

To give support to his argument, General Bastico quotes with praise an author who asserts that the predominant Independent Air Force has to *look for* the battle in order to eliminate *as soon as possible* the major obstacle to the destruction of the enemy bases.

Toward the end of the article General Bastico reaffirms his point.

In each case, as respects the particular conduct of the aerial war, *the battle must be considered the pre-eminent action in the struggle.*

Then, perhaps remembering that he had previously said that to act with intention leading to this pre-eminent action would be to show colossal naïveté, he adds:

The ways of *looking for* the battle will depend upon *contingent circumstances.* Among these ways bombings and poisonings of the vital centers of the enemy nation should be considered as the most effective in the majority of cases.

I do not happen to know of any other *contingent ways,* so I will have to be content with the ones he calls the most effective. According to General Bastico, in order to force the enemy to the desired battle, the stronger Air Force should provoke him by bombing and poisoning his vital centers. The weaker Air Force, thus provoked and playing into the hands of the stronger, would intervene between its threatened vital centers and the stronger Air Force; the clash would occur; the battle would take place; and naturally the weaker would be defeated. Afterward the stronger could bomb and poison the vital centers of the enemy nation with no further worry.

All this could happen, of course; but only if the commander of the weaker Independent Air Force is a ———, as the Neapolitans would say. I prefer to picture the enemy as thrice bad, never as thrice good; so I cannot agree with General Bastico. I say that if a stronger Independent Air Force was bombing and poisoning our vital centers, we should not lead out our weaker Air Force to defeat and destruction. Instead, we should use it to bomb and poison enemy vital centers, the more violently and intensely the weaker we are. Above all, we should always try to avoid that battle in which we would be risking defeat and destruction with no advantage to us.

That point, incidentally, proves also that neither the stronger nor the weaker Air Force should take the defensive attitude—the former because it would be unprofitable to give up hurling spear-thrusts to protect itself from pinpricks; and the latter to avoid being led to an aesthetic but foolish suicide.

It is no use. No matter which way you turn, no matter what the contingent circumstances may be, two and two will never add up to three or five, only four. Anyhow, I have an idea that General Bastico himself must be almost convinced of my contentions, because he writes of the war on the sea:

> In the struggle *on the sea,* the defensive requires a superiority of means. A parity might not be enough because the high speed of modern *naval* units and the consequent possibility of sudden attacks makes larger forces necessary to oppose them. Inferior or even equal forces might not do. Substantially, a *naval defensive* does not mean an economy of forces, but rather a larger expenditure of them.

Later on I will analyze this concept of warfare at sea; right now I wish to point out that if "in the air," "aerial," and "aerial defensive" were substituted for "on the sea," "naval," and "naval defensive" in the quotation above, my conclusions would appear to be justified. Such a substitution is fair, because not even General Bastico would deny that modern aerial units are even faster than naval units, and that they too are likely to launch sudden attacks. If the defensive *does not allow an inferiority of means,* but rather *requires a larger expenditure of them,* may I ask who would be so naïve as to assume the defensive in the air? Therefore, it is best always and everywhere to act offensively. It is no use. Two and two always add up to four.

Somewhere in his article, no doubt by inadvertence, General Bastico attributes to me a statement I have never dreamed of making: namely, that *a weaker* Air Force *is always at the mercy of the enemy.* Nothing of the kind! On the contrary, I have always maintained, and continue to do so, that a weaker Air Force may best a stronger one provided it can compensate for the difference in strength by showing more intelligence, more intensity, and more violence in its offensive actions. But since one should always try to be as strong as possible in war, regardless of any other circumstance, I have always proclaimed: "In the name of charity, do not let any aerial force be diverted from offensive action!"

As ever, to my mind, two and two inexorably add up to four.

CHAPTER IV

The Aerial Field As the Decisive Field

LET US COME NOW to *the decisive field of action,* concerning which the debate has so far developed brilliantly. I have maintained, and continue to do so, that in the wars to come *the decisive field of action will be the aerial field;* and therefore it is necessary to base the preparation for and direction of the war on the principle: *resist on the ground in order to mass your strength in the air.*

My worthy opponents are united against me on this point, but I am secure and confident in the strength of my position. The debate is on, but its outcome is still undecided. Nevertheless, I am more than satisfied with the way it is going; because I have noticed, as everyone else must have too, that all my opponents, in spite of every effort, have been forced to agree that the aerial field *may* become the decisive one in wars of the future. General Bastico has agreed to it, although cautiously. He writes:

... nevertheless, as may happen with any other arm, it [the aero-chemical arm] may become decisive under some especially favorable circumstances.

General Bollati also shows agreement when he writes:

So the aerial field of action may also become [decisive] if it succeeds in effecting so strong an offensive that it will result in a paralysis not only of the enemy's forces on the ground and on the sea, but also of the moral and material strength of the nation attacked, leaving it powerless to retaliate.

Similarly, Engineer Attal writes:

I concede that the Air Force may be the decisive factor, but only relatively.

Captain Fioravanzo also agrees when he writes:

To conclude, it can be said that the massing of strength in the air will constitute the *decisive action* of the war; but only if the attacker has left after attaining command of the air an aerial force large enough to completely subdue the enemy, so that he cannot succeed in invading the territory of the attacker on land.

It is evident from the quotations above, taken from the writings of military, naval, and civilian experts, that they admit the air *may* become the decisive field. I will say more. Both General Bollati and Captain Fioravanzo have in effect qualified their agreement thus: *The aerial field becomes decisive if and when the Air Force can defeat the enemy.*

By these admissions my opponents have clearly surrendered already. When they take the position that the aerial field becomes decisive only when the aerial action defeats the enemy, they completely agree with me. Otherwise their contention would be absurd, as though they were saying, "The aerial field is decisive—when it is decisive."

Someone more modest than I would be satisfied with these admissions. As a matter of fact, who could have hoped two years ago, even a year ago, that the time would come when the stalwart writers of the army and navy would agree that the aerial force—up to yesterday considered simply an auxiliary arm—*could* be the decisive factor in a future war? But when it comes to the aerial force and strategy, I am not modest at all. The admissions I have already forced from them spur me on to exact more and more from them.

Some of my opponents equivocate. They think I am trying to give out a recipe for victory when I voice my ideas. In other words, they think I am contending: "To be victorious, Italy must resist on the ground and mass all her strength in the air." That is not correct. Naturally, my first thought is of our own situation and the eventuality of a possible conflict between Italy and some one of her possible enemies. I admit that the theories I expound have that in the background, and therefore should not be considered applicable to all countries. In all probability, if I were specifically considering a conflict between Japan and the United States, I would not arrive at the same conclusions. To offer a general recipe for victory, applicable to all nations, would be downright presumption on my part. My intention is simply to point out the best and most efficient way for our country to prepare for a probable future war. When I say, "The aerial field will be decisive," I do not mean, "In order to win, we must make the aerial field the decisive one." I am simply stating a factual condition. On that premise I proceed.

According to General Bastico, notwithstanding the value of the aerial factor, the immutable doctrine of war is the following:

> In war the decision is the result of the harmonious use of all available armaments, and it is equal to the sum total of the results obtained by each of them. To attain a harmonious use of all armaments, the constituent parts must be harmonized together; and the secret of victory lies in obtaining the correct proportions of the constituent parts.

Obviously, the secret of victory is a secret, and so is known to no one, and therefore does not consist wholly in the correct proportion among the constituent parts of armament. If the United States should go to war with the Republic of San Marino, it is highly probable that the latter would not win, no matter how harmoniously she might employ the constituent parts of her armament.

If we substitute "the means to obtain the maximum result from one's armed forces" for the words "the secret of victory" General Bastico's formula would be a self-evident eternal truth, applicable everywhere at any time. In other words, it would be a universal truism. But, as is the case with all truisms so general in character, it does not tell us anything concrete about the specific problem under consideration. So it is necessary to come down from eternity to the present in order to find out *the correct proportions among the constituent parts of armaments.*

General Bastico does come down and says that he sees that "just proportion of the parts" in an army, a navy, and an air force, all of them capable of an adequate offensive power." I do not consider this an exact definition. What is the meaning of "offensive power"? Considered in the abstract, every kind of armament has an offensive power, whether a revolver or a dreadnought, a knife or an airplane bomb.

In reference to the army, the navy, and the air force, "offensive power" should mean, in my opinion, "the capacity to act offensively with probability of success." An armed force would have no "adequate offensive power" if it attacked with the likelihood of being defeated. In this case it would be rash and inconsistent. Furthermore, in the same article General Bastico rightly warns that the strongest of all the enemies must always be taken into account. The word "adequate" is then used in reference to the enemy most feared. From this we must infer, then, that General Bastico means a correct proportion among *an army, navy, and air force capable of taking the offensive with probability of success against the strongest enemy*. Good! But in order to take the offensive with probability of success, other things being equal, it is necessary to be *stronger* than the enemy. In the end, therefore, General Bastico must conceive of a correct proportion among *an army, a navy, and an air force, all of them stronger than the corresponding armed forces of the strongest enemy*.

No one can deny, I least of all, that such a proportion is not only the correct one, but obviously the most harmonious and advantageous. But we would have to have the riches of America to put it into practice. What would be practicable for America would be utopian for us, because we have not the necessary means. And General Bastico recognizes this and proves it with figures. He assumes a hypothetical nation, A, which spends 8 billions for armament (of which 2 billions go to her air force) and Nation B, which spends 5 billions (of which 700 millions go to her air force); and from this example he draws the conclusion that Nation B would find herself in a state of *inferiority* in both fields, land and air. May I ask, then, how Nation B could attain for her armed forces that "correct proportion" required for an "adequate offensive power"—that is, that "superiority" for all the three branches of her armed forces which is needed for victory?

This shows that we cannot be guided by my colleague's theory of "correct proportion" in organizing our armed forces.

To find the correct proportion among the parts, that proportion which will implement to the fullest the value of the whole, we must follow a different road. Allow me to give the solution of the problem a mathematical cast.

The resources which a nation can put at the disposal of her armed forces is a constant value which we shall designate with the letter C. The total of these resources is made up of the army, A; the navy, N; and the air force, AF. Then we can put down: $C = A + N + AF$. If we use V to represent the warlike value of the three armed forces, we can say that: $V = A + N + AF$. Our problem now is to give to A, N, and AF such values that V will be the maximum strength, while the total cost of A, N, and AF will not exceed C, which is a constant. In order to implement V to the fullest, we must give the highest value to one of the three factors, A, N, and AF, and the lowest to the other two. Assuming, as I do, that the aerial factor will be decisive in the wars to come, we must give the highest value to AF and the lowest to A and N. This lowest value is the power necessary for them to play a defensive role. Therefore, I say: *resist on the ground in order to mass your strength in the air.*

In arriving at this solution of the problem, we assume that the aerial field of action is the *decisive* one. In that case the solution is true and gives us *the correct proportion among the constituent parts of armament.* But if the assumption is wrong, the solution of the problem is also wrong. In this case, some other assumption should be made, because the correct proportion among the constituent parts cannot spring up like a mushroom, but must stem from a well-thought-out premise. Otherwise it would be an *arbitrary* proportion.

General Bollati says the aerial field *may* become decisive if the aerial forces can carry out an offensive powerful enough to paralyze not only the enemy's armed forces, but "also the material and moral strength of the enemy nation." Does he not believe that the paralysis of his moral forces would be sufficient? What use are the armed forces and material strength of a nation which is *morally* paralyzed?

Captain Fioravanzo admits the decisiveness of the aerial field on condition that the side which masters it has at its disposal enough aerial strength to accomplish the complete ruin of the enemy. It is quite true—an action cannot be considered decisive unless it brings about those conditions which are the essence of a clear-cut decision. This holds good in all fields. Pyrrhus decided nothing with his land victories; and he who is master of the naval field only does not obtain a final decision.

In one of his first articles Engineer Attal wrote:

The mastery of one's own sky is an unavoidable necessity, death being the penalty for failure.

It is hard to improve upon so strong a statement in favor of the decisiveness of the aerial field. It is in the air that the fight takes place for the mastery of the sky, one's own or somebody else's. If the loss of one's sky brings death, what does it matter what is left? On the other hand, in his most recent article he writes:

The aerial field may become decisive *at a certain moment.*

Is this a correction of his earlier article? He accuses me of:

... falling victim to the classical error of giving a pre-eminent and conclusive value to any new element which appears and basing all hopes upon it. History teaches us that on the sea, any new shell finds a new armor; on the surface, the barbed-wire finds the dynamite stick first and then the trench mortar.

It is perfect. But I have never spoken of the chemical and bacteriological elements to which Attal is referring in the above quotation. I know very well that there is an antidote for practically every poison and a serum for practically every microbe. I was not speaking of elements, but of new means. History teaches us that the submarine seized the mastery of the sea from the great warships.

I spoke instead of the aero-chemical arm, which the same Engineer Attal has recognized *to have enough revolutionary power to upset all the fundamental principles so far in use in the art of war.* If this is true, then the history of the basic ideas used up to this time in the art of war cannot teach us anything. To be sure, "a gradation of decisiveness among the various land, sea, and aerial arms is difficult to establish"; nevertheless it should be done so as not to be unprepared when the need for it arises. To be sure, "their ratio of employment will depend upon the geographical configuration of the countries at war"; and it is precisely for that reason I am trying to find out this proportion for our own Italy. To be sure, it can be said in a general way that "all three of them are necessary branches of the ironbound organism of war." But haven't I said that "it is necessary to *resist on the ground* in order to mass our strength in the air"? Does this not mean that all three branches of the armed forces are necessary? Given the necessity of using all these three branches, is it a mistake to try to define the functions of each, so that the whole may acquire the maximum value? It is General Bastico who says that if the aerial is the decisive field, we should pour all our available resources into it. I, on the contrary, say let us mass in the aerial field everything left after organizing the ground defenses. I follow the principle of massing in the decisive field, a principle which does not preclude but integrates resistance on the surface by the other two fields.

In defense of his argument Engineer Attal cites as example the Franco-Moroccan War of 1925-26.

In that war [he writes] aviation was of great assistance; it contributed *preponderantly* to the attainment of victory, but it was not the *sole factor* of victory. By operating closely with the ground forces, in the beginning aviation *co-operated in large measure* in re-establishing interrupted lines by freeing French detachments besieged by the Riffs. Then efficient actions ahead and on the flanks of the attacking columns by aviation helped in carrying out their tasks. But only toward the end, when pressure from surface troops had the enemy wavering, did aviation become the decisive factor and, by energetically cutting the enemy's lines of communication, crushed any further show of resistance and compelled Abd El Krim's men to surrender.

I think, Engineer Attal, there is some misunderstanding here. When I say the Air Force will be *decisive,* I do not mean to say the Air Force will be the *sole factor of victory.* If that were my contention, I should logically advocate the abolition of the army and navy; because, if victory could be won by one factor only, this being the aerial factor, the other two would be completely useless. Consequently, I am in perfect agreement with Engineer

Attal. In the Franco-Moroccan War, aviation was not the sole factor of victory. I will go further and say neither will it be in future wars.

But there is a vast difference between "the sole factor of victory" and "the decisive factor of victory," and aviation may well have been *the decisive factor of victory* in the Franco-Moroccan War without being its *sole factor*. I have not studied that war carefully enough to discuss this point; but the fact that, as Engineer Attal asserts, *aviation contributed preponderantly to the attainment of victory* leads me to believe that aviation was undoubtedly the decisive factor in that war.

But let us not play on words. If, as I think, owing to resistance on the ground in the war to come, the Air Force will decide the war, will not the three armed forces have contributed to the victory? Will not all three of them have been factors of victory? If one of them should fail in its mission, could not victory have been lost? Only one thing could be said: the Air Force contributed preponderantly to victory. Would it not be equally true to say that the Air Force played a decisive role? Did not the navies of the Allies pride themselves, quite rightly, on the fact that their contribution was decisive for victory, since they assured supplies to the armies and life to the Allied nations?

Engineer Attal remarks that things would not be so easy in a European war as they were in the Franco-Moroccan War. Quite so. But not because of aviation being used on both sides, or aerial defense either; but because of the conditions of European life and surroundings. This is proved by Engineer Attal himself.

On June 21, 1925, the aerial bombing of a Moroccan *souk* claimed 800 victims in one minute. A Moroccan *souk* has a population of a few thousand people; a European city usually has several hundred thousand. An aerial attack on one of them with explosive, incendiary, and poison-gas bombs would have terrifying effects. All the Po Valley, all our coastline, all our islands would be under immediate threat of an aerial attack.

That is clear; an aerial action intended to break the morale of a nation is bound to be much more effective when its population is dense and civilized. An aerial action is ineffective, or nearly so, against a nomad people living in the desert; but it would be very effective—terrifying and dreadful—against a highly civilized people living in large centers of population.

After painting this dreadful picture, Engineer Attal asks himself: "Can such an attack have decisive effects against us?" And he answers his own question: "I emphatically affirm that it could not." But after this definite *denial* he appends three "ifs":

> ...*if* our aerial ground defense had been carefully organized; *if* our aviation retained its fighting strength; *if* our land and naval fronts were still strong and menacing.

Evidently so. If our aerial forces could beat off the enemy's aerial offensive, the enemy's aerial action would not be decisive *against us*. But what is all my labor aimed at if not to put "Italy's aerial defense" in condition to prevent any eventual aerial action of decisive effect against us? By "Italy's aerial defense" I do not mean that "aerial defense" Engineer Attal refers to, but the total array of forces which makes up the aerial power of the nation.

Even assuming that our land and naval front would hold firm, we would have to avoid being beaten in the air, because, on account of our geographical position, this would mean our defeat. That is why I advocate our putting ourselves in condition to effect our maximum effort in the air. I wish people could understand that I am thinking primarily of our own situation. When I say that the aerial field of action will be decisive, I refer to Italy. I declare it decisive because if we should be beaten there—and to be beaten in the air implies the impossibility of being able to make effective counteraction—we might be decisively defeated no matter what our situation on the surface. Is there anyone who can logically and in good faith deny this, given the actual development of the aero-chemical arm? Can anyone logically and in good faith assure us that the struggle will not be decided in the air or that the decision on the surface will be made before that in the air? Can anyone assert logically and in good faith that we would have any chance of winning the war on the surface if we were once beaten in the air?

I am sure there is no one who wants to stake the future of the nation on one card. If there are such, they are my opponents who shut their eyes to undeniable truth in the forecasting of the future.

General Bastico writes that my warning "not to forget that airplanes fly and poisons kill" is mere phrase-making. It is nothing of the kind. It expresses a tremendous truth, for which we are in duty bound to make adequate provision so that it may never turn to our disadvantage.

General Bollati declares that the surface field of action is *undoubtedly* decisive, but he is compelled to add an "if":

...if the surface forces succeed in defeating the enemy and in capturing centers so vital that their loss would force him to sue for peace."

But of the aerial forces he writes that they *may* bring about a decision only if they carry on an offensive strong enough to paralyze both the enemy's forces and his material and moral resistance. Those two words, "undoubtedly" and "may," show the General's prejudice, confirmed by what follows.

...a victory in the air is *hypothetical* [all victories are hypothetical until they happen], because the clash between the two aerial fleets may not materialize [did it materialize on the sea in the World War?], because adverse meteorological conditions or other difficulties may influence it. [Still speaking of meteorological conditions in 1929! Do they not influence sea battles too? Have we not read of meteorology in hundreds of communiqués dealing with land battles?] The aerial force is subject to more wastage than any other. [How about the land forces? Did we not hear during the last war of hundreds of divisions so worn out they had to be reorganized? Are not the millions of dead of every country enough to give us some idea of the wastage of human life among the ground troops?] Even a victory in the air or the command of the air would not preclude counteroffensives in other localities paralleling our aerial offensive [do land victories preclude the possibility of enemy land victories in other localities?]; given the destructive power of the airplane, even a few machines could inflict grave losses on us. [Strange, that a few enemy ships could inflict grave losses on us even when we had command of the air! In that case, what kind of aerial fleet would ours be?] The effect of an aerial offensive may be neutralized by an active and passive defense and other means which are now being seriously elaborated. [And are there not active and passive defenses and other means already elaborated against land forces?] In the end we must take into account the *moral field,* which is really decisive and may constitute an unexpected obstacle. [Yes, and now comes the *moral field,* which has been discussed so much there is nothing left to say, especially if we rely on unexpected obstacles, which certainly cannot be discussed.] In conclusion, the aerial field may also be decisive, but the kind of action required in it, though helped and made efficient by its peculiar conditions, is bound to meet with grave difficulties and have serious obstacles to surmount! [Yes, but is this because experience in the World War has shown that surface actions *do not* meet with grave difficulties, *nor* have to surmount serious obstacles?]

Engineer Attal derives some comfort and support for *his* opinion, naturally contrary to *mine,* from an article by Marshal Badoglio, from which he quotes some paragraphs. Here is the concluding one:

And it is exactly the aerial force which will contribute to that form of war which might shorten its duration as much as possible, something for which all nations are searching with feverish haste

He could not have chosen anything better calculated to give comfort and support to *my* opinion and not to *his.* Badoglio's statement contains a clear-cut assertion: "It will be precisely the aerial force which will shorten the war." That is exactly what I have been preaching for years! If one arm can give us a quicker decision than the others, it means it can give us a decision *before* the others. And if it gives us a decision before the others do, it means it will be decisive before the others are. Ergo, the aerial arm will be the decisive arm. If this is so, it is not I, but my opponents, who do not agree with Badoglio's statement; it is they who sweat trying to prove exactly the opposite, and who refuse to admit that the aerial force is bringing about a revolution in the *form of war.* It is not I who am the heretic! What is the synthesis of my opponents' ideas? *"In medio virtus,"* [1] says General Bastico, and General Bollati seconds him. I hope they are both satisfied!

Although Engineer Attal professes to be against this "virtue-in-mediocrity" and to recognize that virtue lies not in the average but *in excelsis virtus,* [2] nevertheless, in practice he also seconds the two preceding authors.

[1] Virtue lies in the middle course.—Tr.
[2] Virtue lies in the best.—Tr.

The *best* must be singular, never plural. "Strengthening all the armed forces of a nation as if each one were the decisive one" is, if you will allow me to say it, nonsense. It means to equalize, to make uniform, to follow an average, to be satisfied with mediocrity. It can never mean the *best*. Generals Bastico and Bollati's theory of the *average* precludes any gradation of value; in fact, it stems from the premise that all fields of action *may* be decisive—which is a possibility, but not a probability.

The theory of the "average" gives a generic solution to the problem of a "correct proportion of the component parts," which does not take into account the respective values of the parts—a solution which may come from deep sagacity, but also from mere indecision. It is as though they asked themselves, "Which one shall we choose?" And the answer came back in unison, "Well, why not all three of them?" It is a recipe which comes in handy in all cases, like some patent nostrum, but will not help in any and essentially puts its trust in Providence. It is like a linear array of forces, which, as everyone knows, is the best way to lose the battle. More than anything else, it betrays uncertainty.

"In excelsis virtus." Precisely, this is my motto. Let us mass our strength in the sky because I say the decision lies in the sky. I wish my opponents would cry out: "You are wrong! The decision lies elsewhere, not in the sky! We must mass somewhere else; we must mass on land, we must mass on the sea!" But nothing of the kind. The only answer I hear is: "We must dilute ourselves everywhere!" No, I cannot be convinced by that.

While Engineer Attal tries to silence me with his own interpretation of the writings of an eminent man, General Bastico tries, of all things, to prove that my ideas are incompatible with *some basic theories of a general character, well known to all who are not ignorant of military matters.*

To beat your head against basic theories is foolish, like beating it against a stone wall. You may break it! But let us see. Are the "well-known basic theories" General Bastico fires at me well founded and reliable? Let us examine them, not for idle curiosity's sake, but to see how sometimes people well versed in military matters cherish deep-rooted prejudices.

BASIC THEORY NO. 1

Every doctrine, though subject to the peculiar characteristics to which it refers, must take into account the actual conditions at the time when it is being applied, and also *how to conduct the war against the most probable enemy; in case there is more than one, against the most dangerous of them.*

This basic theory is a shaky one at the points where I have italicized the words. A doctrine of war must simply correspond to the realities of war obtaining at the time and to the peculiar characteristics of the nation it refers to; and my doctrine conforms precisely to that standard. But it must not be shaped on the pattern of the most probable or most dangerous enemy. If it is, that enemy imposes his own doctrine of war, and everyone else renounces his own ideas and becomes a plagiarist. Further, since every nation has its own probable and dangerous enemy, none of them could evolve a doctrine of war. They would all be waiting to shape it on the pattern of the enemy's doctrine.

If the aerial field has in fact become the decisive one, we should recognize it as such and take all the appropriate measures, even if our most probable and dangerous enemy has not yet realized the possibilities of the new field of action. In case of war, it would be our enemy who would suffer, not we. If our enemy makes a mistake, so much the worse for him. That is no reason why we should make the same mistake.

The historical example General Bastico cites is not apropos. The French doctrine which culminated in De Grandmaison's paradox, "When on the offensive, recklessness is the best safety," brought France to the brink of ruin, simply because it is contrary to reality and common sense. It was based on a sort of offensive mysticism sprung from a strange folly which had seized upon the French High Command at the time, and unf rtunately was copied by others. Everything contrary to reality and common sense is bound to fall, as the mystic French doctrine fell.

If anything, this example proves the opposite of General Bastico's contention, and he himself proves it when he says that the French doctrine *failed when confronted by the German doctrine,*

based on superiority in fire power and method of attack. Therefore, the Germans were wise when they did not *shape their doc-*
trine of war to conform with the doctrine of their most probable
and dangerous enemy.

The first basic theory, then, wobbles like a loose tooth.

BASIC THEORY NO. 2

In preparing the armed forces, it is necessary to keep in mind not
only the geographical and topographical characteristics of the foreseeable theaters of wars, but also *the organization and constitution of*
the enemy's forces. In other words, we cannot regard the preparation
of the armed forces as a problem per se, the solution of which depends
exclusively upon our likes or dislikes, as it must be proportionate to
the size and kind of forces our enemy or enemies might array against
us.

This theory is even wobblier than the first one. Undoubtedly
the preparation of the armed forces cannot be subject to the likes
and dislikes of anyone. It must be based on the criterion of giving
to the whole the maximum strength. Nothing more or better can
be done about it, irrespective of the number of our enemies. To
base the preparation of the armed forces on what our probable
enemy does is not only to give away all initiative, but also to play
into his hands, because if the enemy errs we commit the same
error. We should prepare for the worst. If the worst does not happen when the time comes, so much the better for us.

When I say, "Let us employ all our aerial forces offensively," I
think the worst that may come out of it is that the enemy might
do the same. If I see that he will use them only defensively, I am
glad of it, because then our side will be preponderant. Certainly
I will not copy his defensive organization.

Still worse is to assert that the preparation of our armed forces
should be proportionate to the *size* of the enemy's forces. No
nation can do more than to prepare in proportion to the size of
her own resources.

General Bastico tries to prove by these first two theories that I
am in the wrong because my theory would give our own armed
forces an organization different from that prevailing among the

armed forces of other nations; because, in short, I do not follow fashion. Frankly, I am for an Italian fashion; and I remember that when I had to study history I used to be told that it is always better to be ahead of your enemy than to follow him, because it seems that victory has often gone to those who succeeded in changing from the traditional ways of war, and not to those who clung desperately to them.

BASIC THEORY NO. 3

In regard to surface operations, it is true that defense requires smaller forces than offense, *but only in a slender proportion and provided there has been ample time and opportunity adequately to organize the defensive ground.*

The first statement derives from the fact that the attacker can decide at his pleasure the time and place of the attack, whereas the defender has to maintain an effective defensive along the whole length of the front. As to the second qualification, we must remember that in peacetime any defensive organization on the border must for many reasons remain sketchy today, far from what it should be in wartime, and it would require considerable time to complete it and put it in condition to be of real help to the mobile defense, especially if this were limited in number.

By this basic theory General Bastico tries to prove that there is little to gain in limiting the mission of land forces to resistance, and that therefore this limitation, which I advocate, is valueless. The trouble is that this basic theory, which had a limited usefulness as a thesis subject in war colleges before the World War, has been knocked out by the bloody experience of the war. That experience proved even for the blind that breaking a stalemate between offensive and defensive required a *very great,* not a *slender,* amount of means and men. It proved nearly every day that a few hardy men with a few bullets and some strings of barbed wire could keep imposing enemy forces at bay for months, even years. It showed that at times insignificant topographical obstacles did cost rivers of blood and incalculable tons of steel before they were conquered foot by foot. And now the Alps have suddenly come to be considered a level crossroad impossible to defend!

Yet even the *General Instructions* admit that under certain given conditions, which might easily come into being, *the front would immediately be stabilized*—that is, the same phenomenon which prevailed during the World War.

You had better put your mind at rest, my worthy colleague, for this basic theory is a thing of the past. It is badly worn, and it is time it was relegated to the attic.

BASIC THEORY NO. 4

In naval operations, though it is not generally known, the defensive requires an employment of means and a waste of energy superior to that required by the offensive. On the sea even a fleet which stays on the defensive must protect its lines of communication from the menace, even potential, of the enemy; and since his attacks can come from any direction, the defender must counter them by deploying a great force in actual operation, as well as in reserve. On the sea a defensive stand means substantially a larger expense, not a saving.

By this basic theory General Bastico tries to show that limiting the mission of the naval forces, as I propose, is useless and a disadvantage, because it would be more expensive. But this is not a basic theory. It is merely an opinion of General Bastico's, a respectable but nonetheless strange opinion. In actual fact he affirms that, to be on the defensive at sea, one has to be *stronger*, which is equivalent to saying that the *weaker* side should be on the offensive. Since I maintain that defense would be more expensive than offense in the air, I logically conclude: Go on the offensive in the air, and the weaker you are, the more intensely you should carry it on. But on the sea it seems to me a horse of a different color. At least, history, so often quoted by General Bastico, shows that the weakest naval forces have *always* assumed a defensive attitude. Were they always in the wrong?

General Bastico writes: "Even a fleet on the defensive *must* protect its lines of communication." *Must?* This is not a question of *having* to do something, but of *being able* to do it. It *must* if it *can*. The German navy immediately gave up going on the offensive; but certainly not from fancy or lack of desire or sense of duty. She gave it up because she could not help it; a weaker naval force which would undertake the protection of its lines of communication would not last long unless its opponents were monumental idiots. A weaker navy has to choose between the virtual certainty of being sunk in a few minutes or seeking haven in order to be able to take full advantage of some error on the enemy's part if the chance should come. Giving battle under such conditions would be a bold exploit, but an exploit that would lead straight to suicide without ensuring maritime traffic. This is the attitude a weaker navy is compelled to take—*compelled* because weaker. It is not an attitude deliberately chosen in order to husband strength and energy.

This is so true that I have qualified my idea by saying: "On the sea our aim should be to bar anyone from sailing in the Mediterranean without our consent." This would require fewer forces and of a different type from those needed for the defensive attitude supported by General Bastico. In fact, as Captain Fioravanzo writes:

Less means are needed to attack the enemy's traffic than to protect one's own. In all wars myriads of ships have been mobilized to catch a few raiders, and a few submarines (less than fifty at any given time) have given a world-wide naval organization many sleepless nights and diverted thousands of units from other important tasks.

This is enough to show that, even if the fourth basic theory is a real theory for maritime warfare—others more competent than I can decide that—it still has nothing to do with my contentions. So let us put it aside like the others.

BASIC THEORY NO. 5

Every war preparation must be proportionate to the nation's economic potentiality. To advocate that a nation's military efforts should not be cared for from her general budget, but that the budget should conform to the military needs, is a laudable wish; but ninety-nine times out of a hundred it is simply not feasible. It is proved by the fact that in all the world only the United States is in a position to indulge such a luxury. All other nations must be satisfied with much less.

Here at last is a basic theory which really stands on its own feet. General Bastico must have confused me with Engineer Attal when he quoted it against me. It is Engineer Attal who maintains that the budget should conform to the preparations for defense, so much so that he has rebuked me for giving too much importance to our financial lacks. I simply said: "Our aerial forces should be as powerful *as our national resources allow it to be.*"

The more I think of it, the surer I am that General Bastico must have mistaken me for Engineer Attal. It is he who claims that the safe development of our national life should be guaranteed at all times from any possible enemy. I, much more modest than he, advocate merely a preparation which would enable us to meet an eventual conflict in the best way we can. General Bastico should not waste his time proving to me that it is a material impossibility to crush rapidly the aerial forces of one of our eventual enemies by giving our Independent Air Force a strength one and a half, or twice, or any other number, larger than our enemy's. I do not want to crush anybody. All I want is to put our country in a condition in which she cannot be crushed too easily, if at all.

I would advise General Bastico not to go contrary to this basic theory, as he does when he prescribes as the correct proportion of the component parts "an army, a navy, and an air force, all possessing adequate offensive power." That proportion may be feasible for the Americans, but it is utopian for us, as I have already had the pleasure of pointing out.

BASIC THEORY NO. 6

In the preparation for war one must always take in consideration the most unfavorable situation: the help which might come from a possible alliance should be discounted to the minimum in advance; conversely, the strength of a possible enemy should be evaluated at its maximum.

This is another basic theory which stands firmly on its feet. I subscribe to it without reservation. I have in mind not only our possible enemies' strength, but their wicked natures too. It is just for these reasons I am afraid of the enemy's aerial action. Putting myself in the shoes of our possible enemies, I think as follows:

"Here I am in front of this beautiful garden of Europe. Shall

I attack her through her high mountain rampart? Every stone there, animated with the heroic blood of her sons, would become a fortress against which I should break my horns even if I armored them with the finest steel. Shall I attack her through her seas? Every wave would hide a snare, and behind every shore, every island, every rock, would lurk danger magnified manyfold by the brave hearts of her people. There is only one field in which I have the advantage, not because I shall meet faint hearts there, but because that great garden makes an easy target, and I am strong enough to prevent any retaliation on my own territory. It is therefore in this field that I must unleash a violent, ferocious attack on all the vital centers of this lovely garden. There they are, powerless to stop me."

It is because above all I am afraid that some enemy may reason as I would if I were in his place, that I cry: "Let us mass our strength in the air!" Here again I advise General Bastico not to go contrary to this basic theory, as he does when he propounds that "average" theory of his.

As those readers who are not entirely ignorant of military affairs have had a chance to realize, General Bastico's basic theories in opposition to my doctrine leave me unaffected. The same is true of the other minor arguments he hurls at me. Naturally he finds it logical that our *General Instructions* should assign to the Independent Air Force the task of *carrying the offensive to the heart of the enemy nation;* but he also finds that, since the devil after all does not look so black, an offensive carried to the heart of the enemy, or to ours, can cause at the most only a quickening of the heart-beat.

He says that I want to found a new doctrine of war, based on the principle that "the decisive field of action is the aerial one," forgetting that this may turn out to be a fact and not an abstract principle. He does not realize that a doctrine of war can never be based on principles, but always on realities.

He says that if we put my doctrine into effect, we would be giving to the conduct of war a form and substance not in conformity with established doctrines of war. He forgets that the worth of a doctrine is not measured by its similarity to established doctrines, but by the way it conforms to reality. If no one ever tried to change doctrines for fear of disturbing their similarity, the art of war would become as still and dead as a reef in the middle of the sea.

He says no one would take a chance on putting my doctrine into effect without being sure beforehand of its favorable outcome; but he forgets to prove how it is possible to get a favorable outcome without first putting it into effect.

He says that, even leaving out of account centuries of history, it can be asserted that up to now the struggle has always been between armies and navies *similarly constituted*. I believe it; and I also believe that future history will show that future conflicts will be fought with armies, navies, and aerial forces *similarly constituted*. At present we are living through a period of innovation; tomorrow we will all settle down.

He says that he must logically assume that

...according to my judgment, a two-week period would be enough to bring about the material and moral dislocation which would compel the enemy to call a halt.

But he forgets that I have never said or written anything which could lead anyone to think me capable of so rash a statement. I merely said that a nation which is dominated in the air can be subjected to such moral torment that she would be forced to call a halt *before* the war could be decided on land. He goes on to say:

... but if instead of two weeks, it should take two months, then no changes could be made in the organization of the army; and the army, instead of standing guard on the border, could at least try to advance beyond it, if only because the house door is better defended by standing in front of it instead of behind it.

I, too, think this is obvious; and it is unthinkable that a war on land nowadays could be decided in two months. But it must also be admitted that it doesn't much matter whether one stands in front of the house door or behind it if the enemy is burning the roof, demolishing the walls, and poisoning the family inside.

He says that he does not understand why "it would be against

all elementary principles of war to propose, *a priori,* to attack everywhere at the risk of being defeated everywhere." He says his teachers taught him that, although a war should be fought with singleness of purpose, it would not be an error to fight it offensively on land and sea simultaneously (aviation did not exist at that time).

General Bastico's teachers taught him wrong if they said only, "It would be no mistake to go on the offensive everywhere," without qualifying the statement. It was bad if they did, because the offensive is not an end in itself. One does not go on the offensive in war just for the sake of going on the offensive. If that is done, there is danger of falling into the De Grandmaison theory criticized by General Bastico himself. One always goes on the offensive or on the defensive to attain victory, naturally choosing the one most suitable under the particular circumstances at the time. The French offensive at the beginning of the Franco-Prussian War led France to the brink of ruin; and it would be absurd to go on the offensive to reach such a disagreeable end. One should go on the offensive when one is able to; when one is not, one assumes the defensive.

Naturally, it is preferable to choose the offensive if possible, because it pays better. But one must be stronger, all things being equal, in order to win victory through an offensive both on land and sea. Very likely, therefore, General Bastico's teachers taught him it is advisable to take the offensive simultaneously on land and sea if one is stronger in both fields. I have nothing to say to that.

At the beginning of the World War, the Germans took the offensive on land and the defensive at sea. If they had taken the offensive everywhere, they would have made a great mistake.

It was not wrong to teach General Bastico that one should take the offensive on land and sea when one feels confident of being stronger than the enemy in both fields. Such teaching is not contrary to the elementary principles of war. But it would certainly have been an error to teach him that the preparation for war should be designed for offensive action everywhere, because that implies the necessity of being stronger than the enemy everywhere, something which is not always feasible.

Even when the Air Force did not exist we used to talk about singleness of purpose, which implied the employment of land and sea forces with the single aim of winning. If a nation was likely to be beaten more easily on land than on the sea, singleness of purpose required more strength for the land forces than for the sea forces. It required that one mass one's strength on land, even if it meant compelling the navy to assume the defensive. And vice versa. England has always massed her strength on the sea, and if she had done differently she would have made an egregious mistake. Unfortunately, that singleness of purpose in the past was like the Arabian Phoenix. Everyone knew it existed, but no one knew where to find it.

With the arrival of air power, the armed forces were at last bound in a single whole, because the air force can operate in the sky over land and over sea. For singleness of purpose, a vague, confused formula, *singleness of action* has been substituted. The three armed forces, especially with us who have perfected the necessary organization, must act with singleness of action toward one end—to win. Trying to win everywhere would be ideal. But such an idea is unattainable ninety-nine times out of a hundred, because it means one has to be stronger everywhere. To try to win on only one field is more feasible; and as long as it is enough to win in the decisive field of action, it is enough to try to prepare for victory in that field. All that can humanly be done is to try to have the greater probability of victory on one's own side; and the only way to do that is to mass one's strength in the decisive field of action, no matter which one it happens to be. Therefore, to propose, *a priori*, to attack everywhere is contrary to the most elementary principles of war.

This is true irrespective of whether or not the aerial field is the decisive one. It is irrespective of the "new doctrine which affirms, but does not prove, that the war can be won only in the sky, while on land and sea we must be content with resisting," as General Bastico says, who in parting gives me a *coup de grâce* by exclaiming: "But how many followers of this new doctrine are there?"

Few indeed. But what does it matter? Does my worthy colleague still believe that right is on the side of the majority? He had better beware, because that is a democratic idea at variance with reality. Majorities have the strength of inertia. It takes a lot to move them; but when they do move, they move like an avalanche. Are the followers of the new doctrine few? One need not worry about it. They will increase and multiply, and tomorrow they may be an avalanche.

General Bastico summarizes his idea as follows:

...we are compelled to resign ourselves and face the unknown of a new experience.

He adds in comment, "It is terrible but simple." In fact, it couldn't be simpler! Is there anything simpler than zero? In face of the new realities which press so swiftly in upon us, according to him, we should let well enough alone and placidly wait for a new experience to teach us belatedly what we *should have* done. Because there is nothing else that can teach us. That surely is a fact which should not prove too difficult for any mind to grasp.

Should we really resign ourselves to face the unknown of a new experience? The thought is really terrible. Yes, it is true we could draw many conclusions from it, especially if we happened to be the victims of the new experience. Resign ourselves to the unknown? But to what unknown? Have we not eyes to see and brains to reason? Have we not airplanes and deadly chemicals at our disposal? Can we not practically evaluate their possibilities? Cannot we find out experimentally in advance the effects they can produce? Isn't it possible to lay bare this unknown wholly or in part—this unknown more familiar than Punch and Judy? Shall we always bury our heads in the sand like ostriches? Shall we patiently wait for the storm to break before finding out our umbrella is not strong enough to weather it?

To resign oneself to facing an unknown new experience is like sitting and admiring one's navel, as the ancient Buddhist priests did; and this is an epoch when even Buddhist priests cannot waste time indulging in self-contemplation. I rebel against this passive, resigned, do-nothing attitude. The aggressive spirit must be innate in the soul, the heart, the mind. It cannot be brought to life by mere words. We need it for the events which will take shape in the future; we should not stand by and wait in the idle hope of being able to endure and survive them.

Although reluctantly compelled to admit that the Independent Air Force *may* be decisive in an eventual future conflict, my opponents conclude:

> ...But inasmuch as it has not been proved that it *will* be decisive, let us leave things as they are.

Now, this line of reasoning is fundamentally wrong. As long as the *possibility,* even if not the certainty, that the aerial field of action may be the decisive one is admitted, it should be reason enough for massing our strength in the air. On land a decision is easy to delay; it is not hard to hold the enemy in check and gain time. During the World War great armies were created while the enemy was held at bay—the same armies which decided the issue later on. On the sea small forces kept the most powerful fleets in the world in check. No one now believes that land warfare can be rapidly decided by the forces in existence at the beginning of hostilities. That is why all nations prepare for the mobilization of their industries so as to be ready to transform their national resources into armament during the war. Engineer Attal writes:

> When war is declared, all means will be devoted exclusively to its use. Every necessary expense will be met.

Surely; but that is not enough. It takes time to transform national resources into arms and other war equipment; and it would not be so easy to do under an aerial offensive. Tranquillity and a degree of safety are needed; and therefore it is necessary not to be beaten by the enemy in the air. On land, time can be gained by delaying the decision until one is ready to face it; but nothing of the kind can be done in the air, where there is no place to stop and make a stand. Very likely the aerial forces will clash before the declaration of war, for both sides will realize the great advantages of acting intensely and violently during the critical period of mobilization. The aerial struggle will be decided by the best-prepared and swiftest-acting forces. A stronger aerial force will never give the other side time to get reinforcements, **nor can the weaker** compel the stronger to wait.

My opponents admit that it is *possible* such an aerial action may have a decisive result. That means the war *may* or *may not* be decided in the air. In the first case, to mass strength in the air would be to conform to reality; in the second case it would not, but it would not prejudice the issue. Not to mass strength in the air would conform to reality in the second case, but in the first case it would strongly influence the issue, especially if we take into consideration the topographical peculiarities of our country.

The "average" solution offered by General Bastico and others would put the nation in grave danger if the *possibility* which they admit should become reality. My solution—let us even call it the extreme solution—would bring with it no danger even if the aerial field should not prove to be the *decisive one.* Resignation to the unknown may be labeled dangerous here and now, in view of the admission of that possibility.

But there is more to the question than that. In the first part of this study I affirmed that command of the air will lead to a decision if the conqueror succeeds in breaking the morale of the enemy by his aerial offensives. If the aerial offensives fail to accomplish this, the decision will be made on the surface. But even in the event that command of the air does not prove decisive, it will still be of great help in deciding the war. The side which has command of the air will be able to protect its territory and its armed forces on the surface from any significant aerial offensive; but the other side, the one dominated from the air, will be exposed to aerial offensives without any chance of effective counteraction—offensives which will upset its national activities and prevent freedom of action of its armed forces on the surface. Consequently, massing strength in the air can be advantageous even if the war should not be decided in the air.

I must ask again a question I put first in 1921: "What would be the use of a powerful Italian army deployed on the Alps and a strong navy in command of our surrounding waters, if one of our eventual enemies should conquer the command of the air and launch his aerial forces against our country, destroying our moral and material strength?" The answer is, they could do nothing. Nothing in 1921 and nothing today; and every passing day sees aero-chemical weapons becoming more and more powerful. Our army and navy could fight heroically, but meantime they would be conscious of the nation behind them undergoing torment, and they would have no assurance of safety for their bases and communication lines. In the end they might even win victory; but only at the cost of enormously increased sacrifices. Would we not be putting our nation, our army, and our navy in better condition for the conflict if we directed our efforts to holding the conquest of the air? The most urgent danger should be met and faced first; the others can be attended to in due time.

Let us leave poetry to the poets. The population can and must be inured to the horrors of war, but there is a limit to all resistance, even human resistance. No population can steel itself enough to endure aerial offensives forever. A heroic people can endure the most frightful offensives as long as there is hope that they may come to an end; but when the aerial war has been lost, there is no hope of ending the conflict until a decision has been reached on the surface, and that would take too long. A people who are bombed today as they were bombed yesterday, who know they will be bombed again tomorrow and see no end to their martyrdom, are bound to call for peace at length. It may be two weeks, two months, or six months, depending upon the intensity of the offensive and the stoutness of the people's hearts; but it would be small comfort to that people to know that their army had crossed the border. To get any real relief it would have to know that the army was marching on the double toward the enemy's capital.

Should we then wait for the results of a new experience to provide against such an eventuality? Should we act like the fool who locks the barn door after the horse is stolen? What would be the use of experience then? Our experience in the last war showed we had made a mistake in not recognizing in time the importance of the submarine. This precedent should make us think seven times seven before minimizing the importance of the new aerial weapons, but instead the same thing is happening again; and we, the few who point out the new reality, are considered hotheads, theorists, extremists, iconoclasts, and heretics against the old traditions—the same thing which happened to the few who tried to make people understand the importance of the submarine before the World War.

Why wait for a new experience when past experience has clearly shown that past experience is no help at all, and that history is a monotonous repetition of the same mistakes? Everyone talks about dynamism nowadays. It is human, I admit; but the man who really is dynamic does not wait; he acts, and promptly.

Passive resignation in face of a pressing and dangerous reality is the worst kind of error. Instead we should try to question her. She will answer; for the morrow is not wholly unknown—except for those who do not see, or refuse to see, the causes which shape it.

Despite the grueling experience of the World War, some old conceptions which that experience proved false are still believed in today. For instance, General Bastico writes:

If we must recognize that the aerial arm has changed war to the point where the *objective* of the struggle is no longer the armed forces, but the moral resistance of the enemy nation, et cetera...

By this statement he shows his belief that up to the present time, at least, the objective of war has been the enemy's armed forces. This conception is not peculiar to General Bastico. On the contrary, it is shared by many experts on war, I might even say the great majority of them.

Now, this conception is absolutely wrong. If the *objective* of war were the enemy's armed forces, the aerial force as an arm, as a means, could change nothing. The enemy's armed forces would still be the *objective;* the only change would be in the means of reaching it. But the fact is that the *objective* of war has never at any time been the enemy's armed forces. It has always been, is now, and always will be, to win—that is, to compel the enemy to bow to one's will. *Ultima ratio,* as the ancient Romans called it.

Human will rises above the material field. A country will resist the impositions of the enemy as long as its morale is strong enough to back up its will to counteraction. But moral resistance breaks down in face of intolerable conditions, and in the end they force a country to accept the lesser evil. It is therefore essential to force such intolerable conditions upon the enemy; this is the objective of war, as it has been in the past and will be in the future.

In land warfare the armed forces are employed to defend one's own territory materially and directly, and to try to beat the enemy's armed forces in order to invade his territory. The victorious armed forces on land—that is, the side which succeeds in taking away the enemy's ability to resist—can invade the enemy's territory, occupy its vital centers, seize its riches, impose laws, devastate, burn, kill and enslave its citizens. In other words, it succeeds in imposing those intolerable conditions which will break the people's will and force them to accept whatever peace terms the victor dictates. The objective is thus reached, not because the enemy's armed forces have been broken up, but because of the ensuing consequences. The Pyrrhic victories are proof of this.

But there have been certain differences in the way this fact applied in different circumstances. As long as wars were private affairs, so to speak, between princes, kings, emperors, and other potentates, and the people paid the cost and passively endured them, the heads of governments raised their armies and played their games of war. Often winning a battle was enough to reach the objective and stop the war, because after the victor had defeated the enemy's forces, he was free to impose his will on the enemy country, which was *powerless to put up any further resistance.* When the decisive battle was lost, the head of the government had no alternative but to make peace as best he could. In the Napoleonic era we see battles lasting only a few hours which decided the fates of empires. These wars of the past, superficially interpreted, obscured the reality and brought about a confusion between the aim and the means of attaining it. In other words, the belief grew up from them that the objective of war was the enemy's armed forces.

This belief persisted despite radical changes in the social structure. Thus, the nations came to think they were outside of war, and the citizens took the role of paying spectators looking on at the war. The matter went even further—they were legally excluded from the war and declared to be "nonbelligerents," as though war were none of their business. The phenomenon of war was separate from their life as a nation. Special classes and organizations of citizens, distinct and separate from all others, were entrusted with its preparation and conduct. When war came, the governments, considering it something outside of their province, entrusted its conduct to someone else and then sat back and awaited the outcome. After all, wasn't it an affair between the armed forces? Complete authority for the commander in chief became the rule. Wasn't the objective of war the destruction of the enemy's armed forces? What business had civilians to interfere in such a task? In face of such an objective, what did the rest matter, anyway?

And so the fruits of error ripened. Yet the falsehoods of this conception was apparent even in the Napoleonic era, ardent but often superficial studies of which led reason astray. Napoleon himself, the god of battles, proved at his own expense that a field victory, the rout of the enemy's armed forces, is not decisive when there is something left behind those forces. To his magnificent army and the victories gained by his genius, Russia apposed her climate and the vastness of her territory; to his valorous generals, Spain apposed the resistance of her impassioned partisans; and the Emperor could make neither Russia nor Spain bow to his will. The means failed to reach the objective. Field victories which broke up the enemy's armed forces in the same epoch won against those countries which had only passive unarmed populations behind their armed forces. Napoleon himself lost in the end because there was nothing left behind his armed forces.

These conceptions had not changed when the World War began; but the realities had changed, and so those conceptions failed. Nowadays it is no longer the heads of governments who make war; it is the nations, become living, thinking entities, who make war. The will to fight and win is innate in the people themselves nowadays. The armed forces are nothing but intermediate means between opposed national wills; and behind them is no longer the vacuum of passivity and resignation, but entire populations with all their material and moral resources. War has changed even in its formal aspect, for it has everywhere become a struggle against the resistance of a nation. Nowadays we say, "The victory will go to the one who can resist another quarter of an hour"; and when we say it we refer to nations. We no longer say, "The one who defeats his enemy's army will win." All citizens regard themselves as belligerents, and they all help with the war, which is everybody's business now. The governments themselves feel the enthusiasm of the people and understand that they are as much concerned about it as anyone else.

Military leaders also realized that it is the high morale of the people which gives strength to their armed forces, and they recommend to their governments to build it up as much as possible.

On land the clash between nations takes place in what are still called battle lines, but the battle does not develop in the classical way of Napoleon's time. What happens is a formidable waste of men and armaments which directly affects the warring nations. Spurred on by their will to resist, these nations throw all their resources into these lines, a little at a time, slowly exhausting themselves. Sometimes entire armies are routed and decimated, but the nations behind them are ready to stop and reform them.

It is clear that in order to win one must exhaust the enemy's resistance before one's own is gone. The strategy of the great General Staffs has come down to a "nibbling" strategy. The number of men remaining able to bear arms is anxiously figured on both sides; the greatest consideration is given to industrial production; and great importance is attached to the situation on the naval front. How far we have come from Napoleon's time, only a century ago! As a rule the classic field victory is decisive only when the warring nations have reached the limit of their endurance and despair of victory. Then success in the field becomes the flaming seal of victory.

This phenomenon is still more clearly evident in naval wars. The imposing naval forces contending against each other avoid decisive actions and save their potential strength until the end. Naval action on both sides is limited to attempts to obstruct and impede the enemy's traffic. It is action by war means against civilian means, an action aimed directly at national resistance and not at the enemy's armed forces. And yet it is well known that this kind of action almost decided the last war. The Allied naval forces claimed the distinction of indirectly deciding the outcome of the war; and there is no doubt that if they had failed to control the submarine threat, the Allies would have lost. But actually the credit for controlling the submarine threat belongs partly to the naval forces and partly to the increased production of Allied shipyards. If the shipyards had not first matched the tonnage sunk by German submarines and then surpassed it by intensifying their production, the war would have been lost in spite of the defensive actions of the naval forces. The sea warfare, then, was on the one hand a destruction of factors of national resistance by war means; on the other, production by civilian means to buttress national resistance.

How far we have drifted from the conceptions of war objectives held by Bastico, Bollati, and others of my opponents! And all based on the experience of the last war, not on a vision of the future.

The objective of war has not been changed by the advent of the aerial arm. War objectives will always be the same. The aerial arm will simply modify its form and characteristics, making it easier to act directly against the enemy's national resistance. Land and sea forces can act against it indirectly; but the aerial force can do it directly, and therefore more effectively. That is all there is to it!

No matter what General Bollati thinks of it, Mr. Endres is right when he says that "in the future, war will be waged essentially *against the unarmed populations of the cities and great industrial centers.*" He is right because it is logically destined that it be so. It is logical because if there is any possibility of attacking the enemy's resistance directly where it is found, it will be seized upon by anyone waging war who is trying to reach the objective of bending the enemy's will and knows that it cannot be done unless his resistance is broken. It is destined by the characteristics of the air arm, which, though capable of reaching any given point in the enemy's territory, nevertheless lacks the ability to take any kind of defensive attitude.

If the stronger aerial force is in a position to force the battle, and the weaker hopes to checkmate the stronger by adopting the defensive, the aerial action, before being turned upon the enemy nation, should be directed against his aerial forces. In other words, one Air Force should beat the other first of all. Only after such a victory can the winning aerial force attack the enemy's country.

But since the more powerful of the two opposing aerial forces could not force the battle on the weaker one if it was unwilling to accept it, as has already been demonstrated and is generally admitted; and because the weaker one would have no interest in committing suicide and all the interest in the world in conserving its strength, it is very unlikely that an aerial battle would take place.

Owing to unavoidable necessity, and regardless of men's preferences in the matter, the aerial conflict will therefore develop in actions against the enemy's territory on the part of the stronger force—actions during which it will enjoy complete freedom of initiative; and on the part of the weaker force in similar actions limited only by the necessity of avoiding a clash with the stronger force. Of necessity these parallel actions would be characterized by hideous atrocities, because the immediate aim of the two aerial forces must be to inflict the most possible material and moral damage on the enemy in the least possible time. To bend the enemy's will, one must put him in intolerable circumstances; and the best way to do that is to attack directly the defenseless population of his cities and great industrial centers. It is as sure as fate that, as long as such a direct method of attack exists, it will be used.

And really, General Bollati should not fear that peace, as Mr. Endres says, would be signed "in the cemetery of the enemy." Cemeteries would undoubtedly grow larger, but not as large as they became before the peace was signed at Versailles.

Do we prefer to think that this *fatality* may be only an *eventuality?* Does the thought of so horrible a form of war shock our sensibilities? Well, let it be so. But we cannot expect our eventual enemy to feel as we do, nor that he should think differently from Mr. Endres. But if this *eventuality* should become real and we see the enemy attacking the defenseless population of our cities and industrial centers, could we say to him, "Stop! You aren't playing the game according to rule and we call it off"? What I prophesy as a *fatality* may be simply an *eventuality*, but certainly it is the worst eventuality; and one we should make ready to face.

Will it become reality? If not, so much the better. Then we could be the ones to impose our rules of the game on the enemy if we wanted to. Would we prefer not to? In that case, we would lose nothing. If we were in a position to resist on the surface, we would always have time to improve our preparations, and a strong aerial force would be of great assistance.

I have summarized my thought in the words, *"to resist on the surface in order to mass our strength in the air."* But if there were no doubts as to the meaning of "to resist" as applied to the land forces, it was necessary to specify its application to the sea forces; and I did so by saying that in our particular case, the navy should limit its action to *preventing anyone from sailing in the Mediterranean without our consent.* This conception of mine about our navy's mission did not meet with acceptance. Nevertheless, though I cannot qualify as a naval expert, I feel I can defend it simply by relying on common sense, the more so since it is a conception on general lines only.

Since the end of the World War, experts have been unanimous in declaring that the navy's essential purpose is safeguarding sea lines of communication and hindering or cutting if possible those of the enemy. It is clear that the attainment of such an objective would not only be of great importance, but in some circumstances of decisive importance. As far as Italy is concerned, our sea lines of communication are of primary importance, largely owing to our lack of raw materials. If we were prevented from importing them, the consequences might be fatal. We all agree on that; and undoubtedly the attainment of this objective would be ideal for all the nations of the world, especially since the experience of the World War. In fact, many of the larger naval powers have reached it through well-known naval agreements naïvely masked under the cloak of humanitarianism.

But it is not enough to have an ideal aim; one must also have means and circumstances necessary to nourish some hope of reaching it. One who is not in such circumstances, and who lacks the necessary means, must resign himself to give up his ideal aim and try to reach a more practical one, no matter how modest. When we think of an eventual naval war, we think of a conflict between us and one of the great powers in the Mediterranean, or of a conflict between two coalitions of powers, some of whom, like us, are in this closed sea. We can hardly visualize a war in which Italy would be the only Mediterranean power. Therefore, the powers we must consider in such a contingency are the two largest ones—that is, the one which is in the Mediterranean by nature, and the one which is there by cunning. Let us consider the first probability, a conflict localized between us and one of these two great powers. In this case what *practical* and *feasible* aims could we set for our navy?

To bar the enemy from the Mediterranean? Obviously, yes. To protect our commercial traffic in the Mediterranean? Obviously, yes. To protect our commercial traffic and hinder the enemy's outside the Mediterranean? Obviously, no. We can undertake to carry out the first two aims in the Mediterranean, aided by our geographical position, even with limited forces; but outside the Mediterranean our position is very different. We have no suitable naval bases in the oceans; and our forces, already handicapped by lack of bases, could not be strong enough to be sent out through the gates of the Mediterranean, even if the gates were not in the enemy's possession. Our ocean traffic, compelled to keep to definite routes, would be subject to enemy attacks; and we should therefore have to do without it. I think we cannot cherish any illusions on that score.

Evidently, "to bar the enemy from navigating in the Mediterranean cannot be decisive *against our eventual enemy*." Being barred from the Mediterranean would at the most only hinder and disturb our probable enemy, as Captain Fioravanzo justly says; but it would certainly not defeat him, because he could easily reroute his traffic. But we would gain the advantage of being able to navigate the Mediterranean in comparative freedom ourselves; and this would be a positive result, though a limited one. But it might also turn out to be a very important result, because there are other powers in the Mediterranean, and it is to be hoped that not all of them would be hostile to us, especially in case of a localized war; and they might help us replenish our supplies. It might even be *decisive for* us if and when we could obtain indispensable supplies independently of the ocean routes.

If, instead, we attempted to protect our traffic in the oceans and at the same time attack the enemy's, we would have to decrease our naval forces in the Mediterranean. Then we should find ourselves facing the possibility of being easily beaten there, and consequently subjected to greater limitations on our freedom of navigation in it. Now, if being barred from ocean traffic would leave us with the sole hope of receiving supplies from another Mediterranean power, being barred from Mediterranean traffic would strip even this hope from us, and we would find ourselves completely isolated, which very likely would be *decisive against* us.

In case of a conflict localized between us and one of the other great Mediterranean powers, the minimum program I advocate is a program which will give us the most chance of not being deprived of those supplies without which we could not live. I have considered this case in general—that is, without dividing it into the two possibilities inherent in it: a conflict with the great power which is in the Mediterranean by nature, and a conflict with the one which is there by cunning. But if the reader will himself consider these two possibilities, he will better realize the value of the minimum program I suggest.

Let us now consider the second probability—a conflict between two coalitions of powers, some of them, like us, Mediterranean powers. One or more of these powers may be on our side or against us, or partly on our side and partly against us. In any event, we should not stand alone. There would be one or more navies besides our own. Since all the other powers except the small Balkan states have outlets outside the Mediterranean, by handling the Mediterranean waters ourselves, we would make it possible for our allies to use all their naval forces in the oceans. If no power in the enemy's coalition had any interest in navigating the Mediterranean and this sea became a peaceful lake during the conflict, there would be nothing to stop us from sending our submarines and other small naval units out of the Mediterranean to operate from friendly ocean ports. Mastering the Mediterranean if there are enemy powers there or furnishing a considerable number of naval units for ocean operations if there were no enemy powers in the Mediterranean, would be a good-sized contribution which Italy could make to her allies.[3]

This is my line of reasoning, and I think it very simple. And in contrast I think that if we follow the fashion of standardization which is so popular everywhere, especially in navies, and would form our naval forces on the pattern used by the ocean powers, we would be forgetting that we are shut up in the Mediterranean Sea, and that our position there is a pecular one; and consequently we would reach neither aim, the maximum nor the minimum.

When we feel poetic, we call the Mediterranean "Mare nostrum"; but if we want to be realistic, let us really make it so. As to any aspirations toward making the oceans ours, let us forget them. That is an unrealizable dream, at least as long as present conditions exist. We can make this sea really ours if we make ourselves strong enough to keep anyone from sailing in it without our consent. Even this might have been considered an unrealizable dream before the submarine; but it is no longer a dream. Even with our limited financial resources, we can make it a reality by taking advantage of our matchless location, of our islands and colonies, of the characteristics of the new instruments of naval warfare, and the skill and boldness of our dauntless seamen.

There is another consideration to be taken into account. A small fleet does not require large complicated naval bases such as the great modern naval units need; and they can be hidden easily from the enemy. In times like these, when an offensive can come even from the sky—and all our great naval bases would be exposed to it—it is no mean advantage to hide large and conspicuous targets from the enemy.

---

[3] It would seem that Italy is doing precisely this in the present war, with part of her submarine fleet operating from Germany or German-held bases against United Nations shipping in the Atlantic and possibly elsewhere.—Tr.

But this is not all. A nation's naval forces, like all armed forces, influence international politics by their potentialities. As long as our navy is standardized on the pattern of other navies, it will be considered only *quantitatively*. A navy organized according to my idea would instead be considered capable of mastering the Mediterranean regardless of quantity, which is very different. Captain Fioravanzo writes that being barred from the Mediterranean would be merely a hindrance to our eventual enemies. That is true; nevertheless, the Mediterranean bounds three continents; and possession of it must have great value when we see how it has been fought over through the centuries and how a great power keeps the bulk of her naval forces at its gates most of the time, despite the fact that she is far away. Therefore, ability to dominate the Mediterranean must have great weight in international politics. I have no intention of discussing this point because it is outside my field; but I feel that if Italy could point to the Mediterranean and say, "No trespassing here!" her importance in international affairs would be greatly enhanced.

In a book by a Frenchman advocating a closer *entente* between France and Italy, there is a concept similar to mine. The author tries to show the political value of such a close *entente* in Europe, saying that in case of war it would have the possibility of dominating the Mediterranean through Italy and of acting on the ocean through France. In that case, says the author, it would not be enough for England to reroute her shipping to the Far East around the Cape of Good Hope, because the new route would be anything but secure. This consideration—always according to the French author—would make England stick close to the Franco-Italian Entente, thus forming with Spain and Belgium the cornerstone of the United States of Europe, the necessity for which begins to be felt in order to equilibrate the Old World with the New.

After saying that barring other nations from the Mediterranean would not constitute a decisive objective, Captain Fioravanzo affirms that the fundamental objective would be instead "to safeguard our traffic," an objective which would be reached "through the mastery of the Mediterranean and its entrances"; and he adds that "the impossibility of any nation's carrying on traffic there would be its logical corollary."

I really do not understand how mastery of the Mediterranean's *entrances* could *surely safeguard our traffic,* when it is well known that, above all else, our ships must first reach these entrances. A *sure safeguard,* if I am not mistaken, could only be mastery of the ocean waters beyond the entrances. I do not understand either how mastery of the Mediterranean and its entrances could bring about as a corollary the impossibility of nations' carrying on their traffic, when those nations have outlets on the ocean.

After this affirmation, Captain Fioravanzo seems to assume that we have succeeded in driving all our enemies back into the ocean, so that we can now pass through the Straits; and he writes:

The navy exults; but because it is small—"all dust" [4]—it now has an insoluble problem, safeguarding our traffic in the oceans, or at least in the zone near Gibraltar, and also hindering the enemy's traffic in the ocean.

We cannot occupy Gibraltar...so we must operate in the ocean from Mediterranean bases. Let us suppose we have succeeded in getting hold of one of the Balearic Islands, an objective easier to reach than the conquest of an enemy's harbor on the continent. We have a certain advantage from these islands, but our "dust" does not ride the ocean storms too well, and it has an insufficient autonomy. To solve the problem we would need big, speedy cruisers and large submarines, assisted by ship-based airplanes. But we cannot improvise them, so we have to be content with cruising back and forth in the Mediterranean, emptied even of our merchant ships because our enemies stop them from going in and out.

By these writings, he concludes, he wanted to demonstrate the following thesis:

The stronger Italian aviation is, and the more successful in forcing other naval forces to withdraw to the outer fringes of the Mediterranean during an eventual conflict, the more powerful and better suited to ocean-going our navy would have to be. Therefore, as far as Italy is concerned, "to mass in the air" also requires "to mass on the sea"; and if by this twofold massing we succeeded in safeguarding our supply lines through the seas, in giving our labor on the home front the chance to work undisturbed, and in attacking the enemy's centers of resistance, we should have created all the material and

[4] A term applied to the Italian Navy by a French statesman some years ago.—Tr.

moral circumstances needed to enable our heroic *fante* [5] to plant his foot on enemy territory and make all his dreams come true.

Very true, if we succeeded in doing it! But this is a dream, as the author himself admits; and instead of dreaming we should keep our eyes wide open to reality. The task of compelling the enemy's naval forces to withdraw to the outer fringes of the Mediterranean does not belong to the aerial forces; it belongs to the navy, and if she succeeds, the glory is hers. If, after she succeeds in this task, she is faced with the insoluble problem of safeguarding our traffic in the oceans and hindering the enemy's traffic there, she will not fail because she is too small, but because it would be impossible for us to accomplish anything like that by ourselves on account of our peculiar conditions. [6] We cannot change our peculiar conditions even if we could devote most of our budget to building fairly large ships, for in that case we would run the risk of not being able to stop other nations from navigating in our seas.

Germany was defeated because she was not satisfied with a minimum shipbuilding program, and because she did not concentrate her resources on submarines. Her powerful fleet, suited to ocean navigation, with long range and conveniently located bases, was after all used for nothing but keeping the enemy fleet on the alert; and in the end it failed miserably. If she had not set her goal too high, if she had been satisfied with preventing the other side from navigating instead of trying for the mastery of the sea's surface, then she would have won by making more use of the small units and less of the big ones. This is yesterday's experience.

It is not accurate to say, as Captain Fioravanzo does, that "the navy and aerial forces are so interdependent *in Italy's particular situation* that both must be very strong." Italy's particular situation does not create a relation of *interdependence* between the navy and the aerial forces; it simply points out to both certain practical immediate aims which sound almost alike. For the navy the aim is *mare nostrum,* the domination of the Mediterranean; for the

[5] The Italian foot soldier, a term equivalent to the American doughboy.—Tr.
[6] Mainly geographical, economic, and financial conditions.—Tr.

aerial force it is *aer nostrum*, the domination of the sky above it. Truly if we could build a navy able to dominate the oceans and an aerial force able to dominate the skies, our heroic *fante* could easily plant his foot almost anywhere. But we cannot realize this double ideal because, though we do not lack men, we lack the means—we are not Americans—and so we must be satisfied to keep within the limits of our possibilities. But all this does not imply that we could not greatly facilitate the hard task of our heroic *fante*. We should try to make it possible to tell him in the wars to come:

"Cling to every rock in the mountains which make up our sacred borders and shout your thunderous, 'No trespassing here.' Keep your spirits high because your brothers in the air will prevent the brutal massacre of your people and safeguard them so they can work to send you food and armaments. They will also devastate the enemy's territory while your brothers on the sea sweep our enemies from the Mediterranean and protect the transportation of your supplies. Stand fast, our brother infantryman. Even if the enemy outnumber you, stand fast and let them break their horns on the stones made inviolate by the stoutness of your heart. No matter how hard their horns, they will be blunted, until their exhausted material and moral forces, attacked from the sky, become as soft as wax. Then up and at them. Your advance will be easy and triumphant; and yours will be the joy of unfurling our colors over the enemy territory."

But our heroic *fante* will not be overjoyed if we have to tell him instead:

"Go ahead! Try to advance through the harsh mountainous country, conquering it foot by foot and soaking it with your generous blood. Go ahead, and forget that the enemy is raining fire and poison on your home. Go ahead, and be patient if we cannot send you arms and munitions, because the enemy is destroying our factories, warehouses, and lines of communication from the air. Go ahead, and be patient if hunger torments you. We have tried in vain to dominate the oceans; but instead the enemy has shut us out of even the Mediterranean. Go ahead! You are our only hope. Go ahead and win!"

CONCLUSION

THIS LONG discussion, though it has left the participants immovable in their own convictions, as happens in all discussions, has shown if nothing else the great interest felt in the question, "What will the war of the future be like?" This is the question being asked everywhere nowadays. Everywhere there is a feeling that something new is brewing.

Now, I believe—and I hope that here at last I will find myself in agreement with all my worthy opponents—that this problem is of such vital interest to the whole nation as to need an organization planned to facilitate its solution. And for this I can only quote what I wrote in February 1928:

We find ourselves in a favorable situation as far as such a war organization is concerned inasmuch as we have already achieved the fusion of our armed forces under a single command. But unfortunately, although everyone agrees on the advantages of such a fusion, the thinkers and writers on military affairs seem to find it humanly impossible to see beyond their own special interests.

The army student will deal essentially with the army; the navy student will deal with the navy; the aeronautical student with the aerial forces; and when they deal with war in general, each emphasizes the part which is of more interest to the armed force to which he belongs. There are army experts, navy experts, and aerial experts; but there are no war experts. And war is indivisible, and so is its purpose.

In my opinion this situation makes it difficult to come to any intelligent agreement on a sound doctrine of war. I therefore believe that it will be necessary, especially during the transitional stage through which we are passing, to create *general war* experts, for they are the only ones who can bring into being the new doctrine of war, and only from them can we seek the solution of the fundamental problem of war preparations.

The new war doctrine should of course be based on the combined employment of the armed forces. In wartime the man who directs this combined employment shall consider all the armed forces as parts of a single whole directed toward a single aim. Consequently, we are faced with the necessity of training men capable of handling this triple instrument—namely, to organize a High Command composed of officers who possess competence in the general conduct of war.

The army contains three principal arms: infantry, cavalry, and artillery; but as these three arms are employed together toward a single aim, the need was felt for officers besides infantry, cavlary, and artillery officers, men capable of employing the whole three arms. Therefore the War College—an inaccurate title then, and more so now—was set up to broaden the specialized aptitude of the officers of the three arms.

In my opinion the same thing should be done now in regard to warfare in general, which would employ the three armed forces as a unit geared for a single aim. Certainly it would not be possible to institute what I might call a General War College right now, because we lack the teachers and the doctrine to be taught. First these have to be created; and I think this might be done by an institution which might be called the *War Academy,* in which officers of the armed forces selected from the most intelligent, learned, and open-minded of them, could study these formidable new problems together. In such an academy ideas could be exchanged and approved or rejected; and through this sifting of ideas, through hesitations, uncertainties, and rejections, a final agreement could be born. And on this agreement the new doctrine would be formulated—a doctrine which would easily win recognition and acceptance because of its origin.

Moreover, such an institution would serve the purpose of bringing selected officers of the different armed forces into close and cordial contact, to make each group know and appreciate the true value of the others and that in turn would bring about that warm, close harmony which should always exist between the component parts of a whole.

In conclusion, such an institution would be the very vehicle needed to encourage and organize the efforts of the many people working on these new problems simply from personal inclination. Today this work is unco-ordinated, lacking in means, without direction; and therefore cannot bring satisfactory results. But from it men capable of teaching the new doctrine of war in a real War College could arise to train the officers for the General Staff as natural assistants to the Chief of the General Staff in peacetime, and to the Supreme Commander of the Armed Forces in wartime.

Book Four

The War of 19—

"The War of 19—" was published in March 1930 in Rivista Aeronautica *a few days after the death of General Douhet. It is his last writing, to which he prefaced the following remarks:*

"I have to confess that the invitation extended to me by the editor of this review greatly pleased me, and I accepted it at once, but perhaps thoughtlessly, as I realized as soon as I began to consider the task I had undertaken.

"The subject was to be a description of a hypothetical conflict among the great powers in the near future. A difficult subject in any case, and more so when I considered that it was not a question of idle imaginings or flights of fancy. Rather, I must submit to the tight rein of logic and the strait jacket of reason, since I was to write a serious work for a reputable military review, and I had to achieve the practical end of teaching something to the present by means of imagined happenings in the future. If I had not given the editor my formal acceptance, and, what was worse, if the review had not published an announcement of the forthcoming work, I should gladly have given up the task. But there was no way out, and I had to go on.

"Here is the result of my labor, and I hope the reader will judge it leniently and remember that all the ideas, theories, actions, organization, and events attributed to the great powers hypothetically at war with one another have no foundation in reality. I have no inside information on these subjects; I have only used my imagination to picture two different conceptions of war and two contrasting aeronautical organizations."

Introduction

IN THE GREAT WAR which blazed up in the summer of 19—, formidable air forces took part in warfare for the first time, and it was this which gave the conflict its special characteristics. To trace the development of that conflict, and principally the aerial part in it, is the purpose of this work, compiled from the Official Reports on the War of 19—, published by the High Commands of the belligerent powers, and from other documents which will be mentioned in due course.

But the historian cannot dissociate himself from the man, and every man's personality is likely to be reflected in his works; and so it may be that my personality has led me astray in spite of my firm resolve to be objective. I pray the reader to make allowances if this has happened.

In Part I, after briefly recounting the causes of the war, I shall describe the moral, intellectual, and material preparations of the nations which took the field. In Part II I shall describe the general situation at the beginning of the conflict and the plans of operation on both sides, then go on to narrate the events of the war—briefly as far as land and sea events are concerned, but in greater detail as regards aerial events.

PART I

CHAPTER I

The Causes of the Conflict

The Kellogg Pact: This incident made war inevitable. As our brief narrative shows, events had been rushing pell-mell to a dizzy climax. Inside of a few days the horizon had been darkened by menacing clouds to such an extent that all hope of a peaceful solution had to be abandoned. The tragedy reached a climax so suddenly that all the world was astonished, even the powers who took part in it. It seemed as though they were sucked into it by a relentless destiny.

The Council of the League of Nations: For these reasons the other European powers declared themselves neutral, and they scrupulously observed their neutrality throughout the war. The United States of America reaffirmed her complete disinterest in European affairs and contented herself with sending some observers to the scene.

In view of the fact that we have resolved to consider this war exclusively from the military angle in order to learn as many lessons as possible from the experience, what interests us most of all is that war broke out suddenly, with no appreciable period of incubation. The publication of official documents has proved that the governments of France, Belgium, and Germany had no intimation that the war they had striven to avoid was inevitable until the night of June 15-16. Until that date, therefore, these governments had refrained from taking any startling measures in order not to appear as aggressors. They had limited themselves to secret partial mobilization.

CHAPTER II

The Moral Preparation

ALTHOUGH THE WAR began suddenly, the populations of the nations involved were ready to face it manfully. In spite of the many pacifist and humanitarian theories bandied about during the preceding decade, the people, in their profound common sense, had not gone soft under the influence of these utopian dreams.

The intense patriotism displayed by the peoples who fought in this war revealed that moral preparation of a high order existed on both sides, regardless of racial differences. In fact, subsequent events proved that the moral resistance of the populations reached an almost identical high plane, and the same was true of their armed forces. We who witnessed the epic struggle must bow to the heroic example furnished by the people who fought in it.

CHAPTER III

The Intellectual Preparation

WE MUST remark at once of the intellectual preparation for the war that the two sides held to two different doctrines of war based on deeply divergent conceptions of war.

FRANCE AND BELGIUM

Because these two powers were victorious in the World War, they were led to perfect the armaments and systems of war which gave them the victory then, systems and armaments which experience had proved satisfactory. Consequently, the war doctrine they held to, which was reflected in the organization, instruction, and education of their armed forces, did not much differ from the one which had taken shape during the World War.

This doctrine taught that the aim of war was the destruction of the enemy's land forces; and therefore gave to the army the position of greatest importance as the most suitable and reliable instrument for accomplishing this aim. The offensive was justly considered the right attitude for attaining success in both major and minor actions; and therefore the offensive had been extolled to the skies in the education and instruction of the various war units, from the highest to the lowest. The difficulties of developing offensive actions, as revealed by the World War, had not been forgotten; but the intervening years had somewhat dimmed them. The De Grandmaison theory of the offensive for its own sake was dead and buried by that time. In its place the consensus of opinion was that, before acting on the offensive, one must first put oneself in a position to be able to do it. In consequence, the ways and means of surmounting the difficulties inherent in an offensive attitude had been thoroughly studied; and it was generally thought that they could be overcome by properly arming, organizing, and employing the various war units.

Authoritative military writers had condemned the static form assumed by the war of 1914-18 as a deplorable retrogression in the art of war, and the rules and instructions on the employment of war units were calculated to avoid another stabilization of the battle front, and instead to foster a war of movement, in which maneuvering could easily be done, and bring far more satisfactory results than could be gained by a constant pounding fire between continuous and almost immovable lines.

It was considered essential to successful offensive war to act with speed and decision before the enemy could organize and take up their position on a defensive line. This entailed effective armament and disposition of one's own troops so as to disrupt the enemy's defense speedily. Surprise therefore had come to be considered one of the paramount factors of success; and as surprise depends mainly on speed, the French and Belgians had created great units capable of moving rapidly from place to place and provided with plentiful offensive means.

To avoid slow and wasteful advances and to disrupt the enemy's defense quickly, they had greatly increased the fire power of their war units, which were armed largely with quick-firing automatic arms, light and heavy machine guns, small cannon, trench mortars, and other modern weapons—all this without diminishing the striking power indispensable for deciding the battle. Light artillery to accompany and support the infantry had been improved and increased; all heavy guns had been mounted on tractors so they could be quickly concentrated wherever they were needed. Great numbers of trench mortars were available to destroy quickly the barbed-wire entanglements and accessory defensive works. Due attention had been given to large highly mobile motorized units ("rapid divisions") composed of infantry and artillery on trucks, motorcyclists, cavalry, motorized machine guns, and tanks, destined, as I have already indicated, to forestall the enemy and prevent him from solidly re-forming his lines. Cavalry units, inestimably useful in a war of movement, had been integrated with machine-gun squads, motorized artillery, armored cars, motorcyclists, and other weapons in order to increase their striking power.

In other words, all the experience of the World War had been brought to bear to give their land armed forces the maximum offensive power in order to destroy as quickly as possible the enemy's land forces by a war of movement.

However, this war doctrine had not escaped **its share of criticism**. The Belgian Major Hunsted wrote:

It seems that the World War taught us nothing—or at least that we have failed to learn anything from it. Except for details of secondary importance, our conception of war today is identical with that prevailing before the World War; and that, in its turn, was identical with the conception of the Napoleonic era.

The phenomenon of stabilization of the battle fronts, which came about automatically, against the will of the combatants, was a significant fact with far-reaching consequences. But it was interpreted not in relation to actual reality, but in relation to the ideology of the past. Since this static form was different from what we students of war had expected, it was defined as a retrogression in the art of war, as if reality should follow art instead of art reality. Since the classical maneuvers taught by the great strategists of the past did not work in face of the new conditions, a new maneuver which did suit the facts should have been created. Instead, the new conditions were accused of impeding the maneuver.

Today the ideal is to compel the enemy to fight **a war of movement** —that is, bring the Napoleonic form of war back again, as though it were possible to change reality and go back to the past. As it has always happened in the past, so today the side which feels itself to be the weaker, or for any other reason is interested in delaying the decision, will assume a defensive attitude. Today the defensive attitude leads to the stabilization of the battle front, a condition deriving from the technical factors of the defensive attitude. This form of war which allows time and respite may prove useful for the final purpose; and for this reason it may be used as a maneuver and assume that form of action.

There is no denying that to surprise the enemy will always prove an advantage, just as it always has; but if one is to enjoy this advantage, the enemy must allow himself to be surprised, and one cannot always rely on that. Therefore one must put oneself in condition to beat the enemy even when he cannot be surprised or forestalled. To beat him with dash and force, in the Napoleonic manner, one must have available a very large quantity of arms, munitions, and other means—enough to be able to launch an offensive in great style, keep it up for a long time, and knock the wind out of the enemy, felling him again and again until he is completely exhausted. But no nation can be in a position to keep in store, constantly ready and efficient, so great a supply of arms, munitions, and other means. Therefore, a violent offensive launched at the beginning of a war would rapidly wear itself out against any enemy not entirely inept and unfit for war.

Moreover, such an attempt might also prove to be very dangerous. A wily, cool-headed enemy could, as a matter of fact, take advantage of an unconsidered offensive on the part of his adversary. He might adopt a strong, elastic defense, such as letting the attacker exhaust his strength and then counterattack, fall upon his tired forces on a field not prepared for defense, and then begin a real war of movement himself. It is well to bear in mind that the decisive battles of the World War were more often counteroffensive actions than offensive ones.

The primary object of an army today in wartime is to guard its own dooryard in order to give its people enough time to prepare ways and means of breaking down someone else's front door.

According to the basic conception of the Franco-Belgian war doctrine, their naval and air forces were supposed principally to assist the action of their land forces in their essential task. France had built her navy up to the maximum potentiality allowed by the international convention on limitation of armaments; and as for the air forces, although she recognized that they might weigh heavily in case of war, she did not believe that they could turn out to be predominant.

Since the most essential task of the war had been assigned to their land forces, the principal function of the air force was limited to helping those forces in the accomplishment of their fundamental mission. The World War had shown the importance of auxiliary aviation; and in the years that followed, thanks to the astonishing progress in this branch of the service and to a closer understanding among the various arms, its importance had been fully recognized in navy and army quarters. In fact, an army and navy without auxiliary aviation had come to be inconceivable, and the tendency was constantly to strengthen the land and sea forces with more and more auxiliary aviation.

The generally admitted possibility that in case of war the enemy would launch aerial and perhaps aero-chemical offensives had led to the constitution of a Department of Aerial Defense, to which large means had been granted for neutralizing such offensive actions against the large industrial and population centers. The creation of an Air Ministry in 1928, followed by the organization of an Independent Air Force, had caused vigorous controversy. Military and naval quarters had betrayed great hostility to such an organization. Although they did not underestimate the importance of aerial means, they claimed they could do no more than to integrate and enlarge the radius of action of the land and sea forces, the only forces capable of waging a war and bringing it to a decision. They absolutely denied that the Independent Air Force could revolutionize the form and characteristics of war, nor did they admit the great efficacy of aero-chemical offensives, claiming that defensive means could always be found to neutralize it. The only thing they admitted was that in some special cases an aerial offensive could be of value in co-operation with land and sea actions. It was thought, then, that it was useless to create an Independent Air Force outside the jurisdiction of the army and navy, because it could only function dependent upon one or the other. The Air Ministry was, therefore, created more for political expediency than for technical, military, and aeronautical reasons. Nevertheless, in spite of every kind of difficulty and opposition, the Air Minister succeeded in organizing an air force independent of the army and navy. Out of the funds at his disposal, he had to take care of the auxiliary aviations for the army and navy, the Independent Air Force, aerial defense, and civil aviation.

This situation gave rise to permanent rivalry between the Army and Navy ministries and the Air Ministry. The former clamored for large auxiliary aviations, while the latter tried to reduce them to strengthen the Independent Air Force. In consequence the proportion of aerial forces allotted to auxiliary aviation and the Independent Air Force was being established more by compromise than anything else.

In the opinion of Sir Lyod, the English expert, the war organization of France had a primary fault, lack of unity, as it did not stem from a single root. France had no institution competent to consider war as a whole; she had only three separate and independent authorities charged with the task of preparing for and waging war in three distinct fields. It was inevitable that each one, alive to its own responsibility, tried to put itself in the best possible condition to fulfill its duties, and considered the war from its own particular point of view. Under these circumstances, harmonious preparation and unity of action could have resulted only from real collaboration; but what collaboration there was, was always vague, uncertain, inconstant, because it was essentially a collaboration of individuals rather than institutions.

Sir Lyod wrote:

War undoubtedly requires the most united employment of all national resources. Now, it is strange to see that the necessity for this unity was not felt by even those national forces especially destined for war—namely, the armed forces. Only seldom and sporadically was the complex problem of war faced in its entirety. Theoretically all sides agreed that the strength of the whole depended upon the harmonious proportion of its parts; but in practice each part prepared and acted in its own behalf. Undoubtedly the French system of three independent ministries for the armed forces and three separate Chiefs of the three General Staffs was the least suitable system for bringing about that harmonious proportion which can be attained only from an integrated consideration of the war problem.

The French and Belgian governments had been led by their experience in the World War to stipulate in their treaty of alliance that in case of war their military and naval forces should be under a single allied command. No stipulation was made about the aerial forces, and perhaps it would have been impossible to do so in view of the Franco-Belgian conception of their employment. Very cordial relations free from any partisan spirit existed between the High Commands of the armed forces of the two powers, so it was possible to consider France and Belgium as a single power functioning under a single direction as far as the war is concerned; and so we shall consider them for simplicity's sake.

GERMANY

The restrictions imposed upon her by the Treaty of Versailles and the development of her aeronautical and chemical industries had led Germany to an entirely different conception of war. On the one hand the restrictions gave her no hope of being able to put herself in a position of equality with her probable eventual enemies, in the near future at least. On the other hand, the development of her aeronautical and chemical industries gave her confidence in her ability to compete successfully in the aerial field.

The World War had shown that, owing to rapid-fire arms, especially the small-caliber ones, the success of the offensive could be assured only by a great preponderance of forces over the defensive. Now, such a preponderance of forces would always be necessary even if arms were perfected on both sides and fire power of the offensive and defensive units equally increased. For this reason German opinion held that in a future war, just as in the World War, given equal armaments, small forces would be able to checkmate much larger ones. So, anyone who felt weaker or less well prepared, or for any reason wanted to delay the decision, in land warfare could impose a static war on his enemy, necessitating a long, painful, and expensive waste of superior forces before being conquered.

Germany could not hope to put numerically superior land forces into the field, much less attain enough numerical superiority to break a static form of war. For this reason the concept prevailed that in a war to come Germany should not seek a decision in the field where it would be hard to get. Instead, she should try to prevent the enemy from getting a decision on land until it could be decided in a different field. In other words, she should resist on land until the war could be decided in the air.

After a short period of hesitation, Germany gave up the idea of fighting on the surface of the sea, and instead concentrated on submarine warfare, which, in view of World War experiences, was considered more suitable for inflicting serious losses on the enemy's traffic, while at the same time completely protecting her own coastlines. So, after building a few cruisers, she changed her naval policy to intensification of her submarine-building program. Germany knew that she would have to give up her own sea trade in case of war, but the World War had taught her she would have to do so anyway even if she had at her disposal a large surface fleet. Her problem for a future war, therefore, was how to live without her sea traffic until the end of the war.

Better to clarify German thought on a conception of the future war, I shall quote part of a document contained in the Report of the War of 19—, recently published by the German General Staff. It is a memorandum sent to the Chancellor by General Reuss, Chief of the General Staff, in January 1928.

It is not in the armed forces of the enemy but in the nation itself that the will and capacity to make war is found. Warfare must therefore be waged against the people, to break their will and destroy their capacity to make war. The armed forces of the enemy do not possess an absolute importance in and for themselves; their importance is only relative, in the degree to which they prove capable of opposing our warfare against their country or of acting against ours. Consequently, from the point of view of the absolute, it is not necessary at all to destroy the enemy's armed forces. If our submarine campaign in the World War had been prosecuted with more vigor, we would have won the war—without destroying the enemy's armed forces—because we would have made the enemy materially incapable of carrying on the war.

The aerial arm makes it feasible to strike directly at the heart of the enemy, striking at all his interior activities without land and sea armed forces, and up to a point independently even of the same aerial forces. Such a means, therefore, affords the best chances of good results.

A decision on land necessitates one side's succeeding, through the action of the armed forces engaged in the struggle, in depriving the enemy's ground forces of all capacity to resist, so that they can no longer protect their country and the way is opened for invasion of their territory, occupation of the most important centers, and the imposition of the victor's law. Thus, on land one must first strike at and break down the maximum moral and material strength of the enemy and shatter its armor, in order later to act against the nation itself. The World War showed that a decision can be reached in this way only by long, painful, and expensive toil.

A decision on the sea necessitates one side's succeeding, through the action of its naval forces, in imposing on the other side an intolerable condition of life, by cutting off most if not all of its sea-borne supplies. But except in special circumstances, it would take a long time to bring about such a situation. In the World War we fought on for years, although we had to give up our maritime traffic right at the beginning.

But for a decision in the air, it is only necessary to put the people themselves in an intolerable condition of life through aerial offensives.

Aerial action enjoys the advantage of unrestricted choice of objectives. Land action can be exercised only against the enemy's land forces; naval action, only against the enemy's maritime resources, warlike or otherwise; but aerial action can be exercised against the objectives which best suit one's purpose—that is, against the enemy's land armed forces, his maritime resources, his aerial forces, or his country itself. It can therefore be employed against the point of his least resistance, which is undoubtedly the wide-open, defenseless territory of the nation itself.

By integrating the aerial arm with poison gas, it is possible today to employ very effective actions against the most vital and vulnerable spots of the enemy—that is, against his most important political, industrial, commercial, and other centers, in order to create among his population a lowering of moral resistance so deep as to destroy the determination of the people to continue the war.

To force the decision in the aerial field, the war on the surface must be neutralized to prevent the enemy from gaining a decision there. In other words, it is necessary to hold the enemy's land armed forces and keep one's own national life going on in spite of deficiency in or lack of maritime traffic.

All this is along general lines. As to what particularly concerns us, we should keep in mind:

1. Owing to our political and geographical situation, we cannot hope to safeguard our maritime traffic in case of war with any sea power. In any event, the safety of one's maritime traffic cannot be assured nowadays even by a preponderance of naval surface means. We ourselves have given the best proof of that to our former enemies. Consequently, even if we had a naval surface force stronger than our enemy's, we should have to give up our maritime traffic just the same if he knew how to use his submarine forces. Besides, even if our surface naval forces did prevail and succeeded in stopping the enemy's maritime traffic, it would be decisive against only one eventual enemy power—England. All other powers have land borders through which more or less adequate supplies could be imported; and the one power against whom the result would be decisive happens to be the strongest one on the seas, and to contend with her would be, if not impossible, certainly very difficult.

Therefore, practically speaking, our surface fleet could attain no positive result, just as it happened to our great fleet in the World War. In consequence, the best solution is to give up the fleet and devote our resources to something else. By not having a fleet, we should be spared seeing it beaten or having to tie up somewhere for shelter. In this way we would annul the enemy's naval surface power, as it would find nothing to fight against but empty space.

What interests us primarily is keeping the enemy's fleet from attacking our coastline from the sea; secondarily to hamper the enemy's traffic. All this can be done by our submarine arm. As far as the sea is concerned, then, our efforts should be in that direction.

The impossibility of safeguarding our maritime traffic compels us to look for means suitable for waging war without such traffic. In this regard we should consider that we could always establish trade with neutrals, unless we again suffer the complete encirclement to which we were subjected in the last war. Anyway, because it is our duty to prepare for the worst, the Government should take timely steps to meet this extreme contingency. The experience of the World War shows that it can be solved; and the shorter the war, the easier to solve.

2. On land we will find ourselves confronted by formidable armies which, even according to the best hypothesis—that is, that they would be compelled to take the defensive—will have such enormous power of resistance that we would find it very expensive to break down. The nations behind them would keep on replenishing their supplies from neutrals because we would not be able to blockade them by sea, and they would continue to throw all their resources on the battle lines, thus lengthening the struggle in space and time. To decide the war in our favor on land—that is, to succeed in destroying this enormous resistance—in the best hypothesis we would have to fight fiercely for a long time and use up enormous quantities of money and resistance—and, what is worse, always be handicapped by inability to get supplies by sea. In the most favorable issue, we might achieve victory; but we would find ourselves in an exhausted condition at the end, just as our enemies of the last war were.

Moreover, it is well to keep in mind that we might not be able to put preponderant forces in the field, and that very probably, for obvious reasons, we might be confronted by superior forces of an enemy. Experience has shown that a great superiority of forces and means is required to break a static condition of war. So, although we could easily stand on the defensive, it would be hard for us to take the offensive with any probability of success.

On land the war will present much the same characteristics as the World War, because no substantial changes have taken place in armament or organization of land forces. The side most interested in the defensive will take advantage of the efficacy of a defensive system to force the enemy to a static form of war.

This static form has been judged, especially abroad, as a retrogression in the art of war, but as a matter of fact it is simply a state of affairs stemming from special technical conditions to which the art of war must be adapted. There is a tendency, especially abroad, to return through various artifices to a war of movement, but the tendency is destined to fail because no artifices can alter the deep causes which lead to the static form of war. The frontiers of the great powers are not long enough to allow full deployment to the huge modern armies—this leads to the continuous front—and the efficacy of rapid-fire arms has gone on increasing, thus enhancing the value of the defensive. Against the will of those who will fight it, the next war will have the same static form as the World War presented, also against the will of those who fought it. It can be said with certainty that in a future war, a few will be able to resist the many on land. Therefore it is not to our interest to try for victory on land.

3. In the air we find ourselves in better case than on land and sea, because, quite independent of the development of our technical knowledge and our industry, we are on an equality with our eventual enemies. This is the field in which we should seek a decision, even against the will of our enemy. To do this we will have to be able to hold our enemy's land forces and live without maritime trade while the aerial conflict develops. To be in a favorable position to win the war, we must mass the bulk of our forces there.

By limiting the aims of our land and naval forces to those strictly needed for the full development of the mission of the aerial forces, we will automatically be able to increase the air force and decrease the army and navy correspondingly. To reach the decision in the shortest possible time, we must direct our warlike actions with the utmost intensity and violence against the most vulnerable and vital centers in the enemy's territory. The aim of our aerial forces will be to break down as speedily as possible the enemy population's will to fight.

The report relates that the concepts and ideas set forth in this memorandum from the General Staff were accepted by the German Government only after heated discussion. The employment of the aero-chemical arm had been banned by an international convention, and the use of such atrocious means against unarmed populations had been condemned by world opinion. To base its war organization precisely on the unrestricted use of the aero-chemical arm against unarmed populations, in accordance with General Reuss's ideas, seemed to the Government antisocial and politically inexpedient. Nevertheless, General Reuss triumphed in the end, owing to the following considerations:

1. All the powers were busily equipping themselves with aero-chemical arms, each solemnly promising not to use them unless the enemy did so first. This clearly demonstrated that no power trusted the others to respect the convention's prohibition of the use of aero-chemical weapons. This general mistrust was only

natural and logical, for no one would be justified in trusting his enemy's renunciation of any arms which might prove useful. All nations will prepare for aero-chemical warfare, and in case of war all of them will be ready to wage aero-chemical war. How could these arms remain unused while all other national resources were thrown into the struggle? It is fated that the side which for any reason believes it to be to its interest will not hesitate to override any convention; and naturally it would not be willing to forego any chance of victory. Then the other side will be compelled to retaliate in kind, and the aero-chemical war with all its horror would be on. In either case, whether one expects to abide by the convention's prohibition or defy it, one must be ready to face aero-chemical warfare.

2. One who prepares to face an eventuality must do it in a way calculated to make him reasonably sure of success. Hence it is necessary to put oneself in condition to win the aero-chemical war wherever and whenever it strikes if one wants to meet it successfully. To wait for the enemy to begin it and then rush to parry it would be conceding a great advantage; it would be beginning the war by putting oneself passively in an unfavorable position from the very outset.

3. In face of instinctive self-interest, of national survival, every convention loses its value, every humanitarian sentiment loses its weight. The only principle to be considered is the necessity of killing to avoid being killed.

Since 1927 a sweeping military reform has taken place in Germany through the creation of the Ministry of National Defense and the Supreme General Staff, which led to the abolition of the various military ministries. The functions of the Chief of the General Staff were very important. On him depended the proper allocation among the three armed forces of all resources assigned to national defense. Since he knew the complex problem of war, it was his task to establish the importance of the three armed forces so as to give the maximum potentiality for war to the whole.

The Chief of the General Staff did not exercise this important function in complete independence, for he had to submit his plans for approval to the Chief of State. A veto automatically brought the resignation of the Chief of Staff, because it was inconceivable that he could prepare the armed forces according to concepts at variance with his own. On the other hand, approval of his ideas made his authority paramount, for the Ministry of National Defense was essentially an administrative institution charged with the organization of the armed forces according to policies laid down by the Chief of Staff. His importance was further enhanced by the fact that in case of war he became commander in chief of all the armed forces of the nation.

In the beginning the German General Staff consisted of a number of officers selected from the better educated, more intelligent and open-minded men of the armed forces. They were to assist the Chief of Staff in the exercise of his duties in peacetime as well as in wartime. At the same time the War Academy was created, in which a certain number of General Staff officers were to study the problem of integrated war under the personal direction of the Chief of Staff. In 1930 the first officers came out of the War Academy. The fundamental purpose of this organization was to centralize in the hands of one man the preparation and employment of all the armed forces in order to give them a single directive in view of their single aim. This emphasized still more strongly for all the component parts of the armed forces that the paramount necessity in war is to win. This made each branch of the armed forces understand that, whatever the task assigned to it in wartime, it was just as valuable as any other, for all tasks would be indispensable to the attainment of victory.

This central organization enabled General Reuss to put his ideas into effect once they were approved by the Chief of State, and to inculcate that mental discipline which constitutes the moral foundation of every war potentiality.

The preparation of the land armed forces was inspired by the concept that they were to be in condition to resist firmly, with the smallest possible expenditure of resources, so that most of the resources could be given to the forces entrusted directly with reaching the decision. The ideas predominating abroad were well known, and it was a foregone conclusion that the German Army would have to face the shock of great offensives from the outset. But it was believed that, no matter how great the offensives, they would rapidly exhaust themselves against a tenacious defensive; for at the outset of the war no power would have ready at hand the immense quantity of means necessary for protracted offensive action. In fact, no power was confident of being able to do so, and all of them were preoccupied with plans for industrial mobilization to turn out the means needed for the war machine.

It was therefore principally a question of surviving the critical initial period—i.e. the action of the forces the enemy had ready at the beginning of the war. Once his initial strength had been exhausted, there would be time to provide for other contingencies if the war had not meantime been decided in another field.

It was necessary to confine the enemy to a stabilized battle front, and this could be done fairly easily by a firm but elastic resistance directed not toward obstinately contesting each foot of ground, but toward putting the enemy in a difficult position. It would be enough to establish as fast as possible a continuous line of rapid-fire small-caliber arms, and to reinforce it continually to make it stronger and stronger. It was also necessary to study in detail during peacetime the nature of this line, outlining in advance its main points, such as the proper location of arms, munitions, and other equipment, how to make use of the people living nearest the borders, especially the youth of the sport clubs, assigning everyone his place and task, and concentrating reserves behind the danger spots as rapidly as possible so they could be thrown into action when and where they were needed. In this way everything could probably be made ready before the enemy could mobilize enough means and forces to make his offensive really dangerous. All this task of preparation would after all be simply a work of minute organization.

The employment of land forces was based on these criteria; but the planned defensive attitude did not preclude or lessen the offensive spirit in the German Army. On the contrary, it was made paramount in the education of the troops and officers by teaching them that the defensive attitude was to be adopted as a means for passing eventually to the offensive and schooling each unit, no matter how small or unimportant, never to lose any chance of taking the offensive.

The naval forces limited their ambition to defending the coasts against enemy offensives from the sea and hampering his maritime traffic by developing the submarine and other insidious weapons. Cruisers already built were kept in active service, but they were to be laid up at the outbreak of hostilities on the theory that valuable men were needed for primary tasks and should not be wasted on secondary ones.

Since it had been decided to seek the decision in the aerial field and to concentrate the maximum effort there, the Independent Air Force had been organized exclusively for the offensive, not only in materials and arms, but also in the minds and hearts of the men. All secondary aims were subordinated to giving the Independent Air Force the maximum power, and so auxiliary and defense aviations were abolished.

CHAPTER IV

The Material Preparation—France and Belgium
[The preparation of land and sea forces followed traditional lines.]

AERIAL FORCES—FRANCE

Auxiliary Aviation for the Army: The Franco-Belgian war concept had assigned the army the most essential task of the war, and therefore considerable aerial forces had been allocated to the large ground units. These aerial auxiliaries were made up of the following specialties:

1. Strategic reconnaissance
2. Tactical reconnaissance and liaison
3. Artillery observation
4. Attack—against fighting, marching, and encamped enemy troops.
5. Pursuit—to police the sky in the sphere of activity of the various units.
6. Bombing—to execute aerial offensives against objectives directly related to land actions.

The inclusion of pursuit and bombing groups had been discussed at length by the Council for National Defense, as the Air Ministry had been loath to concede aerial means to the auxiliary aviation for arms which in his opinion belonged to the Independent Air Force. But the opinion of the Minister of War had prevailed because he contended that the army could not always rely upon the Independent Air Force for the necessary close collaboration unless it was made dependent upon the army command.

Irrespective of the specialty to which it belonged, each Squadron was made up of 6 first-line planes, with 2 in reserve. Two squadrons constituted a Group; 3 groups a Regiment; and 2

regiments a Brigade. The organic strength of the various units
was as follows:

| | FIRST-LINE | | |
	SQUADRONS	PLANES	IN RESERVE
1. FOR EACH GROUP OF ARMIES:			
1 regiment for strategic recon- naissance	6	36	12
1 group for tactical reconnais- sance	2	12	4
1 regiment for attack	6	36	12
1 brigade for pursuit.........	12	72	24
1 brigade for bombing	12	72	24
Total for group of armies	38	228	76
2. FOR EACH ARMY:			
1 group for strategic recon- naissance	2	12	4
1 group for tactical reconnais- sance	2	12	4
1 regiment for attack	6	36	12
1 regiment for pursuit	6	36	12
Total for army	16	96	32
3. FOR EACH ARMY CORPS:			
1 group for tactical reconnais- sance	2	12	4
1 group for artillery observa- tion	2	12	4
1 group for pursuit	2	12	4
Total for army corps	6	36	12
4. FOR EACH INFANTRY DIVISION:			
The Command of the army corps allots aerial means to its divisions according to need.			
5. FOR EACH MOTORIZED OR CAV- ALRY DIVISION:			
1 squadron for tactical recon- naissance	1	6	2
1 squadron for pursuit	1	6	2
1 squadron for attack	1	6	2
Total for motorized or cav- alry division	3	18	6

As it had been decided that the first mobilization would call for 3 groups of armies, consisting of 7 armies, 30 army corps, 10 motorized divisions, and 12 cavalry divisions, the constitution of the following had been foreseen:

		FIRST-LINE	
	SQUADRONS	PLANES	IN RESERVE
1. FOR STRATEGIC RECONNAISSANCE:			
3 regiments (for the groups of armies)	18	108	36
7 groups (for the armies) ...	14	84	28
Total for strategic reconnaissance	32	192	64
2. FOR TACTICAL RECONNAISSANCE:			
3 groups (for the groups of armies)	6	36	12
7 groups (for the armies)	14	84	28
30 groups (for the army corps)	60	360	120
10 squadrons (for the motorized divisions)	10	60	20
12 squadrons (for the cavalry divisions)	12	72	24
Total for tactical reconnaissance	102	612	204
3. FOR ARTILLERY OBSERVATION:			
30 groups (for the army corps)	60	360	120
4. FOR PURSUIT:			
3 brigades (for the groups of armies)	36	216	72
7 regiments (for the armies) ..	42	252	84
30 groups (for the army corps)	60	360	120
10 squadrons (for the motorized divisions)	10	60	20
12 squadrons (for the cavalry divisions)	12	72	24
Total for pursuit	160	960	320

5. FOR ATTACK:

3 regiments (for the groups of armies)	18	108	36
7 regiments (for the armies)..	42	252	84
10 squadrons (for the motorized divisions)	10	60	20
12 squadrons (for the cavalry divisions)	12	72	24
Total for attack	82	492	164

6. FOR BOMBING:

3 brigades (for the groups of armies)	36	216	72

Therefore the army auxiliary aviation included:

SQUADRONS		AIRPLANES	IN RESERVE
32	for strategic reconnaissance	192	64
102	for tactical reconnaissance	612	204
60	for artillery observation	360	120
160	for pursuit	960	320
82	for attack	492	164
36	for bombing	216	72
472	for a total of	2,832	944

This was the French aerial organization in time of war. In peacetime it had half as many squadrons (236), each composed of 4 planes (944 in all). In peacetime the auxiliary units were under the Army Corps Commands in the territories where they were located—in discipline, command, and instruction of personnel. For technical aeronautical instruction and specialized materials they depended upon the Aeronautical Inspectorates of Specialties—one for strategical reconnaissance, one for tactical reconnaissance, and so on through the list of specialties. These Inspectorates, in turn, were dependent on the General Aeronautical Inspectorate with the Air Ministry.

A General Direction of Aeronautics, part of the Ministry of War, also functioned as a liaison organ with the Air Ministry. According to agreement between the two ministries, the General Direction of Aeronautics requisitioned and received from the General Aeronautical Inspectorate all specialized personnel and materials, and distributed them to the units which it controlled through the Army Corps Commands.

When war came the following were to be created:

1. A General Command of Aeronautics attached to the Army High Command

2. Three Aeronautical Commands for the groups of armies

3. Seven Aeronautical Commands for the armies

4. Thirty Aeronautical Commands for the army corps

5. Ten Aeronautical Commands for the motorized divisions

6. Twelve Aeronautical Commands for the cavalry divisions

In case of war the General Inspectorate of Aeronautics and its dependent Inspectorates of Specialties, through an Aeronautical Intendency dependent on the Army Command, would continue to take care of the replacement of specialized personnel and materials, and of the creation of new units, according to an agreement between the War Minister and the Air Minister.

This system [remarks a Report from the French High Command] seemed rather cumbersome and faulty, as it made auxiliary aviation dependent on two different hierarchies, which was bound to raise bureaucratic complications and lead to divided responsibility; and this would certainly have serious consequences in war if not in peace. On the other hand, if auxiliary aviations had been placed under the Ministries of War and Navy respectively, the result would have been a multiplication of similar organs, from which more complications and inconveniences of a different sort would have ensued.

The lesser of the two evils had to be chosen—that is, the system of centralizing the direction of personnel and aviation materials production under a single institution, the Air Ministry, and then have them distributed to the organizations which employed them—the Ministry of War, the Ministry of the Navy, the Independent Air Force, and Aerial Defense.

Upon mobilization each squadron was to fill up its quota and form another squadron from reserve personnel and materials. As organized, each squadron already in being had to be prepared for instant action within twelve hours, and each of the reserves for action within twenty-four hours.

Auxiliary Aviation for the Navy: To the Navy's auxiliary aviation were entrusted the following tasks:

1. For the aerial forces not ship-based:

1. Aerial defense of naval bases
2. Submarine scouting and convoy duty
3. Long-range reconnaissance
4. Participation in the Fleet's action

2. For ship-based aerial forces (on catapults or on airplane carriers):

1. Defense against aerial attacks on the naval forces while in navigation
2. Aerial reconnaissance while in navigation
3. Tactical co-operation during action

To this end were envisaged:

1. For the aerial defense of naval bases: 60 hydro-pursuit squadrons with 360 first-line planes and 120 in reserve.

2. For submarine scouting and convoy duty: 20 short-range hydro-reconnaissance squadrons with 120 first-line planes and 40 in reserve.

3. For long-range reconnaissance: 20 long-range hydro-reconnaissance squadrons with 120 first-line planes and 40 in reserve.

4. For participation in the Fleet's action: 20 hydro-bombing squadrons with 120 first-line planes and 40 in reserve; 6 hydro-torpedo squadrons with 36 first-line planes, and 12 in reserve.

A total for the aerial forces not ship-based of 126 squadrons with 756 first-line planes, and 252 in reserve.

Aerial forces ship-based:

1. For defense against aerial attacks directed against the naval forces while in navigation: 80 hydro-pursuit catapult planes.

2. For aerial reconnaissance while navigating: 80 hydro-reconnaissance catapult planes.

3. For tactical co-operation during the action: 80 hydro-pursuit planes, 40 hydro-bombing planes, 20 hydro-torpedo planes, all on airplane carriers.

A total of 300 planes ship-based.

General total of naval auxiliary aviation, including reserves: 1,308 planes.

As for dependency, the situation was analogous to that of the army auxiliary aviation.

Independent Air Force: The Independent Air Force had been entrusted with the following tasks:

1. To attack, in order to gain or consolidate aerial superiority over the enemy aerial forces.

2. To carry the offensive to the enemy's territory.

3. To co-operate directly with the land and sea forces, and eventually to reinforce the auxiliary aviations organically assigned to said forces.

The Independent Air Force was exclusively and completely under the Air Ministry, and in the event of war its commander, appointed by the Council of Ministers, was invested with rank and authority equal to the army and navy commanders.

The nucleus of the Independent Air Force consisted of bombing and pursuit units; and to this nucleus had been added special reconnaissance units in order to give it its own reconnaissance service.

The war organization of the Independent Air Force was as follows:

BRIGADES	SQUADRONS	FIRST-LINE PLANES	IN RESERVE
5 pursuit	60	360	120
2 day-bombing	24	144	48
4 night-bombing	48	288	96
1 strategic reconnaissance regiment	6	36	12
Total	138	828	276

Aerial Defense: Due consideration had been given to the eventuality that the enemy might launch great aerial and aero-chemical offensives, and therefore the aerial defense of the nation's territory had been diligently organized and richly endowed by the General Direction of Aerial Defense working with the Air Ministry. Under this direction had been placed all the aerial defense, anti-aerial and aerial protection means, and in case of war, a General Command of the Territorial Aerial Defense was to be constituted to take charge of it.

It was known in France that other nations, Germany among them, were constituting offensive aerial units of battleplanes powerfully armed for air combat and able to carry great bomb loads; but not much importance was attached to this novelty, as it was thought that the experience of the World War did not justify it. It was said that such planes, being slow and incapable of quick maneuvering, could not keep in formation during the battle, and that they would always find themselves isolated in front of pursuit squadrons attacking them in formation, and therefore in a condition of absolute inferiority. Moreover, it was thought that their possible superiority of armament (in caliber and range) could be easily offset by attacking pursuit planes which, owing to superior speed and maneuverability, could always avoid their fire, and that such big planes would be ideal targets for antiaircraft artillery. It was also thought that it would be sufficient to send highly maneuverable single-seaters against them, the more so as, taking comparative costs into account, it would always be more effective to oppose each large plane with several small ones, thus distributing among the latter the task of attacking the various vital parts of the former.

For aerial defense—that is, the pursuit action taking place in one's own sky against enemy planes coming to attack territorial centers—they had adopted the alert type of pursuit plane capable of climbing at a very high speed and possessing a radius of action of 50 to 60 minutes, time enough for it to rise to the attack, fight the enemy, and return to its airfield.

Defense Aviation: This included 50 groups of alert pursuit planes, each group composed of two squadrons, each squadron having 6 planes (total, 100 squadrons, 600 planes).

As for anti-aerial artillery, the gun was a 75-millimeter, its high-explosive and shrapnel shells weighing about 7 kilograms each. It was mounted on a mobile platform and had a useful maximum range of 5,000 meters.

The Anti-Aerial Artillery comprised 10 anti-aerial regiments, each including:

2 brigades of anti-aerial batteries
1 battalion of anti-aerial searchlights
1 company of signalmen

In their turn, each brigade of anti-aerial batteries included:

3 anti-aerial batteries (divided into 4 sections of 2 75-mm. guns, and an anti-aerial machine gun each)

1 section of anti-aerial machine guns (8 machine guns to a section)

Each battalion of anti-aerial searchlights included:

4 companies of anti-aerial searchlights (divided into 6 sections of 1 searchlight, 1 sound locater, and 1 anti-aerial machine gun each)

Each company of signalmen included:

2 sections of signalmen

3 sections of telegraph operators

In total, each anti-aerial regiment was composed of:

48 75-mm. guns

168 anti-aerial machine guns

96 searchlights

96 sound locators

The general total was, then, 480 guns and 1,680 machine guns.

In time of peace, only the nucleus of the alert pursuit groups and the anti-aerial regiments existed, namely:

1. Fifty alert pursuit squadrons of 4 planes each. Upon mobilization each squadron was required to fill up its quota of 6 planes and to create a twin squadron and its Group Command. The needed materials were ready, stored in the mobilization depots; and the personnel kept in the territorial reserve were required to reach their squadrons within six hours. All the personnel were kept in perfect training by periodical recalls to the colors.

2. Ten brigades of anti-aerial batteries (each including 3 batteries of 2 sections each) with a searchlight company, a signalmen section, and a telegraph operators section. These 10 brigades when mobilized were required, by completing and doubling themselves, to constitute the 10 regiments called for by the war organization. All the needed matériel was stored in depots, and the personnel were kept in the territorial reserve and always efficiently trained. Upon mobilization they were required to reach their brigades within 6 hours. The alert aerial units, as well as the anti-aerial units, were located, even during peacetime, in the immediate vicinity of the centers to be protected, so that at the beginning of the hostilities the only thing to be done was to take units from localities less exposed and shift them where the enemy's attacks would be concentrated.

The General Command of the Territorial Aerial Defense through these means at its disposal (50 alert pursuit groups and 10 anti-aerial regiments) was required to take care of the aerial defense of the territory outside the army and navy jurisdictions. The defense of the territories located in the army's and the navy's zones of activity was considered a task belonging to these two institutions, and they were required to take care of it through their respective auxiliary aviation and anti-aerial artillery.

The strength of the French aerial forces when fully mobilized was as follows:

PLANES

CATEGORY	SQUADRONS	FIRST-LINE	RESERVE	UNATTACHED	TOTAL
Army auxiliary aviation	472	2,832	944	....	3,776
Naval auxiliary aviation	126	756	252	300	1,308
Independent Air Force	138	828	276	....	1,104
Aerial defense	100	600	....	....	600
Total	836	5,016	1,472	300	6,788

Colonial aviation has not been taken into account, because it was required to remain in the Colonies in time of war.

AERIAL FORCES—BELGIUM

The Belgian aerial forces were organized almost exactly like those of France.

The army auxiliary aviation included:

	SQUADRONS	FIRST-LINE PLANES	IN RESERVE
1. FOR THE ARMY HIGH COMMAND:			
1 group for strategical reconnaissance	2	12	4
1 group for tactical reconnaissance	2	12	4
1 regiment for attack	6	36	12
1 brigade for pursuit	12	72	24
1 brigade for bombing	12	72	24
Total	34	204	68

2. For the army corps and the motorized and cavalry divisions, the allotments of aerial forces were identical with those of the corresponding large French units.

As the mobilization, at the beginning, envisaged 5 army corps, 2 motorized divisions and 2 cavalry divisions, the organization of the aerial forces was established as follows:

	FIRST-LINE		
---	SQUADRONS	PLANES	IN RESERVE
1. FOR STRATEGIC RECONNAISSANCE:			
1 group (for the Army High Command)	2	12	4
2. FOR TACTICAL RECONNAISANCE:			
1 group (for the Army High Command)	2	12	4
5 groups (for the army corps)	10	60	20
2 squadrons (for the motorized divisions)	2	12	4
2 squadrons (for the cavalry divisions)	2	12	4
Total	16	96	32
3. FOR ARTILLERY OBSERVATION:			
5 groups (for the army corps)	10	60	20
4. FOR PURSUIT:			
1 brigade (for the Army High Command)	12	72	24
5 groups (for the army corps)	10	60	20
2 squadrons (for the motorized divisions)	2	12	4
2 squadrons (for the cavalry divisions)	2	12	4
Total	26	156	52
5. FOR ATTACK:			
1 regiment (for the Army High Command)	6	36	12
2 squadrons (for the motorized divisions)	2	12	4
2 squadrons (for the cavalry divisions)	2	12	4
Total	10	60	20
6. FOR BOMBING:			
1 brigade (for the Army High Command)	12	72	24

Therefore the army auxiliary aviation was constituted by:

SQUADRONS		FIRST-LINE PLANES	IN RESERVE
2	for strategical reconnaissance	12	4
16	for tactical reconnaissance	96	32
10	for artillery observation	60	20
26	for pursuit	156	52
10	for attack	60	20
12	for bombing	72	24
76	squadrons with a total of	456 and	152

The naval auxiliary aviation included:

1. For the aerial defense of the naval bases: 10 hydro-pursuit squadrons with 60 first-line planes and 20 in reserve.

2. For submarine scouting and anti-submarine convoying duty: 10 hydro-reconnaissance squadrons with 60 first-line planes and 20 in reserve.

3. For long-range reconnaissance: 2 strategic hydro-reconnaissance squadrons with 12 first-line planes and 4 in reserve.

A total of 22 squadrons, with 132 first-line planes and 44 in reserve.

The Independent Air Force: For aerial offensives against the enemy's territory, use would be made of the forces at the disposal of the Army High Command.

Aerial Defense: This was constituted as a separate institution and included: 6 pursuit groups of 2 squadrons each (72 planes in all) 1 anti-aerial regiment (48 75-mm. guns and 168 machine guns)

The total strength of the Belgian aerial forces, after the first mobilization, is given in the following table:

		PLANES		
CATEGORY	SQUADRONS	FIRST-LINE	RESERVE	TOTAL
Army auxiliary aviation	76	456	152	608
Naval auxiliary aviation	22	132	44	176
Aerial defense	12	72	. . . .	72
Total	110	660	196	856

The war organization of the Allied aerial forces, classified by specialities, was as given in the following table:

NUM-BER	SPECIALTIES	FRANCE SQUAD-RONS	FRANCE PLANES	BELGIUM SQUAD-RONS	BELGIUM PLANES	TOTALS SQUAD-RONS	TOTALS PLANES
1	Strategical reconnaissance	38	228	2	12	40	240
2	Tactical reconnaissance	102	612	16	96	118	708
3	Artillery observation	60	360	10	60	70	420
4	Pursuit	220	1,320	26	156	246	1,476
5	Attack	82	492	10	60	92	552
6-7	Day- and night-bombing	108	648	12	72	120	720
8	Hydro-pursuit	60	360	10	60	70	420
9	Hydro-strategical reconnaissance	20	120	2	12	22	132
10	Hydro-tactical reconnaissance	20	120	10	60	30	180
11	Hydro-bombing	20	120	..	..	20	120
12	Hydro-torpedo	6	36	..	..	6	36
13	Hydro-aboard-ship	..	300	..	..	..	300
14	Defense pursuit	100	600	12	72	112	672
	Total	836	5,316	110	660	946	5,976

The peacetime organization was as follows:

France:

SQUADRONS		PLANES
236	Army auxiliary aviation	994
63	Naval auxiliary aviation	252
69	Independent Air Force	276
50	alerts	200
418	*total*	1,722

Belgium:

SQUADRONS		PLANES
38	Army auxiliary aviation	152
11	Naval auxiliary aviation	44
6	alerts	24
55	*total*	220

MOBILIZATION

By timely measures a successful mobilization of the aerial units had been assured. Through them a personnel twice as large as the war organization required was always ready and duly trained.

The reserves of matériel needed for the units envisaged by the war organization were also available and stored in the mobilization depots.

As already mentioned, every squadron of 4 planes would be required to increase the number of its planes to 8, of which 6 were first-line and 2 in reserve. Furthermore, it was required to double itself by creating another squadron of the same size. Therefore, in the mobilization depots of each squadron 12 planes and all accessories were stored.

It had been estimated that each squadron would lose one-third of its strength for each month of war, and that consequently the French aerial forces would need about 2,000 new planes every month for replacement. There was grave doubt that industry could turn out that many planes, especially in the first months of the war, so it was decided to have 2 more planes in reserve for each squadron as a second-line reserve. Thus, for each 4-plane squadron, 16 planes and accessories were stored in the mobilization depots. That was considered sufficient to keep all squadrons up to full war efficiency without replacements for at least the first two months of war.

These large stores of aviation matériel necessitated great expense for storage, upkeep, and custody. Besides, as time went by, they became obsolete and had to be discarded without ever seeing service. Nevertheless, it was impossible to follow any other system, since everything had to be on hand at the moment of mobilization. These large quantities of matériel had to be continually replaced with later models to keep aviation abreast of scientific and industrial progress; and therefore it was decided to completely renovate all matériel every five years. This meant 3,000 new planes every year, and still some of the stored machines would be five or even six years old.

This situation gave rise to criticism from military critics who claimed that it was wrong to spend huge sums every year to buy planes and motors, only to let them grow obsolete in military depots. They maintained that better counsel was to have industry always ready to turn out the most modern and improved planes with mass-production methods and limiting the strength of the aerial forces to peacetime requirements or only slightly higher. But this criticism was based on the doubtful assumption that the war would give France time enough even for mass-production methods to function. Other critics lamented the multiplicity of plane types adopted by French aviation, a situation caused by so many specialized services and the number of competitive firms in the airplane industry.

Shortly after the beginning of the war, the magazine *Les Ailes* carried an article which created a furor in the aeronautical world, although the author, who signed himself Commander X, remained anonymous.

It seems that in France [wrote Commander X] military aviation is built for everything but war. Technical experts see it only as an aero-dynamic phenomenon. New models of planes with new and improved characteristics are continually being thought out and designed, just as aeronautical science and industry constantly progress. A new model is accepted by the military aviation in order, it is supposed, to be used for some purpose or other. But for what purpose? Well, that is not yet known; first the machine must be studied and experimented with. So another set of technicians will gather round the plane to see what can be done with it. Then, by shifting something here and something there, cameras, machine guns, bomb racks and other accessories are attached to it, and at last the new model becomes a military plane.

Then there are the specialized tacticians, who see things from one point of view only. They are always for specialization. There are many ways to make use of a plane in war, from bombing to transportation of goods. The man who has more imagination will invent new uses for it, and naturally each time he will want the proper machine for that use. And, of course, who can dispute that bombing racks, for instance, are superfluous for transportation of goods?

Then there are the firms which build airplanes, motors, and accessories. According to them, they have a right to do business and make a living, so it is the government's duty to do business with them. Well, in that case it is the Government's duty to order from them what it wants, regardless of what they want to produce.

Thus, owing to technical progress in aeronautics and the most varied forms of specialization, and thanks to competition among the plane builders, the most evident characteristic of our military aviation is its variety. Barring errors, it presents fourteen specialties, namely: strategical reconnaissance, tactical reconnaissance, day bombing, night bombing, artillery observation, attack, pursuit, alert pursuit, long-range hydro-reconnaissance, short-range hydro-reconnaissance, hydro-pursuit, hydro-bombing, hydro-torpedo, and hydro-catapult. Theoretically, then, we have fourteen types of matériel for our squadrons.

Theoretically, yes; but in actuality the variety of our plane types is fantastic. In our mobilization depots we have matériel up to six years old; so for each type we have several varieties, according to age. For instance, we have three different models for the tactical reconnaissance plane: the 1927, the 1929, and the 1930 models. But the 1927 model was built by firms A and B, the 1929 by C and D, and the 1930 by E and F; so for this type we have no less than six varieties. And this without taking into account the different varieties of engine.

Other specialties offer still more variety. Let us consider the pursuit specialty. As is well known, this must always be up to date, and so its rate of aging is very fast. In fact, new models come out one right after the other, and today we have nine varieties, exclusive of the alert pursuit specialty, which has another six varieties of its own.

If I am not mistaken, the fourteen specialties into which our aviation is divided have all told more than sixty varieties of matériel. Since our peacetime organization has about 400 squadrons, we can say that, on the average, only six or seven squadrons for each variety can be considered homogeneous.

But what will happen to us tomorrow, in case of war, with our varied sample-case of arms?

Undoubtedly the French aeronautical industry, with its well-tooled factories, capable technicians, and skilled workmen, could furnish first-class planes and motors, while scientific institutes with a glorious tradition contributed largely to the technical improvement of aerial means. But perhaps these excellent efforts were not always well directed. The authorities responsible for the organization of the aerial forces were deeply preoccupied with the great variety of types lamented by Commander X. This variety resulted in differing war values for the various squadrons, depending on the type of their armament. A pursuit squadron of the 1932 type was certainly more efficient than one of the 1928 type. But the 1928 squadron could not be discarded simply because a better type of armament had come into use. It had to be kept until it could be replaced with a better type. It was decided, therefore, that the most modern matériel should go to the Independent Air Force, and that which became obsolete should be handed down to the auxiliary aerial forces. As a consequence, at the opening of hostilities, the pursuit matériel was distributed as shown in the following table:

ARMAMENTS

UNITS	NEEDED SQUADRONS	TYPE 1932	TYPE 1931	TYPE 1930	TYPE 1929	TYPE 1928	TYPE 1927
Independent Air Force	60	42	18				
Groups of armies	36		22	14			
Armies	42			26	16		
Army corps	60				24	36	
Motorized divisions	10					4	6
Cavalry divisions	12						12
Total	220	42	40	40	40	40	18

If this system of allocation answered to a logical criterion of employment [remarks the report of the French High Command], on the other it nevertheless gave way to two types of deficiency, one moral and one material.

1. To follow the order of preference in allocating the most modern matériel, it had to keep moving down from the major to the minor units. When the armaments of an Independent Air Force squadron were replaced, the old ones were shifted to a group-of-armies squadron, and so on until this replacement reached the cavalry divisions. Only then was the old matériel definitely eliminated. For obvious reasons of instruction and morale, the personnel were not shifted. This shifting of matériel was a complicated and costly affair, but it was inevitable if the order of preference was to be kept. Otherwise we might find ourselves with an Independent Air Force armed with obsolete matériel when war broke out.

2. This order of preference was undoubtedly harmful to the morale of the flying personnel. A cavalry division squadron, for example, could not help feeling slighted in having to use old matériel when other squadrons up the line had better and more modern equipment.

This situation was made worse by the fact that most of the new matériel was stowed away in the mobilization depots. Thus, out of 20 new planes delivered by the factories, only 4 were given to a squadron, while 12 were stowed away in that squadron's mobilization depot (4 to complete the squadron eventually, 8 to create a new squadron), and the remaining 4 were sent to the second-line depot. But if all the new matériel was given out to the squadrons in being during peacetime, it would be impossible to mobilize homogeneous squadrons in case of war.

AIRFIELDS, AERONAUTICAL CENTERS, AND
GROUPING CENTERS

Numerous airfields had been established throughout French and Belgian territory for quartering aerial forces during peacetime and for storing matériel needed to bring them up to full wartime quota. They were divided into two kinds: first line and second line. First line included all the airfields destined to be used as bases for active aerial units in war; second line were those planned as replacement centers, instruction fields, organization centers for new aerial units, and other minor tasks.

All the Belgian fields had been classified as first line. The French first-line ones were located along a zone 100 to 150 kilometers deep, paralleling the land and sea borders, thus being in a position to meet any possibility of war. These zones had been subdivided into smaller zones, one next to the other, and within them the Aeronautical Centers functioned.

All Aeronautical Centers facing a given border had been grouped into distinct Grouping Centers designed to meet the various eventualities of war. The Eastern Grouping Center, where the prospective war was against Germany, included the Aeronautical Centers of Amiens, St. Quentin, Soissons, Rheims, Châlons, St. Dizier, Chaumont, and Dijon.

The Grouping Centers, the Aeronautical Centers, and the airfields were regarded as supply centers and were dependent upon the Air Ministry.

In Belgium there was only one Grouping Center, integral with the French Eastern Center. It included the Aeronautical Centers of Ghent, Brussels, and Namur.

All the airfields in each Grouping Center, especially the Eastern, were built to accommodate all the aerial forces contemplated by the war organization for the Independent Air Force as well as for the army auxiliary aviation. In fact:

1. In the permanent airfields of Châlons, St. Dizier, Chaumont, and Dijon, 69 squadrons of the Independent Air Force were located in peacetime. In the corresponding depots was stored all the matériel needed to complete these 69 squadrons and create

their 69 twin squadrons. The Independent Air Force thus could mobilize along the same line of deployment they would use in war. The personnel called back from the reserves were expected to arrive there within six hours after the call to mobilization.

2. In the permanent airfields of the Eastern Grouping Center about a third of the squadrons of the army auxiliary aviation were located even during peacetime. To be exact, these were the squadrons belonging to the Eastern Army Corps, motorized and cavalry divisions, and in their depots all the matériel needed to complete and double them was stored.

3. During peacetime the other two-thirds of the army auxiliary aviation were located on permanent second-line airfields, always facing the eastern frontier. At mobilization time these units were expected to complete and double themselves, then fly to their stations at the Front.

4. Besides the permanent airfields in the territory of the Eastern Grouping Center, there were other fields called war fields, so large and so numerous they could accommodate the whole of the Independent Air Force and the army auxiliary aviation.

5. Besides the 69 squadrons of the Independent Air Force and 80 of the auxiliary aviation, and mobilization depots, the permanent airfields of the Eastern Grouping Center contained administration buildings, offices, warehouses, shops, and so on; and therefore they made easily identified and vulnerable targets. For obvious reasons of prudence, these airfields were to be vacated as soon as mobilization was completed, and the aerial forces were to be transferred to the operating bases.

An operating base was simply a landing field, usually left grass-covered; and on its outskirts supply depots had been built for gasoline and oil—all of them scattered and well camouflaged. The Chief of the Army High Command had selected the locations of the auxiliary aviation's operating bases, and they were coordinated with the line of deployment of the army. The Commander of the Independent Air Force selected the operating bases for his organization. All of them were well served by telegraph, telephone, and radio. When we consider that these airfields had to take care of more than 610 squadrons, we can see the enormous labor that went into their establishment and organization.

SUPPLY SERVICE—GASOLINE AND OIL

It had been decided that the depots of the operating bases should have a permanent supply of motor fuel, enough for at least 30 hours' flying. Since there were approximately 5,000 planes averaging 500 horsepower, the total was 2½ million horsepower. In the Eastern Grouping Center the airfield depots kept permanently stored from 15,000 to 20,000 tons of gasoline and from 1,000 to 1,500 tons of lubricating oil. This figured out to an average of 25 to 30 tons of gasoline for each squadron. The problem had been solved by making the gasoline and lubricant companies build and service a complete service station at each operating base, each service station to be large enough to handle between 25 and 30 tons of gasoline. In addition, measures had been taken to assure in war a continuous daily supply service for enough gasoline and oil for three hours of flying time (2,000 tons of gasoline and 100 tons of oil). For this service the Eastern Grouping Center had a supply even during peacetime of 200 four-ton trucks, which in wartime would be increased to 600 trucks requisitioned from private concerns, besides the tank trucks belonging to the gasoline and oil companies. With these trucks the Aeronautical Centers would draw off what they needed from the advanced depots to replenish the storage tanks of the airfields.

The advanced depots for gasoline and oil for aviation were located in the neighborhood of Noilles, Senlis, Villers-Cotterets, La Ferté, Vadonis, and Melun. There were six of them, and their total capacity was 120,000 tons of gasoline and 6,000 of oil, enough to last for 200 hours for all the planes of the Independent Air Force and auxiliary aviation. These advanced depots had been completed in 1930. They were strong, partly underground structures, bomb-proofed and hard to locate from the air, since the fuel was carried by pipe to an outlet two or three kilometers away. Although their existence and location were supposed to be a military secret, some information about them had leaked out.

They, in turn, were supplied by rail from the great central deposits located in the zone between Laval, Chartres, Orléans, Bourges, Limoges, Angoulême, and Angers, where the products of the great refineries located near the ports arrived.

To fill the needs of aviation kept up to full war efficiency including the needs of training schools, repair shops, automobiles, and trucks, it was estimated that 5,000 tons of gasoline and 250 tons of oil every day the war lasted could be made available—figuring an average of three hours of flying time a day. In three months of war 450,000 tons of gasoline and 23,000 tons of oil would be required, which meant the importation of 2,250,000 tons of crude oil.

FLYING MATÉRIEL—ARMS AND MUNITIONS

The replacement of matériel presented difficulties because of the variety of armaments in the various squadrons. The job devolved upon the Aeronautical Centers, which drew the matériel from the advance warehouses and distributed it to the operating bases. In these warehouses were stored repair and replacement parts for each type of armament. They were replenished from central warehouses, and the latter from the factories. For each type of armament a certain proportion of parts was kept constant in peacetime; but the plan was that as soon as war began the production of all obsolete matériel had to stop, and the factories to put all their productive capacity into improved and modern matériel. To qualify as manufacturers of aviation matériel, the factories had to prove their ability to increase production fourfold within eight days from notification.

THE ORGANIZATION OF SURFACE AERIAL
DEFENSE

The principal idea had been to prevent if possible the scattering of aerial defense on pre-determined centers, but instead to create defensive aerial lines for the general protection of the national territory. Paris would naturally be the chief target of aerial offensives, especially if the war was with Germany, for it lay only two hours' flying time from the frontier. Consequently, two great lines of aerial defense had been drawn to shield the capital and protect the territory in between them.

As we have already seen, France had ready 50 alert pursuit groups (100 squadrons, 600 airplanes), and Belgium had 6 groups (12 squadrons, 72 airplanes). These groups were distributed among the Aeronautical Presidios as follows:

AERONAUTICAL PRESIDIO	BELGIAN DEFENSE PURSUIT GROUPS
Brussels	1st & 2d
Liéges	3d & 4th
Namur	5th & 6th

AERONAUTICAL PRESIDIO	FRENCH DEFENSE PURSUIT GROUPS
Mézières	1st & 2d
Stenay	3d & 4th
Metz	5th & 6th
Nancy	7th & 8th
Épinal	9th & 10th

These eight Aeronautical Presidios (32 squadrons, 192 airplanes) constituted the first line of aerial defense and were under the direct command of the unit stationed at Stenay.

AERONAUTICAL PRESIDIO	FRENCH DEFENSE PURSUIT GROUPS
Amiens	11th, 12th, & 13th
St. Quentin	14th, 15th, & 16th
Laon	17th, 18th, & 19th
Rheims	20th, 21st, & 22d
Châlons	23d, 24th, & 25th
Troyes	26th, 27th, & 28th
Auxerres	29th, 30th, & 31st
Nevers	32nd, 33d, & 34th

These eight Aeronautical Presidios (24 groups, 48 squadrons, 288 airplanes) constituted the second line of aerial defense and were under the direct command of the unit stationed at Châlons.

AERONAUTICAL PRESIDIO	FRENCH DEFENSE PURSUIT GROUPS
Houdoin	35th, 36th, 37th, & 38th
Rambouillet	39th, 40th, & 41st
Étampes	42d, 43d, & 44th
Malesherbes	45th, 46th
Nemours	47th, 48th
Villeneuve	49th, 50th

These six Aeronautical Presidios (16 groups, 32 squadrons, 192 airplanes) constituted the direct aerial defense of Paris and were under direct command of the Paris aerial defense. The Commands of the two lines of aerial defense and of the Paris aerial defense depended from the General Command of Aerial Defense.

In the territory where aerial offensives of some significance might take place, the Independent Air Force and the army auxiliary aviation could be found in wartime in addition to the Aeronautical Presidios. These 220 squadrons were to locate themselves on the operating bases of the Eastern Grouping Centers (Aeronautical Centers of Rouen, Amiens, St. Quentin, Soissons, Rheims, Neufchâtel, Chaumont, and Dijon)—that is, they had to deploy themselves almost on the first line of aerial defense. In Belgium the 26 pursuit squadrons of the auxiliary aviation were to locate themselves in the centers of Brussels, Namur, and Liége. Altogether more than 240 squadrons (1,440 airplanes) were available, which, in case of need, could co-operate with the 112 squadrons (672 airplanes) of the aerial defense.

The pursuit matériel had been given close attention, and it was excellent.

	SQUADRONS	MODEL		SQUADRONS	MODEL
Independent Air Force	42	1932	and	18	1931
Groups of armies	22	1931	and	14	1930
Armies	26	1930	and	16	1929
Army corps	24	1929	and	36	1928
Motorized divisions	4	1928	and	6	1927
Cavalry divisions	12	1927			

The 1932 model, of 1,000 horsepower, carried in front of the fuselage a 20-mm. cannon. The other models, of 500 horsepower (with the exception of the 1927 model), carried two machine guns. There were very few differences between the various models; and in speed, climbing, maneuverability, and ceiling they showed good characteristics in the main. The alert pursuits of the defense pursuit groups, 1929, 1930, and 1931 models, differed from the others only by having more speed in climbing, a result obtained by limiting their range to one hour instead of three.

The technical and tactical training of all the pursuit and alert pursuit units was perfect. Besides the formation attack, a cavalry-charge type of attack against the big bombing planes had been studied.

In order to execute it, the pilot had to rush at full speed with his plane upon the enemy's and bail out an instant before the crash, then parachute to earth.

A perfect observation service had been organized all along the frontier, integrated with a complete system of communications which reached all interested authorities.

The anti-aerial regiments had been distributed between Paris (6 regiments) and other important centers to protect indispensable industrial factories located there.

CHAPTER V

The Material Preparation—Germany

AERIAL FORCES

WHEN HOSTILITIES began, the German Independent Air Force consisted of 15 aerial groups, each composed of 10 battle divisions and 1 explorer squadron. All aerial groups were homogeneous; and there were 8 2,000-horsepower groups, 6 3,000-horsepower, and 1 6,000-horsepower. Every battle division was made up of 3 squadrons of 3 planes each and 1 in reserve. In all there were:

BATTLE DIVISIONS	HORSEPOWER	PLANES
80	2,000	800
60	3,000	600
10	6,000	100

The tactical unit was the battle division.

The organization of the Independent Air Force had been worked out by General Reuss, Chief of the General Staff, and put into effect in the spring of 1928. Before that time, owing largely to the restrictions imposed by the Treaty of Versailles, the German aerial forces had been anything but notable. According to General Reuss's concepts, the Independent Air Force had to be a suitable instrument for carrying out over the enemy's territory an offensive strong enough to break down quickly the enemy people's resistance, especially their moral resistance. Therefore, the Independent Air Force had to be able to (1) fly over the enemy's territory, overcoming resistance; and (2) execute efficient aerial offensive while flying over the enemy territory.

The first requirement was fighting capacity. In his *Private Instructions* General Reuss wrote:

The fighting capacity of the Independent Air Force lies in the integration of the fighting capacity of its parts. The tactical unit, the squadron, must be considered the unit of fighting capacity; therefore, by nature and definition the squadron must be an indivisible whole. [This was written in 1928. In 1930 newly acquired experience dictated the change to the battle division, composed of 3 squadrons, as the tactical unit.]

The fighting capacity of the tactical unit is measured by the armament of the individual planes in it.

In the minds of all personnel, from pilots to technicians, the idea must be firmly fixed that the aim of the Independent Air Force is not flying for flying's sake, but the execution of war operations while flying; and that therefore the warplane is an integral whole of arms capable of flying, not a flying machine with arms attached. The efforts of technicians should be directed toward the creation of the most powerful integral whole of arms, because it is with arms that fighting is done. The task of the flying personnel is the efficient employment of this most powerful integral whole of arms in the aerial field, because it is with arms that the conflict is decided.

The Air Force must be made up entirely of a single type of plane, the battleplane. Technicians must study battleplane types, always striving for perfection and more power, beginning with the principle that a plane of this type is more perfect as the following characteristics are better co-ordinated: radius of action, speed, armament—in the air as well as against ground troops—and protection.

Through subsidies and substantial prizes, the national aeronautical industry must be spurred on to produce always more perfect aeronautical matériel. The selection of the kinds of matériel for the Independent Air Force is the exclusive business of the flying personnel. They are the ones who have to fly the machines, and they are the ones best fitted to judge their worth. It should never be forgotten that technicians should listen to the experience of fliers, never the other way round.

The types or models chosen will be ordered in the desired quantities from the aeronautical industry, which should merge into a cartel, to distribute the government orders among its members.

The technical offices of the Independent Air Force should never engage in any planning or experimental activity. It is inconsistent for technicians who evaluate the products of others to produce themselves. Therefore, the technical offices of the Independent Air Force should confine themselves to their natural functions of testing and control.

The efficiency of aerial offensives on land should be based more on the quality of the weapons than on their quantity. Chemists should always keep in mind that the offensive power of an Air Force can be doubled simply by doubling the efficiency of its chemical weapons.

These definite rules show clearly just what the Air Force expected of industry; and therefore industry knew where it stood and exactly what it should do. Since the warplane was conceived as an integral whole of arms, its armament became its essential part and was no longer regarded as an accessory. Industry stopped producing planes with certain stereotyped aeronautical characteristics and began producing warplanes with excellent aerodynamic characteristics.

The warplane's armament had to be planned so as not to leave any dead angles of fire and to allow of easy handling. The arms had to be powerful, with perfect sighting and firing mechanisms. Knowing what the Independent Air Force wanted, the technical offices of the aeronautical industry worked intensively and produced planes with complete armament, which were submitted to the High Command of the Independent Air Force for approval.

In 1928 the 2,000-horsepower type of plane was built and adopted by the Independent Air Force. Its main characteristics were as follows: [1]

> Wing surface—115 square meters
> Weight empty—4,500 kilograms
> Armament weight—500 kilograms
> Crew weight (5 men)—400 kilograms
> Weight with armament and crew—5,400 kilograms

With a take-off weight of 8,000 kilograms, its ceiling was 7,000 meters and it could be loaded with 2,600 kilograms of fuel and bombs. Its autonomy was 7 hours without bombs and 5 hours with 700 kilograms of bombs.

With a take-off weight of 9,000 kilograms, its ceiling was 6,500 meters and it could be loaded with 3,600 kilograms of fuel and bombs. Its autonomy was 7 hours with 1,000 kilograms of bombs and 5 hours with 2,000.

With take-off weight of 10,000 kilograms, its ceiling was 5,600 meters and it could be loaded with 4,600 kilograms of fuel and bombs. Its autonomy was 12 hours with 1,000 kilograms of bombs and 9 hours with 2,000.

With a maximum take-off weight of 11,000 kilograms, its ceiling

[1] The data on planes which follows is from an article, "War Airplanes of Medium and Large Tonnage," by Captain G. A. Corrado Custosa in *Rivista Aeronautica,* May 1929, No. 5.

was 4,800 meters and it could be loaded with 5,600 kilograms of fuel and bombs. Its autonomy was 12 hours with 1,000 kilograms of bombs and 9 hours with 2,000.

Its armament consisted of two 20-mm. cannon, one mounted forward and the other behind the wing; one 12-mm. machine gun which fired from the lower sector of the tail surface.

A first series of 200 planes of this type was ordered and given the name type "2,000/1928." They were delivered in 1929 and allocated to the first and second groups. At the same time the type 2,000/1929 was produced. It was similar to the 2,000/1928, with some improvement. A series of 200 planes of this type was also ordered.

In the spring of 1929 the 3,000-horsepower type was produced and accepted, and a series of 200 ordered. The characteristics of the 3,000-horsepower type was as follows:

> Wing surface—230 square meters
> Weight empty—9,000 kilograms
> Armament weight—1,660 kilograms
> Crew weight (9 men) —720 kilograms
> Weight with armament and crew—11,380 kilograms

With a take-off weight of 16,000 kilograms, its ceiling was 6,000 meters and it could be loaded with 4,620 kilograms of fuel and bombs. Its autonomy was 1 hour without bombs and 6 hours with 1,000 kilograms of bombs.

With a take-off weight of 18,000 kilograms, its ceiling was 4,900 meters and it could be loaded with 6,620 kilograms of fuel and bombs. Its autonomy was 8 hours with 2,000 kilograms of bombs and 6 hours with 3,000.

With a maximum take-off weight of 21,000 kilograms, its ceiling was 3,500 meters and it could be loaded with 9,620 kilograms of fuel and bombs. Its autonomy was 12 hours with 2,000 kilograms of bombs and 8 hours with 5,000.

Its armament consisted of one 37-mm. cannon mounted forward, two 20-mm. cannons mounted on the sides, one 25-mm. cannon mounted behind the wing, and one 12-mm. machine gun firing from the lower sector.

In the spring of 1930 the third and fourth 2,000-horsepower groups and the first and second 3,000-horsepower groups received their armaments.

During that period the 6,000-horsepower type was also produced and accepted. Its characteristics were:

Wing surface—460 square meters
Weight, empty—20,000 kilograms
Armament weight—2,500 kilograms
Crew weight (16 men)—1,300 kilograms
Weight with armament and crew—23,800 kilograms

With a take-off weight of 36,000 kilograms, its ceiling was 5,000 meters and it could be loaded with 12,200 kilograms of fuel and bombs. Its autonomy was 9 to 10 hours without bombs, 8 hours with 2,000 kilograms of bombs, and 6 hours with 4,600.

With a take-off weight of 39,000 kilograms, its ceiling was 4,000 meters and it could be loaded with 15,200 kilograms of fuel and bombs. Its autonomy was 12 hours with 2,000 kilograms of bombs and 9 hours with 5,000.

With a take-off weight of 42,000 kilograms, its ceiling was 3,500 meters and it could be loaded with 18,200 kilograms of fuel and bombs. Its autonomy was 15 hours with 2,000 kilograms of bombs and 9 hours with 8,000.

Its armament consisted of two 37-mm. cannon, two 20-mm. cannon, and three 12-mm. machine guns.

A series of 50 planes of the 6,000-horsepower type was ordered, and with it 200 of the 2,000/1930 type and 200 3,000/1930's. In the spring of 1931, then, the fifth and sixth 2,000-horsepower groups, the third and fourth 3,000-horsepower groups, and half of the 6,000-horsepower group received their armament. No new types were accepted that year, but orders were placed for 200 of the new 2,000/1931's, 200 of the 3,000/1931's and 50 of the 6,000/1931's. They went into service in the spring of 1932, allocated to the seventh and eighth 2,000-horsepower groups, the fifth and sixth 3,000-horsepower groups, and the other half of the 6,000-horsepower group. When war began the decision had already been made to do away with the 2,000-horsepower types and orders had been placed for 200 of the 3,000/1932 type and 50 of the 6,000/1932.

Consequently, when war began the Independent Air Force was constituted as follows:

GROUPS	TYPE OF PLANE	NUMBER OF PLANES
I and II	2,000/1928	200
III and IV	2,000/1929	200
V and VI	2,000/1930	200
VII and VIII	2,000/1931	200
I and II	3,000/1929	200
III and IV	3,000/1930	200
V and VI	3,000/1931	200
½	6,000/1930	50
½	6,000/1931	50

All together, 1,500 planes of three types with six variations of type. There were also 15 explorer squadrons—one for each group—of 12 planes each. These explorer groups were composed of high-speed single-seaters (300 kilometers per hour) armed with fixed machine guns with a 3-hour range. They had been organized to give full play to the initiative of exceptionally skilled pilots; their mode of employment had not been exactly determined, since it was to be based essentially on the daring of individual pilots.

The Independent Air Force was kept always ready for war, not only matériel, but also personnel (12,800 men). At mobilization this personnel would be doubled to provide for replacement of losses. Flying matériel was to be kept in service for four years, and all the time they were maintained at full efficiency.

It was estimated that in wartime a plane would be good for 1,000 hours of flying—barring total loss, of course. This estimate was cut down to 750 hours for planes which had already had one year of service, to 500 for those with two years, and 250 for planes with three years of service.

The normal productive capacity of the aeronautical industry could supply a fourth of the entire Independent Air Force every year; but it had been put into condition to increase rapidly if an emergency arose.

The Independent Air Force had at its disposal a total armament of 800 37-mm. cannon, 3,600 of the 20-mm., and 1,700 12-mm. machine guns; and a bomb-carrying capacity of 3,000 to 4,000 tons for each flight of an average distance of 500 kilometers from its take-off points. It had a total of 4,000,000 horsepower, and its cost was reckoned 4 billion lire.

In peacetime the groups of the Independent Air Force were located on the large permanent airfields of Potsdam, Neuruppin, Magdeburg, Leipzig, Erfurt, Braunsberg, Bamberg, Kassel, and Fulda, and in the permanent hydro-basins of Fahrlander See (near Potsdam) and Ratzeburg See (near Lübeck).

In case of war they had at their disposal other designated airfields, depending upon which enemy they had to face. Thus, in case of war against France, each squadron had been assigned to a certain territory where there were already special war airfields (simply landing fields with deposits of gasoline, lubricants, arms, and munitions), many more than needed.

The eight 2,000-horsepower groups were to be located as follows:

GROUP	TERRITORY
I	Astride the Wesel-Münster line
II	Astride the Düsseldorf-Hagen-Wesel line
III	Astride the Köln-Olpe line
IV	Astride the Linz-Siegen line
V	Astride the Koblenz-Wetzlar line
VI	Astride the Mainz-Hanan line
VII	Astride the Mannheim-Aschaffenburg line
VIII	Astride the Breisach-Biberach line

The six 3,000-horsepower groups would be located as follows:

GROUP	TERRITORY
IX	Astride the Münster-Osnabrük line
X	Astride the Wesel-Paderborn line
XI	Astride the Siegen-Warburg line
XII	Astride the Warburg-Kassel line
XIII	Astride the Hanan-Fulda line
XIV	Astride the Würzburg-Meiningen line

The 6,000-horsepower groups would be located on the Steinhunder, Dümmer, Schweiziner, and Plauer lakes.

In each of these territories there was a Replacement Section which, in turn, was replenished from the second-line warehouses. To each section was entrusted the task of having supplies ready for a group, a comparatively easy task, since every group had a homogeneous armament.

The deposit of fuel and oil at each operating base was enough to ensure 30 hours of flight to any aerial unit which could land at it, and the arms and munitions were sufficient for 5 flights of 30 hours each. Since there were more of these bases than necessary to accommodate the Independent Air Force, in actual fact they provided the wherewithal for 10 flights of 40 to 60 hours each. In the fuel and oil deposits there were stored about 50,000 tons of gasoline and 2,500 tons of oil.

For replacement of bombs, it was calculated that the average consumption for each flight would be 1, 2, or 3 tons for each plane, depending upon whether it was a 2,000-, 3,000-, or 6,000- horsepower machine. On this basis it was calculated that the Independent Air Force would need 3,100 tons of bombs for each flight; and in the operating bases there were 30,000 tons.

In the second-line storehouses was enough fuel and oil to ensure 100 hours of flight for the whole Independent Air Force, and enough bombs for 20 flights. This was considered a sufficient supply to wage war for at least 30 days; and in that time munitions factories could produce 3,000 to 4,000 tons of bombs a day. At the outbreak of hostilities those groups which were permanently on a war footing could go into action immediately according to sealed orders already in their possesssion.

The maintenance personnel for the operating bases were recruited from the vicinity. The storehouse depots of the second line furnished their own personnel and means of transport. Each group was trained by peacetime exercises to reach its own operating base; thus each group was thoroughly familiar with its base, especially from the point of view of supply services.

General Reuss's idea was that the Independent Air Force, as soon as war was about to begin, should launch themselves on the enemy's territory, like a tightly wound spring suddenly released, possibly without warning, and attack with the greatest intensity, giving no respite to the enemy, nor to themselves, in order to concentrate the offensive into as short a period of time as possible, and obtain the most shattering effect.

Owing to methodical preparation, materially everything was ready to enable the Independent Air Force to spring to the attack at the first call. Morally, General Reuss had taken special care to imbue all the personnel of the Air Force with a sense of the high importance of their mission. The Commanders of the various groups, divisions, squadrons, and airplanes, besides the pilots, machine-gunners, bombardiers, and mechanics, were all inspired by the same unshakable faith in the decisive value of their arm; and all of this highly selected personnel were deeply conscious of the importance of their mission, and of the certainty that its fulfillment implied a dangerous task, requiring the gravest sacrifices and the most heroic self-abnegation.

The great size of the airplanes had brought about the creation of the plane commander, whose tasks aboard were the same as those of a naval commander aboard his ship, thus assuring better discipline and teamwork among the crew.

The battle division (3 squadrons, 9 planes) had been designated as the tactical unit, instead of the squadron, in order better to impress the personnel with the concept of mass action. According to the 1930 *Private Instructions for Action*, the battle division had to be employed always as a whole, without exception. The flying formation of the division was always the same— a stepped-up row of aligned squadrons. The squadron commander flew in the center of his line, and the division commander with the commander of the center squadron. The plane at the center of the formation, bearing the division commander's insignia, was the leader of the formation, and very few signals were needed for the few necessary maneuvers. The principal signals were for (1) changing from close (normal) formation to open formation— to reduce the vulnerability to antiaircraft fire—or vice versa; and (2) changing direction by shifting from line to file formation, or vice versa.

It was a fundamental principle that the battle division had to accept combat irrespective of the enemy's numbers. When the enemy was sighted, regardless of the direction of his attack, the division was to keep flying on its route without breaking formation but ready to fire as soon as the enemy came within range. This tactic answered to the unalterable facts of the situation. The battle division could not compete in speed and maneuverability with the attacking pursuit units, and neither could it avoid combat, so any maneuver to this end would be a waste of energy. Since the division had to accept combat, willing or unwilling, the only thing to do was to put itself in the best position to face it; and this consisted in keeping the original formation, which allowed every plane to co-operate with the others in repelling the attack. So when the attackers approached, all the division could do was to keep to its formation and fly calmly on its way.

Keeping formation was the division's best protection against attack; and the knowledge of this had been firmly fixed in the minds and hearts of all the flying personnel. Even in peacetime they were always required to fly in formation after the briefest of training periods. In time of war, to fly out of formation without the most urgent reasons, was considered dereliction of duty in face of the enemy. According to the above-mentioned *Private Instructions for Action,* the battle divisions were given well-defined instructions about the tasks they were to perform, and they had to perform them to the limit of human ability (*bis Erschöpfung von allen menschliche Kräfte*).

Upon returning to the airfield, aerial units were to prepare to take off again as soon as possible. As I said before, the flying personnel was doubled at mobilization, and so fresh crews were always ready to take off. The idea was to get the maximum use of the flying matériel. As soon as a plane landed, squads of mechanics took it in hand, refilled the fuel tanks, loaded arms, ammunition, and bombs aboard, and otherwise put them in condition to go up again with a fresh crew if necessary.

Each division had one plane in reserve. In emergencies caused by losses or crippling damages, the division could take off with only four planes. But if the losses had cut the division's strength to less than six planes, the group commander was authorized to reduce the number of divisions in order to keep them up to a strength above the minimum allowed.

The problem of giving the planes greater elasticity of action had been diligently studied; and therefore it was easy to increase the planes' autonomy according to circumstances, by decreasing the bomb load or vice versa; or increasing the bomb load and correspondingly decreasing the weight of arms, or vice versa.

An offensive against political, industrial, communication, and other centers does not require great precision in firing in order to achieve terrifying effects—especially upon morale. For this reason one very simple type of bomb had been adopted, all weighing 50 kilograms, but of three different kinds—explosive, incendiary, and poisonous (of the yperite type), used in the proportion of one, three, and six, respectively. The system of dropping bombs one by one had been abandoned. Bomb racks had been installed so that each squadron could release 20 tons (one ton to a plane) of bombs at a time, one after the other with an interval of 15 to 25 meters between them. The switch for the bomb rack was located on a panel facing the commander of the plane.

Every release of bombs caused 20 explosions in a row over a distance of approximately 300 to 500 meters. Bombing operations were executed by squadrons according to orders from the division commander. Every release of bombs effected by a squadron caused three series of 20 explosions each over an area 200 meters wide and 300 to 500 meters long. Bombings could be carried on simultaneously by two or even all three of the squadrons in a division; and therefore a division could cover an area 200 to 300 meters wide to 600 long, using a ton of bombs from each plane. By having squadrons fly one after another in a bombing operation, each plane releasing a ton of bombs, a division could blanket a zone 200 to 300 meters wide and 2 or 3 kilometers long. Therefore, a division whose planes could carry a bomb load of 2, 4, 6, or 8 tons, could blanket areas from 200 to 300 meters wide and 3, 6, 9, or 12 kilometers long.

This system lent itself well to laying smoke screens, and therefore the planes were supplied with smoke bombs. Smoke screens were considered useful in blinding antiaircraft batteries. They were laid with one-half smoke bombs and one-half poison bombs, naturally taking the direction of the wind into account.

All means of civil aviation had to be put at the disposal of the Independent Air Force the moment war broke out. This applied to both matériel and personnel. All the planes used by the numerous air lines had been built with a view to their eventual employment in war. Suitable armaments were kept in stock for each of their various types, ready to be installed as soon as mobilization was ordered. Their flying personnel was to be militarized at once and would make up the war crews and squadron and division commanders for these planes. Through periodic recalls to service with the divisions of the Independent Air Force, all this personnel was kept in training for war. Obviously, civil planes converted to military use would not be as efficient as planes built expressly for war, but the civil aviation could be relied on to carry out operations of secondary importance.

Even the employment of amateur aviation for sport had been visualized. The purpose was to utilize the ardor and youthful energy devoted to this kind of flying. No definite arrangements had yet been made, but the belief was confidently held that a place for them in the scheme of war would present itself spontaneously at the opportune moment.

Aerial defense had been restricted to the employment of antiaircraft batteries located in the most important centers, but hope was cherished of being able to prevent a resolute enemy from carrying out his offensive.

Suitable propaganda had been used to convince the people that it was physically impossible to protect them from aerial attacks, and that therefore it would be a waste to immobilize armaments and other means which could be more effectively employed in offensive action. The best thing to do was to counteract the enemy's offensive against one's own territory by resolute large-scale offensives against his, and keep the morale of one's people high by the impressiveness of their own large aerial forces invading the enemy's sky. But, even as other powers had done, Germany nevertheless took all the steps which might be considered useful in protecting the population to some degree from the effects of aerial offensives.

PART II

CHAPTER VI

The Allies' Plan of Operation

THE PLAN OF operation worked out by the French and Belgian General Staff was very simple—to defend the Rhine line and attack on the rest of the front. Their ground forces had been divided into three large groups of armies:

1. *The Northern Group:* This group included the Belgian Army and 2 French armies under one command. The Belgian army was composed of 5 army corps, 2 motorized divisions, and 3 cavalry divisions; the 2 French armies of 8 army corps, 5 motorized divisions, and 6 cavalry divisions. In total the Northern Group consisted of 13 army corps, 7 motorized divisions, and 8 cavalry divisions. Mobilization requirements demanded that this group deploy itself along two lines, the Belgian Army between Liége and Neufchâtel, the 2 French armies between Lille and Stenay. At the beginning of the war the second line was to make contact with the first line by prearranged movements.

2. *The Southern Group:* This group included 3 French armies, with 14 army corps, 5 motorized divisions, and 6 cavalry divisions. It was to deploy along the border between Montmédy, where it made contact with the Northern Group, and Mulhouse.

3. *The Central Group:* This group was composed of 2 French armies with 8 army corps. It was to mobilize on the second line on the left of the Meuse between Chaumont and St. Menchould, waiting to proceed according to circumstances.

AERIAL FORCES

As I have already said, the French Independent Air Force was stationed and activated during peacetime on the permanent airfields in the Aeronautical Centers of Châlons, St. Dizier, Chaumont, and Dijon. Its operating bases were distributed along both sides of the Meuse from Stenay to Belfort.

The choice of this deployment line answered to the concept of employment of the Independent Air Force in the war. Although created to perform independent actions of war with its own forces, the Independent Air Force—according to the French concept—had to collaborate in attaining the final result, and therefore had to function in a way calculated to facilitate the principal mission, which had been entrusted to the army.

One of the war aims was to hurl back the enemy beyond the Rhine, and in order to facilitate this task for the army, the enemy had to be harassed on the left of that river by destroying the bridges spanning the Rhine, and disrupting his rail communications on his left.

The deployment lines pre-established by the French Independent Air Force were good, as from them all the territory between the Rhine and the Franco-Belgian borders could be reached by bombing planes in a one-hour flight, thereby affording them the advantage of protection by their own pursuit planes.

AUXILIARY AVIATION

The group of armies, especially during the mobilization period, had to have their auxiliary aviation, and especially their pursuit planes, ready to answer their call so they could face foreseen and unforeseen eventualities. With this aim in view, the disposition of the pursuit and bombing units of the auxiliary aviation was as follows:

Northern Group:
Army group's aviation—I pursuit brigade, based south of Fourmies.

Army group's aviation—I bombing brigade, based south of Guise.

Belgian Army's aviation—Belgian pursuit brigade, based north of Rochefort.

Belgian Army's aviation—Belgian bombing brigade, based north of Namur.

Belgian Army's aviation—Pursuit groups (5), based at the front.

I French Army's aviation—I pursuit regiment, based south of Maubeuge.

II French's Army aviation—II pursuit regiment, based south of Mézières.

II French Army's aviation—Pursuit groups (8), based at the front.

Southern Group:

Army group's aviation—III pursuit brigade, based north of Nancy.

Army group's aviation—III bombing brigade, based south of Metz.

III Army's aviation—III pursuit regiment, based south of Thionville.

IV Army's aviation—IV pursuit regiment, based south of St. Avold.

V Army's aviation—V pursuit regiment, based south of Sarrebourg.

V Army's aviation—Pursuit groups (14), based at the front.

Central Group:

Army group's aviation—II pursuit brigade, based north of St. Dizier.

Army group's aviation—II bombing brigade, based north of Vitry.

VI Army's aviation—VI pursuit regiment, based south of Suippes.

VII Army's aviation—VII pursuit regiment, based south of St. Dizier.

VIII Army's aviation—Pursuit groups (8), based at the front.

The employment of the auxiliary aviation pertained exclusively to the command of the army group to which it was attached, and in general the Army Group Commands had to provide their own means of policing the sky above their deployment lines; nevertheless, in case of large-scale air raids, the commander of the Aerial Defense was empowered to give orders directly to the pursuit units of the auxiliary aviation, provided he simultaneously apprised the respective Army Group Commands of it. The pursuit units of the auxiliary aviation could act on their own initiative, in some especially grave circumstances.

SECRET MOBILIZATION

During the week before the beginning of the war, the aeronautical authorities had been able to effect a secret mobilization of part of their aerial forces—specifically, the part which might be needed immediately and which, being mobilized on the spot, did not require a too-noticeable movement of men and matériel. Thus, on the evening of June 15 the French Independent Air Force had its 5 pursuit brigades on a complete war footing. Of the 6 bombing brigades, only the permanent squadrons had been mobilized but not their doubles, so the bombing forces were only half of what they were expected to be when fully mobilized. The same thing was true of the reconnaissance regiments. And all the Independent Air Force units had been ordered to remain on the permanent airfields instead of transferring to their operating bases, in order not to arouse suspicion. As to the auxiliary aviation, the Allies had brought up to war strength only their pursuit forces, so as to be ready to repel probable enemy raids from the beginning.

Therefore, on the evening of June 15 the following were on a complete war footing: 3 pursuit brigades attached to the groups of armies, 7 pursuit regiments assigned to the armies, and the Belgian pursuit brigade. Along the borders, already mobilized, were 30 pursuit squadrons assigned to the army corps—the squadrons which would have constituted the 30 groups belonging to the army corps after complete mobilization. Similarly, all the defense pursuit groups, French and Belgian, the anti-aerial regiments, and all the look-out, information, and signal services had been mobilized and were ready to function.

To sum up, on the evening of June 15, owing to the secret mobilization, all the strength and resources of aerial defense, French and Belgian, were on full war footing and ready to act. All pursuit units belonging to the Independent Air Force and the auxiliary aviation had been completely mobilized with the exception of the 30 auxiliary pursuit groups of the army corps for which the twin squadrons had not yet been constituted. In other words, only 30 pursuit squadrons were not ready, and they were to be mobilized the next day, the sixteenth.

Because of Germany's minor position in the naval field, the naval auxiliary aviation had not taken any steps toward secret mobilization.

DISPOSITIONS FOR JUNE 16

Although all hope of averting the war had been abandoned by 10 P.M. on June 15, the Allies still hesitated to take any decisive step. For the sake of humanity and their repute in history, they were reluctant to take the responsibility of starting the war, and several hours were consumed in a feverish exchange of telegrams between Paris and Brussels, until at 2 o'clock in the morning the famous German radiogram arrived, stating that from that moment Germany considered herself at war with France and Belgium, and between 6 A.M. and 7 A.M. her Independent Air Force would invade their sky and *would be compelled by the hard necessity of war to bomb all centers where mobilization, concentration, or other movements of armed forces would be taking place.*

Although the warning was so short, it was tantamount to giving up the advantage of surprise. Everyone realized that it had been given so that Germany could claim some sort of justification for unrestricted use of aero-chemical weapons at the tribunal of world opinion. Especially in the first days of war, concentration and movements of armed forces will take place in all centers, from the largest to the smallest, so that all centers of the Allied nations were equally threatened.

Discounting the arrogant tone of the enemy's threat, the Allied military authorities decided to take the initiative and invade the enemy's territory, and to that end the following orders were dispatched:

1. The first and fourth pursuit brigades of the Independent Air Force were to be cruising over the Koblenz-Mainz-Aschaffenburg-Wurzburg section at 6 A.M. to repel any German forces trying to advance to the border.

2. The first regiment of the Belgian pursuit brigade was to be cruising the Köln-Koblenz front at 6 o'clock for the same purpose.

3. The four night-bombing brigades of the Independent Air Force were to take off at once with the squadrons at their disposal —half of their war effectives—and destroy the bridges and most important railroad stations on the Rhine, according to plans already prepared.

4. The two day-bombing brigades of the Independent Air Force were to cross the border at 6 o'clock with the planes at their disposal—half their war effectives—to bomb the cities of Hanover, Magdeburg, Leipzig, and Dresden.

5. The reconnaissance regiment of the Independent Air Force with the planes at its disposal—half of its war effectives—was to reconnoiter toward Berlin.

6. All pursuit units belonging to the Independent Air Force and auxiliary aviation were to be under the direct command of the General Command of the Aerial Defense until further orders.

In order to put the responsibility for first violating the agreement of the international convention on Germany, the Allies ordered that bombing operations should be confined to railroad stations, and that only high-explosive bombs should be used. The personnel of the Franco-Belgian aviation, when apprised of the enemy's threats, resolved to fight and humble Germany's arrogance.

CHAPTER VII

Germany's Plan of Operation

THE GERMAN PLAN of operation has already been outlined in its general lines. In brief, it was to beat the enemy in the air, meanwhile holding him on land, thereby being able to inflict such severe losses on the enemy country as to make it stop fighting. The Independent Air Force plan of operation envisaged a series of offensive actions with the double object of beating the enemy's aerial forces and carrying out offensives over his territory. The first offensive action had to be launched at the very beginning of the war in an effort to catch the enemy's aerial forces in the process of mobilization. Anyway, it had to be tried with the whole of the Independent Air Force in order to beat the enemy's forces more easily and give them a sense of their own inferiority. The units of the Independent Air Force were to be kept constantly on a war footing, and therefore ready for action. Since they were located on permanent airfields in peacetime, they were instructed in case of war to take off from those fields and land on their operating bases upon their return from executing their first assignment.

In order for the Independent Air Force to function properly on its mission against the enemy, its huge mass—150 divisions, 1,500 great battleplanes—had to be articulated and at the same time flexible. It was articulated in columns of attack and made flexible by dividing each column into waves of attack. The offensive action had to develop on a large front—generally the whole length of the frontiers—both to give ample space to the aerial units and to make the enemy extend himself as much as possible. Therefore, the mass of the Air Force was articulated in parallel columns of attack distributed along the whole front.

Each column was to develop its action in a given direction toward assigned tasks, and it was divided into detachments which followed one another at a specific distance, generally a half-hour's flying time, 100 kilometers. All columns were to go into action at the same time, and so all the leading detachments had to be stationed at the same hour along an assigned line of take-off. In this way the mass would enter into action in waves of attack at regular intervals, generally half an hour.

This was the method of attack for the mass employment of the Independent Air Force worked out in advance, and this was the method actually used except for some variations in the number of columns and waves of attack, variations suggested by circumstances.

By the first offensive action of the Independent Air Force, General Reuss wanted to achieve the double goal of beating the enemy's aerial forces and giving the people of the enemy nation the feeling of being dominated from the air. To accomplish this the Independent Air Force had to invade the enemy's sky; but it could not be hoped that the Allies would stand idle while the enemy entered their sky, flew there for hours, and attacked at will their territorial centers. Undoubtedly the Allies would throw their own forces into action and try to down the German Air Force or drive it off. But which aerial forces would the Allies use? Those suited to that purpose, of course—that is, their alert pursuit and pursuit units. Given the determination of the German Air Force to fly over the enemy's territory, and assuming an equal determination on the part of the Allies to stop it, a real aerial battle was inevitable, a battle between the mass of the German Air Force and all the pursuit and alert pursuit units the Allies could muster against it.

As I have already said, each column of attack had to accomplish its own particular action, follow a given itinerary, and perform its tasks according to the instructions contained in the orders of operation. Each column was divided into detachments, and each detachment included a certain number of divisions. Each division, according to the order of operations, received from its column commander definite instructions as to the itinerary to follow and the tasks to perform, with the express understanding that such orders had to be executed as far as humanly possible. Therefore, each of the Independent Air Force divisions in the attack, although it was part of the great organic whole, preserved its own individuality for the performance of the task; it did not have to rely on the help of other divisions, but only to act for itself. As long as it existed, it had only one thing to do—to go ahead, no matter what happened, along the route assigned to it.

By apportioning the divisions to each column of attack and making them flexible by subdivision into waves, the orders of operation put in motion, perfectly synchronized, all the Independent Air Force units, each one of them, although isolated, with the feeling that similar units were flying on its left, right, front, and back. However, during action, no division was in a position to know what was happening to the other divisions in the waves ahead or behind it. A whole wave could be destroyed by the enemy without the following one being aware of it, because they were separated by a distance of 100 kilometers. From the take-off to the landing, for long hours, each division was left entirely on its own with a task to perform, unless prevented by destruction or serious damage.

At first thought, this situation of the divisions not being able to co-operate and help each other might be construed as a weakness. On the contrary, it was the very strength of the organization, because the co-operation among the units existed outside of them and independently of the will of the individual commanders; they ensued logically from the flexibility given to the whole organism; they were inherent to it; they did not happen from time to time and according to circumstances; they were there all the time and functioned continuously and uninterruptedly.

Each unit of the Independent Air Force which escaped destruction flew to its destination and performed the task assigned to it, thus demonstrating the imposition of its will on the enemy. In these cases, each unit going back to its own airfield could consider itself victorious.

In face of a mass attack by the Independent Air Force, launched along the whole front in successive waves, the Allies' action could not but prove disorganized and chaotic [writes General Reuss in his *Memoirs*]. The Allies entertained an old concept of aerial war, as though they were still living in the year 1918. Their conviction was that it would be fought more or less along the same lines of the World War, with the single difference that the planes this time would be larger and more powerfully armed; in fact, their air organization had been modeled approximately on that of the 1914-18 period. Faced by our mass action pursuing a definite aim, the Allies found themselves completely unprepared and disorganized.

Many people have strongly criticized the measures taken by the Allies to meet our offensive. But what else could they have done besides throwing their pursuit forces against us?

It must be kept in mind that the Allies had at their disposal for air fighting, pursuit and alert pursuit units; but these units were supposed to carry on special and distinct aerial actions. The pursuit units of the French Independent Air Force were to be used essentially to open the way for and facilitate the performance of tasks assigned to the bombing units; units of the auxiliary aviation had essentially the task of facilitating the action of their own auxiliary aviation in fighting the enemy's; the alert pursuit units had been entrusted with the mission of fighting against enemy bombing units which threatened the centers under their protection. All these aims were of particular and episodic nature; the principal aim, that of beating the enemy's aerial forces, was not found among them at all. Consequently, the Allies had no suitable effective means with which to oppose an enemy bent on beating them in the air, and therefore had no other choice but to use what they had available, whatever its worth.

Were the Allies' Defense Commands in a position to give instructions to their depending units? What could they see or know about events taking place in the sky on a front of from 500 to 600 kilometers long? Only what reached them from various information posts stationed far away; but such information, even if correct when transmitted, was about situations which had already greatly changed by the time they could hear of them. Only on the basis of such information, already old and superseded, could they transmit orders to units located, very likely, hundreds of kilometers away. In their turn, the pursuit units, on the receipt of those orders, had to interpret them and adapt them to the situation as changed by that time, and certainly not at all like the one on which the orders received had been based. Furthermore, such an interpretation by the pursuit units had to be made on the ground before their take-off, perhaps before they sighted the enemy, without precise data, and even without being sure of meeting the enemy. Units flying like that were units flying to an unknown destiny.

The first wave is sighted; against it a pursuit force is dispatched. Either this wave is destroyed, or it is not; in the latter case it would go on to its task. Then the next wave would come into sight. This game would go on for hours. After a certain period of fighting, the pursuit units would have to land because of their limited flying autonomy (the alert pursuit units, for instance, have only a one-hour autonomy) but where would they find themselves after being compelled to abandon the fight?

How, then, to employ effectively one's own forces? How to use and apportion them against the unknown number and size of the waves which will follow? What instructions can be given? All is uncertain, and in the face of so terrible an uncertainty, nothing can be done except hurl one's own forces against the enemy as he comes into view, as long as they last, without being able to follow a definite and coordinated plan. As long as an Independent Air Force attacks as an organic whole, perfectly articulated, the opposing defense will always be shapeless and disorganized.

In their turn, how were the pursuit units to perform? They could act only in the way they actually did. Once they were in the air, they had to attack the first formation they sighted. The struggle between a pursuit unit and a battle unit necessarily presented, in view of their different ways of combat at a certain moment, this characteristic aspect: dissolution of the pursuit unit into its component elements; permanency in the battle-unit formation. Irrespective of the outcome of the attack, even if the pursuit unit suffered no losses, for the time being, it had ceased to exist as a unit, while the battle unit remained permanent, no matter what its losses. After the attack was over, a cerain number of pursuers remained; in order for them to be able to re-engage the same battle unit or to attack the next one, they had first of all to reconstitute their unit, or be satisfied with becoming isolated pursuers, and in this case to have to attack by themselves against units in regular formation, thereby placing themselves in a position of grave inferiority. The pursuit unit was fated by its very nature to lose most of its offensive power in offensive action.

Necessarily, at a certain moment a certain number of waves entering the Allied Nations' sky, more or less strong according to losses suffered, would have been confronted by Allied pursuit forces, not only decreased in strength by losses suffered but also lacking any organic bond, divided into their elements, whittled down to a number of lone planes compelled to land before being able to fly again. Naturally, at that moment the battle would have been won by our Independent Air Force because, as the waves continued to enter and fly over the enemy's sky, the defense could offer only a disorganized and chaotic resistance, with no possibility of changing the outcome of the struggle.

The advantage to the attacker, who had a definite aim and the means to attain it, who knew where he wanted to go and what he wanted to do, who could assign to each of his units a clear and definite task co-ordinated with those assigned to the others, was an advantage absolutely decisive against a defense placed in the position of having to fend off lightning thrusts of unknown strength coming from unknown directions.

The Commander of the German National Armed Forces was more than confident that his Independent Air Force (150 divisions strong, including in its organic units, materially and morally indivisible, 1,500 great battleplanes in a single articulated and flexible mass) would succeed in defeating the enemy's forces, and in doing it very easily. However, the operating plan provided that all units and reserve planes, without exception, had to take part in the action.

Later on, someone criticized this arrangement, remarking that General Reuss had staked everything on a gamble; and that in case of adverse fortune, always possible, Germany would have been left with no aerial forces at all. General Reuss answers this criticism by saying that the best way to make not only possible but very probable an "adverse fortune" is engaging in a battle and keeping forces in reserve, the lack of which contributes greatly to defeat, and which, in case of defeat, would be easily swept away by a victorious enemy.

The invasion of the enemy's sky by the Independent Air Force did not have to take place as a gesture, that is, for the simple purpose of demonstrating one's ability to fly there. If that were the case, the enemy might have opposed it, but probably not in a very determined fashion. Therefore, beginning with its very first action, the Air Force had to act offensively against surface objectives. These offensive actions would spur the enemy to react with the utmost intensity, which was what the Commander of the National Armed Forces really wanted, as his strategy was to force the enemy to a decisive battle immediately, and as he was not interested in having the enemy conserve his energies.

Therefore, it had been decided that in its very first action, the Independent Air Force had to be in condition to act offensively against the enemy's territory. Because the first waves of attack would suffer more from the effect of the enemy's opposition, it was decided that the division in the first wave would carry no bombs, but would increase their armament quota. But all the successive waves had to carry their prescribed bomb load.

While flying to the attack, the divisions had to keep normally at the highest elevation possible with their load weight to compel the enemy to climb and fight at high altitudes. Even bombing, especially at the beginning, had to be executed from high altitudes in order to avoid the antiaircraft artillery, and even because, especially during the first action, the idea was to obtain a moral effect.

In view of the general concept of the attack, it had been thought advisable to extend the front as much as possible so as to compel the Allies to a greater dispersion of their forces; that is, it would be advisable, once over the frontier, to have the attacking columns keep spreading out fan-shaped all over the Allies' territory. As the detachments belonging to the columns of attack would automatically follow their prescribed itinerary, unless destroyed, it was possible to assign to them the most profitable ones—namely, after having beaten the enemy's aerial forces, they had to proceed ahead, fly over the enemy's sky as long and as far as possible, cause to the enemy the greatest possible damage, materially and morally, and provoke him to further attacks in order further to exhaust his energies. For these reasons, the itineraries of the various columns were predicated on the criterion of giving the enemy the immediate sensation of being dominated from the air, by attacking the political and railroad centers far from the borders, and even the capital cities.

The plan of attack for the first action by the Independent Air Force had been gone over minutely in all its smallest details and commanders of all units, from the largest to the smallest, knew what they had to do when the commander of the Independent Air Force gave the signal to go ahead.

Assuming that the initial offensive action would be successful, it had been established that, during those following it, the Independent Air Force's task was to be cutting off the operation zones of the Allied armies from their respective territories, that is, more precisely the cutting off of the road and rail communications leading to the French and Belgian territories on the Belfort, Épinal, Toul, Rheims, Charleville, Givet, Dinant, Namur, St.

Trond, and Tongres line, in order to prevent an easy and orderly flow of troops and supplies and to hamper the armies' activities between that line and the border.

As he says in his *Memoirs,* this was one point on which General Reuss's ideas prevailed only in part. When the enemy's aerial forces had been reduced to a negligible force, he wanted to utilize his Independent Air Force to attack directly the national resistance of the enemy. In other words, he wanted to realize the ultimate results of his theory by hurling the Independent Air Force on an unrestricted offensive against the most vital and vulnerable centers in order to put the enemy populations under intolerable conditions of life, making them sue for peace. According to General Reuss, this would have been the quickest and most economical way of ending the war, entailing the minimum loss of blood and wealth on both sides, because the collapse of the enemy would have been brought about by moral compulsion more than anything else. But these extreme ideas of General Reuss had not been accepted by the Government, or at least they were accepted with reservations. In the face of a strong opposition, General Reuss yielded and agreed, once the Command of the Air had been won, to use the Independent Air Force to hinder and harass the concentration and the action of the Allied armies on their line of deployment at the front.

To attain this aim it was necessary to cut off a certain number of road and rail communications leading from the Franco-Belgian territories to the front, and to keep these communications interrupted for a predetermined length of time. It was not easy, but it could be done, especially if, after the conquest of the air, the Independent Air Force had enough strength left for such an offensive. If the attempt did not succeed, then General Reuss's extreme theories might be put into effect.

Selecting as a separation line between the Allied armies' deployment zones and the rest of the Franco-Belgian territories, the one running through Belfort, Épinal, Toul, Rheims, Charleville, Givet, Dinant, Namur, St. Trond, and Tongres, a zone of from 80 to 100 kilometers deep would be enclosed paralleling the Franco-Belgian borders, which, if cut off from the rest of their territories, would certainly have placed the Allies in a very difficult situation.

Naturally, the idea was not to attempt the cutting off of all road and rail communications at once. That was not considered necessary. When we think that the whole number of men and the quantity of matériel constituting the Allied armies would have to pass through that oblique line in the first few days, and after them everything needed for the life and action of the armies, we can easily realize that even a partial cutting off of those road and rail communications would have played havoc with the mobilization and concentration of the Allied armies and any subsequent war actions on their part. By keeping even a portion of these vital communications interrupted it was reasonable to expect it would weaken the enemy's front so that defeating it would be easier at the opportune moment. Apart from these material effects, we must also take into account the moral effects of such traffic interruptions on troops marching or traveling toward the operation zones, compelling them to halt until the raiding enemy had flown away.

A complete and itemized plan had been elaborated to attempt the isolation of the Allies' zone of operations through the Independent Air Force.

The railroad traffic needed in case of mobilization and concentration had been thoroughly studied. Railroads cannot be hidden, and everything pertaining to them can be easily figured out. The approximate number of men likely to be mobilized was no secret. On the basis of such information, even if not precise, it had been possible to estimate the major or minor importance of the railways going through the chosen line of separation. In the same way it had been possible to estimate the major or minor importance of ordinary roads.

For each of the ordinary roads and railroads passing through that oblique line, and especially for the most important ones, a particular plan of operation had been prepared containing a detailed explanation of the offensive to be carried out against it in order to reach the desired result. In general, the destruction of bridges, tracks, and other road facilities was not contemplated;

the idea was to create prohibited zones along the communication lines themselves, by bombing those centers through which the ordinary roads and the railroad passed with chemical, incendiary, and poison bombs, thus creating zones of fire and poison difficult to approach and still more difficult to travel through. In the interruption plans for each road or railroad the centers to be bombed were indicated, besides the quantity of bombs to be thrown on each one of them (10, 20, or 30 tons of bombs for a center). Where and when bombings had to be repeated in order to keep transportation and traffic interrupted were also indicated. With an Independent Air Force capable of carrying on each flight 2,000 tons of bombs, 150 centers for each flight could be bombed, using an average of 20 tons of bombs for each bombing.

As a certain strength of aerial forces would be needed for the carrying out of this interruption plan, General Reuss had reserved for himself the decision as to whether the remaining strength of his Independent Air Force, after conquering the command of the air, would be sufficient for the need. If it would not, he would have felt free to employ them according to his extreme theories.

It was known in Germany that the enemy had at their disposal day- and night-bombing units. Certainly these units would be employed, the more so as Germany had no pursuit or alert pursuit planes. How to safeguard their own centers from such an offensive on the part of the Allied bombers? Here is what General Reuss writes about the problem:

Once the enemy's aerial defense forces had been destroyed, even the Allies would be left without pursuit planes, and so the struggle would continue between the bombing units of the Allies and the German battle units.

Evidently our battle units would have lost no time in trying to prevent the enemy's bombing units from carrying on their offensive. From this would have ensued two parallel actions in which each of the two sides would have tried to inflict as much damage as possible on its enemy. Which one of the two sides would have prevailed? Naturally, under equal conditions, the one possessing the greatest offensive capacity against ground objectives.

Just for this reason I had devoted all national resources to the Independent Air Force and tried to give them the maximum offensive capacity against ground objectives.

Notwithstanding this power conferred on our Independent Air Force, we were not theoretically in a position to prevent the bombing of our centers. Theoretically, I say, because in practice our superior offensive capacity against ground objectives, even in its potential state alone, could have been relied on and utilized to dissuade the enemy from offensive actions against our own territory. In fact, this is precisely what did happen.

DISPOSITIONS FOR JUNE 16

The German Ambassador von Taupritz's telegram arrived from Paris at 11 P.M. on June 15, while the Reich Council was still sitting. It meant war; no human force could have stopped it from exploding in all its fury. Even those most opposed to extreme measures had to bow to the inevitable. Time for discussion was past and gone, and there was no other way open but action. The order for general mobilization was issued at midnight, and General Reuss, having assumed the Command of the National Armed Forces, announced to the Council that the Air Forces would invade the enemy's sky that same day, June 16, between 6 A.M. and 7 A.M., in order to begin the disintegration of the enemy's national resistance.

In order to prevail over the last-minute hesitations of some members of the Council anent the unrestricted employment of the aero-chemical arms, General Reuss proposed to inform the adversary of his intentions so that they could take the necessary countersteps. Since the means to hinder the mobilization and concentration of the enemies' armed forces were available, it would have been a crime against the Fatherland to fail to use them and wait until they were ready to fight. It was up to the enemies to defend and protect those centers where they meant to carry on acts of war such as mobilization and concentration; it was the duty of the enemies to evacuate civilians from those centers. It would have been naïve to believe that unarmed citizens, women, children, and old men could have served as a shield; as a matter of fact, the warning was superfluous, because everyone knows, or should know, that war is war.

This is what originated the famous German radiogram broadcast of June 16, at 2 A.M.

To the Minister of Foreign Affairs who had remarked that such a warning meant giving up the advantage of surprise, General Reuss answered that it was the Independent Air Force which would constitute the real surprise, and not the hour at which it would go into action.

As soon as he assumed command of the National Armed Forces, General Reuss radioed to the Independent Air Force the following order:

To All Commanders of Aerial Units:
    The X-hour will be 6 o'clock this morning.
    I am sure that all of you will do your duty, and that, therefore, at sundown the Independent Air Force will have decided the war.

The orders of operation to which "X-hours" referred contained the following principal instructions:

Concept of Operation: To attack in mass all along the frontier, in successive waves, with the left wing reinforced to envelop Paris from the south, and to beat the enemies by bombing their main lines of communication, thus giving them the immediate impression that they are being dominated from the air.

Forces: All the strength of the Independent Air Force, including the divisions' reserve planes.

Distribution of Forces: Eight columns of attack to be formed, that is:

1st column—Constituted by the I 2,000-horsepower group in 3 detachments of 4, 4, and 2 divisions.

2d column—Constituted by the II 2,000-horsepower group in 3 detachments, as the first.

3rd column—Constituted by the III 2,000-horsepower group in 3 detachments, as the first.

4th column—Constituted by the IV 2,000-horsepower group in 3 detachments, as the first.

5th column—Constituted by the V 2,000-horsepower group and the IX 3,000-horsepower group in 8 detachments of 2, 2, 2, and 4 2,000-horsepower divisions, and 2, 2, 2, and 4 3,000-horsepower divisions.

6th column—Constituted by the VI 2,000-horsepower group, and the X 3,000-horsepower group in eight detachments as the V, plus a detachment of the 6,000-horsepower division.

7th column—Constituted by the VII 2,000-horsepower group, the XI and XII 3,000-horsepower group, and the XV 6,000-horsepower group in 8 detachments of 2, 2, 2, and 6 2,000-horsepower divisions, 4, 4, 4, and 8 3,000-horsepower divisions, and 4 6,000-horsepower divisions.

8th column—Constituted by the VIII 2,000-horsepower group, and the XIII and XIV 3,000-horsepower group, in 7 detachments of 2, 2, 2, and 6 2,000-horsepower divisions, 4, 4, 4, and 8 3,000-horsepower divisions, plus one detachment of 3 6,000-horsepower divisions.

Each detachment to keep a distance of one-half hour's flying time (100 kilometers), and in each detachment the divisions to fly in formation.

Waves of Attack:

At the X-hour the leading detachments of the eight columns of attack are to deploy on the line Paderborn, Korbach, Giessen, Hanan, Aschaffenburg, Wurzburg, Ansbach, and Ulm.

Therefore, eight waves of attack are to be formed:

1st wave—Leading detachments of the 8th columns, 24 2,000-horsepower divisions

2d wave—Leading detachments of the 8th columns, 24 2,000-horsepower divisions

3d wave—Leading detachments of the 8th columns, 23 2,000-horsepower divisions

4th wave—Leading detachments of the 5th, 6th, 7th, 8th columns, 8 2,000-horsepower divisions and 8 3,000-horsepower divisions

5th wave—Leading detachments of the 5th, 6th, 7th, 8th columns, 12 3,000-horsepower divisions

6th wave—Leading detachments of the 5th, 6th, 7th, 8th columns, 12 3,000-horsepower divisions and 3 6,000-horsepower divisions

7th wave—Leading detachments of the 5th, 6th, 7th, 8th columns, 20 3,000-horsepower divisions and 4 6,000-horsepower divisions

8th wave—Leading detachments of the 5th, 6th, 7th, 8th columns, 8 3,000-horsepower divisions and 3 6,000-horsepower divisions

Itineraries and Tasks for Each Column:

The itineraries as here assigned to the various columns of attack are general directions for the whole of each column, and, similarly, the tasks assigned to each one are global tasks. On this basis, the column commanders, through their group commanders, shall trace the itineraries for, and allot the tasks of, the depending divisions.

1st Column—Itinerary: Paderborn, Eupen, Liége, Brussels, Lille, Abbeville, Rouen, Dreux, Corbeil, Châlons, operating bases (10-hour flight). Task: to bomb some great northern center of France for moral impression.

2d Column—Itinerary: Göttingen, St. Vith, Namur, Valenciennes, Gisars, Meulan, Étampes, Melun, St. Dizier, operating bases (10-hour flight). Task: to bomb some great northern center of France for moral impression.

3d Column—Itinerary: Giessen, Merzig, Stenay, Rheims, Villeneuve, then follow same itinerary as the 5th column. Task: to bomb airfields in the Stenay and Rheims regions (10-hour flight).

4th Column—Itinerary: Hanan, Saarbrucken, Verdun, Châlons,

Sens, then following same itinerary as the 6th Column. Task: to bomb airfields in the Verdun and Châlons regions (10-hour flight).

5th Column—Itinerary: Aschaffenburg, Pirmasens, Nancy, St. Dizier, Romilly, Le Mans, Alençon, Rouen, Amiens, Laon, Verdun, operating bases (10-hour flight). Task: to bomb rail communications between Paris and the west and southwest of France Tours-Paris; Angers-Paris; Orléans-Paris; Le Mans-Paris; Le Havre-Paris railroad lines).

6th Column—Itinerary: Wurzburg, Bergzabern, Charmes, Chaumont, Troyes, Sens, Orléans, Chartres, Gisars, Beauvais, Soissons, Épernay, Toul, Nancy, operating bases (10-hour flight). Task: to bomb the following rail communications: Troyes-Paris; Dijon-Paris; Nevers-Paris; Tours-Paris; Angers-Paris and Le Mans-Paris railroad lines.

7th Column—Itinerary: Ansbach, Strasburg, Remiremont, Nevers, Paris, operating bases (10-hour flight). Task: to terrorize the capital and sow destruction in its suburbs, especially where the big industries are located. To give a vivid demonstration of our command of the air, the divisions belonging to the XI, XII, and XV groups, keeping themselves at high altitude, shall fly around Paris and its suburbs, releasing their load (1,200 tons). The first two detachments of the XI and XII shall carry smoke bombs in order to blind the anti-aerial defense, if needed, but anyway to impress the population.

8th Column—Itinerary: Ulm, Breisach, Besançon, Châlons, then various itineraries (12-hour flight). Task: to carry the offensive on the following faraway centers to impress their populations: Clermont-Ferrand, Limoges, Bordeaux, Roanne, Toulouse, Lyon, St. Étienne, Valence, Avignon, Nîmes, Montpellier, Arles, Aix, Borg, and Grenoble.

Directions: The first two waves shall carry no bomb loads, but an armament load at least double the usual. The waves shall always fly at the highest altitude possible with their loads. Objectives defended by antiaircraft artillery shall be generally avoided.

Explorers.—The 15 explorer squadrons shall reach about the H + 2 [1] hour the sky above Rheims, Stenay, Chaumont, and Charmes, where it is estimated that the battle will be most furious, and there they shall act on their own initiative.

These orders of operation were to start on its way the great offensive machine which, once started, could not possibly be stopped.

On leaving its airfield in order to lead the waves at the given hour each division (Paderborn, Göttingen, Giessen, Ansbach, Ulm) had this well-defined mission to accomplish: to proceed along the established itinerary and execute the prescribed bombings.

---

[1] A military code for designating the time factor.

No other care needed to be taken by the division; it knew that on its sides, front, and back other divisions were similarly flying, and the only other task it had was repelling any possible enemy's attack while flying on its route.

To oppose these actions, the enemies could do nothing more than to attack the divisions with their pursuit units. In case of such attacks, the divisions were not to change their own route—it would have been useless, anyhow—no matter what the enemies might be, no matter what losses they should suffer, no matter how far over the enemies' territories they were. The divisions had to accept combat on their routes, always remembering that they were parts of an organic mass of attack whose final aim could be reached only through the individual action as designated of all its component elements.

When reduced in strength to only two planes, the division could fall back, but only in order to join the following detachment, which they could reach in 10 to 20 minutes.

A division could fly back (it could, but it was not expected to) once it had exhausted all the ammunition of its planes and on orders given by its commander. In that case it had to fly back over its original itinerary and land on its own operating base. Flying back before the established time was left to the commander's discretion, but he had to keep in mind that, except for special cases, such returns must be avoided if possible, because the mere presence of the divisions on the enemies' territories was witness to strength.

From the distribution of the forces, it appears clear that their deployment, at first, seemed the stronger on the right wing, perhaps to draw the enemy's forces toward the north, but afterward the left wing became the strongest—that is, the one which was to invade all the French territory south of the Paris parallel and around Paris itself from the west.

Notwithstanding that the fortune of war had been on his side, this plan of operation was violently criticized by eminent war historians for its scholastic rigidity.

General Reuss, author of that plan, answered these critics as follows:

I certainly never entertained the idea that my Independent Air Force would succeed in flying over the enemy's sky always keeping that symmetrical order it showed when my plans were diagrammed on paper. Better than anyone else, I was conscious of the fact that my battle divisions were not inert pawns shifted mechanically on an inert chessboard, but that they were living entities. Into these living entities, and into each one of them, with my plan of operation, I had infused a will stronger than iron to follow to the end the road I had pointed to them. And that was enough for me!

What mattered if the waves, flying in succession one after the other, could not keep exactly at the prescribed distance from one another? As long as the divisions would be flying, the ones which had left first would necessarily precede those which left later. If I gave to each division a definite itinerary and definite tasks, I did so because I knew that all my divisions would adhere to that itinerary unless the enemies destroyed them. Besides, I knew the valor of my crews. I knew that my divisions, once on their way to attack, could not do anything different unless they were destroyed. Through my four columns on the left, inside of three and a half hours I was able to hurl, on one sector of the enemies' front, more than four-fifths of my forces. Our enemies had to lose, and they did!

During the day before the war, the German Independent Air Force had nothing to do outside of routine matters, brass-polishing, as the saying goes; but to make those great machines of war spring into instant action, the order issued by General Reuss at 1 o'clock in the morning of June 16 was enough.

CHAPTER VIII

The Battle of June 16

To GIVE A brief but correct idea of the formidable clash which went down in history under the title of the Battle of June 16, is a difficult task, but I shall attempt it, basing my account on official documents recently published and personal testimony from witnesses and actors in the great tragedy.

In the preceding pages I have outlined the situation on both sides during the evening of June 15 and the following day; and now, in order to orient properly my narrative, I will recount the events in their correct time and space.

Properly speaking, the battle began between 6 o'clock and a quarter after 6 in the morning when the first aerial units from both sides made contact. Nevertheless, some acts of war had taken place before that time which, although part of this battle, did not influence its outcome. An example is the actions carried out by the four night-bombing brigades of the French Independent Air Force. According to orders, between 3 o'clock and half-past that morning, these brigades crossed the Franco-Belgian border between the Luxembourg and the Rhine and went to bomb the Köln, Bonn, Koblenz, Bingen, Worms, Mannheim, and Speyer objectives. The purpose of these bombings was the destruction of the ordinary and railroad bridges on the Rhine.

These night-bombing French brigades presented, at that moment, a strength only one-half that of their war effectives (the permanent squadrons had been completed, but the twin squadrons had not been mobilized yet—that is 6 squadrons (36 planes in all) for each brigade. The bombings were executed by regiments (3 squadrons), and went unopposed by the enemy, who, judging by appearances, at least, had limited himself to black out all lights.

Explosive bombs of 500 kilograms and 1,000 kilograms were used and extensive damages were done, especially to the Köln and Koblenz bridges.

The four brigades, intact, landed back on their operating bases between 6 o'clock and half-past of that same morning.

At 6 o'clock the German Government broadcast to all radio stations of the world its first war communiqué. It is worth quoting.

Berlin, June 16—6 o'clock.

Between 4 o'clock and 5 o'clock this morning, French Aerial forces, after having flown over the Rhenish region, have thrown hundreds of tons of explosive, incendiary, and poison bombs on the cities of Köln, Bonn, Koblenz, Bingen, Mainz, Worms, Mannheim, and Speyer. Damages to persons and buildings are incalculable; thousands of citizens, aged people, women, and children have been killed or lie dying.

The German Government has ordered its Independent Air Force to act in reprisal.

This communiqué greatly exaggerated the effects of the French bombings. If citizens had been struck, their number had not been very great, and the French had not used poison bombs.

But the German Government took advantage of these bombings to accuse the Allies, before world public opinion, of having begun unrestricted use of the aero-chemical arm, and only for the purpose of justifying its use on their part, as they had already decided to do.

This communiqué, published in special editions by all newspapers in the world, made a great impression which could not be canceled by denials issued by the Allied governments, as in these denials they could only try to explain and justify the way they had acted. Even, later on, when the German Independent Air Force unleashed their terrible aero-chemical offensives, the impression lingered, and in many minds the conviction remained that it had been the Allies who had first broken the international con-, ventions, and that Germany had only exercised a justified right of reprisal.

THE SITUATION AT 6 O'CLOCK

As a result of the dispositions made on both sides, the situation at 6 o'clock was as follows:

Allies:

1. The I regiment of the Belgian pursuit brigade (6 squadrons, 36 planes) is cruising in the sky over Köln-Koblenz, on a front of about 80 kilometers, at about the 5,000-meter altitude.

2. The II and IV French pursuit brigades (4 regiments, 24 squadrons, 144 planes) are cruising, the first in the sky over Koblenz-Mainz, and the second over Mainz-Aschaffenburg, on fronts of over 100 kilometers each, at about the 5,000-meter altitude.

(In order to describe the situation in the sky, we always have to refer to some fixed points on the surface. The reader must make the necessary reference in his own mind. Considering the peculiarities of the air, an aerial situation can only be the situation at a certain moment in reference to fixed points on the ground, and therefore the ground reference must be taken, more than anything else, only as a general indication. When we say, for instance, that such and such an aerial force was at such and such a time on the Koblenz-Mainz front at the 5,000-meter altitude, we do not mean to say that that force was really there with all its units deployed and aligned on a vertical plane drawn between Koblenz and Mainz at an altitude of 5,000 meters, but we mean that the units constituting that force found themselves, at that moment, approximately some 10 kilometers outside or some 10 kilometers inside an alignment running from the Koblenz vertical to the Mainz vertical at an altitude of about 5,000 meters.)

Germans:

1. Four divisions of the I 2,000-horsepower group (1st column) have arrived in the Paderborn sky, and are flying toward Köln; these 4 divisions (40 2,000-horsepower planes) will clash at about 6:30 A.M. with the I regiment of the Belgian pursuit brigade.

2. Four divisions of the II 2,000-horsepower group (2d col-

umn) have arrived in the Göttingen sky, and are flying toward Honnef (Rhine); these 4 divisions (40 2,000-horsepower planes) will clash with the I regiment of the Belgian pursuit brigade.

3. Four divisions of the III 2,000-horsepower group (3d column) have arrived in the Giessen sky, and are flying toward St. Goar (Rhine); 4 divisions of the IV 2,000-horsepower (4th column) have arrived in the Hanan sky, and are flying toward Mainz. These 8 divisions will soon clash with the French II pursuit brigade.

4. Two divisions of the V 2,000-horsepower group (5th column) have arrived in the Aschaffenburg. Two divisions of the VI 2,000-horsepower group (6th column) have arrived in the Wurzburg sky.

These 4 divisions (40 2,000-horsepower planes) have made contact with some elements of the VI French pursuit brigade.

5. Two divisions of the VII 2,000-horsepower group (7th column) have arrived in the Ansbach sky, and are flying toward Strasburg.

6. Two divisions of the VIII 2,000-horsepower group (8th column) have arrived in the Ulm sky, and are flying toward Breisach.

For the time being, these two last columns are finding their way open, with no opposition.

At 6 o'clock the battle has begun between the leaders of the 5th and 6th columns and some elements of the IV French pursuit brigade. Between 6 and 6:30 it develops gradually, always toward the north, until at about 6:30, fighting is going on over a front from Köln, through Koblenz, Kreuznach, and Ludwishm, to Heidelberg.

In the sky over Köln and Honnef the I regiment of the Belgian pursuit brigade attacks the 8 2,000-horsepower divisions which constitute the first wave of the first and second columns of attack. There are 6 pursuit squadrons (36 planes) pitted against eight battle divisions (80 2,000-horsepower planes). In the sky over Koblenz and Kreuznach the second French pursuit brigade attacks the 8 2,000-horsepower divisions which constitute the first wave of the first and second columns of attack. There are 12 pursuit squadrons (72 planes) against 4 battle divisions (40 2,000-horse-power planes).

From the many memoirs and accounts published in France and Germany, by officers who fought on that tragic June 16, we can gain a sufficiently correct idea of what took place.

The Allied pursuit units which were cruising or were being sent up against the enemy's masses, tried to take an advantageous position for the attack as soon as they sighted them. But the German divisions, whether they had sighted the enemy or not, proceeded on their route, keeping their formation intact. This allowed the pursuit units, possessing a higher speed and maneuverability, to choose easily their direction of attack, as the enemy's formations did not attempt to avoid the attack, nor executed any maneuver to change their positions. Since they had to assault compact formations, the pursuit units tried to get on top of them and envelop them with all their planes to make them face in all directions and disperse their fire.

The pursuit planes operated through squadrons or groups (2 squadrons) in the sense that they kept in such a formation until the moment of attack. The squadrons were subdivided into half-squadrons (3 planes), and each half-squadron generally operated in one direction of attack. The four directions of attack, in the case of a group, or the two directions, in the case of a squadron, had to synchronize while converging on the enemy. During peace-time training, a great deal of attention had been given to this sort of maneuver, and in practice it proved effective; in fact, every time the Allied units succeeded in employing this method, they obtained the best results.

The German divisions, faithful to their instructions, kept in close formation and did not deviate from the prescribed routes, regardless of what forces attacked them or from which direction the attacks came.

Each division that day was 10 planes strong, instead of 9, as designated by the war organization, because the reserve plane was included. Now, when a division was attacked simultaneously by the 12 pursuit planes of one group—which seldom happened—the fire effectiveness of the division was generally superior to the frontal fire of the pursuit planes. When the division was attacked by one squadron alone, or still worse by a half-squadron, the disadvantage of the attackers would increase enormously, because in those cases the formation could concentrate its fire in fewer directions. On the great German airships the armament had been placed with great care, it was easily handled, not influenced by the wind, and manned by a perfectly trained personnel. Furthermore, as the formation was not obliged to maneuver in any way while sustaining an attack, the planes functioned for firing purposes almost like stable platforms. For a lone airman to attack a division, even if it had lost one-third or one-half of its effectives, was sheer folly; nevertheless several Allied airmen attempted this heroic feat.

When a pursuit unit, whether a group or a squadron, was through with its attack, no matter what its results, it found itself disorganized, with its planes scattered in all directions, and with no hope of being able quickly to reassemble its formation to attempt another assault against the same division or against others. On the other hand, the division which had gone through the attack, even if it had suffered losses, would keep going on its route, maintaining its formation, original or reduced, according to its losses. And then, unless it allowed the enemy to proceed undisturbed, each pursuer had to attack individually. And the great majority of the Allied pursuers, to whom the idea of letting the enemy go on unopposed was repugnant, would keep on attacking and re-attacking alone, after the attack by unit was ended. These heroic acts, especially during the June 16 battle, caused only insignificant damages to the battle divisions, and perhaps most of the losses suffered by the Allied pursuit forces.

The apparent impassivity displayed by the German divisions while flying to their destination and keeping their formations intact irrespective of losses, greatly puzzled the Allied airmen used to maneuver, but this impassivity constituted the great strength of the divisions themselves, and their entire personnel were intimately and deeply conscious of it.

From the moment they left their airfields, the divisions' crews knew that they could do nothing but accept combat in case of contact with the enemy. Therefore, the only thing left for them to do was try to face it under the most favorable conditions—namely, by keeping that close formation which allowed reciprocal help among all the airships in the formation, and by enabling them easily to discover the enemy and shoot at him straight and true. Therefore, there was nothing aboard to distract them from their task, the task of looking around and using their weapons properly to the maximum advantage. To the pilots belonged the task of keeping in formation and following the prescribed route; all the rest of the crew had only one thought in mind, to discover and hit the most dangerous enemy as quickly as possible. The formation was arranged so that the field of observation was divided into as many sectors as there were planes, and this dividing of the firing task made the division a powerful instrument of war even when its effectives were reduced.

Even when numerous units on both sides clashed, the fighting would result in a series of attacks carried on by pursuit units against battle units. Just as the German divisions could not fly with all their planes aligned along a frontal line, so the Allied pursuit units could not attack all at the same time. Thus it happened that in a certain zone a division would be attacked successively by two, three, and even four pursuit groups or squadrons, while in another zone the attack would come only from isolated airmen, and in still others the divisions would meet no opponents at all.

Combat in the sky often presented a chaotic and disordered appearance with pursuit units or single planes hurling themselves from time to time against the divisions bent on proceeding as long as they could fly, while all around battleplanes and pursuit planes would be crashing or trying to land. Little by little the intensity of the fight would slow down; as the pursuit units were destroyed, the attacks would cease; and their few survivors, having exhausted their ammunition or their fuel, especially in the case of alert pursuit planes, would try to land to rearm and refuel; while the divisions, reduced in their effectives, would proceed to their destination.

As we have seen, it was in the sky around Köln and Honnef, about 6:30 A.M., that the first clashes occurred between the 8 2,000-horsepower divisions leading the first and second columns of attack, and the first regiment of the Belgian pursuit brigade.

The fight between these 6 pursuit squadrons and the 8 divisions took place more exactly in the sky above Köln, Honnef, Eupen, and St. Vith. The Belgian squadrons performed miracles of valor, attacking repeatedly in spite of their great numerical inferiority (there were 36 planes against 80) ; but about 7 o'clock the surviving pursuers (only a quarter of those who had attacked) were compelled to land, having exhausted their ammunition, while the 2,000-horsepower divisions, having lost a dozen of their planes, were flying in the sky above Verviers and St. Vith at an altitude of about 6,000 meters.

About 6:30 the lookout service stationed at the Belgian frontier had informed the Belgian Aerial Defense Command of the advance of a great German aerial mass coming over the border, and that the first regiment of the Belgian pursuit brigade had been compelled to quit the fight. The Command of the Belgian Aerial Defense already apprised from other sources of the magnitude of the enemy's forces crossing the borders, at about 7:15 o'clock ordered the II regiment of the Belgian pursuit brigade and the Brussels, Namur, and Liége Aeronautical Presidios (12 alert pursuit squadrons) to attack the enemy's forces which had invaded Belgium.

These forces began to take off between 7:30 and 8 o'clock.

At 7:30 the 8 battle divisions of the first wave of the first and second columns are flying over Brussels at a very high altitude beyond reach of the anti-aerial batteries, on their way to Lille and Valenciennes, some of the Belgian pursuit trying to overtake them.

But at about 7:30 the Belgian Aerial Defense Command is informed by its lookout service on the frontier that another great German aerial mass is crossing the border between Eupen and St. Vith. There were the 8 battle divisions of the second wave of the first and second columns.

The Belgian Aerial Defense Command is barely on time to

change its order to its pursuit forces and to send half of them (6 alert pursuit squadrons) against this second wave. The 8 divisions of the first wave (which had already suffered some losses during previous fights) are overtaken by the first pursuit units sent up after them at about 8 o'clock, over Lille and Valenciennes, while at about the same time the 8 divisions of the second wave are met by the other 6 alert pursuit squadrons in the sky over Brussels and Namur. At the same time, the frontier lookout service is sending out the information that still another German mass is crossing the border. They are the 4 battle divisions of the third wave of the first and second columns.

The Belgian Aerial Defense Command has now only 5 army corps pursuit squadrons left, but it does not think it prudent to risk these remaining auxiliary forces. The French Aerial Defense Command has already been apprised of the events in the Belgian sky, as by 8 o'clock the battle divisions of the first wave were crossing the border between France and Belgium at Lille and Valenciennes. It ordered the first auxiliary pursuit brigade (of the Northern Group of Armies) and the Aeronautical Presidios of Amiens, St. Quentin, and Laon to take off and engage the enemy. There are 12 pursuit squadrons and 18 alert pursuit squadrons, a total of 30 squadrons with 180 planes, when at 8:30 these forces take off against the battle divisions of the first wave, which were already being attacked from the rear by the second regiment of the Belgian pursuit brigade (6 squadrons) and by 6 Belgian alert pursuit squadrons, in all 12 squadrons with 72 planes.

In the sky over Arras, Cambrai, Amiens, and Péronne, between 8 and 9 o'clock a terrible mêlée ensues between the 8 battle divisions of the first wave (already weakened by losses) and 42 squadrons of French and Belgian pursuit planes. There are 252 pursuit planes fighting against about 70 battleplanes. The 8 battle divisions are literally destroyed, not one plane surviving. But this victory cost the Allies about 150 planes.

Also between 8 and 9 o'clock, the battle between the 8 divisions of the second wave and the 6 Belgian alert pursuit squadrons begins in the skies above Brussels, Namur, Charleroi, and Renaix. There are 80 battleplanes against 36 pursuit planes. About 9 o'clock, the 8 divisions of the second wave, which had lost about a dozen of their own planes and destroyed about 30 of the enemy's, arrive in the sky over Arras and Cambrai, where they are attacked by the Allied pursuit forces which had already destroyed the 8 divisions of the first wave. These Allied forces—about 80 planes—are in confusion after the battle they have sustained. Nevertheless they attack courageously, but individually. At about 9:30 the 8 divisions of the second wave, reduced to little more than half of their effectives, have reached the sky above Amiens and Abbeville, while the surviving Allied pursuers are landing to refuel and reorganize.

At 9 o'clock the French Aerial Defense Command is informed that another German aerial mass has been sighted in the sky over Roubaix and Lille, and is bombing Roubaix. They are the 4 battle divisions of the third wave, which had crossed Belgium almost unopposed. One of these 4 divisions releases 10 tons of bombs on Roubaix.

The French Aerial Defense Command orders the first auxiliary pursuit regiment (of the first army) to attack it. The first auxiliary pursuit regiment takes off about 9:30 and flies toward Lille. But, after roaming the sky for a long time, it fails to contact the enemy; therefore, between 12 and 12:30 it returns to its own airfields.

At 10 o'clock the 8 battle divisions of the second wave find themselves in the sky above Rouen, and the 4 divisions of the third wave in the sky above Abbeville. They release 10 tons of bombs on this center.

At about the same time, the French Aerial Defense Command sends the first auxiliary pursuit regiment (of the second army) in the direction of Rouen.

We have followed the events which took place in the sky over Belgium and northern France from 6 to 10 o'clock, events which stand by themselves in the general picture of the June 16 battle. On this partial theater of the war, 20 battle divisions (200 2,000-horsepower airplanes) had clashed with 24 pursuit squadrons and 30 alert squadrons, a total of 324 planes.

At 10 o'clock the situation was as follows:

Germans:

The first wave of the first and second columns (8 divisions, 80 planes) had been totally destroyed.

The second wave (8 divisions) had lost about one-half of its effectives, and was flying in the sky above Rouen.

The third wave (4 divisions, 40 planes), almost intact, was flying above Abbeville, and had bombed Roubaix and Abbeville.

On the whole, the first and second columns of attack had lost about one-half of their effectives, 100 2,000-horsepower airplanes.

Allies:

Of the Belgian pursuit brigade and the three Aeronautical Presidios of Brussels, Namur, and Liége (12 pursuit squadrons and 12 alert squadrons, total 144 planes) about 40 planes were left.

The 5 auxiliary pursuit groups of the Belgian army corps, which were about to mobilize their twin squadrons, were left intact. The first auxiliary pursuit brigade (of the Northern Group of Armies), numbering 72 planes, had been left with about 30 planes. The Aeronautical Presidios of Amiens, St. Quentin, and Laon (18 squadrons, 108 alert planes) had lost about one-half of their effectives. The two auxiliary pursuit regiments (of the First and Second Armies) were flying in quest of the enemy. Also available were the auxiliary pursuit groups of the army corps, which were about to mobilize their twin squadrons.

On the whole, the Allies had lost more than 200 planes.

About 6:30 A.M. in the sky over Koblenz, Kreuznach, Kaiser-lantern, Speyer, and Heidelberg the battle is joined between the leaders of the 3rd, 4th, 5th and 6th columns of attack (12 2,000-horsepower divisions) and the second and sixth pursuit brigade of the French Independent Air Force. The clash takes place above the Rheinish region—144 pursuit planes against 120 2,000-horse-power battleplanes.

At 7 o'clock the 12 divisions of the first wave, reduced to two-thirds of their effectives, cross the frontier between Merzig and Bergzabern, flying due southwest, pursued by about 50 pursuit planes which exhaust their ammunition during valorous but scarcely profitable individual actions, and afterward they have to land.

Also at 7 o'clock, 4 battle divisions (40 2,000-horsepower battleplanes) cross the frontier between Strasburg and Breisach, flying due southwest.

At that time, the Command of the French Aerial Defense orders:

1. The I and II pursuit brigades of the Independent Air Force to attack the enemy's mass crossing the frontier between Merzig and Bergzabern. This mass has already suffered some losses;

2. The V pursuit brigade of the Independent Air Force to attack the enemy's mass crossing the frontier between Strasburg and Breisach:

3. The Aeronautical Presidios of Verdun, Metz, Nancy, and Épinal to stand by ready to attack, where the enemy might advance with other masses.

4. The auxiliary pursuit brigades of the central and southern groups of armies, the auxiliary pursuit regiments of the armies, and the pursuit squadrons already mobilized by the army corps to stand by for orders.

At 7:30 the 12 battle divisions of the first wave (third, fourth, fifth, and sixth columns), reduced to about two-thirds of their former strength, by losses, arrive on the Stenay-Verdun-Nancy-Charmes front, and here they have to sustain the first attacks by the units of the first and second pursuit brigades of the Independent Air Force. At the same time, 12 other battle divisions of the second wave of the same columns of attacks are crossing the border between Merzig and Bergzabern.

Also at 7:30, the 4 divisions of the first wave of the seventh and eighth columns are arriving undisturbed in the sky above Remiremont and Besançon, where they are assaulted by elements of the fifth pursuit brigade of the French Independent Air Force, while 4 other divisions of the second wave of the same columns are crossing the frontier between Strasburg and Breisach.

Between 7:30 and 8 o'clock a combat takes place in the sky over Rheims, Stenay, Verdun, Charmes, Chaumont, St. Dizier, and Châlons, between the divisions of the first wave and the two pursuit brigades. There are 12 battle divisions reduced to two-thirds of their normal effectives against 24 pursuit squadrons.

The French airmen attack with violence and audacity; they seem eager to sacrifice themselves; most of the 80 German battle-planes are destroyed; only a few survivors succeed in falling back to join the following wave. But the two pursuit brigades also suffer heavily and find themselves completely disorganized when, at 8 o'clock the 12 divisions of the second wave appear intact in the Stenay, Verdun, Toul, and Charmes sky. Only a few isolated airmen with scarce ammunition offer them any resistance.

Between 7:30 and 8 o'clock the battle is also joined between the 4 divisions of the first wave of the seventh and eighth columns and the fifth pursuit brigade of the French Independent Air Force in the sky above Vesoul, Dijon, and Besançon. There are 72 pursuit planes against 40 battleplanes.

At 8 o'clock, after having lost about half of their strength, these four divisions arrive in the sky above Dijon and Châlons, while 4 other divisions of the second wave have reached the Remiremont-Besançon front.

The remnants of the fifth pursuit brigade, which also attacks this second wave, are completely destroyed.

At about 8 o'clock the 15 German explorer squadrons arrive in the sky above Rheims, Stenay, Chaumont, and Charmes. They have 180 very fast pursuit planes, piloted by the ablest German airmen. As soon as they arrive on the scene of battle, they engage, each on his own, the French airmen who are attacking the battle divisions.

To the Commander of the French Aerial Defense, at about 8 o'clock the situation looks like this:

On the Stenay, Verdun, Toul, and Charmes front a great mass of large enemy planes, almost intact, is traveling due east at high altitude. About 100 kilometers behind it, almost in line with the border, another great mass of big enemy planes seems to be following on the same route. Toward the south, on the Dijon, Châlons front, there is a mass of enemy planes which has suffered relevant losses; behind it another mass almost intact, and still further back, on the Rhine, another similar great mass.

From information originating with units of the reconnaissance regiment of the French Air Force, other great aerial masses following those which have already invaded the French sky have been located.

The pursuit brigades of the French air forces have suffered great losses, and the units need time to reorganize. For the present no further demands can be made on them.

Faced by such a situation, the commander decides to mass his two forces and orders all those still at his disposal to launch themselves against the enemy as immediately as possible. The forces still available are:

The Aeronautical Presidios of Stenay, Metz, Nancy, and Épinal; 16 squadrons with 96 alert planes. The second-line Aeronautical Presidios of Rheims, Châlons, Troyes, and Auxerre; 24 squadrons with 144 alert planes. The first and second auxiliary pursuit brigade of the southern and central groups of armies; 24 squadrons with 144 planes. The 7 auxiliary pursuit regiments of the armies; 42 squadrons with 252 planes. The 20 pursuit squadrons of the army corps; 20 squadrons with 120 planes. In total, 126 squadrons with 756 planes.

The order to attack is issued at 8 o'clock, and a few minutes afterward the first units begin to take off. About 8:30 the great struggle begins.

At 8:30 the situation of the German columns is as follows:

A. 3d, 4th, 5th, and 6th columns:

1. First wave—destroyed.

2. Second wave—12 2,000-horsepower divisions, almost intact, have reached the Rheims-Châlons-St. Dizier-Chaumont front.

3. Third wave—8 2,000-horsepower divisions, intact, have reached the Stenay-Toul-Charmes front.

4. Fourth wave—8 2,000-horsepower divisions, intact, have reached the frontier between Merzig and Bergzabern.

B. 7th and 8th columns:

5. First wave—reduced to very few planes, have reached the Nevers-Moulins front.

6. Second wave—4 2,000-horsepower divisions, almost intact, have reached the Dijon-Châlons front.

7. Third wave—12 2,000-horsepower divisions, intact, have reached the Remiremont-Besançon front.

8. Fourth wave—8 3,000-horsepower divisions, intact, are crossing the border between Strasburg and Breisach.

At the moment, then, not including the losses suffered, there are 44 2,000-horsepower divisions and 8 3,000-horsepower in full efficiency (440 2,000-horsepower planes and 80 3,000-horsepower) in the French sky.

Seven hundred and fifty-six French pursuit planes hurl themselves against these 520 great German battleplanes. Naturally the German waves deeper into the French sky are the first to feel the brunt of this violent attack. Thus, the second wave of the third, fourth, fifth, and sixth columns (12 2,000-horsepower divisions, almost intact) is defeated in the sky over Rheims and Auxerre; and the very few planes which survive fall back on the third wave (8 2,000-horsepower divisions). This in turn also loses most of its planes and falls back on the fourth wave (8 2,000-horsepower divisions); which in the meantime has reached the Stenay-Toul-Charmes front. The fourth wave is also vigorously attacked, but by this time the French pursuit planes have performed an enormous task (about 200 German battleplanes have been brought down), have suffered very serious losses, and all the remaining planes are scattered all over the sky. At this time a fifth wave, of 4 3,000-horsepower divisions, enters French territory between Merzig and Bergzabern. The first and second waves of the seventh and eighth columns are defeated and almost destroyed; the third wave is also violently attacked but, as in other sectors, the French assaults weaken here too; and the third wave, whittled down to about one-half of its effectives, arrives on the Dijon-Châlons front, while the fourth follows it in the sky above Remiremont and Besançon, and the fifth (8 3,000-horsepower divisions) is crossing the frontier between Strasburg and Breisach.

At 9 o'clock the situation of the German Independent Air Force in the French sky, south of the Paris parallel, is as follows:

A. 3d, 4th, 5th, and 6th columns:

1. First, second, and third waves—destroyed.

2. Fourth wave (8 2,000-horsepower divisions), reduced to

about one-half of its effectives, are on the Stenay-Charmes front, flying toward the Rheims-Auxerre front.

3. Fifth wave (4 3,000 divisions) are on the frontier between Merzig and Bergzabern.

B. 7th and 8th columns:

1. First and second waves—destroyed.

2. Third wave (12 2,000-horsepower divisions) reduced to about one-half of its effectives, are on the Dijon-Châlons front.

3. Fourth wave (8 3,000-horsepower divisons) are on the Remiremont-Besançon front.

4. Fifth wave (8 3,000-horsepower divisions) are on the Strasburg-Breisach front.

In this sector of the sky, the German Independent Air Force have lost about 500 battleplanes of 2,000 horsepower; but the French Aerial Defense has left at its disposal only a few alert pursuit groups and about 100 isolated and scattered individual pursuers; while 10 2,000-horsepower divisions and 20 3,000-horsepower divisions are proceeding along the designated itineraries in the French sky. The sixth, seventh, and eighth waves will arrive with another 40 3,000-horsepower divisions and 10 6,000-horsepower divisions.

At about 10:30, then, 10 2,000-horsepower divisions, 60 3,000-horsepower divisions, and 10 6,000-horsepower divisions, a total mass of 800 great battleplanes, will be flying in the French sky south of the Paris parallel. And the French Aerial Defense will be in no position to offer any appreciable resistance.

Since 9 A.M., then, the Battle of June 16 can be considered as won by the German Independent Air Force; and, in fact, from that hour on no aerial clash of importance takes place. The various columns of attack can follow their designated itineraries almost unopposed, execute the bombings assigned to them, and then return to their operating bases with only insignificant losses.

The German war communiqué, issued at 8 P.M., reads as follows:

The Independent Air Force, which entered the sky of France and Belgium at 7 o'clock this morning, has defeated the Allied Aerial

Forces, then bombed the cities of Bordeaux, Limoges, Clermont-Ferrand, Toulouse, Roanne, Lyon, St. Etienne, Valence, Avignon, Nimes, Montpellier, Arles, Aix, Bourg, Grenoble, Dijon, Nevers, Bourges, Tours, Le Mans, Rouen, Amiens, Roubaix, and some others; besides dropping more than 1,000 tons of bombs on the suburbs of Paris.

No one and nothing can now prevent our Independent Air Force from dropping, daily, wherever it may see fit, at least 3,000 tons of bombs; and beginning tomorrow, our Independent Air Force will carry on this daily task until the enemy nations acknowledge their defeat.

Today, at about 8 o'clock, some Allied squadrons dropped bombs on the cities of Hanover, Magdeburg, Leipzig, and Dresden. Acts of this sort which, owing to their insignificance, cause only useless damages which cannot contribute to a decision, must not be repeated if serious reprisals are to be avoided. From now on, for each German center struck by even one bomb alone, our Independent Air Force will receive orders to destroy completely an enemy center of equal importance.

The events of June 16 made a deep impression on the Allied governments.

The news which began to arrive in the early hours of the morning at once gave them a feeling of their own inferiority in the air. This sensation became deeper and more painful when the 3,000- and 6,000-horsepower divisions began to unload bombs on the Paris suburbs, causing serious material and moral damage. From every sector of the country news kept arriving of the bombing of faraway centers which had been considered safe from enemy incursions; and from everywhere clamorous requests for prompt measures of aerial defense were being received. It seemed that the enemy were everywhere in the sky.

Most of the pursuit and alert pursuit units had been destroyed. Only a few hundred pursuit planes were left, and they needed to be reorganized in squadrons, but they could bring no assurance of being able to face any further attack successfully. Many other squadrons existed, but they were specialized for other duties and not for air combat, especially against the German battleplanes. However, during the night of the sixteenth, the aeronautical authorities tried to make available all possible aerial means, even makeshift ones, in order to oppose further enemy attacks.

The reprisal threat contained in the 8 o'clock communiqué angered the French leaders, who decided to ignore it. In fact, orders were given to the night-bombing brigade of their Independent Air Force to bomb the German cities of Köln, Koblenz, Mainz, and Frankfurt that same night.

During the 16th, the German Independent Air Force had lost:

1. About 600 2,000-horsepower planes.
2. About 40 3,000-horsepower planes; and
3. 3 6,000-horsepower planes.

During the night of the sixteenth the remnants of the 2,000-horsepower divisions were·reorganized into two groups (I and II), of 10 divisions, of 9 planes each.

The orders of operation to the Independent Air Force for the seventeenth set them the following task:

To disrupt rail and road communications crossing an oblique line extending from Belfort, through Épinal, Toul, Rheims, Charleville, Givet, Dinant, Namur, and St. Troud to Tongres.

The attack had to be executed by 8 columns in 3 waves each, flying one-half hour apart. As the flight would last about 5 hours, the 2,000-horsepower planes had to load 3 tons of bombs, and the 3,000- and 6,000-horsepower planes 5 and 8 tons of bombs, respectively.

The first and second columns had to include in each of them one 2,000-horsepower group (10 divisions, 90 planes) and one 6,000-horsepower division (9 planes) in 3 waves of 4, 4 and two 2,000-horsepower divisions each, plus a 6,000-horsepower division. These two columns, carrying a total of 600 tons of bombs, had to take care of the disruptions to be effected in Belgium, from Tongres to Dinant.

Each of the other 6 columns had to include one 3,000-horsepower group (10 divisions, 90 planes) in 3 waves of 4, 3, and 3 divisions respectively. Two 6,000-horsepower divisions (18 planes) had to be added to the last wave of the fourth, fifth, sixth, and seventh columns. Each of these columns would carry about 500 tons of bombs.

The third and fourth columns had to take care of disruptions between Rheims and Givet; fifth and sixth, of disruptions between Rheims and Toul; and the seventh and eighth, of those between Toul and Belfort. The first wave had to cross the frontier at 5 o'clock, and the divisions, as soon as their task had been performed, had to return to their own airfields flying at the highest altitude by the shortest route.

CHAPTER IX

Operations of June 17

ABOUT 1 A.M. of the seventeenth, the cities of Köln, Mainz, Koblenz, and Frankfurt were bombed by the 4 night-bombing brigades of the French Independent Air Force. During the sixteenth, these brigades had completed their mobilization and come up to their regular war strength (12 squadrons, 72 planes in each brigade), so that each one carried out the bombing of one of the four cities, releasing about one hundred tons of explosive, incendiary, and poison bombs. The damages were very serious. Great fires were caused everywhere, and, as the spreading of poison gas prevented the bringing of help, the four cities were almost completely destroyed.

About 6 o'clock the German Command issued the following communiqué:

During the night, between 1 and 2 o'clock, the Allies bombed Köln, Koblenz, Mainz, and Frankfurt.

Consequently, today, between 4 P.M. and 5 P.M., the German Independent Air Force will completely destroy the cities of Namur, Soissons, Châlons, and Troyes, and their inhabitants are hereby warned to evacuate them.

In case another German city should be bombed to any degree by the Allies, the Independent Air Force will be ordered to destroy Brussels and Paris completely.

In the meantime, at 7 o'clock, the first wave of the German Independent Air Force had crossed the frontier. There were 250 great battleplanes (exactly 288, of which 72 were of 2,000-horse-power and 216 of 3,000), and it was against them that the few surviving pursuit units, reorganized during the night by the Allies, hurled themselves. A few German planes were brought down by this attack, but the task assigned to the columns was performed.

In fact, by 8 o'clock, over more than 150 centers, where road and rail communications passed through, an average of 20 tons of bombs each had been released.

Since 6 o'clock in the morning the explorer squadrons of the Independent Air Force had been flying over the cities of Namur, Soissons, Châlons, and Troyes, dropping leaflets of the threatening German communiqué. Several thousands more of these leaflets had been scattered over Paris, Brussels, and several other Allied cities.

News reports which began to arrive at 6 o'clock in the morning to the Allied governments appeared at once as most ominous. They helped to convince them of the physical impossibility of preventing and counteracting the enemy's aerial action, which was evidently developing according to a predetermined plan which soon became clear.

There was no doubt that the enemy's purpose was to make the mobilization and concentration of the Allied armies as difficult as possible. The interruptions of road and railroad communications, in fact, were already numerous and widespread, and at many points they were stopping or severely hindering railroad traffic.

From everywhere civil and military authorities had begun to ask anxiously for means of aerial defense. More than 100 important centers crossed by railroad lines or great arterial roads were in flames and smothered in clouds of poison gas, which in some cases were carried by the wind, spreading death and terror all around the countryside.

Many detachments of troops had been compelled to stop, finding themselves unable to advance and bring help to the stricken cities. Impressed by the terrible effects of the bombings and by the sight of the enemy planes flying freely and unopposed in their own sky, though they cursed the barbarous methods of their enemy, they could not help feeling bitter against their own aeronautical authorities, who had not taken enough protective measures against such an eventuality.

Under such conditions the Allied authorities had to take seriously the threat contained in the German communiqué, and the question gave rise to a sharp divergence of views between the political and military authorities.

The latter viewed the evacuation of the threatened cities as a public admission of aerial helplessness on their part, and were absolutely opposed to it. But, when asked whether they were in a position to guarantee an adequate defense of those same cities, they were compelled to admit that they were not. Who, then, was going to shoulder the responsibility of not ordering the evacuation of cities which could not be defended? The reality, the terrible reality, of their aerial impotence had to be faced and acknowledged. It was only the second day of the war; during the first day already great masses of enemy battleplanes had flown over Paris and Brussels with almost complete immunity and dropped hundreds and hundreds of tons of bombs on centers, even the farthest away from the frontiers. Now, the humiliation of having to bow to an enemy ultimatum; tomorrow, very likely, if it suited the enemy, Paris and Brussels might have to be evacuated! What would be the end of it all? Why had the aerial forces, which had cost so much, been pulverized in so short a time? Whose fault was it? The discussion was long, bitter, sometimes tragic; but finally, about 10 o'clock, the evacuation of the threatened cities was ordered.

The impression made by this order, which could not be kept hidden from the capital cities, was, as expected, enormous; the Allied nations felt definitely that they had been defeated in the air, and that they were hopelessly at the enemy's mercy. In the threatened cities, where the reading of the leaflets dropped by the enemy's aviators had naturally stirred up plenty of agitation, the order of evacuation caused some disorder and panic. However, it was carried out calmly by the majority of the inhabitants, while around those cities the remaining Allied aerial forces were being feverishly concentrated.

The orders of operation to the German Independent Air Force for the punitive expedition contemplated the same distribution of forces as the preceding one; the only change was in the tasks which were assigned as follows:

1. The 1st and 2d columns—destruction of Namur.
2. The 3rd and 4th columns—destruction of Soissons.
3. The 5th and 6th columns—destruction of Châlons.
4. The 7th and 8th columns—destruction of Troyes.

About four hours had been allowed the Independent Air Force for refueling and reloading bombs. The designated bomb-load was 2, 3, and 6 tons for each airship of 2,000-, 3,000-, and 6,000-horsepower, respectively. This figured out at 500 tons of bombs for each one of the cities to be destroyed.

According to the *Private Instructions for the Independent Air Force,* bombings for the purpose of integral destructions had to be executed while flying at the highest possible altitude; the divisions had to fly over the target along lines cutting it in various directions, and by bombing a surface zone larger than the target itself. Owing to the power of the chemical (incendiary or poisonous) bombs, there was no doubt that, by dropping ten thousand 50-kilogram bombs (total 500 tons) on a city of average size, it was possible to destroy it completely.

The start from the airfields had to be made allowing time enough for the leading wave of each column to reach its targets at 4 P.M.

It is useless for us to elaborate on this episode, which has been amply described by eyewitnesses in writings, some of which have become famous for vividness and descriptive power. It is enough to relate that between 4 P.M. and 5 P.M., in spite of the heroism displayed by the few Allied pursuers available, the four cities became unapproachable flaming braziers and burned to the ground under the eyes of their former inhabitants, who had sought refuge and shelter in the neighboring countryside.

The German communiqué issued at 9 P.M. read as follows:

This morning, between 6 and 8 o'clock, the Independent Air Force began the task of disrupting the road and rail communications in the zone of operations of the enemy armies by dropping more than 3,000 tons of bombs over about 150 centers astride said road and rail communications.

This afternoon, between 4 and 5 o'clock, the Independent Air Force, in defense of German cities, has been compelled to destroy the cities of Namur, Soissons, Châlons, and Troyes, whose population, as per our warnings, had been evacuated by the Allied governments.

Tomorrow the Independent Air Force will resume its methodical action, meant to prevent the concentration of the Allied Armies. . . .

From this moment on, the history of the war of 19— presents no more interest.